Basic Skills in English

Purple Level

Yellow Level

Blue Level

Orange Level

Green Level

Red Level

Basic Skills in English

Red Level

McDougal, Littell & Company

Evanston, Illinois

New York   Dallas   Sacramento   Raleigh

AUTHORS

Joy Littell

Edward Hagelin Pearson, Lincoln Junior High School, Park Ridge, Illinois

Kraft and Kraft, Developers of Educational Materials, Newburyport, Massachusetts

CONSULTANTS

Carole B. Bencich, Coordinator of Secondary Language Arts, Brevard County School Board, Rockledge, Florida

Dr. Sheila F. S. Ford, Coordinator for Secondary Language Arts, Spring Branch Independent School District, Houston, Texas

Marietta H. Hickman, English Department Chairman, Wake Forest-Rolesville High School, Wake Forest, North Carolina

Mary Evans Roberts, Supervisor of English and Language Arts, Savannah-Chatham Public Schools, Savannah, Georgia

ISBN 0-8123-5475-3   TE ISBN 0-86609-477-6

Acknowledgments

Simon & Schuster: for entries from *Webster's New World Dictionary,* Students Edition; copyright © 1981 by Simon & Schuster, Inc. Macmillan Publishing Company: the Handbook section contains, in revised form, some materials that appeared originally in *The Macmillan English Series, Grade 5,* by Thomas Clark Pollock et. al., © 1963 by Macmillan Company. Used by arrangement.

1 2 3 4 5 6 7 8 9 10 11 12 13 14 15 / 90 89 88

Composition

HANDBOOK

Words: Building Your Vocabulary

It Grows on You

Learning About Language

Here's the Idea   English is a living language. Like other living things, it grows and changes. Some words outlive their usefulness and are dropped from the language. From time to time, new words are added. These changes occur in many ways.

Borrowed Words   Many English words are borrowed from other languages. English has borrowed words from the American Indian languages (squash), from French (garage), Spanish (cigar), German (noodle), and Dutch (cookie), among others.

Compound Words   Other new words come from combining two words. *Motor* and *cycle* for example, were combined to form *motorcycle*. Other examples of compound words are *halfback*, *downtown*, *outdoors*, and *birthday*.

Words from People's Names   Sometimes a person's name becomes a word. An example is *sandwich*, named after the Earl of Sandwich. It is believed that he ate such a snack while he gambled so he wouldn't have to leave for meals. Words from the names Charles *Boycott*, Rudolf *Diesel*, Gabriel *Fahrenheit*, and Louis *Pasteur* are also part of the English language.

In these and other ways, words have been added to English. Some of these words are so common today that it is hard to imagine that they were not always used. However, new ideas and inventions need new words. English changes as the world changes.

Building a good vocabulary will help you to express your thoughts and ideas clearly. A good vocabulary will help you communicate better with others.

Check It Out Read the following sentences. Notice the words that have been added to English.

1. Sometimes I *doodle* on my paper.
2. Hamburgers taste better with *ketchup*.
3. A *tornado* picked up Dorothy's house.
4. The pitcher left the *dugout* to warm up in the *bullpen*.
5. Dad's blue *cardigan* is old, but it's still his favorite sweater.

- How is English enriched by these new words?
- How can these words help you to communicate ideas more clearly?

Try Your Skill Read the following English words. Some were borrowed from other languages. Others are compound words or words made from names. Using a dictionary, try to find out how these words came into English.

tea	vampire	anteater	bloomer	zeppelin
pajamas	outfield	watchdog	watt	bookcase

Keep This in Mind

- English is a living language. It changes and grows.
- A good vocabulary will help you to express your thoughts and ideas clearly. It will help you communicate better with others.

Now Write Label your paper **It Grows on You.** Choose any five words that are mentioned but not explained in this lesson. Write the words on your paper. Check the meanings of the words in a dictionary. Then write a sentence using each word. Keep your sentences in your writing folder.

Look Around

Learning Word Meaning from Context

Here's the Idea English has so many words, no one can know all of them. Every reader comes across unfamiliar words from time to time. Sometimes you must look up a word in a dictionary. At other times you don't have to. The context can tell you the meaning.

The **context** of a word is the words and sentences around it. A word's context will often help you figure out what the word means. It may not tell you the exact meaning, but it can give you a general idea.

Read the following example. Try to figure out what the *italicized* word means.

> Australia has some strange native birds, like the *kookaburra*.

You couldn't draw a picture of a kookaburra from the information in this sentence. You do know, though, that it is an Australian bird. The context has helped you understand the meaning of an unfamiliar word.

You cannot always depend on the context to help you with unfamiliar words. Sometimes the context is no help. The example below gives no hints about the meaning of *kookaburra*.

> On the postcard was a picture of a *kookaburra*.

From the information in this sentence, a *kookaburra* could be a mountain, a kind of house, or almost anything.

When you see an unfamiliar word, look for context clues to its meaning. You may find clues in the same sentence as the new word. Sometimes you may have to read two or three sentences to find them. Here is a paragraph that provides context clues.

> You will rarely see pets on a farm. Every animal has a job to do. If a cat is not a good *mouser*, it has no place on a farm.

If you had read the word *mouser* in a list of words, you might not have known what it meant. However, from the context, you can tell it has something to do with a cat's job on a farm. From this you can guess that a *mouser* catches mice.

Check It Out Read the following sentences. Try to figure out what each italicized word means. Use context clues to help you.

1. Jill loves *jalapeños*, which are Mexican hot peppers.
2. The *galleon*, like all large ships, had a crew of hundreds.
3. We heard the *oriole* sing and saw its nest in the tree.
4. Everyone else hurried out, but Elaine *lingered* after class.

   · What is the general meaning of each word in italics?
   · What context clues helped you figure out the meaning?

Try Your Skill In each of the following sentences, there is a word in italics. Use context clues to figure out what that word means. Write what you think each italicized word means.

1. These streets *intersect*; that is, they cross one another.
2. *Icons*, or religious statues, filled the room.
3. Some blood diseases, like *hemophilia*, are inherited.
4. *Nocturnal* creatures, such as bats, sleep during the day.
5. The pony was not one color; instead, it was *piebald*.
6. If you don't obey the rule, you will be forced to *comply*.

Keep This in Mind

· Context, the words surrounding a word, often gives clues to the meaning of that word.

Now Write Label your paper **Look Around**. List four words you know. Write a sentence using each word. In each sentence, give context clues that would help a reader understand your word. Save the sentences in your folder.

Spell It Out

Definition and Restatement

Here's the Idea   There are several kinds of context clues. The most direct clues to the meaning of a word are definition and restatement.

In a **definition,** the meaning of a word is given directly.

> We sailed the boat near Longboat Key. A *key* is a low-lying island or reef.

In a **restatement,** the meaning of a word is usually signaled by key words like *or, is called, that is, which is,* or *in other words.* Sometimes the meaning of the word is signaled by a comma or a pair of commas.

> At the zoo we saw a *gnu,* which is a large African antelope.
> Carbon monoxide is a *noxious,* or poisonous, gas.

Writers use definition and restatement to help readers understand unfamiliar words. If you stay alert for context clues, you will learn new words more easily.

Check It Out   Read these sentences. Each uses definition or restatement as a clue to the meaning of the italicized word.

1. A mammal that carries its young in a pouch is called a *marsupial.*
2. The horse's coat had a healthy *gloss,* or shine, when it stood in the sunlight.
3. We ate *scrapple,* which is a food made from cornmeal and scraps of pork.
4. Our garden has spiky, colorful flowers called *gladioli.*
5. Jill saw a colony of *gannets,* large white sea birds, on the beach.

- What is the meaning of each italicized word?
- What is the clue in each sentence that signals a definition or restatement?

Try Your Skill   Each of the following sentences has one word in italics. You can find context clues that tell what that word means. Write each word and its meaning.

1. A *cowlick* is a patch of hair that sticks up and won't lie flat.
2. I bought a *yucca*, a plant with stiff, pointed leaves.
3. Jim is *indecisive*; that is, he has trouble making up his mind.
4. The *smelt*, a small, silvery fish, has a delicate taste.
5. At first, McCall Junior High seemed like a *labyrinth*, a maze, to me.
6. Our cycling club stayed in *youth hostels*, which are inexpensive places for young travelers to spend the night.

Keep This in Mind

- The most direct context clues to the meaning of a word are definition and restatement.
- A definition or a restatement usually comes after key words or phrases, like *or, is called, that is, which is,* or *in other words*. A definition or restatement may be set off by commas.

Now Write   Label your paper **Spell It Out**. List four unusual words that you can define. For example, the words might name special objects, tools, or foods. Imagine that each word you choose is unfamiliar to your reader. Write a sentence for each word. Use definition or restatement in the sentence. Use a key phrase or punctuation to alert the reader. Check your sentences by having a classmate see if your meanings are clear. Save your sentences in your folder.

Look Again

Using Context Clues: Examples

Here's the Idea Another kind of context clue is an **example.**
When you read, check to see if an unfamiliar word is explained
by one or more examples. The examples may give you a clue to
the meaning of the word. Read this sentence.

Legumes, such as peas, beans, and peanuts, are rich in protein.

The context tells you that peas, beans, and peanuts are examples of *legumes.* The words *such as* alert you that one or more
examples are used as context clues.

There are several key words and phrases that tell you to look
for an example. These include *especially, like, other, this, these,
for example, for instance,* and *such as.*

Read two more sentences in which examples give you the
meaning of the word *legumes.*

Many legumes, beans and peanuts *for instance,* are rich in protein.

Include peas, beans, peanuts, and *other* legumes in your diet.

None of these sentences tells you exactly what legumes are.
However, they all use examples to make the general meaning
of the word clear.

Check It Out Read the following sentences. In each sentence the context clue is an example.

1. *Herbs,* for instance mint and basil, have fragrant odors.
2. *Pit vipers,* such as rattlesnakes and copperheads, are poi-
sonous.
3. The *produce,* especially the lettuce and tomatoes, is always
fresh.

- What is the meaning of each of the italicized words?
- Which words or phrases signal an example is used?

Try Your Skill   In each sentence, use the context to help you get the meaning of the italicized word. Number your paper from 1 to 5. Then write a definition of each italicized word.

1. *Crustaceans*, including lobsters, crabs, and shrimp, were displayed in a large aquarium.

2. *Quinces*, like many hard fruits, taste best when they are cooked.

3. The *sari* and other items of traditional Indian clothing are often very colorful.

4. *Carbonated* beverages, such as root beer and ginger ale, give some people the hiccups.

5. Guitars, *zithers*, and other stringed instruments are fun to play.

Keep This in Mind

- Examples are sometimes used as context clues.
- Several key words and phrases will alert you to look for an example. These words include *especially, like, other, this, these, for example, for instance*, and *such as*.

Now Write   Label your paper **Look Again.** Choose three of the following words to use in sentences: *fish, mammals, board games*, and *vegetables*. Write a sentence using one or more examples as a context clue to the meaning of each of the words you have chosen. Make sure your examples are clear.

Put your work into your folder.

Make It Clear

Learning About Synonyms and Antonyms

Here's the Idea Many English words are close to each other in meaning. Such words are called **synonyms.** Synonyms may not mean *exactly* the same thing, however. One of them will usually have a meaning closer to the idea you want to express. Read the following sentence.

Helen ran around the track.

You may want to use a synonym for *ran* in this sentence. The synonym could give more specific information.

Helen **sprinted** around the track.
Helen **jogged** around the track.
Helen **loped** around the track.

Sprinted, jogged, and *loped* all have the same general meaning. They are all ways of running. But each word suggests a different way of running. *Sprinted* suggests that Helen ran at full speed. *Jogged* suggests that she ran at an easy, steady pace. *Loped* suggests that Helen ran with a long, swinging stride. One of these words is the best word to describe how Helen ran.

Knowing **antonyms** will also help you to choose the best words when you write. Antonyms are words with opposite meanings. *Long* and *short* are antonyms. So are *stop* and *go.*

Antonyms are useful when you want to make a contrast in order to emphasize an idea. For example, look at the following sentence: "Roberta was so *generous* that she made me feel *stingy.*" In this sentence, the word *stingy* helps to emphasize the meaning of its antonym, *generous.*

When you write, think about exactly what you want to say. What idea or feeling do you want to give the reader? When these ideas and feelings are clear in your mind, decide which words would best express them.

Read the following sentences.

1. Joan is a *fast* walker.
2. Dr. Brown was *quick* to take notice of Martha's symptoms.
3. The deer made a *swift* retreat when Jerry approached it.
4. We noticed a *rapid* change in temperature.
5. Don's remark was *hasty*, and he regretted making it.

   - Notice that the word *fast* and its synonyms have their own special meanings. Can you explain each meaning?
   - What is an antonym for the word *fast*?

Try Your Skill   Decide which synonym would best fit in each blank. Then write the complete sentence.

1. We are studying the art of _____ Rome.
   antique   ancient   old
2. We need _____ approaches to old problems.
   immature   young   fresh
3. Our Thanksgiving turkey was _____, not plump.
   little   small   scrawny
4. The _____ sound of the speaker's voice was soothing.
   loud   deep   thunderous
5. I heard Kim _____ when I made the same mistake again.
   talk   murmur   mutter

Keep This in Mind

- Synonyms are words that have similar meanings. Decide which synonym best expresses your idea.
- Antonyms are words that have opposite meanings.

Now Write   Label your paper **Make It Clear.** List two synonyms for the word *quick*. Write a sentence for each synonym, using the special meaning of that synonym. Then write antonyms for the words you chose. Use a dictionary or thesaurus to help you. Save your work in your folder.

Get Down to Bases

Learning Word Parts: Base Words

Here's the Idea One way that language grows is by the addition of word parts to base words. A **base word** is a word on which other words can be built. If you can recognize a base word within a larger word, you will have a good idea what that larger word means.

Some base words have parts added in front of them. The word *untie*, for instance, is built on the base word *tie*. Other base words have parts added to the end of them. *Hopeless* is built on the base word *hope*. A word part added to a base word can change the meaning of the word. A base word may have a word part added at the beginning and at the end. The word *removable* is built on the base word *move*.

Recognizing base words helps you understand the meanings of many unfamiliar words. You may see what appears to be a strange word. If you look again, you may recognize its base word. If you know the meaning of the base word, you can probably figure out the meaning of the entire word. This becomes even easier when you learn the meanings of the word parts that are added to the base words.

Some base words are easy to spot. In the word *joyful*, the base word *joy* is easy to see. In some words, the base word may be harder to see. One letter may be changed or dropped. The word *famous*, for example, is based on the word *fame*. The letter *e* from *fame* has been dropped from the longer word.

When you look for base words, remember that the final letter or letters in base words may be changed or dropped. The word *persuasive* is based on *persuade*. *Beautiful* is based on *beauty*. Sometimes a letter may be doubled when an ending is added. For example, *runner* is based on *run*.

Check It Out   Read these three sets of words.

changeable	unlikely	misfit
changeless	likable	fitting
unchanging	likeness	fitness

- Can you find the base words?
- In which words has the spelling of the base words been changed?

Try Your Skill   Find the base word in each word listed below. On your paper, write the base word. Remember that the spelling of a base word can change when a word part is added.

1. traveler
2. careful
3. prewash
4. nonstop
5. harmless
6. worrier
7. misspell
8. comfortable
9. reopen
10. defenseless
11. nonviolent
12. rebuild
13. unwanted
14. eventful
15. unwrap
16. preschool
17. unforgettable
18. boxer
19. sensible
20. unlawful

Keep This in Mind

- Word parts can be added at the beginning or end of a base word to make new words.
- The spelling of a base word may change when an ending is added. Often the final letter is changed or dropped.

Now Write   Label your paper **Get Down to Bases.** Open one of your textbooks to any page. Find and copy five words that contain base words. Underline the base words. Then make another word from the same base, and write it on your paper. You may use a dictionary. Save your words in your folder.

Small Beginnings

Learning Word Parts: Prefixes

Here's the Idea   In the last lesson you learned about base words. You learned how to recognize them in longer words. A word part added to the beginning of a base word is called a **prefix.** For instance, the word part *un-* is the prefix in *uncertain.*

There are many different prefixes. The meaning of the prefix changes the meaning of the base word. The prefix *un-* means "not," so *uncertain* means "not certain, doubtful."

Some words may seem to have a prefix, though they do not. The word *under*, for example, does not contain the prefix *un-.* How do you know this? Look at the word. If you cover the letters you think make a prefix, do you have a base word? No, you have only a nonsense syllable, *-der.* Therefore, the word *under* does not have a prefix. Not all words do.

Look at this list of common prefixes. If you learn these prefixes, you will be able to figure out what many words mean.

Prefix	Meaning	Examples
pre-	"before"	preschool
non-	"not"	nonsense
un-	"not"	unhappy
mis-	"wrong"	mistreat
re-	"again"	reappear

Check It Out   Notice how these prefixes and base words work together to make new words.

precook	—	"to cook before"
nonfiction	—	"not fiction"
uneasy	—	"not easy"
misjudge	—	"to judge wrongly"
renew	—	"to make new again"

- What is the base word in each example?
- Does every prefix change the meaning of the base word?

Try Your Skill Number your paper from 1 to 20. Look at each word below. Decide whether it has a prefix or not. If the word does have a prefix, write the meaning of the prefix plus the base word. For example, next to the word *unhappy* you would write this: not + happy.

1. replay	8. unity	15. unnecessary
2. misty	9. prerecord	16. prejudge
3. unfair	10. misplace	17. recipe
4. pressure	11. unskilled	18. nonviolent
5. none	12. reelect	19. rebuild
6. receive	13. nonswimmer	20. miserable
7. mispronounce	14. ready	

Keep This in Mind

- A prefix is a word part added at the beginning of a base word.
- Each prefix has its own meaning or meanings. The prefix changes the meaning of the base word to which it is added.
- Some words appear to have a prefix but do not. Check to see if a base word follows the word part that looks like a prefix.

Now Write Label your paper **Small Beginnings**. Find five words. Each should contain one of the five prefixes you have learned in this lesson. Use a dictionary. List the words on your paper.

Write five sentences, each one using one of the five words you found. Finally, study the words so that you can add them to your vocabulary. Save your sentences in your folder.

Last, but Not Least

Learning Word Parts: Suffixes

Here's the Idea A word part added at the end of a base word is called a **suffix**. In the word *wonderful*, the suffix is *-ful*. Like a prefix, a suffix has a meaning of its own. A suffix also changes the meaning of the base word to which it is added.

In this lesson you will study five of the most common suffixes. When you learn the meanings of these five, you will have made a good start toward understanding many words.

Suffix	Meaning	Examples
-er (or **-or**)	"a person or thing that does something"	helper, reflector
-less	"without"	fearless
-able (or **-ible**)	"having this quality, able to be"	washable, sensible
-ful	"full of, having"	hopeful
-ous	"full of, having"	dangerous

When suffixes are added to base words, the spelling of the base word may change. A letter may be dropped from the base word. For example, *cure* becomes *curable*. Sometimes the final letter of the base word will be changed. For example, *beauty* becomes *beautiful*. At other times, the final consonant may double. For example, *swim* becomes *swimmer*. If you are not sure how to spell words when adding suffixes, check the correct spelling in a dictionary.

Check It Out Look at the following words and their definitions. Notice how the suffix and base word work together to make a new word.

winner — "a person or thing that wins"
operator — "a person who operates"
worthless — "without any worth"
reasonable — "having the quality of reason"
horrible — "having the quality of horror"
useful — "having a use"
famous — "having fame"

- Does every suffix change the meaning of the base word?
- In which words is the spelling of the base word changed?

Try Your Skill   On your paper write each word below. Next to each, write the base word and the suffix. For example, next to the word *famous*, you would write this: fame + ous. Remember that the spelling of a base word may change when a suffix is added to it.

1. dryer	7. thriller	13. lovable
2. tearful	8. actor	14. pitiful
3. joyous	9. homeless	15. runner
4. counselor	10. admirable	16. poisonous
5. penniless	11. breakable	17. generator
6. readable	12. carrier	18. glamorous

Keep This in Mind

- A suffix is a word part added to the end of a base word.
- A suffix changes the meaning of the base word.
- A letter in the base word may be dropped, changed, or doubled when a suffix is added.

Now Write   Label your paper **Last, but Not Least.** Write five words, each containing one of the five suffixes you have learned. You may use a dictionary. Then write five sentences, each using one of the five words. Save your work in your folder.

Keep Up with the Times

New Language for Special Fields

Here's the Idea   The world around you is constantly changing. People think of new ideas. They invent new machines. They have dreams, and they try to figure out ways to make those dreams become real.

As the world changes, you need to be able to describe the new things in it. The English language grows and changes to help you do so. New words are created. Old words are given new meanings.

The space industry, for example, has added a whole new vocabulary to our language. Can you tell what the following words mean?

countdown	astronaut	zero gravity
liftoff	launch pad	reentry

Computers are changing the world so fast that people speak of the *computer revolution*. The English language has grown to keep up with that revolution. Do you know what each of these terms means?

printout	keyboard	printer	software

Science and technology also add new words to your language. How many of these words do you know?

laser	pacemaker	bionic
videotape	digital	synthesizer

Remember, the world does not stand still. Neither does the English language. If you want to be a part of the modern world, you need to know the new words that describe it.

Check It Out   Look carefully at the following words. They are all space, computer, or science and technology terms. Some of them have older, more familiar meanings. Others are made up of two familiar words.

monitor	bioengineering	satellite
bit	booster	ultrasound
printout	word processor	heat shield

- Do you see how English words can take on brand new meanings to describe new ideas and inventions?

Try Your Skill   Look up the following words in a dictionary. Write one familiar meaning for each word. Then write each word's space or computer meaning.

1. shuttle
2. memory
3. burn
4. hardware

Keep This in Mind

- The English language changes as the world changes.
- English changes in different ways. New words are created, and old words take on new meanings.

Now Write   Label your paper **Keep Up with the Times.** Make a list of two space words, two computer words, and two new science and technology words that you know. Next to each word, write its meaning. Share your words with your classmates. Perhaps you and your classmates could make your lists into a *Dictionary of New Language.* Save your work in your folder.

Using
a Dictionary

Look It Up

How To Use a Dictionary

Here's the Idea   English has over 600,000 words, more than any other language. Few people know more than a small fraction of them. Everybody needs a dictionary.

What is a dictionary? It is a reference book containing a list of words and information about those words. A dictionary can tell you if a word exists. It can also help you to use words correctly.

The words in a dictionary are listed in alphabetical order. Words that begin with *a* come before words that begin with *b*, and so on. If two words begin with the same letter, they are alphabetized by the second letter. If the first and second letters are the same, the words are alphabetized by the third letter. The following columns of words are in alphabetical order:

admire	hold	schedule	yank
always	holdout	scheme	yarn
at	holiday	school	yawn

There are many kinds of dictionaries. Some dictionaries list only words in special fields, such as music or medicine. Bigger dictionaries may contain more words and a more detailed explanation of each word. The biggest dictionaries, like those on stands in a library, are *unabridged*. That means they contain nearly all the words in the language. An unabridged dictionary is useful when you want to look up an uncommon word.

Most of the time, through, a desk- or pocket-size dictionary, which is *abridged*, will suit your needs. It's helpful to keep one of these handy when you're reading or writing. It will help you to understand difficult words when you're reading. It will also help you to use words correctly when you're writing.

Dictionaries also vary in the ways they are organized and in the kinds of symbols and abbreviations they use. For this reason, it's a good idea to become familiar with the dictionary that you will use most often. Learn how the information for each word is organized. Study the explanatory material in the front of the dictionary to learn what the abbreviations and symbols stand for.

Check It Out Look at this portion of a dictionary page.

---

firefly   358   **fish and chips**

fire·fly (-flī′) *n., pl.* **-flies′** a small, flying beetle whose lower body glows with a light that goes off and on
☆**fire·house** (-hous′) *n. same as* FIRE STATION
fire insurance insurance against loss or damage resulting from fire
fire·light (-līt′) *n.* light from an open fire
fire·man (-mən) *n., pl.* **-men** 1. a man whose work is fighting fires 2. a man who tends a fire in a furnace, locomotive engine, etc. ☆3. *U.S. Navy* a nonrated enlisted man whose duties are concerned with the ship's engines, etc. ☆4. [Slang] *Baseball* a relief pitcher
Fi·ren·ze (fē ren′dze) *It. name of* FLORENCE, Italy
fire·place (fīr′plās′) *n.* a place for a fire, esp. an open place built in a wall, at the base of a chimney
fire·plug (-plug′) *n.* a street hydrant to which a hose can be attached for fighting fires
fire·pow·er (-pou′ər) *n. Mil.* 1. the effectiveness of a weapon in terms of its accuracy and the number of shots it can fire 2. the number of shots a given unit can fire in a short time
fire·proof (-prōōf′) *adj.* that does not burn or is not easily destroyed by fire —*vt.* to make fireproof
☆**fire sale** a sale of goods damaged in a fire
fire·side (-sīd′) *n.* 1. the part of a room near a fireplace; hearth 2. home or home life
fire station the place where fire engines are kept and where firemen stay when on duty
fire·storm (-stôrm′) *n.* an intense fire over a large area, as one caused by an atomic explosion
fire tower a tower, usually in a forest, where a lookout is posted to watch for fires and give the alarm
fire·trap (-trap′) *n.* a building that would be unsafe in case of fire because it will burn easily or does not have enough exits
☆**fire wall** a fireproof wall for preventing the spread of fire, as from one room to the next
☆**fire·wa·ter** (-wôt′ər, -wät′ər) *n.* [prob. transl. of AmInd. term] alcoholic liquor: now humorous
☆**fire·weed** (-wēd′) *n.* any of various plants that grow readily on cleared or burned-over land
fire·wood (-wood′) *n.* wood used as fuel
fire·works (-wurks′) *n.pl.* 1. firecrackers, rockets, etc. used, as in celebrations, to produce loud noises or a fancy show of lights:

FIREFLY
(to ½ in. long)

highest in pitch or the leading part —*adv.* 1. *a*) before any other person or thing [guests are served *first*] *b*) before doing anything else [*first* we had soup] 2. as the first point [*first*, let me say this] 3. for the first time [I *first* met him yesterday] 4. sooner; preferably [when told to beg, he said he'd starve *first*] —*n.* 1. the first person, thing, class, place, etc. 2. the first day of the month 3. the beginning; start [at *first*, I believed him] 4. a first happening or thing of its kind 5. [*pl.*] the best quality of merchandise 6. the winning place, as in a race 7. the first or lowest forward gear ratio of a motor vehicle
first aid emergency treatment for injury or sudden illness, given while waiting for regular medical care —**first′-aid′** *adj.*
☆**first base** *Baseball* the base on the pitcher's left, the first of the four bases a runner must touch in succession to score a run
first·born (furst′bôrn′) *adj.* born first in a family; oldest —*n.* the firstborn child
first-class (-klas′) *adj.* 1. of the highest class, rank, quality, etc.; excellent 2. of the most expensive kind [a *first-class* cabin on a ship] ☆3. designating or of mail that is sealed and that carries the highest regular postage rates —*adv.* 1. with the most expensive accommodations [traveling *first-class*] 2. as or by first-class mail
first cousin the son or daughter of one's aunt or uncle
first finger the finger next to the thumb
first·hand (-hand′) *adj., adv.* from the original producer or source; direct [a *firsthand* report]
☆**first lady** [*often* F- L-] the wife of the U.S. president
first lieutenant a U.S. military officer ranking above a second lieutenant
first·ling (-liŋ) *n.* 1. the first of a kind 2. the first fruit, produce, offspring, etc.
first·ly (-lē) *adv.* in the first place; first
first mate a merchant ship's officer next in rank below the captain: also **first officer**
first offender a person found guilty for the first time of breaking the law
first person that form of a pronoun (as *I* or *we*) or verb (as *do*) which refers to the speaker or speakers
first-rate (-rāt′) *adj.* of the highest class, rank, or quality; excellent —*adv.* [Colloq.] very well [I feel *first-rate*]
☆**first sergeant** *U.S. Army & Marine Corps* the noncommissioned officer, usually a master sergeant, serving as chief assistant to the commander of a company, battery, etc.
☆**first-string** (-striŋ′) *adj.* [Colloq.] *Sports* that is the first choice for regular play at a specified position [our *first-string* quarterback]

- How are the words listed?
- What special symbols are used?
- What words are new to you?

Try Your Skill   On your paper, write each of the following lists in alphabetical order. Then look up one word from each list in a dictionary and write the first meaning given.

1.	2.	3.	4.
cake	goat	none	stick
easy	give	now	still
army	get	noon	stitch
friend	great	note	stiff
barn	glum	nod	stir
duck	ghost	nose	sting

Keep This in Mind

- Dictionaries are reference books that list words alphabetically. They give explanations of each word.
- Have a dictionary nearby when you're reading and writing.
- Become familiar with the organization, symbols, and abbreviations of the dictionaries you use.

Now Write   Imagine that you are a person who compiles dictionaries. On your paper, write the title of this lesson, **Look It Up.** Write ten words that begin with the first letter of your last name. Then put the words into alphabetical order.

Write a short definition for each word. Check your work in a dictionary. Save your word lists in your folder.

Show Me the Way

How To Use Guide Words

Here's the Idea   In most dictionaries there are two **guide words** at the top of each page. They are in large, bold print. The left guide word is the same as the first word at the top of the page. The right guide word is the same as the last word at the bottom of the page. All the other words on the page are arranged alphabetically between the guide words. Look at this top portion of a dictionary page. *Grew* is the first word on the page. What would the last word be?

grew   417   **gripe**

where, formerly, many eloping English couples went to be married **2.** any similar village
grew (grōō) *pt. of* GROW
grew·some (grōō′səm) *adj. same as* GRUESOME
grey (grā) *adj., n., vt., vi. Brit. sp. of* GRAY
Grey (grā) **1. Charles,** 2d Earl Grey, 1764–1845; Eng. statesman; prime minister (1830–34) **2. Sir Edward,** Viscount Grey of Fallodon, 1862–1933; Eng. statesman; foreign secretary (1905–16) **3. Lady Jane,** Lady Jane Dudley, 1537–54; queen of England (July 10–19, 1553); beheaded
grey·hound (grā′hound′) *n.* [OE. *grighund*] any of a breed of tall, slender, swift hound with a narrow, pointed head and a smooth coat
grid (grid) *n.* [short for GRIDIRON] **1.** a framework of parallel bars; gridiron; grating **2.** a network of crossing parallel lines, as on graph paper **3.** a metallic plate in a storage cell for conducting the electric current **4.** an electrode, usually a wire spiral or mesh, for controlling the passage of electrons or ions in an electron tube —☆*adj.* [Slang] of football
☆**grid·der** (grid′ər) *n.* [< GRID, & GRIDIRON] [Slang] a football player
grid·dle (grid′'l) *n.* [< Anglo-Fr. *gridil* < OFr. *graïl* < L. < *craticula*, gridiron < *cratis*: see CRATE] a flat, metal plate or pan for cooking pancakes, etc. —*vt.* **-dled, -dling** to cook on a grid-

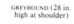

GREYHOUND (28 in. high at shoulder)

grill·room (gril′rōōm′) *n.* a restaurant that makes a specialty of grilled foods
grill·work (-wurk′) *n.* a grille, or something worked into the form of a grille
grilse (grils) *n., pl.* **grilse, grils′es:** see PLURAL, II, D, 2 [<? OFr. dim. of *gris*, gray] a young salmon on its first return from the sea to fresh water
grim (grim) *adj.* **grim′mer, grim′mest** [OE. *grimm* < IE. base *ghrem-*, angry] **1.** fierce; cruel; savage *[war is grim]* **2.** hard and unyielding; relentless; stern *[grim courage]* **3.** appearing stern, forbidding, harsh, etc. *[a grim face]* **4.** frightful or shocking; ghastly *[grim jokes about death]* —see SYN. at GHASTLY —**grim′ly** *adv.* —**grim′ness** *n.*
gri·mace (gri mās′, grim′əs) *n.* [Fr. < OFr. *grimuche*, prob. < Frank.: for IE. base see CHRIST] a twisting of the face in fun or in a look of pain, disgust, etc. —*vi.* **-maced′, -mac′ing** to make grimaces —**gri·mac′er** *n.*
gri·mal·kin (gri mal′kin, -môl′-) *n.* [earlier *gray malkin* (cat)] **1.** a cat; esp., an old female cat **2.** a spiteful or harmful old woman
grime (grīm) *n.* [prob. < Fl. *grijm:* for IE. base see CHRIST] sooty dirt rubbed into or covering a surface, as of the skin —*vt.* **grimed, grim′ing** to make very dirty or grimy
Grimm (grim), **Ja·kob (Ludwig Karl)** (yä′kôp), 1785–1863 & **Wil·helm (Karl)** (vil′helm), 1786–1859; Ger. brothers who worked in language studies and together made a collection of fairy tales

Guide words help you find words quickly. Look at them as you flip the pages searching for your word. Suppose that the word you want is *newt*. First, look for guide words beginning with *n*. Next, look for guide words beginning with *ne*. After that, look for guide words beginning with *new*. Soon you'll come to a page where the left guide word comes alphabetically before *newt*. The right guide word comes alphabetically after *newt*. Now you have found the right page.

Check It Out   Look at the portion of a dictionary page on page 25.

- What are the guide words for this page? Would you find the word *grin* on this page? Which way would you turn the pages to find *great*?

Try Your Skill   At the top of a sheet of paper, write the following sets of guide words: *back/boat, break/but, tab/tall,* and *tame/tax*. Look at the list of words below. Find the words that go below each set of guide words. Write them under the correct set in alphabetical order.

brave	tan	tape	bite
tag	take	bark	target
tarnish	brink	tactic	beef
blue	big	tacky	tax
break	breath	bring	taste

Keep This in Mind

- Dictionary guide words show the alphabetical range of words on each page. The left guide word is the same as the first word on the page. The right guide word is the same as the last word on the page.

Now Write   Imagine that you are writing a composition about airplanes. You want to look up the following words: *aileron, elevator, fin, fuselage, landing gear, rudder, stabilizer,* and *wing*.

On your paper, write the title of this lesson, **Show Me the Way.** List the words above. Find each word in the dictionary. Next to each word, write the guide words that appear at the top of the page where the word is found.

Save your work in your folder.

It's All There

How To Read a Dictionary Entry

Here's the Idea   You know that a dictionary entry gives the meaning of a word. It also gives other helpful information about a word. Take a look at all the information a dictionary entry can give you.

The **entry word** is the word you are looking up. It is in bold type. It is divided into syllables. For example, *mathematics* is entered as **math·e·mat·ics**.

The **pronunciation** of the word is often put inside parentheses following the word. Symbols are used to help you sound out the word. An accent mark tells which syllable to stress. *Science,* for example, appears as (sī′əns).

The **part of speech** is shown by an abbreviation in bold type. For example, *noun* is abbreviated *n*. *Adverb* is abbreviated *adv*. If you do not recognize an abbreviation, look in the front of the dictionary for an explanation. You will usually find a complete list of the abbreviations used in the dictionary.

If a word can be used as more than one part of speech, the other parts of speech will also be given in the entry.

If a word has **special forms** or **endings,** they will be included next in the entry. For example, the entry for the irregular verb *swim* would include the forms **swam, swum,** and **swimming.** Plural forms are given for nouns.

The **origin,** or **history,** of a word is given next, often in brackets. Symbols and abbreviations are used. The symbol < means "came from." The abreviations *ME., Gr.,* and *L.* stand for "Middle English," "Greek," and "Latin." Look up unfamiliar abbreviations in the complete list at the front of the dictionary.

27

Definitions are given in a numbered list. Often, the most common definition is given first. Sometimes a word will have a special meaning in one field. The dictionary will show this by naming the field. For example, one definition of *guard* is "*Sports*—to keep an opponent from making a gain or score."

A word may have a special meaning when it is used in speaking or in informal writing. This is a colloquial meaning. The dictionary shows this by using an abbreviation. For example, one definition of *story* is "[Colloq.] a falsehood or fib."

Synonyms and **antonyms** may also be listed. For some words there may also be a *synonymy*—a group of synonyms and their shades of meaning. Or, the notation "**SYN.** *see*" may refer you to another entry.

Entries in one dictionary may differ from entries in another. Become familiar with the way an entry is given in the dictionary you use.

Check It Out   Look at the dictionary entry below.

> **fam·i·ly** (fam′e lē, fam′lē) *n., pl.,* **-lies** [L. *familia,* household < *famulus,* servant] **1.** orig., all the people living in the same house; household **2.** *a)* a social unit consisting of parents and their children   *b)* the children of the same parents **3.** a group of people related by ancestry or marriage; relatives **4.** all those claiming descent from a common ancestor; tribe or clan; lineage **5.** a group of things having a common source of similar features; specif.,   *a) Biol.* a category that is used in classifying plants or animals and that ranks above a genus and below an order   *b) Linguis.* a group of languages having a common ancestral language   *c) Math.* a set of curves, etc. with some shared property —*adj.* of or for a family

- How many syllables are there in *family*? How many pronunciations are given? What part of speech is *family*? Is it used as any other part of speech? From what language did the word come? What is the most common definition? Are there special meanings for use in particular fields? Are any synonyms given?

Try Your Skill   Turn back to the sample dictionary page in the last lesson, **Show Me the Way.** Answer the following questions.

1. How would you pronounce *grimace*? What does it mean?
2. What parts of speech are listed for *grid*?
3. What are the other forms of the adjective *grim*?
4. Where would you find synonyms for *grim*?
5. What is the most common definition of *grid*?

Now Write   On your paper, write the title of this lesson, **It's All There.** Find the words *back, gorilla,* and *uniform* in a dictionary.

Copy two different definitions for each word. Then write a sentence telling any other information you find about each word.

Save your work in your folder.

Does It Fit?

How To Find the Meaning of a Word

Here's the Idea   If you see a word that you don't know, you look it up in a dictionary. The word may have several meanings. Which is the right one? Usually the sentence in which you found the word, the context, will help you out.

In each sentence below, the context helps you to know the meaning of the word *glass*.

   1. I cannot read without my *glasses*. (In this sentence, *glasses* means "eyeglasses, spectacles.")

   2. Would you like a *glass* of strawberry milk? (In this sentence, *glass* means "a quantity of something.")

   3. She smiled at her reflection in the *glass*. (In this sentence, *glass* means "a mirror.")

When you look up a word in the dictionary, read through all the definitions given. Try to find the meaning that best fits the word in context.

Check It Out   Here is part of a dictionary entry. Study it. Then read the sentence that follows.

> **court** (kôrt) *n.* [OFr. <LL. <L. *cohors:* see COHORT] **1.** an un-covered space wholly or partly surrounded by buildings or walls **2.** a short street, often closed at one end **3.** *a)* an area for playing any of several ball games [a tennis *court*]   *b)* a part of such an area ☆**4.** a motel: in full, **motorcourt 5.** *a)* the palace of a sovereign   *b)* the family, advisers, etc. of a sovereign, as a group *c)* a sovereign and his councilors as a governing body   *d)* any formal gathering held by a sovereign **6.** attention paid to some-one in order to get something **7.** courtship; wooing ˙**8.** *a)* a per-son or persons appointed to examine and decide law cases, make investigations, etc.; judge or judges   *b)* a place where trials are held, investigations made, etc.   *c)* an assembly or meeting of the judge or judges, the lawyers, and the jury in a law court

We reserved a handball **court** for four o'clock.

   • Which definition of *court* fits the context of this sentence?

Try Your Skill   Read the entry. Some meanings are for *plug* as a noun, and some are for *plug* as a verb.

> **plug** (plug) *n.* [MDu. *plugge*] **1.** an object used to stop up a hole, drain, etc. **2.** *a*) a cake of pressed tobacco   *b*) a piece of chewing tobacco **3.** a device, as with prongs that stick out, for fitting into an electric outlet, etc. to make electrical contact **4.** *same as:* *a*) SPARK PLUG   *b*) FIREPLUG   **5.** [Colloq.] a defective or shop-worn article ☆**6.** [Slang] an old, worn-out horse ☆**7.** [Colloq.] a boost, advertisement, etc., esp. one slipped into the entertain-ment part of a radio or TV program, a magazine article, etc. —*vt.* **plugged, plug′ging 1.** to stop up (a hole, etc.) with a plug (often with *up*) **2.** to insert (something) as a plug [he *plugged* the putty in the hole] **3.** [Colloq.] *a*) to promote (a song) by frequent performance ☆*b*) to promote with a plug (*n.* 7) **4.** [Slang] to shoot a bullet into —*vi.* [Colloq.] to work or study hard and steadily; plod —**plug in** to connect (an electrical device) with an outlet, etc. by inserting a plug in a socket or jack —**plug′ger** *n.*

On your paper, write the number of each sentence below. After it, write the meaning from the entry that matches the use of the word *plug*.

1. The painters *plugged* putty into the holes.
2. This lamp needs a new cord and *plug*.
3. Although math is difficult for Rob, he *plugs* away at it.
4. The performer *plugged* her new album.
5. A mechanic replaced the *plugs* and points on the car.

Keep This in Mind

- If you don't know the meaning of a word, look it up. Read all the definitions. The context of the sentence will help you find the right meaning.

Now Write   Look up the word *strike* in your dictionary. On your paper, write the title of this lesson, **Does It Fit?** Copy four meanings of *strike*. For each meaning, write a sentence. Save your work in your folder.

The Right Language at the Right Time

Up to Standards

Writing and Speaking Standard English

Here's the Idea   Do you use the same language with your friends as you do with your teachers? Probably not. Most people speak and write the English language in more than one way.

When you speak before a group or write a paper for class, you probably try to speak as correctly and precisely as possible. In other words, you try to use standard English. **Standard English** follows all of the rules of good grammar and usage. It is the language you use when you want to be understood by everyone. When you use standard English, people tend to listen more carefully to what you have to say.

There is also another type, or "level," of language. It is called nonstandard English. **Nonstandard English** does not follow all of the rules of good grammar and usage. It is often found in friendly letters or casual conversation. Slang is one type of nonstandard English. So are words such as *ain't* and *hisself.* Phrases like *I seen it* and *she gone now* are also nonstandard.

Learn to be aware of the type of language you are using. Remember that nonstandard English is acceptable only in very casual situations. Use standard English in school and in all your writing. Also use it whenever you want to present yourself or your work in the best possible way.

Check It Out   Compare these examples.

Standard	Nonstandard
1. *Sit* down and rest.	1. *Set* down and rest.
2. Tim *has gone* to school.	2. Tim *gone* to school.
3. She *doesn't* want to go.	3. She *don't* want to go.
4. I *am* studying for the test.	4. I *be* studying for the test.
5. I didn't learn *anything.*	5. I didn't learn *nothing.*

- What is nonstandard about each sentence in the second column?
- Say the standard sentences to yourself until they sound natural to you.

Try Your Skill Read the following pairs of sentences. Choose the correct standard English sentence in each pair.

1. They were late this morning.
   They was late this morning.
2. Come in and set down.
   Come in and sit down.
3. Ain't it a nice day?
   Isn't it a nice day?
4. I seen the movie already.
   I saw the movie already.
5. He doesn't know anything.
   He don't know nothing.

Keep This in Mind

- Standard English is correct in any situation. Learn to speak and write standard English.

Now Write Make each sentence below show standard usage. Choose the correct word from the two shown in parentheses. Write the complete sentence. Then compare your work with that of your classmates. Correct any mistakes you made. Save your finished work in your folder.

1. They (was, were) hurt badly.
2. Marnee and her sister (aren't, ain't) going to the basketball game.
3. The team doesn't have (no, any) good pitchers.
4. I (saw, seen) the hot air balloon fly away.
5. Frankie (has written, has wrote) me a funny letter.

Staying Cool

Using and Misusing Slang

Here's the Idea   Not too long ago, the words *grody* and *far out* were often heard in conversation. Within a few months, however, they were no longer being used. These words, and others like them, are called **slang.** Slang is a type of nonstandard English. It is made up of colorful, descriptive words and phrases. Some slang terms are known by everyone. Some are familiar only to certain groups.

Slang changes rapidly. Most slang terms disappear quickly from our language. The words below were all very popular slang expressions at one time. Do you know what each one means?

groovy	vamoose	bummer	uptight
rap	heavy	marvy	drag

Some slang terms do become permanent parts of our language. *Hot dog,* for example, was once a slang term. Now it is an accepted part of our vocabulary.

Always remember that slang is nonstandard English. Never use slang in a report for school, in a business letter, or when speaking in formal situations. Use it only in casual conversation with your friends.

Check It Out   Read the list of activities below.

1. Writing a letter to your principal asking to use the gym for a seventh grade basketball game.
2. Making a phone call to your best friend.
3. Writing an advertisement for a book sale for the junior high classes.

4. Giving an oral report in class.
5. Telling your cousin about the popular styles at your school.

- Which situations require standard English?
- In which situations would slang be acceptable? Why?

Try Your Skill   Complete each sentence in two ways. First, complete it with a slang term. Then complete it using standard English. The word or words in parentheses will give you an idea of the types of words you should use.

1. That group's music is really _____. (good)
2. Do you _____ what I'm saying? (understand)
3. His outfit is _____. (in style)
4. This movie _____. (is bad)
5. We _____ last Saturday. (had a good time)

Keep This in Mind

- Slang is current, popular, nonstandard English.
- Slang should never be used in situations that call for standard English.

Now Write   Listen to the dialogue on several popular television shows. Write down the slang terms that you hear. Then write down the meaning of each term. Compare your list with the lists of your classmates. What standard English words or phrases could be used in place of these terms? Save your list of slang terms in your folder.

Writing Better Sentences

Put It Together

Learning About Sentences

Here's the Idea   You have seen how a good vocabulary helps you to express ideas clearly. You know that using the right word in the right place can make a big difference. So can using the right word at the right time.

Now you are ready to put your words together in the most effective way. You are ready to create sentences.

A sentence is a group of words that expresses one complete thought. You can use sentences to express many different kinds of ideas. If you write carefully, your sentences can be very powerful. Read these examples of powerful sentences.

Common sense is not so common.—VOLTAIRE

That it will never come again is what makes life so sweet.
—EMILY DICKENSON

When one door closes, fortune will usually open another.
—FERNANDO DE ROJAS

Not every writer can write a sentence that becomes famous. However, you can learn to write good sentences. A good sentence states an idea in a clear, direct, and lively way.

Check It Out   Read the following sentences.

1. A junk is a flat-bottomed Chinese boat.
2. The pale moon rose over the snow-capped mountains.
3. We have a haunted telephone.
4. Computers can do almost anything.
5. The Mahoney family celebrates Christmas in July.

- Does each sentence express a complete thought?
- Is each sentence clear and direct?

Try Your Skill   Read the ten sentences below. Each one asks you to tell about something. Choose five directions to follow. Write a single sentence to answer each direction. Try to make each sentence clear, direct, and lively. Use details from your memory or your imagination.

1. Tell one event that happened in this class.
2. Describe your favorite object.
3. Explain one way to cheer someone up.
4. Explain what a best friend is.
5. Explain why a person should get enough sleep.
6. Tell how you came to school this morning.
7. Describe how your head feels when you have a cold.
8. Explain what a broom does.
9. Explain why people should vote.
10. Tell one of your favorite wishes.

Keep This in Mind

- A sentence is a group of words that expresses a complete thought.
- A good sentence expresses an idea clearly and directly.

Now Write   Write five sentences. Write a sentence that tells how to do something. Write one that describes something. Write one that tells what something is. Write one that tells why something should be done. Finally, write one that tells about some action.

Try to write sentences that you would enjoy reading. When you've written your sentences, read them over. Are they clear and direct? Are they strong? If not, rewrite them. Save your work in your folder.

Getting Nowhere

Avoiding Empty Sentences

Here's the Idea   Some sentences get nowhere. They are written as sentences, but they do not say anything. Such groups of words are called **empty sentences.**

There are two kinds of empty sentences. The first repeats an idea from an earlier sentence, or states one idea twice.

> I was thirsty and I wanted something to drink.

If you are thirsty, it is understood that you want something to drink. The sentence above needlessly repeats the same idea. A sentence like this can be revised by adding more information.

> I was thirsty because I had eaten a bag of salty pretzels.

The second kind of empty sentence gives an unsupported opinion. The writer makes a strong statement that captures a reader's attention, but leaves the reader asking "Why?"

> Most TV news programs are second-rate.

Such strong statements must be supported with details. These details may be facts, reasons, or examples. Supporting evidence may be given in the same sentence or in following sentences.

> Most TV news programs are second-rate because newscasters act like entertainers, not like journalists.
>
> Most TV news programs are second-rate. Newscasters devote too little time to explaining news events. Instead, they try to entertain.

When you give an opinion, you must also give a reason for your opinion. Otherwise, your writing will seem empty. Your readers may not agree with you, but at least they will know *why* you think as you do.

Read the following empty sentences.

1. The forest was quiet because there wasn't a sound.
2. You should always try to eat a good breakfast.
3. Exercise can be enjoyable.
4. I didn't like the movie because it was terrible.
5. This record is broken, and it is unplayable.

- Which sentences repeat an idea? Which sentences give an unsupported opinion?
- How could you improve these empty sentences?

Try Your Skill Copy the following sentences. Decide why each one is empty. Then try to improve each sentence.

1. The wind was freezing, and I was cold.
2. My feet were sore from walking, and they hurt.
3. The city is the best place to live.
4. We shouldn't waste our natural resources.
5. The book was so dull that it bored me.
6. Writing is the most important skill you will ever learn.

Keep This in Mind

- There are two kinds of empty sentences. One kind repeats an idea. The other kind states an opinion without supporting it.
- Improve sentences that repeat an idea by taking out the repeated idea. Complete sentences that give an opinion by supporting the opinion with facts, reasons, or examples.

Now Write Read some advertisements in magazines and newspapers. Find two examples of empty sentences. Write down the sentences. Then write why you think each one is empty. Finally, improve each sentence. Save your work in your folder.

Cut It Out!

Avoiding Padded Sentences

Here's the Idea   Every word in a sentence should say something about the main idea of the sentence. Some sentences will be longer than others. However, a good sentence should have no extra words.

Sentences that contain useless words or phrases are called padded sentences. A padded sentence is not clear and direct. It takes too long to get to the point. Padded sentences can be improved by trimming. Read the following example.

> Due to the fact that I didn't have shoes on, I couldn't go into the museum.

The phrase *due to the fact that* is unclear. It adds nothing to the sentence. It gets in the way of the main idea. The sentence could be improved by leaving out the padding.

> Because I didn't have shoes on, I couldn't go into the museum.

Phrases such as *you know, you see, what I mean to say is,* and *well, what I think is* are sometimes used in conversation. However, they don't help you to state ideas clearly. You should avoid them when you write and speak.

Remember that padding gets in the way of your ideas. Good writers revise their work to leave out unnecessary words.

Check It Out   Read the following pairs of sentences. Notice how each padded sentence has been revised.

Padded   What I mean to say is that I agree.
Improved   I agree.

Padded   I am going to write about whales,
which are not fish, but mammals.
Improved   Whales are not fish, but mammals.

Padded What I want to do is catch the four
o'clock bus.

Improved I want to catch the four o'clock bus.

- Do you notice how much clearer and more direct the improved sentences are?

Try Your Skill Decide which sentences are padded in each of the following groups. Copy each padded sentence. Draw a line through each unnecessary word or phrase. Then write the improved sentences.

1. What I want to say is that bees are social insects. They live together in large groups. Each insect in the group has one job to do.

2. Never go to bed angry. The reason that you shouldn't is because your anger may keep you awake or give you nightmares. Then your night will be as bad as your day was.

3. What I think is that Willie Mays was one of the greatest ballplayers of all time. He played twenty-two seasons in the major leagues. Mays had a career batting average of .302 and hit 660 home runs.

Keep This in Mind

- A padded sentence has more words than are necessary to express an idea.
- Leave out words and phrases that add nothing to the idea in a sentence.

Now Write Improve the following padded sentences by rewriting them.

Well, you see during World War II, Navajo Indians sent secret messages for the United States Marines. You see they used a code that substituted the Navajo names of animals for military terms. On account of the fact that the Navajo language is so varied, the enemy never broke the code.

All Join Hands

Combining Sentences

Here's the Idea   You know that a sentence states a complete idea. Sometimes you may write two or more short sentences that have similar ideas. These sentences can often be combined. The new sentence will include the ideas stated in the shorter sentences.

Sometimes two sentences contain similar ideas that are equally important. You can combine sentences like these by using a comma and the word *and*.

> Diane plays the flute. Her brother plays the piano.
> Diane plays the flute, **and** her brother plays the piano.

Other sentences may state contrasting ideas of equal importance. You can combine sentences like these with a comma and the word *but*.

> Ted barely finished the test. He got the highest grade.
> Ted barely finished the test, **but** but he got the highest grade.

Sometimes, two sentences state a choice between ideas. You can combine sentences like these with a comma and *or*.

> We can wait for the bus. We can start walking.
> We can wait for the bus , **or** we can start walking.

Check It Out   Read the following sentences.

1. Do you want to order Chinese food, or should we make some?
2. Jean mopped up the water, and Andy called the plumber.
3. The work was hard, but the results were worth it.

- Which sentence combines closely related ideas of equal importance?
- Which sentence combines contrasting ideas of equal importance?
- Which sentence combines ideas of equal importance and offers a choice between them?

Try Your Skill   Combine each pair of sentences. Follow the directions in parentheses.

1. Nick brought the camera. Sheila took all the pictures. (Join with **, but.**)
2. The wind was brisk. The water was rough. (Join with **, and.**)
3. Did Inspector Clouseau know the truth? Was he only guessing? (Join with **, or.**)

Keep This in Mind

- Use a comma and *and* to combine sentences that express closely related ideas of equal importance.
- Use a comma and *but* to combine sentences that express contrasting ideas of equal importance.
- Use a comma and *or* to combine sentences that offer a choice between ideas of equal importance.

Now Write   Combine the following pairs of sentences, using **, and** or **, but** or **, or.**

1. Joyce chopped the vegetables. Adam sliced the cheese.
2. Aluminum is lighter than steel. It is more expensive.
3. Lisa weeded the garden. I watered the plants.
4. The metal must be painted. It will rust.
5. The shoes fit. They don't feel comfortable.

A Look at Paragraphs

What Is It?

Learning About Paragraphs

Here's the Idea   You want your reader to understand what you have to say. Your reader will understand your ideas if you organize them well. The basic tool for organizing ideas in writing is the paragraph.

What is a paragraph? A **paragraph** is a group of sentences that work together. Each sentence says something about one main idea.

Read each of the following groups of sentences. See if the sentences in each group work together.

1   Kit knew that she had to warn her friend. She snatched her cloak from the peg and, carrying her leather boots in her hand, crept down the stairs. She dared not try to unbolt the great front door. Instead, she tiptoed cautiously through the cold company room into the back chamber. She let herself out the shed door into the garden. She could hear shouts in the distance. Slipping hurriedly into her boots, she fled along the roadway.

—ELIZABETH GEORGE SPEARE

2   The young boy turned over on the thin mattress as the summer sun edged its way over the East River. The sun moved slowly. It spread a soft, gray light down the boy's face, and he was awakened. His eyes opened quickly, hurrying sleep away. He lay still a moment, smelling and hearing the morning all around him.

3   You can create your own T-shirt design. Use a plain T-shirt, a piece of cloth, an apple, a stiff paintbrush, and textile paint in any colors of your choice. Begin by slicing an apple in half lengthwise. Brush a thick layer of textile paint over the cut side of the apple halves. Press the apple, paint side down, on a piece of cloth. Keep practicing until you have it just right. Then print your T-shirt.

Check It Out   Look again at the three groups of sentences above. The first group tells a story. The second group describes a person. The third explains a process. Are they all paragraphs?

- Does each group of sentences deal with one idea?
- Does every sentence in each group say something about the main idea?

Try Your Skill   Below are two groups of sentences. One is a paragraph. One is not. Read each group and decide which one is not a good paragraph. Write a sentence or two explaining why that group of sentences does not make a good paragraph.

1   I'll never forget the championship game of the baseball season. That night our family had fried chicken for dinner. Chicken is my favorite food. There were two outs in the last inning and I was batting. I like batting better than fielding. We were behind, but the tying run was at third base. Unfortunately, I popped the ball up to the infield for the final out.

2   To change a flat tire, first secure the emergency brake, then loosen the nuts on the wheel rim. Next use the jack to raise the car. Then replace the flat tire with the spare. Turn the nuts until they are almost tight. Finally, lower the car and tighten the nuts.

Keep This in Mind

- Each paragraph should deal with one main idea.
- Every sentence in the paragraph should say something about the main idea.

Now Write   Find one of the groups of sentences in **Try Your Skill** that does not make a good paragraph. Look it over, using **Keep This in Mind** as a guide. Find the sentences that do not belong. Copy the remaining sentences in the form of a paragraph. Put your paragraph into your folder.

United We Stand

Recognizing Unity in a Paragraph

Here's the Idea   You have learned that a paragraph is a group of sentences that work together. This means that all of the sentences tell about one main idea. When all of the sentences in a paragraph work together to express one main idea, the paragraph has **unity.**

Check It Out   Read this paragraph:

> Tracy Austin is one of the few athletes who achieved greatness at an early age. By the age of ten, she had won age-group titles in national tennis tournaments. She was one of the youngest contenders ever to play at Wimbledon. In 1981, Austin became the youngest woman ever to win the U.S. Open, beating such tennis greats as Chris Evert Lloyd and Martina Navratilova. She was just sixteen years old at the time.

- Do all of these sentences work together? Do they all tell about one main idea? Does this paragraph have unity?

Try Your Skill   Here are four paragraphs without unity. In each, one sentence does not work with the others. Write the sentence in each paragraph that does not belong.

1   I guess I've been on every kind of diet ever invented. Many books on diets have been published recently. I remember the time I resolved to eat only fruit and cottage cheese. I gained three pounds, and to this day I hate the sight of cottage cheese. Then there was the B diet: boiled eggs and bananas. I ate so many bananas that I felt like King Kong. The trouble was, I was still shaped like him, too.

2   Thomas Jefferson and Alexander Hamilton did not get along. The tall, red-headed lawyer from Virginia had little use for the

ideas of the smaller, dark-complexioned former lawyer from New York. The two disagreed on the idea of democracy. Jefferson was in favor of it, Hamilton against it. They disagreed, too, on which group the national government should favor—farmers, or those who owned factories and businesses. Hamilton was killed in a duel.

3   My cousin and I learned most of our family's history by playing in Grandmother's attic. In one corner stood a brass-bound trunk, filled with dolls once treasured by aunts and mothers. Grandfather's World War I uniform hung on a metal rack, along with once-stylish dresses. The clothing now is much more comfortable than it was thirty years ago. When we played with the toys our mothers had played with, or dressed up in the old-fashioned clothes, we felt that the past was truly part of our lives.

4   Senses are so basic that all animals have them, but not all animals use their senses in the same way. Many people have lost their sense of hearing. A frog's eye, for instance, does not see a fly as we see it. In fact, a frog won't spot a fly at all unless the fly moves. Put a frog into a cage with dead insects, and it will starve.

Keep This in Mind

- All of the sentences in a paragraph should work together. They should all say something about the main idea. Then a paragraph has unity.

Now Write   Label your paper **United We Stand.** Choose one of the paragraphs from **Try Your Skill** that does not have unity. Look at the sentence on your paper that does not belong with the others. Now write the paragraph so that it has unity. Save your paragraph in your folder.

What's It All About?

Using a Topic Sentence

Here's the Idea To write a paragraph that has unity, you must have a **topic sentence.** The topic sentence tells what the paragraph is about. It states the main idea in a clear and interesting way. The topic sentence is often the first sentence in a paragraph.

There are two good reasons for using topic sentences. First, a topic sentence helps you to keep track of your ideas. Make sure that all of your sentences tell about the main idea stated in the topic sentence. Then you will not make the mistake of bringing in unrelated ideas. All your sentences will work together. Second, the topic sentence helps your readers. It tells them what the paragraph is going to be about.

Check It Out Read the following paragraph.

> When Manolo was nine he became aware of three important facts in his life. First, the older he became, the more he looked like his father. Second, he, Manolo Oliver, was a coward. Third, everyone in the town of Arcangel expected him to grow up to be a famous bullfighter, like his father. —JAMES RAMSEY ULLMAN

- Does this paragraph have a topic sentence?
- Does the topic sentence state what the paragraph is about?

Try Your Skill Write the topic sentence from each group.

1. (a) My toes became numb inside my boots.
   (b) As I walked home, the biting cold pierced my body.
   (c) Even under a heavy jacket, my skin had goosebumps.
   (d) My face felt as if it would never thaw.
   (e) I exhaled in huge bursts of steamy fog.

2. (a) In first-class sections, there were elegant dining cars, homey parlor cars, and comfortable sleepers.

   (b) However, dust from the plains swept over the passengers.

   (c) Railroads brought new speed to travel.

   (d) In addition, floods and blizzards often destroyed sections of track, causing delays.

   (e) Early railroads were both enjoyable and unpleasant.

3. (a) She applied it to everything I did.

   (b) Sometimes she'd say it barely loud enough to hear, and I'd stop and think about what I was doing.

   (c) At other times she'd write it on a piece of paper and put the paper where I'd be sure to find it.

   (d) "An ounce of prevention is worth a pound of cure" was my grandmother's favorite saying.

   (e) I used to tease her about her "all-purpose" advice, but I never questioned the wisdom of that advice.

Keep This in Mind

- Be sure that every paragraph has a topic sentence.
- Be sure that the topic sentence states clearly what the paragraph is about.

Now Write Look at the sentences below. They all tell about one main idea. However, they do not have a topic sentence. Write a clear and interesting topic sentence that states the main idea these sentences tell about. Share your topic sentence with your classmates. Save your paragraph in your folder.

Our English language includes *skunk* and *pecan* from the Algonquin Indians. *Persimmon* came to us from the Powhatan Indians of Virginia. *Moose* came into English from the Narragansett tribes, *woodchuck* from the Cree Indians, and *toboggan* from the Micmacs of New England.

Follow the Leader

Developing a Paragraph

Here's the Idea The sentences that follow a topic sentence should tell about the main idea of the paragraph. That means that these sentences should add important information about the main idea. This information can include **details, examples,** and **facts and figures.**

Details can be used to develop a topic sentence.

> My uncle's stall in the market is a feast for the senses. The aromas of sweet strawberries and pungent onions rise above the rows of lettuce in every shade of green. Uncle Max shouts, "Get your berries, two pints a dollar," waving his arms to signal the crowds to come take a look. He tumbles potatoes into a scale which responds with creaking springs and a rattling chain, while the black arrow swings downward—one, two, three pounds.

An **example** develops the topic sentence in this paragraph:

> Dolphins can solve simple problems. At Marineland of Florida, gates separate the dolphins' small pools from the big show pool. One night some dolphins must have wanted to play in the big pool. They figured out how to use their snouts to open the gates.—*National Geographic World*

Facts and figures are used to develop the topic sentence in this paragraph:

> The open mouth of a killer whale is a frightening sight. An adult may have as many as fifty teeth. The teeth are cone-shaped, three inches long and one inch in diameter. They curve inward toward the throat and interlock when the jaw is closed. The teeth are used for grasping, ripping, and tearing food, but not for chewing. The food is swallowed whole or in large chunks.
>
> —SEYMOUR SIMON

Check It Out   Read this paragraph about the Mayan Indians.

The Mayan Indians excelled in many fields. They created pyramid-shaped buildings, covered with stone carvings and filled with painted murals. They developed a written language based on pictures and used it to write books. They created a number system that included zero. But their greatest accomplishment was their calendar. It was as accurate as ours is today.

- Is the topic sentence developed by details? Is it developed by examples? Is it developed by facts and figures?

Try Your Skill   Find and write the topic sentence in this paragraph. Write whether it is developed by details, examples, or facts and figures.

Even in a small area of the desert there can be a tremendous variation in temperatures. Temperatures on the ground are often 30 to 60 degrees higher than air temperatures in the shade. The National Park Service has recorded some astounding ground temperatures in Death Valley. In 1974 a reading of 176° was recorded and in 1978 a reading of 182°. In 1972 a reading of 201° was recorded. This is almost the boiling point of water.

Keep This in Mind

- The main idea of a paragraph can be developed by using details, an example, or facts and figures.

Now Write   Find the topic sentence in the following paragraph and write it. Then write whether the topic sentence is developed with details, examples, or facts and figures.

A white mare galloped west along the strand against the fierce spring wind. Her tail was stretched out stiff and motionless. Flecks of foam dropped from her jaws with each outrush of her breath. Her wide-open nostrils were blood red. Hailstones, carried slantwise at a great speed by the wind's power, struck with a loud noise against the canvas of her saddle. —LIAM O'FLAHERTY

What's in a Name?

Recognizing Three Kinds of Paragraphs

Here's the Idea   When you write, you may want to tell a story. You may want to describe someone or something. You may want to explain. For each of these times you would use one of the three kinds of paragraphs: narrative, descriptive, or explanatory.

A **narrative** paragraph tells a story about something or someone. It tells that story in the same order that it happened.

A **descriptive** paragraph is a picture drawn with words. It appeals to your senses of sight, sound, taste, smell, and touch.

An **explanatory** paragraph explains something as clearly as possible. It may tell "how" or "why." A "how" paragraph explains what is to be done first, what is to be done next, and so on through all the steps in a process. A "why" paragraph gives reasons why something is so. It begins with an idea or an opinion. Then it is expanded with reasons that tell why the idea or opinion is true.

You will learn more about narrative, descriptive, and explanatory paragraphs in Sections 8–11.

Check It Out   Read the following paragraphs.

1   In the roads where the teams moved, the dirt crust broke and the dust formed. Every moving thing lifted the dust into the air. A walking man lifted a thin layer as high as his waist. A wagon lifted the dust as high as the fence tops and an automobile boiled a cloud behind it. The dust was long in settling back again.

—JOHN STEINBECK

2   Keith was suspicious when he opened the front door. No one was supposed to be home, but he had heard strange, shuffling noises. Then some lights in the kitchen went off. Keith was worried. He headed towards the door. Suddenly his friends burst

into the room. "Surprise! Happy birthday!" they shouted. Then Keith laughed.

- Do these paragraphs tell stories, describe, or explain? Are they narrative, descriptive, or explanatory?

Try Your Skill   Read each paragraph. Write whether it is narrative, descriptive, or explanatory.

1   Dean had invented a new kind of pizza. On the bottom was a thick, crispy crust. On top of the crust were tangy tomatoes, then juicy sausage and pepperoni. Next came a second layer of tomato-covered crust to make a double-decker pizza. Thick, gooey cheese topped the creation.

2   All people would be happier as pet owners. Whether the pet is a dog, a rabbit, or a hamster, it is fun to watch and to play with. In its own way, a pet shows affection. In addition, it can teach its owner how to care for other living things. Certainly, no one is lonely with a pet.

Keep This in Mind

- A narrative paragraph tells a story.
- A descriptive paragraph describes someone or something.
- An explanatory paragraph explains "how" or "why."

Now Write   Below is a list of topics. For each topic, write *Narrative, Descriptive,* or *Explanatory* to show the kind of paragraph you would write for it. Then, briefly explain why. Label your paper **What's in a Name?** Save it in your folder.

my father's garden	why I like spring
why I enjoy hiking	Lake Geneva in winter
my first airplane ride	how to sail a boat
how to make papier mâché	the surprise of my life

Writing a Paragraph

Step by Step

Writing as a Process

Here's the Idea You have learned that a paragraph is a group of sentences that work together to express one main idea. You know that the main idea of a paragraph can be developed with details, examples, or facts and figures. You also know that a paragraph can tell a story, describe someone or something, or explain something. Now you are ready to start writing some paragraphs of your own.

You may have some questions as you get ready to write. What will you write about? Where will you get your ideas? Once you have begun, how can you improve what you have written? You can find the answers to these questions if you follow a plan when you write. This plan is called the **process of writing.**

The process of writing has three stages. The first stage is **pre-writing.** Pre-writing is all of the planning that you do before you write. This includes choosing a subject, gathering ideas, and putting those ideas into a logical order.

The second stage of the writing process is **writing the first draft.** This is your first attempt to put your ideas down on paper. At this stage you use the ideas you have gathered and organized to write a rough version of your paragraph.

The third and final stage of the writing process is **revising.** *Revise* means "to look over again in order to improve." At this stage of the writing process you try to make your paragraph better.

The lessons in this chapter will show you how you can use the writing process to improve your writing.

Check It Out Here are some things a writer does when writing a paragraph.

1. organizes ideas
2. corrects spelling errors
3. chooses a subject
4. puts ideas in sentence form
5. gathers information
6. improves sentences

- Which of these activities are part of pre-writing? writing the first draft? revising?

Try Your Skill Answer these questions about the writing process.

1. How many stages are there in the writing process? What is each stage called?
2. Name some things you would do during pre-writing.
3. What is the purpose of a first draft?
4. What is the reason for revising what you have written?

Keep This in Mind

- **Pre-writing** includes all the planning you do before you write.
- **Writing the first draft** is the stage where you write a rough version of your paragraph.
- **Revising** is the stage where you improve what you have written.

Now Write In order to become better at something, you have to practice. One of the best ways to get practice in writing is by keeping a journal. A *journal* is a notebook that you write in every day. It is a place where you can write about the things you do, think, or feel.

Get a notebook that you can use as your journal. Try to write in it each day. For today, write down the most interesting thing that you saw or did last week. Include as many details as you can.

What Do You Know?

Pre-Writing: Choosing a Subject

Here's the Idea   Have you ever stared at a blank piece of paper and grumbled, "I can't think of *anything* to write about?" Choosing a good subject for a paragraph or a composition can be hard. You can make the job easier, however, by learning what a good subject is and how to find one.

A good subject is something that interests you and is important to you. A good subject is also something that you know about.

Knowing what makes a good subject is the first part of choosing something to write about. The second part is knowing where to look for ideas. Here are two ways you can find good subjects to write about.

Journal Writing   In your journal you write about your ideas, your feelings, and your experiences. These are subjects that interest you and are important to you. They are also subjects you know something about. Read over what you've written in your journal. You'll find many good writing ideas there.

Brainstorming   Brainstorming is an enjoyable way to search for a subject. You can do it by yourself or with friends. Start out with a general idea such as *school*. Then build on that idea by writing down everything about school that comes into your mind. As you brainstorm, you will probably think of several subjects, such as "the food in the cafeteria," "the time the frog escaped from biology lab," and "why I like gym."

Check It Out   Here is what one student wrote in his journal during a brainstorming session on the subject *sports*.

- Do you see how brainstorming can lead from one idea to another?
- Can you find some subjects in these notes that this student might write about?

Try Your Skill Here are four very general subjects. Choose one, and spend about fifteen minutes brainstorming about it. As you brainstorm, make notes in your journal. Try to find two or three good subjects among the ideas you wrote down.

school   friends   family life at home   hobbies

Keep This in Mind

- Choose a subject that is important to you and that you know something about.
- Use journal writing and brainstorming to help you find good subjects for writing.

Now Write In the next few lessons you will be writing a paragraph of your own, one step at a time. Your first step, of course, is to choose a subject. Use what you have learned in this lesson to help you. When you have chosen your subject, write it on a piece of paper. Save it in your folder.

In Focus

Pre-Writing: Narrowing a Topic

Here's the Idea   Choosing a subject is the first step in writing a paragraph. Sometimes, however, you may choose a subject that is too broad or general to be covered well in a single paragraph. You will need to narrow your subject. This means that you will have to make it more specific.

The subject "vacations," for example, is too general. If you tried to write a paragraph about it, you might end up with something dull like this:

> I like vacations. I like being out of school.
> It's fun to go different places and do fun things.
> I wish my vacations were longer.

The subject "vacations" needs to be narrowed. One way to narrow a subject that is too general is by asking questions about it. Such questions might begin with *who, what, when, where, how,* and *why.*

> *Vacations*
>
> *Who?* me
> *What?* learned to ski
> *When?* last winter
> *Where?* Toll House slopes,
>   Stowe, Vermont
> *How?* lessons, practice
> *Why?* outdoor fun?

Now the general subject "vacations" has been narrowed to "my first attempts at skiing." Narrowing the subject in this way could lead to an interesting paragraph like this one:

> I've discovered that learning to ski can be a painful experience. When my family took a winter vacation to Stowe, Vermont, I decided to take skiing lessons. For five days, I climbed up the Toll House slopes and strapped on my skis. Each time, I soon found myself sliding along on my back or tumbling into a tree. On the sixth day, I sat and watched everyone else make it look easy.

Check It Out   Now it's your turn to work with the general subject "vacations." Try to narrow it to a more specific topic. Jot down your ideas.

- Did you narrow the subject by asking *who? what? when? where? how?* and *why?*
- Can your narrowed topic be covered in one paragraph?

Try Your Skill   Choose two of the general subjects below. Narrow each one by answering the questions *who? what? when? where? how?* and *why?*

family traditions	best friends
school rules	cafeteria food
my pet	gym class

Keep This in Mind

- Choose a subject that you can cover well in one paragraph.
- Narrow general subjects by asking *who? what? when? where? how?* and *why?*

Now Write   Think about the subject you chose in **What Do You Know?** Narrow that subject by asking *who? what? when? where? how?* and *why?* Write your narrowed topic in your journal.

A Better Birdfeeder

Pre-Writing: A Good Topic Sentence

Here's the Idea   Once you've narrowed your topic, you will have a good idea of what you want to write about. To make your idea clear to your reader, you will write a topic sentence for your paragraph.

A topic sentence states the main idea of a paragraph. It tells the reader what the paragraph is going to be about. When you write a topic sentence, keep the following points in mind.

A good topic sentence is direct and interesting.   Avoid unnecessary words in your topic sentence. These are words that introduce *you* instead of your topic. Don't write sentences like these:

> I am going to write about birdfeeders.
> My paragraph is about how dolphins talk to each other.

Instead, write direct and interesting statements like these:

> Building a birdfeeder takes just three easy steps.
> Dolphins have their own special language.

A good topic sentence is informative.   Your topic sentence should give specific information about your paragraph. Don't write general statements like these:

> Playing baseball can be exciting.
> Cheetahs run fast.

Instead, write specific and informative statements like these:

> I'll never forget my first pony league home run.
> The cheetah is the fastest land animal in the world.

Read this topic sentence.

In this paragraph, I'm going to write about why I like sports.

- Does this topic sentence avoid extra words that introduce you and not the topic?
- Is this topic sentence interesting?
- Does this topic sentence give specific information?

Try Your Skill Below are four poorly-written topic sentences. Rewrite two of them. Make each topic sentence direct and informative.

1. I want to tell you about my best friend George.
2. It is my opinion that school should be closed on Wednesdays.
3. My paragraph is going to be about the hardships of the early sailors.
4. I think I can tell you in this paragraph how to fry a fish.

Keep This in Mind

- A topic sentence should be direct, interesting, and informative.
- Avoid extra words in a topic sentence that introduce you and not the topic.
- Give specific information in a topic sentence.

Now Write Think about the topic you narrowed in the last lesson, **In Focus**. Now write a good topic sentence that tells what your paragraph is about.

Writing a good topic sentence may take some time. Be patient. Try writing several different topic sentences. Which one does the best job of stating your main idea? Choose the best topic sentence. Be sure it is direct, interesting, and informative. Save your topic sentence in your folder.

Bits and Pieces

Pre-Writing: Gathering Ideas

Here's the Idea   The topic sentence introduces the main idea of a paragraph. The sentences that follow the topic sentence *develop* that main idea. That is, they add information that tells about the main idea. This information may be descriptive details. It may be examples, or facts and figures.

One way to gather information for a paragraph is through **personal observation.** Suppose that you want to describe the cafeteria at school. You would go to the cafeteria and write what you see, hear, smell, taste, and so on. These are the descriptive details you would use to develop your main idea.

Another way to gather information is by **brainstorming.** Perhaps you are writing a paragraph about all the rules a student has to follow at school. Think about your subject and write down all of the examples, incidents, and ideas that come into your head. These details will help you to explain your main idea when you write your paragraph.

A third way to gather information is by **doing research** in the library. Maybe you want to write a paragraph about how fast some animals can travel. You would find the facts and figures you need to explain your main idea by looking up different animals in an encyclopedia.

Check It Out   Read these pre-writing notes.

> *Uncle Dom's Butcher Shop*
> Smells: · sausage, sawdust, cheese
> Touch : · rough, greasy butcher blocks
> · cold display cases / razor-sharp knives

Lights: · rows of steaks, chops / mounds of ground beef
· Uncle Dominick – his gold tooth in front
· freezer cases (chrome and glass)
Sounds: · knives being sharpened
· meat cleaver on butcher block
· slap of meat on the scale
· slicer

- How do you think these descriptive details were gathered?

Try Your Skill Here are four topic sentences. Read each one and decide what kind of information is needed to develop it. Would you use descriptive details, examples, or facts and figures? Would you gather this information through personal observation, brainstorming, or research?

1. Paramedics help people in many kinds of emergencies.
2. My neighbor's kitchen is a most comfortable room to be in.
3. Television programs get sillier each year.
4. Chicago has some of the world's tallest buildings.

Keep This in Mind

- You can gather ideas through personal observation, by brainstorming, and by looking things up.
- The kind of ideas you gather depends on what your paragraph is about.

Now Write Gather some ideas and information for your paragraph. First read your topic sentence. Then ask yourself what kind of information you need to develop it: descriptive details, examples, or facts and figures. Use personal observation, brainstorming, or research to gather this information. Write your information. Save your notes in your folder.

First Things First

Pre-Writing: Organizing a Paragraph

Here's the Idea Once you have gathered information for your paragraph, you must make another decision. How should this information be arranged?

There are basically three ways to organize information in a paragraph. The method you choose will depend on the purpose of your paragraph. One way is to arrange details in *the order that they happened or should happen.* This is called **chronological order.** You would choose this order if your purpose were to tell a story or explain how to do something.

A second way to organize details is to arrange them in *the order that a viewer would notice them.* This is called **spatial order.** You would use this order if your purpose were to describe something—the objects in your room, for example.

A third way to organize details is to arrange them in **the order of their importance.** You might start with the least important idea and work toward the most important. Or you could do just the opposite. You would use this kind of order if some of your ideas are more important than others.

When you are organizing the details for a paragraph, choose an order that fits the type of paragraph that you are writing.

Check It Out Read the following paragraph.

Making a delicious chocolate milkshake is as easy as one, two, three. First, drop two scoops of creamy vanilla ice cream into a blender. Second, add about one cup of milk and as much chocolate syrup as you like. Third, blend the ingredients at high speed for a minute or two. Now pour the milk shake into a chilled glass, and enjoy a mouth-watering, warm-weather treat!

- What is the purpose of this paragraph?
- In what order have the details been arranged?

• Does the arrangement fit the purpose of the paragraph?

Try Your Skill   Here are some pre-writing notes for a paragraph explaining how to paint a bike. Organize the notes so that a good paragraph can be written from them. Remember to choose an order that fits the purpose of the paragraph. When you have finished, write the kind of order that you used.

- finally, wax the newly-painted bike
- after primer dries, spray on metal paint
- begin by cleaning bike with steel wool
- before applying metal paint, spray on coat of primer paint
- after sanding, use masking tape to cover all parts you don't want to paint
- when bike is clean, sand all parts you want to paint
- when metal paint dries, remove masking tape

Keep This in Mind

• The details in a paragraph can be organized in three ways:
1. chronological order, or the order in which they happened or should happen.
2. spatial order, or the order in which a viewer would notice them.
3. the order of their importance.
• Details should be organized to fit the type of paragraph you are writing.

Now Write   Look over the details you gathered in the last lesson, **Bits and Pieces.** Organize these details so that you can write a good paragraph from them.

First ask yourself what type of paragraph you are writing. Then choose an order that fits your purpose. Save your organized details in your folder.

Part 7

Roughing It

Writing the First Draft

Here's the Idea   All the work you've done on your paragraph up to now has been part of pre-writing, the first stage of the writing process. Now you are ready to begin the second stage of the process, **writing the first draft**.

The first draft is the first time you write your ideas down in paragraph form. It is a chance for you to experiment. You may find out as you write your first draft that your topic sentence is weak. If that is the case, go ahead and rewrite it. You might decide that the order of your details needs to be changed. Feel free to move them around. You may even discover that you need more information. If so, stop writing and look for more details. Remember, your first draft is not your final paragraph. You can change it as much as you want to. You may even write several drafts before you are satisfied with your paragraph.

As you write your first draft, concentrate on explaining your ideas as well as you can. Don't worry about whether a word is spelled correctly, or whether you need a comma in a sentence. You will have time later on to fix your spelling and punctuation. Skip lines as you write so you will have room to make corrections.

Check It Out   Read this first draft. It was written from the pre-writing notes on pages 70–71.

> My favorite place to spend a Saturday afternoon is my uncle Dominick's butcher shop. I love the smell of the sausages and cheeses. Uncle Dom is always smiling and talking to the customers. Aunt Christina is there too. She arranges the steaks into rows

in the display cases. I can hear the knives click as she sharpens them. The customers always tell her say hello to your family. Everybody is friendly. That's why I like my uncle Dom's butcher shop.

- Does this first draft have a clear topic sentence?
- Does this draft use ideas from the pre-writing notes on pages 70–71?
- Has the writer added any new details to the draft that weren't in the pre-writing notes?

Try Your Skill Look over the pre-writing notes that you organized in **Try Your Skill** on page 73. Use your organized notes to write a first draft of a paragraph about painting a bike. Write a topic sentence for the paragraph. Remember, you can add new details if you want to.

Keep This in Mind

- A first draft is the first written version of your paragraph.
- A first draft is a chance for you to experiment with your ideas.
- When you write a first draft, don't worry about spelling and punctuation. Just get your ideas down in paragraph form.

Now Write Take out your organized notes from the last lesson, **First Things First.** Write a first draft of your paragraph. Don't be afraid to change your ideas as you write. Feel free to experiment. Remember to skip lines as you write. Save your first draft in your folder.

Saying Goodbye

The First Draft: Ending a Paragraph

Here's the Idea   Once you have written your ideas in paragraph form, your first draft is nearly finished. All that it needs is a good ending sentence.

A good ending sentence should follow naturally from what you have already written. It should tie the paragraph together by summing up the main idea. The ending sentence should not add any new information to the paragraph.

A good ending sentence should also be interesting. Don't just repeat your topic sentence. Put a new twist on your words. Try to make your ending as interesting as your beginning.

Check It Out   Read the following paragraph.

> My friend George is a "gopher." George works for his father during the summers. George and his father build and repair houses. Most of the time, George's father does the carpentry. When he needs nails, he yells, "George, go for the nails." When he wants coffee, he says, "George, go for some coffee." George is my best friend.

- Does the paragraph have an ending sentence?
- Does the ending sentence follow naturally from the rest of the paragraph? Does it sum up the idea of the paragraph?
- Is the ending sentence interesting? Explain your answer.

Try Your Skill   Revise the ending sentences of these two paragraphs. Be sure each ending sentence sums up the main idea of the paragraph. Try to make each ending sentence interesting.

1   Susan joined the sea of subway riders. Clutching her purse, she went down the escalator. She was pushed along with the crowd, first to the ticket booth and then to one of the screeching trains. Once inside, she saw that there was no chance of getting a seat. The subway was powered by electricity.

2   Homemade gifts are the best gifts. Not only are they less expensive than bought gifts, but they can also be more personal. Homemade gifts show that the giver cares, because they require time, energy, and creativity. They are appreciated more than gifts that are bought from a store. I made my own Christmas gift two years ago.

Keep This in Mind

- A paragraph should have an ending sentence.
- A good ending sentence is interesting and sums up the main idea of the paragraph.
- A good ending sentence should not add any new information to the paragraph.

Now Write   Reread your first draft. Write an ending sentence that is interesting and that sums up the main idea of the paragraph. Save your draft in your folder.

Icing the Cake

Revising Your First Draft

Here's the Idea   You have finished writing your first draft. Now you are ready to begin the last stage of the writing process: **revising.**

The purpose of revision is to improve what you have written. All writers have to revise their first drafts. They know that careful revision will make their writing the best it can be.

When you begin revising your rough draft, first work on your ideas. Then work on your organization. Check to see that your paragraph begins with a good topic sentence. Be sure all of the details you have used help to develop the main idea of your paragraph. Look at the arrangement of those details. Does the order make sense? See that you have ended your paragraph with a good ending sentence.

When you are sure that your ideas are strong and in good order, look at the language you have used. Is it lively? Is it interesting? Does it make your paragraph come alive for your readers? Replace any dull language that you find.

Finally, you will want to proofread your draft. Is your grammar correct? Have you used capital letters where they are needed? Have you used the right punctuation? Are all of the words spelled correctly? Use a dictionary and the Handbook sections of this book if you need help.

When you are satisfied that your revised paragraph is as good as it can be, make a final copy of it. Proofread this final copy one last time to correct any mistakes.

Check It Out   Read this revised version of the first draft on pages 74–75.

My favorite place to spend a Saturday afternoon is my uncle Dominick's butcher shop. I love the smell of the spicy sausages and the sharp cheeses. Uncle Dom is always smiling as he talks to his customers. His gold tooth gleams in the bright white light. Aunt Christina helps out, too. She arranges the steaks and chops into neat rows in the shiny display cases. I can hear the click and scrape of the knives as she sharpens them. The customers always tell her, "Say hello to your family." Everybody is so friendly. Who wouldn't enjoy a place as warm and happy as my uncle Dom's butcher shop?

- How is this version different from the one on pages 74–75? Why is it better?

Try Your Skill Revise this draft. Improve the topic sentence. Add interesting details. Replace any dull language. Add a good ending sentence. Compare your revision with those of your classmates.

The best time is lunch. We all go from class to the lunchroom. Sometimes we bring lunch from home. Then we can trade. Sometimes we buy lunch. Everyone talks about what to do after school. There is music on the loudspeaker.

Keep This in Mind

- When you revise, try to improve your ideas, organization and word choice.
- Proofread to correct any errors in grammar, capitalization, punctuation and spelling.

Now Write Revise your first draft. Use the guidelines you studied in this lesson. When you are satisfied with your revision, make a good copy of your paragraph. Save your paragraph in your folder.

The Process of Writing

The Process of Writing

In the last section, you learned about the three main stages in the process of writing. You learned how to choose and narrow subjects. You learned how to gather and organize information during pre-writing. You learned how to write a first draft, and how to revise.

Now you can begin practicing your writing skills. In the next few sections, you will be writing many different kinds of paragraphs and compositions. However, no matter what kind of writing you do, the process of writing remains the same.

In this lesson, you will review the process of writing from beginning to end. First, read about each step in the process. Then look at the example that shows how one student followed each step.

Pre-Writing   Sometimes you write in response to an assignment. Sometimes you choose to write in order to communicate something that is important to you. No matter what or why you write, you will find the pre-writing, or planning, stage to be very important.

Before you write, you may want to brainstorm for subject ideas. Perhaps you have kept a journal. Look through it for interesting subjects to write about. When you choose a subject, narrow it. That is, make it specific enough so that it can be covered well in a given length.

Jot down some notes and ideas about your topic. These notes may include lists of descriptive details, examples, or facts and figures that you can use to develop your topic. You can gather this kind of information through personal observations, by brainstorming, or by using the library.

When you have gathered enough details, you need to organize them. You may not need to use all of the information you have collected. Look over your details and cross out any that do not relate directly to your main idea. Then arrange your details in the best order for the kind of writing you are doing. Three kinds of order you might use are chronological order, spatial order, and the order of importance.

Pre-Writing

You list possible topics and choose one.

You list details, choose the most important ones, and organize them.

topics

(Rocky to the vet)   Red Sox win

history test   the beach   moving day

details

① Rocky needed shots
⑥ rabbit on a leash
② Rocky hides under bed (he knew!)
⑦ four cats
⑧ heartworm (false alarm)
④ smell of disinfectant

③ Rocky won't get in car
spotless office
⑤ pet photos on wall
collie on way to surgery
⑨ Rocky gets doggie treat
smiling assistant

Writing the First Draft   At this point in the process of writing, you are ready to write your first draft. Simply put your pencil to paper and write. Don't try to make anything perfect at this stage. Don't worry about spelling or punctuation. Let whatever happens, happen. Just put your ideas down in paragraph form, following the order you decided on. You will have time later to revise. Skip lines as you write, so that you will have space to make corrections.

You write a paragraph about your topic.

I had to take Rocky to the vet for his shots. I knew I was in for trouble. I had to drag him out from under the bed. He refused to get in the car. At the office, we waited to see the doctor. The office smelled like disinfectant. There were pet photos on the wall. In the waiting room was a lady with four cats. A boy had a rabbit on a leash he was shaking. When the doctor looked at Rocky, he thought Rocky might have a case of heartworm. It was a false alarm. After his shots, Rocky got a doggie treat. He couldn't get out of the doctor's office fast enough. And that was my trip to the vet with Rocky.

Revising   At this stage of the process, you have to check what you have written. You should read your first draft carefully and decide how you can make it better. Here are some questions you should ask yourself about your first draft.

1. Have I written a topic sentence? Is it interesting, direct, and informative?
2. Have I included enough details to develop my topic?
3. Do all of my details tell about the main idea of the paragraph?
4. Have I organized my details well?
5. Have I used lively, interesting language?
6. Have I written a strong ending?

As you answer these questions, you will discover how to improve what you have written.

Proofreading   Proofreading is the last stage of revising. Check your draft to see that you have used correct grammar, capitalization, punctuation, and spelling. Use the Handbook sections of this textbook and a dictionary to check your work.

As you revise your first draft, use the following proofreading marks to show your corrections and changes.

Proofreading Symbols

Symbol	Meaning	Example
∧	add	would gone
≡	capitalize	United states
/	make lower case	our club President
∾	reverse	thier
✗	take out	finished the the race
¶	make new paragraph	....be over. New ideas
⊙	period	....and stop Before we
⋏	add comma	Red, blue and green are

Here is how the paragraph about Rocky was revised.

You
rewrite.

When Mom said
I had to take Rocky, to the vet ,my collie
for his yearly shots, I knew I was in for
trouble. First, I had to drag him out
from under the my bed. Then, He refused to
get in to the car. At the office, we
waited to see the doctor. The office
smelled like disinfectant. There were
pet photos on the wall. In the
waiting room sat was a lady with four
fat cats. They hissed at Rocky, and he barked right back.
A boy had a rabbit on a leash.
The rabbit
he was shaking. When the doctor
examined
looked at Rocky, he thought Rocky
might have a case of heartworm. It
turned out to be
was a false alarm. After he got his shots,
was given Then he dragged me to the door.
Rocky got a doggie treat. He couldn't
get out of the doctor's office fast
a trip to the vet with Rocky can be an
enough. And that was my trip to
exhausting experience.
the vet with Rocky.

You
express
your
idea
in a
different
way.

Making the Final Copy Finally, when you are satisfied that your writing is clear and correct, make a final copy. Write carefully. Make your work as neat as possible.

When you have finished your final copy, proofread it one last time. If you discover a mistake, correct it neatly.

Final Copy

> When Mom said I had to take Rocky, my collie, to the vet for his yearly shots, I knew I was in for trouble. First, I had to drag him out from under my bed. Then, he refused to get into the car. At the office, we waited to see the doctor. The office smelled like disinfectant. In the waiting room sat a lady with four fat cats. They hissed at Rocky, and he barked right back. A boy had a rabbit on a leash. The rabbit was shaking. When the doctor examined Rocky, he thought Rocky might have a case of heartworm. It turned out to be a false alarm. After he got his shots, Rocky was given a doggie treat. Then he dragged me to the door. He couldn't get out of the doctor's office fast enough. A trip to the vet with Rocky can be an exhausting experience.

You can learn to write only by writing. Whenever you write, follow the steps in the writing process that you have learned. Each time you write, you will be learning something about writing and about yourself.

The Narrative Paragraph

Details, Details

Pre-Writing: Developing a Narrative

Here's the Idea   No matter what kind of paragraph you write, the three stages that make up the process of writing always remain the same. The choices you make at each stage of the process, however, will change. You want to make choices that best suit the kind of paragraph you are writing. In this section you will learn about some of the choices you might make as you develop a narrative paragraph.

A **narrative paragraph** tells a story. When you choose a subject for this type of paragraph, choose an interesting or exciting event. You might, for example, write about something that happened to you on a weekend camping trip or in your science class. You could also write a story that you make up, such as a space adventure.

When you have chosen a subject for your narrative paragraph, you must gather supporting ideas to develop your story. The best way to develop a narrative paragraph is to use **specific details.** These should be vivid, interesting details. They should make the story seem real to your readers.

You can find details to develop your story by doing what newspaper reporters do. Reporters ask *who? what? when? where? why?* and *how?* to discover the details that make up a story. Ask yourself these same questions about the story you want to tell. The answers to these questions will give you the details you need to write a good narrative paragraph.

Check It Out   Read these pre-writing notes for a paragraph about a toboggan ride.

Who?	Chris, David, Drew, and I
What?	tobogganing for the first time
Where?	Bemus Woods, twenty-foot high slide, six-foot long toboggan
When?	last weekend, during subzero cold, $-13°$
Why?	to try a new daredevil challenge
How?	bundled like mummies, laughing and shrieking

- Do you see how asking *who? what? when? where? why?* and *how?* can help you to find vivid, interesting details for your narrative paragraph?

Try Your Skill   Read the topics listed below. Ask *who? what? when? where? why?* and *how?* to gather specific details for one of the topics. List as many details as you can.

1. a sports event I attended
2. a birthday party
3. a funny incident in class

Keep This in Mind

- Develop narrative paragraphs by using specific details.
- The details for a narrative paragraph can be gathered by asking *who? what? when? where? why?* and *how?*

Now Write   Choose one of the two topics you did not use in **Try Your Skill.** Narrow the topic to a specific event you can tell about in one paragraph. Ask yourself questions to gather vivid, specific details that will make the story seem real to your readers. Save your pre-writing notes in your folder.

Then What Happened?

Pre-Writing: Using Chronological Order

Here's the Idea   After you have gathered details for your narrative paragraph, the next important pre-writing step is deciding how to organize those details. Remember, narrative paragraphs tell stories. As the narrator, or person who tells the story, you will want to tell your story in the same order that the events took place. This type of organization is called **chronological order.** *Chronological* means "arranged in the order of time."

Use a natural time sequence to organize the details of your story. Tell what happened first, what happened next, and so on. This will help the reader understand the story.

Look at this narrative paragraph. Notice that the events are told in the same order that they happened.

> He crawled through the doorway. He pulled the ankle flaps of his new winter moccasins up and tied them tightly. He fastened the thongs of the snowshoes firmly around his toes and around his ankles. He moved out onto the snow with wide, swinging steps and flapped his arms to make his blood flow fast and warm. It was good to be out in the open again, not just to push to the stream for water or to the storehouse for food, but out in the open and free to swing anywhere throughout his canyon.
>
> —JACK SHAEFER

Check It Out   Now read this narrative paragraph:

> Huck began to dig and scratch now. Some boards were soon uncovered and removed. They had concealed a natural chasm which led under the rock. Tom got into this and held his candle as far under the rock as he could, but said he could not see to the end of the rift. He proposed to explore. He stooped and passed

under; the narrow way descended gradually. He followed its winding course, first to the right, then to the left, Huck at his heels. Tom turned a short curve, by and by, and exclaimed: "My goodness, Huck, looky here!"

—MARK TWAIN

- In what kind of order are the details of this narrative arranged? How do you know?

Try Your Skill   Arrange the following pre-writing notes into a chronological order.

- My grandparents' 50th wedding anniversary party was wonderful.
- Before dinner, my grandparents opened gifts from friends and family.
- To end the evening, the band played polkas and waltzes.
- The evening began with everyone shouting "Surprise!" as my grandparents walked through the door.
- Then, there was a huge meal with a special cake for dessert.
- After dinner, my father gave a toast to the couple.

Keep This in Mind

- In a narrative paragraph, use chronological order to organize details.

Now Write   Look at the topic you chose and the pre-writing notes you gathered in the last lesson, **Details, Details.** Organize these notes in chronological order. Save your organized notes in your folder.

Who Said That?

Pre-Writing: Choosing a Point of View

Here's the Idea   You have chosen a story to tell. You have gathered and organized the details you need to tell your story. Before you can begin writing the first draft of your narrative, however, you have one more decision to make. You must choose a point of view.

Point of view means the eyes and mind through which something is written. You may decide to use first-person point of view or third-person point of view.

When you use **first-person point of view,** you use the first-person prounoun *I*. *I* becomes the person telling the story. The reader can see and know only what *I* sees, knows, and thinks about. You will usually use the first-person point of view when you write about things that happened to you. You may also use first person in an imaginary story. In an imaginary story, you can let *I* be the main character, or any character.

When you use **third-person point of view,** you often use the third-person pronouns *he* and *she*. The narrator is not part of the story. You use the third-person point of view to tell about things that happened to other people.

Choose the point of view that best suits the type of narrative you are writing. Be sure to use the same point of view throughout your paragraph.

Check It Out   Read the following paragraphs.

1   I wished that my first day of school at Hunter Junior High had been my last. Because I had transferred from a school three hundred miles away, I knew no one. The large building with its maze of halls confused me. Worst of all, no one talked to me or even smiled. I wondered if I would always feel like a stranger.

2   When Jane spotted a glowing mass in the dark sky, she shouted a warning to her friend Anita. She dived to the ground and pulled Anita with her. The reddish disc seemed to come closer. The girls blinked. Then the painful light disappeared. As they got up, Jane said she had never believed in flying saucers.

- Which of these paragraphs uses first-person point of view? Which uses third-person? How do you know?

Try Your Skill   Copy this paragraph twice. The first time, fill in the blanks with the correct pronouns for the first-person point of view. The second time, use correct pronouns for the third-person point of view

_____ sat on the bleachers, nervously tapping _____ feet and twisting the jersey of _____ uniform around _____ finger. The coach was calling out the names of the kids who had made the varsity squad. _____ knew _____ tryout had gone well, but there were so many talented players in the gym that day. Suddenly, _____ heard it. The coach was calling _____ name. _____ leaped to _____ feet and let out a whoop. _____ dream had just come true.

Keep This in Mind

- With first-person point of view, the first-person pronoun *I* is used. *I* tells the story.
- With third-person point of view, the third-person pronouns *he* and *she* are used. The narrator is not a part of the story.

Now Write   Think about the narrative paragraph you have been developing throughout these lessons. Decide whether you want to write it using first-person point of view or third-person point of view. Write your decision on the paper where you organized your pre-writing notes. Save these notes in your folder.

First, Then, Finally

Writing the First Draft

Here's the Idea All the work you've done so far has been part of the pre-writing stage. You are now ready for the next stage, writing the first draft. This is where you write your ideas in paragraph form for the first time.

As you write your first draft, remember that you are telling a story. In order to tell the story as it happened, you need special words and phrases to help you to show time order. These words and phrases are called **transitional words.**

Good transitional words show your readers when things happened in your story. Read this list of transitions.

first	now	at the beginning	before
then	soon	in the middle	after
next	later	at the end	by the time

As you write your first draft, include some of these transitional words. Also, use any other words and phrases, such as *suddenly* or *a few minutes later,* that help show time order.

Check It Out Read the following narrative paragraph.

Yesterday I headed the supermarket's "Ten Most Wanted" list. First, because I entered the store through the exit door, I set off the burglar alarm. Then I slipped and fell into a pyramid of citrus, sending grapefruit flying. Afterward, I was so nervous that I dropped a dozen eggs. Finally, I didn't bring enough money to pay for my groceries. Needless to say, I was not the supermarket's favorite customer that day.

- Find the transitional words. Do they help make the story clear?
- Do the transitional words show time-order?

Try Your Skill   Stories can be told with pictures as well as with words. Comic strips usually combine words with pictures. Some comic strips tell stories in pictures only. Here is one.

© 1971 Publishers Newspaper Syndicate

You are going to add words to these pictures. Tell what happens, frame by frame. Describe the action. Try to keep the humor of the cartoon.

First, jot down notes on your paper for each frame. Number each note to match the number of the frame it refers to.

Now write a few good transitional words for each frame. These should help you tell the story in the correct order. Use these transitional words along with your notes when you write about the cartoon.

Keep This in Mind

· Transitional words that show time-order help to make a narrative clear.

Now Write   Write the first draft of your narrative paragraph. Use the details you gathered. Put these details in the order you decided on. Use transitional words to show time order.

Don't worry about grammar, spelling, or punctuation as you write. Just get your ideas down on paper in paragraph form. Save your first draft in your folder.

Prance or Trudge?

Revising Your Narrative Paragraph

Here's the Idea When you revise your narrative paragraph, you want to make it the best it can be. Here are some questions you should ask yourself as you revise your narrative.

1. Have I included enough details to tell my story well?
2. Are my details arranged in chronological order?
3. Have I included transitional words to show time order?
4. Have I used the same point of view throughout?

One other thing you should look at as you revise is your choice of verbs. You can make your narrative come alive by using strong, specific verbs.

Some verbs, like *trudge* and *prance,* are strong and show action. Linking or state-of-being verbs, such as *is, become,* and *seem,* are weaker. It is stronger to write "Mary *won*" than "Mary *was* the winner."

You will also want to use verbs that are specific rather than general. For example, think of all the ways to say *look* that are more interesting and more specific. A detective, for example, might *spy, snoop, pry,* or *peep.* The detective might also *stare, survey, inspect,* or *examine.* Any one of these verbs is stronger and more specific than *look.*

As you revise your narrative paragraph, replace weak, general verbs with strong, specific ones.

Check It Out Notice the verbs in this paragraph.

> The skydiver *ignored* her fear. She *leaped* from the hatch of the plane and *arched* her body for a free fall. Her arms and legs *stretched* spiderlike. Suddenly, she *whirled* to the right, then the left, and *looped* backwards. She *had sailed* through a figure-eight stunt. Then, she *popped* her parachute.

- How do the verbs in italics make this narrative paragraph come alive?

Try Your Skill   Imagine that you walked to school on Monday and Friday last week. On Monday you were facing a tough math test. On Friday you were looking forward to videotaping a class play. Copy the following paragraph twice. The first time, write about Monday morning. Then write about Friday morning. Use strong, specific verbs to express your different moods on these two mornings. Compare your paragraphs with your classmates'.

On (Monday, Friday) morning, I _____ out the door on the way to school. I _____ around the corner and _____ down the street. When the light changed, I _____ across the street. I _____ up the school steps. The bell was ringing as I _____ into class.

Keep This in Mind

When revising a narrative paragraph:
- Use enough specific details to tell the story.
- Use clear chronological order and strong transitional words.
- Use the same point of view throughout.
- Use strong, specific verbs.

Now Write   Revise your first draft. First follow the guidelines presented in this lesson. Then proofread your draft. Be sure you have used correct grammar, capitalization, punctuation, and spelling. When you are satisfied that your narrative is the best it can be, make a final copy. Save your narrative paragraph in your folder.

The Descriptive Paragraph

Part 1 **Observe!**
Pre-Writing: Gathering Sensory Details

Part 2 **Top to Bottom**
Pre-Writing: Using Spatial Order

Part 3 **In, Out, and Around**
Writing the First Draft

Part 4 **The Choice Is Yours**
Revising Your Descriptive Paragraph

Observe!

Pre-Writing: Gathering Sensory Details

Here's the Idea When you write a descriptive paragraph, you are painting a picture with words. You want your reader to get to know the person, place, or thing you are describing as well as you know it. Once you have chosen a subject for your descriptive paragraph, how can you make that subject come alive for your readers?

The best way to develop a descriptive paragraph is through the use of sensory details. **Sensory details** tell about things that can be seen, heard, felt, tasted, and smelled. Sensory details can help paint a clear, real picture for your readers.

You can gather sensory details for your descriptive paragraph through **observation.** For instance, you might want to describe a place, such as the school cafeteria. Go to that place, or close your eyes and picture the place in your mind as clearly as possible. Write down the things you *see*. List the noises you *hear*. Make notes about how the food *tastes*, how the cafeteria *smells*, how objects in the cafeteria *feel* (greasy table, hot soup). When you have finished making your notes, you will have gathered many good sensory details. These details will make your readers feel as if they are right in that cafeteria with you.

Check It Out Read this descriptive paragraph.

Just as we were getting weary, we spotted a clear stream. The banks surrounding the stream were carpeted in thick, spongy moss. Shallow water bubbled and gurgled as it rushed across rocks. Sunlight glistened off the clear water. We hurriedly filled our cups and found the water numbingly cold. It tasted fresh as a liquid icicle. We dipped our burning feet into the blue water, resting them on the sharp stones that lined the bottom of the stream. We inhaled the crisp mountain air, lightly scented with the perfume of spring's first wildflowers.

- What sensory details are included in this descriptive paragraph?

Try Your Skill   Use your senses to create specific, lively descriptions. Try to imagine each of the sensations listed below. Then write two vivid words or phrases to describe each one.

1. the smell of soap
2. the feel of your hairbrush
3. the sounds of a football game
4. the taste of potato chips

5. the way a tennis ball looks
6. the taste of an orange
7. the way your nose looks
8. the feel of sand

Keep This in Mind

- When you write a descriptive paragraph, develop your description with sensory details.
- Gather sensory details through observation or memory.

Now Write   Think about some possible subjects for a descriptive paragraph. Make a list of persons (your best friend, a passenger on a bus), places (a locker room, a crowded beach), and things (a race car, a camel) you might want to describe.

Choose one of these as the subject of your descriptive paragraph. Observe your subject. Gather as many sensory details as you can about it. List each detail under the sense it is related to. Save your list of sensory details in your folder.

Top to Bottom

Pre-Writing: Using Spatial Order

Here's the Idea   When you organized the details of your narrative paragraph, the order you needed to use was clear. You wanted to tell your story in the same order that it really happened. How should you arrange the sensory details for your descriptive paragraph?

Whenever you describe something, you want your readers to see it in a special way. You should organize your details in the order that you want your readers to notice them. Start with the first detail you want them to notice. Then add the other details as they relate to this first one. This is called **spatial order.** Using spatial order, you might describe your subject from top to bottom, side to side, front to back, or near to far.

For example, you might be describing the driver of a bus. What do you want your readers to notice first? Her drab, brown uniform? Her friendly smile? Her strong, clear voice? What did *you* notice first? Then continue your description, leading your readers from one detail to another in the order that you want your readers to see them.

Read this descriptive paragraph. Notice how the details are organized.

> Professor Lookit invented a unique squirtgun. The barrel and trigger below it pump water like any other water pistol. From the bottom of the grip, a rubber tube runs down to a balloon-like tank, which is filled with water. At the side of the tank is a plug for filling. The main advantage of this gun is that it gives more squirts with fewer refills.

Check It Out   Read this description:

My family calls my dresser "Danny's dump." The top of the dresser is usually piled high with clothes, sports equipment, and a few leftover snacks. The top drawer is jammed so full of old comic books that I can't open it. The drawer below has socks and T-shirts spilling out over the sides. I leave the bottom drawer open for my dog's bones, toys, and scraps. My dresser might not be orderly, but I know where everything is.

- How does this description use spatial order?

Try Your Skill   Make notes for a description of someone or something in your classroom. First observe your subject, listing as many sensory details as you can. Then put these details into the order you would want a reader to notice them.

Keep This in Mind

- Use spatial order to organize the sensory details for your descriptive paragraph.
- Put your details in the order that you want your readers to notice them.

Now Write   Look over the sensory details you gathered in the last lesson. Decide the order in which you want your readers to notice them. Then arrange the details in that order. You may want to try several different arrangements until you find one that best suits your subject. Save your organized details in your folder.

In, Out, and Around

Writing the First Draft

Here's the Idea   Now that you have organized your sensory details, you are ready to write the first draft of your descriptive paragraph. As you write your first draft, remember that you want your readers to see your subject in a special way. Try to make your description as clear as possible.

If you think you need to make some parts of your description clearer, you may want to add transitional words. When you wrote your narrative paragraph, you used transitional words to tell *when*. In a descriptive paragraph, you use transitional words to tell *where*.

Here are some examples of transitional words and phrases used in description:

in	ahead of	down	to the right
on	outside	by	back and forth
above	downstairs	front	at the end of
under	close to	north	side by side
behind	between	east	in back of

Look at how this description of a dog uses transitional words and phrases to show spatial order.

> My dog Duke came inside last night looking as if he had lost a major battle. On top of his head two patches of fur were missing. Over one ear was a long scratch, and his matted tail hung down behind him. He limped because he was holding his injured left rear leg up under his belly. Duke needed first aid and my kindly attention.

Check It Out   Now read this description of a dungeon:

> The prisoner found himself in a dark, musty cell. A tiny vent high on the wall in front of him was the only opening. A leaky pipe above him dripped onto an iron cot, and a puddle of foul water stood in the center of the cell. Insects skittered around the edges of the dirt floor. He shivered in disgust, as the solid iron door slammed behind him.

- What transitional words in this descriptive paragraph tell *where*?

Try Your Skill   Write a brief description of the objects in the front of your classroom, including anything on the wall. Use transitional words from the list in this lesson to make your description clear. Compare your description with those of your classmates.

Keep This in Mind

- To make your description clear, use transitional words that tell *where*.

Now Write   Write the first draft of your descriptive paragraph. Describe your subject as you want your readers to see it. Use transitional words to make your description clear. Save your first draft in your folder.

The Choice Is Yours

Revising Your Descriptive Paragraph

Here's the Idea As you revise your descriptive paragraph, remember that you are trying to paint a word picture for your readers. Here are some questions to ask yourself to help make your description better.

1. Have I used strong sensory details in my description?
2. Are the details arranged in the order that I want my readers to notice them?
3. Have I used transitional words to make my description clear?

Another way you can improve your description is through your word choice. Be sure you use strong, specific verbs. Also pay special attention to your use of adjectives. Adjectives, you will remember, are words that describe. They can help your descriptive paragraph come alive for your readers.

You must choose adjectives carefully. There is usually one adjective that says just what you want to say better than any other word. For example, if you were describing a big park, you might use the adjective *big.* However, you could also describe the park as *huge, enormous, large, sprawling, gigantic, vast,* or *immense.* Always search for the best adjectives to make your description clear.

Be careful not to overuse adjectives in your descriptive paragraph. Too many adjectives can make your writing wordy. There is no need to say "the dark, inky, black sky," when "the inky sky" says just what you want to say.

Check It Out Read the following description.

The steamy jungle teemed with life. Monstrous trees were home to agile monkeys and colorful parrots. Long, thick snakes slithered along low-lying branches. Exotic frogs hopped from limb to limb. Graceful flying squirrels launched themselves from treetops and glided to the forest floor. The air was filled with the harsh cries, sudden screeches, and excited babble of a thousand strange creatures.

- Name some vivid adjectives and strong, specific verbs that are used in this paragraph. Do you see how these words make this description more interesting?

Try Your Skill   Beside each number below, there are three adjectives that have similar meanings. Number your paper from 1 to 8. Arrange the adjectives from the weakest to the strongest. For example, you would rearrange the adjectives *frightened, uneasy, terrified* to *uneasy, frightened, terrified.* Look up any words you are not familiar with.

1. hot, warm, blistering
2. cold, cool, freezing
3. beautiful, pretty, gorgeous
4. soggy, damp, soaking

5. huge, enormous, large
6. blackness, shady, dark
7. love, adore, like
8. thunderous, noisy, loud

Keep This in Mind

When revising your descriptive paragraph:
- Use strong sensory details.
- Arrange details in the order that you want the reader to notice them.
- Use transitional words that tell *where.*
- Use strong, specific verbs and vivid adjectives.

Now Write   Revise the first draft of your descriptive paragraph, using the guidelines in this lesson. When you are satisified that your description is as clear as it can be, proofread it. Correct any errors in grammar, capitalization, punctuation, and spelling. Then make a final copy. Save this final copy in your folder.

The Explanatory Paragraph

Telling *How*

How Do You Do?

Pre-Writing: Listing the Steps

Here's the Idea   Some paragraphs tell a story. Other paragraphs give a description. Still other paragraphs present an explanation. A paragraph that explains is called an **explanatory paragraph**. When such a paragraph explains how *something is done* or *how something happens,* it is called an explanatory *how* paragraph.

Sometimes an explanatory *how* paragraph tells how to do something. You might write a how-to paragraph to explain how to type a message on a computer, how to shoot a free-throw, how to make a pizza, or how to play a flute.

An explanatory *how* paragraph can also tell how something happens or how something works. This kind of paragraph might explain how a cell divides, how snow is formed, how volcanos erupt, or how a caterpillar becomes a butterfly.

Whether you are explaining how to do something or how something happens, or works, you are explaining a process. A process is made up of a series of steps. The details you gather for your pre-writing notes should include all of these steps. As you record these steps, be sure you don't leave any out. Also, make each step simple and specific. Otherwise, your readers won't understand your explanation.

Check It Out   Read the following pre-writing notes for a paragraph explaining how to build a tree house.

need a big tree	ladder for climbing up tree
get lots of scrap lumber	need nails and a hammer
tree must have strong branches	get a saw

- Do these notes for an explanatory *how* paragraph include all the steps needed to explain how to build a tree-house? What other details should be included?

Try Your Skill A six-year old child gave the following explanation of how to make pizza. Explain what is wrong with these directions. On your paper, list at least three errors.

Pizza
½ of white cheese
1 full thing of red gravy
A lot of dough
   Get the dough into a circle about size 14. Then throw it up in the air over your head.
   Cook the gravy for a couple of hours or minutes. Then put it on the dough with a cookin' spoon—and pat it all around.
   Take your gold square thing that makes the cheese all crumble up.
   Then put on the gravy and cook it for a real long time.
   If you don't get it out on time, it gets kind of blackish, but you still have to eat it.
   Have it in the summer with ice cream.—*Smashed Potatoes*

Keep This in Mind

- An explanatory *how* paragraph can explain how to do something. It can also tell how something happens or works.
- An explanatory *how* paragraph must include all of the steps of the process being explained.
- Each step must be simple and specific.

Now Write Think of a simple process that you would like to explain. You might explain how to do something or how something happens or works. Make a list of all the important steps that are a part of the process. Save your list in your folder.

What's Next?

Pre-Writing: Using Step-by-Step Order

Here's the Idea   In an explanatory *how* paragraph, you need to explain a process step-by-step. You must start with the first thing that happens or that must be done. Then you must follow that with the next step, and so on. Having a step out of order could confuse your reader as much as leaving out a step.

If you were explaining how to play Frisbee, you would not start out by saying "To catch a Frisbee, you should . . . ." Catching is the last step in the process. Instead, you would begin by first explaining how to hold a Frisbee properly. Then you would explain how to throw it and, finally, how to catch it. That would be the correct step-by-step order to explain how to play Frisbee.

Step-by-step order is very much like the chronological order you used when you wrote a narrative paragraph. In both cases you need to use a natural time order to organize your paragraph.

Check It Out   Read the following paragraph.

> Sewing a button on clothing is a simple task. First, gather a needle, straight pins, scissors, and thread that matches the color of the clothing. Second, remove any loose threads where the button used to be. Thread your needle. Next, mark the space for the button with a straight pin. Then, put the button in place and hold it there with one hand. Now, with your other hand, sew in and out of the holes in the button until it is firmly attached. Finally, knot the thread on the underside of the clothing. Snip the thread close to the clothing.

- Does this explanatory *how* paragraph explain a process step-by-step?
- Are the steps listed in natural time order?

Try Your Skill   Read the following pre-writing notes. They are for a paragraph that explains how to build a jar garden. Organize them into step-by-step order.

Making a Jar Garden

1. drop plants into jar and cover roots with soil using long stick
2. lightly mist newly planted plants with a sprayer
3. to prepare jar, put a layer of charcoal on bottom of jar
4. add light potting soil on top of pebbles using paper funnel
5. set garden in a sunny spot
6. cover charcoal with clean, small pebbles
7. after spraying, add tiny decorative rocks or ornaments to newly planted garden
8. take plants out of original pots and shake roots clean
9. screw the top on your new jar garden
10. first choose a large water bottle or jar with narrow lip

Keep This in Mind

- In an explanatory *how* paragraph, explain a process step-by-step.
- Organize the steps in the natural time order of the process.

Now Write   Using the notes you gathered in the last lesson, **How Do You Do?,** organize your explanatory *how* paragraph. Place your notes in step-by-step order. Make sure all of your steps are in the correct order. Save your organized notes in your folder.

Watch Your Step!

Writing the First Draft

Here's the Idea   As you write the first draft of your explanatory *how* paragraph, you want to be careful to make your explanation as clear as possible. Remember to include all of the important steps. Be sure you follow the order you decided on in the last lesson. Try to make each step in your explanatory paragraph simple and specific.

Another way you can make your explanation clear is by using transitional words. Transitional words can help you to show your reader how the steps in your explanation are related to each other. Transitional words can show which step comes first, which comes second, and so on. If two steps in the process you are explaining happen at the same time, transitional words can help you to make that idea clear.

Here is a list of transitional words. Use them as you write your first draft to help make your explanation clear.

first	then	at first
second	now	to start with
third	when	after that
fourth	while	at the same time
next	until	the next step
last	finally	at last

Check It Out   Read the following paragraph.

Scrambled eggs make a delicious light meal that is easy to prepare. First, gather the necessary utensils. You need a mixing bowl, an egg beater or wire whisk, a spatula, and a frying pan. Second, collect the ingredients. You need eggs, milk, butter, salt, and pepper. The third step is to break the eggs into the bowl. Use one egg for each person you are serving. Next, add a small amount of milk, and beat the mixture until it is fluffy. Then, over low heat, melt a tablespoon of butter in the frying pan. Add the eggs. Cook the eggs slowly until they are firm. While they cook, mix them a few times with the spatula. Finally, season them with salt and pepper and serve hot.

- What transitional words and phrases in this explanatory *how* paragraph help to make the explanation clear?

Try Your Skill The sentences below belong in a paragraph, but their order has been jumbled. First of all, find the topic sentence and write it on your paper. Then write the remaining sentences of the paragraph in step-by-step order. Finally, fill in the blanks with precise transitional words to show the order.

_____, get a group of hardy bikers together.

_____, enjoy the fresh air and scenery _____ you are traveling.

Bike trips are fun, but they require careful planning.

_____, have the group use maps to plan each day's routes.

_____ you set out, have the group check the brakes, gears, and tires on all the bikes.

_____, make a list of needed supplies and _____ gather them together.

Keep This in Mind

- In an explanatory *how* paragraph, use transitional words and phrases to make your explanation clear.

Now Write Using your organized notes from Part 2, write the first draft of your explanatory *how* paragraph. Include all of the important steps in the right order. Use transitional words to help make your explanation clear. Save your first draft in your folder.

Clear the Way

Revising Your Explanatory *How* Paragraph

Here's the Idea   After you have written the first draft of your explanatory *how* paragraph, read it carefully. Remember that your purpose is to explain a process to your readers as simply and as clearly as you can. Here are some questions you should ask yourself as you read your first draft. If you can't answer *yes* to a question, then you will have to revise that part of your first draft.

1. Have I included all of the important steps in the process I am explaining?

2. Have I arranged those steps in a natural, step-by-step time order?

3. Have I made each step simple and specific?

4. Have I used transitional words to make my explanation clear?

You might want to ask one of your classmates to read your first draft. Ask him or her to answer the four questions above. The answers you get will help you to know how you should revise your first draft.

Check It Out   Read the following explanatory *how* paragraph.

It's easy to play checkers. First, get the right kind of board and playing pieces. One player is red. The other player is black. You have to move the pieces across the board. You try to jump your opponent's pieces that are in front of you. At the other side of the board, your pieces are crowned. Then you win.

- Is this a good explanatory *how* paragraph? Explain your answer.

Try Your Skill   Revise the paragraph in **Check It Out**. Make it as clear as possible. Use the guidelines in this lesson as you revise. When you are finished, compare your revision with those of your classmates.

Keep This in Mind

When you revise an explanatory *how* paragraph:
- Include all the important steps.
- Arrange the steps in natural time order.
- Make each step simple and specific.
- Use transitional words to make your explanation clear.

Now Write   Read your first draft carefully. Revise it, using the guidelines in this lesson. Remember to proofread your draft to be sure you have used correct grammar, usage, capitalization, punctuation, and spelling. When you have finished your revision, make a good copy of your explanatory *how* paragraph. Save this final copy in your folder.

The Explanatory Paragraph

Telling *Why*

Part 1 **State Your Case**
Pre-Writing: Developing an Opinion

Part 2 **Save the Best for Last**
Pre-Writing: Organizing an Opinion

Part 3 **Build Your Case**
Writing the First Draft

Part 4 **In My Opinion**
Revising Your Explanatory *Why* Paragraph

State Your Case

Pre-Writing: Developing an Opinion

Here's the Idea   How do you feel about math, your uncle Harry, spinach, softball, or the school lunch program? Having strong feelings or beliefs about things is only natural. Expressing your opinion is something you do often.

The purpose of an explanatory *why* paragraph is to present your opinion in writing. You may want to explain why something is so, or why it should be changed. In either case, the first pre-writing step is to make your opinion clear in your own mind so that it will be clear to your readers. You can do this by writing a sentence that states your opinion simply and directly. Later, when you write your first draft, you can use this statement as the topic sentence of your paragraph.

Here are some typical statements of opinion.

The school lunchroom should serve food from other countries.
All students should take science classes.

Now you have to make your readers understand why you hold this opinion. To do this, you have to list specific reasons or facts to support your opinion. Your reasons must sound logical. Your facts must be accurate. Here are some examples of good supporting reasons and facts.

Opinion: The school lunchroom should serve food from other countries.

Reasons/Facts: Food teaches us about other cultures.

We have many foreign students in our school: 10% are from Asia, 15% are from Latin America, 5% are from India.

Having their own food served in the lunchroom will make foreign students feel more at home.

It's interesting to try different foods.

Check It Out   Read the following paragraph.

Students should be allowed to use calculators in math class. Calculators are not a form of cheating. Even with a calculator, a student must know what to do to solve a problem. The calculator simply saves time by doing the addition, multiplication, subtraction, or division. It does this quickly and accurately. Since electronics is the way of the future, today's students should keep pace. They should use the most efficient method, the calculator.

- Does this paragraph state an opinion clearly?
- Is the opinion supported with logical reasons and accurate facts?

Try Your Skill   Below are three opinions that could be developed in explanatory *why* paragraphs. Choose one opinion and develop some pre-writing notes for it. List at least three logical reasons or accurate facts to support it.

1. Smoking is dangerous to your health.
2. All students need to learn computer skills.
3. A balanced diet is important to good health.

Keep This in Mind

- In an explanatory *why* paragraph, you present and support an opinion.
- Use logical reasons and accurate facts to support the opinion.

Now Write   Title a piece of paper "I Believe." Then do some brainstorming. Write down your opinions on different subjects. List as many opinions as you can.

Choose one opinion you would like to write about. In your pre-writing notes, list all the reasons and facts you can think of to support your opinion. Be sure your reasons are logical and your facts accurate. Save your pre-writing notes in your folder.

Save the Best for Last

Pre-Writing: Organizing an Opinion

Here's the Idea   Now that you have a list of supporting reasons and facts, you have to decide how to present them. You want your reasons to have the greatest impact on your reader. One good method is to save your strongest reasons until the end. This method of organization is called **least important to most important idea.** When you use this type of organization, you leave the most convincing reason fresh in your reader's mind.

For example, below are three reasons why private cars should be banned from large cities.

1. Pleasant pedestrian malls could replace some streets.
2. Energy is saved when people use public transportation.
3. Air pollution would be reduced, and cities would be healthier places to live.

The first reason is a good one, but it isn't as important to the nation as the second reason, saving energy. The last reason is probably the most important of all, since it affects people directly. We are all concerned about our health. You can see that these reasons have been listed in order, from the least important to the most important.

Check It Out   Read the following explanatory paragraph.

More junior high schools should offer soccer. A fast-moving game, soccer is fun to play and to watch. Soccer is also inexpensive for a school, since it requires little equipment. Most important, soccer is a sport that anyone of any size can play. For all these reasons, soccer is a popular sport all over the world. Junior high school students should have a chance to try it.

- Is the opinion supported by specific facts or reasons?
- Is the evidence given in order of importance, from the least important to the most important?

Try Your Skill   In the last lesson, **State Your Case,** reasons were listed that support the opinion "The school lunchroom should serve food from different countries." Organize these reasons from the least important to the most important. Compare your organization with that of your classmates. Save these organized notes in your folder.

Keep This in Mind

- The most convincing way to organize an explanatory *why* paragraph is to list reasons and facts in the order of their importance. Start with the least important idea and end with the most important.

Now Write   In the last lesson, **State Your Case,** you chose an opinion to write about. Then you listed reasons and facts to support that opinion. Now arrange these reasons or facts in the order of their importance. Save your organized list in your folder.

Build Your Case

Writing the First Draft

Here's the Idea   An explanatory *why* paragraph has two purposes. One is to present your opinion. The other is to give good reasons that support your opinion. Keep these two purposes in mind as you write your first draft.

You present your opinion in your topic sentence. Write a clear, direct sentence that tells your readers how you feel about a subject. Do not, however, use the first person in your topic sentence. Don't write "I think . . ." or "I believe . . ." or "In my opinion. . . ." When you state an opinion, your reader already knows that it is what you think.

In the body of your paragraph, offer reasons and facts to support and develop your topic sentence. As you write, use transitional words to help make your opinion clear. Here are some transitional words you may find helpful. One kind helps you to state reasons and facts. The other kind helps you to put your reasons and facts in the order of their importance.

To State Reasons and Facts:	because, so, since, therefore, as a result, if (something) . . . then (something)
To Put in Order of Importance:	the first reason, second, more important, most important, finally

Finally, you want to end your paragraph with a strong ending sentence that sums up your opinion and your reasons.

Check It Out   Read this paragraph.

The highway speed limit should not be raised from 55 miles per hour. The first reason is that passengers can see more and are more relaxed at slower speeds. More important, lower speeds save fuel because engines are working efficiently. Most important, if motorists drive slowly they have more time to react to dangerous situations and lives will be saved. The savings in headaches, fuel, and lives speak strongly for keeping the speed limit at 55 miles per hour.

- Does the topic sentence state an opinion clearly?
- Which transitional words and phrases show the reasons? Which show their order of importance?
- Does the concluding sentence sum up the argument?

Try Your Skill Write a first draft using the pre-writing notes you organized in the **Try Your Skill** section of **Save the Best for Last.** Be sure that the opinion is stated in the topic sentence. Use transitional words in the body of the paragraph. Write a strong ending sentence. Save the first draft in your folder.

Keep This in Mind

- State your opinion in the topic sentence.
- Use transitional words that show the supporting reasons and facts and their order of importance.
- Sum up your argument in the ending sentence.

Now Write Using your organized notes from the last lesson, write a first draft of your explanatory *why* paragraph. State your opinion in the topic sentence. Use clear transitional words. Write a strong ending sentence. Save your first draft in your folder.

In My Opinion

Revising Your Explanatory *Why* Paragraph

Here's the Idea   When you revise the first draft of your explanatory *why* paragraph, try to make it clearer and more convincing. Ask yourself the following questions as you revise.

1. Have I presented my opinion clearly and directly in the topic sentence?

2. Have I supported my opinion with reasons and facts?

3. Are my reasons logical? Are my facts accurate?

4. Have I arranged my details from the least important to the most important idea?

5. Have I used transitional words to state my reasons and organize them?

6. Does my ending sentence sum up my opinion and reasons?

You may want to ask a friend to read your paragraph. Ask your friend to tell you if your opinion is presented clearly and strongly and if you have supported your opinion with good reasons and facts.

Check It Out   Read the following explanatory *why* paragraph.

All bicyclists should be required to wear safety helmets. Each year, thousands of cyclists are injured in accidents. Because many riders do not wear helmets, they suffer serious head injuries. As a result, some of these riders are paralyzed for the rest of their lives. Some even die from their injuries. If more bicyclists wore safety helmets, then fewer riders would suffer serious and sometimes fatal head injuries.

- Does the topic sentence state the writer's opinion clearly and directly?
- Are the reasons and facts arranged from the least important to the most important?
- What transitional words has the writer used to help state the reasons and facts?
- Does the ending sentence sum up the argument?

Try Your Skill   Revise the first draft you wrote in **Build Your Case** about serving food from different countries in the lunchroom. Follow the guidelines presented in this lesson.

Keep This in Mind

When revising your explanatory *why* paragraph:
- State your opinion clearly and directly in your topic sentence.
- Use logical reasons and accurate facts to support your opinion.
- Use transitional words to state your reasons and to show the order of their importance.
- Be sure your concluding sentence sums up your argument.

Now Write   Revise the first draft of your explanatory *why* paragraph using the guidelines presented in this lesson. Proofread your paragraph for correct grammar, usage, capitalization, punctuation, and spelling. Neatly rewrite your revised paragraph. Save this final copy in your folder.

A Look at Compositions

It's a Long Story

Learning About Compositions

Here's the Idea   There are times when you cannot say everything you want to say in one paragraph. You may have a long story to tell or a lot of information to present. A subject that is too big for a paragraph may be just right for a composition.

A **composition** is a group of paragraphs that tell about one idea. A composition has three parts: an introduction, a body, and a conclusion.

The **introduction** is a paragraph that tells what the composition is about. The introduction does the same job in a composition that the topic sentence does in a paragraph.

The **body** of a composition is made up of paragraphs that develop the main idea. The main idea can be developed with descriptive details, examples, or facts and figures.

The **conclusion** of a composition is a paragraph that sums up the important ideas in the composition. The conclusion does the same job as the ending sentence of a paragraph.

Check It Out   Read the following composition.

The Jacobs' Specialty

At first glance, there doesn't seem to be much that's special about the Jacob family. However, something sets them apart from every other family I know. It's their refrigerator.

From the outside, the refrigerator looks like a big, white box next to the sink. Open the door, though, and the inside is unlike anything you've ever seen before. Every shelf and space is always crammed with tempting foods. The top shelf has colorful containers of pickles, jelly, cold meats, milk, and juices. The middle shelf is always heaped with plates of sandwiches. The bottom shelf is packed with cheeses, homemade breads, and fruit of every kind.

Getting an invitation to the Jacobs' house is like being invited to a banquet. One day the snack might be ham and Swiss on rolls with sharp dill pickles on the side. Another day, it might be rich cream cheese on thick slices of rye bread. On a rainy Saturday, the feast might include homemade pizza.

Whenever I think of that refrigerator, I think of the Jacob family itself. Every member of that family is friendly, generous, and affectionate. Everyone seems to contribute something to the comfort of family and friends. I guess that makes the family special. Their hearts are as open as their refrigerator door.

- What is the main idea of this composition?
- Which part is the introduction, which is the body, and which is the conclusion?

Try Your Skill   Write which part of a composition you think this paragraph is. Write the reasons for your answer.

A good-luck charm may be anything from a rabbit's foot to a shiny penny. It's not the shape or size that matters. What counts is that the owner believes in the charm. That belief gives confidence, and confidence often assures success. In that respect, anyway, good-luck charms have really worked.

Keep This in Mind

- A composition is a group of paragraphs that tell about one idea.
- A composition has three parts: an introduction, a body, and a conclusion.

Now Write   Write a paragraph that explains what a composition is. In your paragraph, define the term *composition*. Tell how many parts a composition has. Tell what each part does. Be sure your paragraph has a good topic sentence and an ending sentence. Save your paragraph in your folder.

Decisions, Decisions

Pre-Writing: Choosing a Topic

Here's the Idea   The first step in planning a composition is choosing a topic. You want to choose a topic that you are interested in and that you know something about. You also want to choose a topic that you can cover thoroughly in four or five paragraphs.

One place you might find ideas for your compositions is in your journal. Perhaps you made some notes about topics that you later decided were too long for just one paragraph. You might use them now for compositions. The books, magazines, and newspapers that you read might also suggest some composition ideas to you. Finally, you may want to discuss some possible topics with your classmates or do some brainstorming.

Once you have chosen a subject to write about, you may have to narrow it. Even though a composition is longer than a paragraph, some subjects are still too general to be covered well in a short composition. One way to narrow a topic is to ask questions such as *who? what? where? when? how?* and *why?* about it. The answers to these questions will give you information to make your topic more specific.

For example, the subject, "a challenging adventure," is too general. By asking the questions *who? what? where? when? how?* and *why?* about this subject, you might come up with narrowed topics like these:

> –the time Sandy and I hiked from the rim of the Grand Canyon down to the canyon floor
> –winning the canoe race last summer at camp
> –when Rob and I explored the old Hickock coal mine in Lester County

Check It Out   See how one writer narrowed a general subject to a more specific topic by asking questions.

General subject — an outdoor adventure
        Who? — Rob and I, with the Portland Hiking Club
       What? — camping trip
      Where? — Acadia National Park
       When? — summer vacation July, 1990
        How? — open-air camping
        Why? — to see what living outdoors for a week is like
Specific topic — my week-long camping trip to Acadia
                National Park with the Portland
                Hiking Club in July, 1990

- How is the specific topic different from the general subject?

Try Your Skill   Each of these subjects is too general for a composition. Choose one. Then ask *who? what? where? when? how?* and *why?* about it. Write the answers below the subject. Then use your notes to write a specific topic.

a big surprise   a difficult challenge
a long, hard day   a new invitation
a real accomplishment   a funny incident

Keep This in Mind

- Choose a topic that is interesting and that you know something about.
- Narrow your topic so that it is specific enough to be covered well in a composition.

Now Write   Choose a subject that is suitable for a composition. Narrow your subject by asking *who? what? where? when? how?* and *why?* Then write a specific topic. Save your topic in your folder.

135

Getting It Together

Pre-Writing: Organizing Ideas

Here's the Idea   Once you have chosen and narrowed your topic, you must gather ideas for your composition. These ideas will include specific details, sensory details, examples, and facts and figures. You can gather these ideas through brainstorming, personal observation, and research in a library.

Before you can use the ideas you gather to write your first draft, you must organize them. Look at your pre-writing notes. Which notes seem to belong together? That is, which notes seem to be about the same main ideas? Try to group your pre-writing notes around two or three main ideas. Each group of notes can then become a paragraph in the body of your composition.

Check It Out   Look at these pre-writing notes for a composition about soccer.

–oldest sport
–I lift weights for strength
–Roman soldiers brought game to England
–you must kick or bounce ball into opponent's goal
–world's most popular game

–only goalkeeper can touch ball with hands
–players always running
–boys and girls can play
–players need good physical conditioning
–players use feet, bodies, heads to move ball

These notes could be grouped around three main ideas:

History
oldest sport
Roman soldiers brought
    game to England
world's most popular game

Players
boys and girls can play
I lift weights for strength
players always running
players need good physical
    conditioning

Rules
players use feet, bodies, and
    heads to move ball
only goal keeper can touch
    ball with hands
you must kick or bounce ball
    into opponent's goal
2 teams of 5 to 11 players

· What three main ideas are these notes grouped around?
· Do you see how each group of notes could be developed into a paragraph?

Try Your Skill   Read the following pre-writing notes for a composition about the early settlers in America. Decide what two main ideas these notes could be grouped around.

came to make a better life   came to find religious freedom
some were adventurers   some were criminals
came to make a fortune   some were persecuted minorities

Keep This in Mind

· Gather ideas for your topic through brainstorming, personal observation, or research in a library.
· Organize your ideas by grouping them around several main ideas. Use each grouping as a paragraph in your composition.

Now Write   Make a list of pre-writing notes for the topic you chose in the last lesson, **Decisions, Decisions**. Then group your notes around two or three main ideas. Save your notes.

First Try

Writing the First Draft

Here's the Idea   Once you have organized your ideas, you can begin writing your first draft. Remember that this draft is just your first attempt to put your ideas into paragraphs. As you write, you may take out some ideas or add new ones. You may even change your organization. Don't worry about details such as grammar, punctuation, or spelling. You can make any necessary corrections when you revise your composition.

As you write your first draft, remember the three parts of a composition and the purpose of each part.

Introduction   Your first paragraph introduces your composition. This paragraph should capture your reader's interest. It should also let the reader know what you will be writing about.

Body   The body of your composition is made up of paragraphs that develop your topic. Each group of ideas from your pre-writing notes will become a paragraph in your composition. Each of these paragraphs should have its own topic sentence.

Arrange the paragraphs and the ideas within them logically. You can use chronological order, spatial order, or the order of importance. Use transitional words and phrases within and between paragraphs to make your ideas flow smoothly.

Conclusion   End your composition with a concluding paragraph. The conclusion may be a summary or a general statement about your story, description, or explanation. The conclusion may also be just a group of sentences that clearly signal an ending to the idea you have developed. Be sure not to introduce any new ideas in your concluding paragraph.

When you have finished writing the first draft, give your composition an interesting title.

Check It Out Read the following first draft.

I found out that soccer is the most popular game in the world. It is also the oldest sport. The Chinese played the game over 2,000 years ago. Roman soldiers played the game, to. They brought it to England when they conquered England. I play soccer on our school team.

In the game, players use their feet, bodies, and heads to move the ball. The only ones who can touch the ball with their hands are the goalkeepers. Each team tries to put the ball into the opponent's goal to get points. I like to play goalie.

Boys and girls can play this game. It is a very active game. They need to be in good physical condition.

Soccer is a popular game. It has lasted so long because it is easy to learn and is a game everyone can take part in and enjoy.

- Has the writer made each group of ideas from the pre-writing notes into a paragraph?
- Are the ideas in a logical order?
- Has the writer added any new ideas that weren't in the pre-writing notes? Has the writer taken out any ideas?

Try Your Skill Reread the first draft of the composition on soccer. What are some things you could do to improve this first draft? Discuss your idea with your classmates.

Keep This in Mind

- Your rough draft should have an introduction, a body, and a conclusion.
- Organize the paragraphs and the ideas within them logically.

Now Write Use your organized ideas to write a first draft of your composition. Make sure you have an introduction, a body, and a conclusion. Be sure the paragraphs are arranged logically. Give your composition a title. Save your first draft.

Nobody's Perfect

Revising Your Composition

Here's the Idea   All writers, even experienced ones, have to revise their first drafts. When you revise, you can improve your ideas, your organization, and your word choice. You can correct any errors you find in grammar, capitalization, punctuation, and spelling. Revising helps you to make your composition better than it was when you first wrote it.

Here are some questions you should ask yourself as you revise.

1. Have I included enough details to develop my topic? Are there any unrelated details that should be taken out?

2. Have I organized my details around two or three main ideas?

3. Is my introductory paragraph interesting? Does it tell the reader what my composition is about?

4. Does each paragraph in the body contain details about just one main idea? Are the paragraphs and the ideas within them arranged logically?

5. Have I written a strong concluding paragraph that sums up the ideas in my composition?

6. Have I used good transitional words to lead the reader from one idea to another?

7. Have I used verbs that are strong and specific? Have I used vivid adjectives?

Check It Out   Notice how the first few paragraphs of the composition on soccer have been revised.

- Do you see how these paragraphs have been improved through revision?

¶ There was a time when football, baseball, and basketball were the only sports Americans cared about. Now soccer has joined the big three as one of the country's most popular sports.

I found out that soccer is the most popular game in the world. It is also the oldest sport. The Chinese played the game over 2,000 years ago. Roman soldiers played the game, to. They brought it to England the game with them. when they conquered England, I play soccer on our school team.

soccer,
In the game, players use their feet, bodies, and heads to move the ball. The only ones who can touch the ball with their hands are the goalkeepers. Each team tries to kick or bounce the ball into their opponent's goal to get points. I like to play goalie.

Try Your Skill   Use proofreading symbols (See Section 7, p. 85) to correct the errors in these sentences.

1. We new that it nearly ten o clock.
2. Independence Day is a Major holiday in the united states.
3. My Brother and Sister found there shoes in the closest.

Keep This in Mind

- Revise your composition to improve your ideas, organization, and word choice.
- Proofread your composition to correct errors in grammar, capitalization, punctuation, and spelling.

Now Write   Use the guidelines in this lesson to revise the first draft of your composition. Save the revised copy.

Wrap It Up

The Final Copy of a Composition

Here's the Idea   You have put a great deal of effort into writing your composition. However, you are not quite finished. Now you have to write your **final copy.** This is the only copy of your composition that your readers will see. Therefore, it is important to take your time with this final step in the writing of your composition.

Always write your final copy on clean, white, lined paper. Use a pen, not a pencil. Put your name, the subject, and the date in the upper right-hand corner of your paper. On the second line of your paper, center the title for your composition.

Copy each line of your composition carefully. Include all of the changes you made when you revised your composition. Leave at least one inch on the right and left sides of the paper for a margin. Leave at least one line blank at the bottom of your paper. Write on only one side of a piece of paper. If you need more than one sheet, number each sheet after the first one in the center at the very top.

When you are done, proofread your final copy one last time. Use a single line to cross out any errors you find. If you have made more than three or four mistakes, you may want to rewrite your composition. Remember, you want your final copy to be as neat as possible.

Check It Out   Look at this beginning of the final copy of the soccer composition.

- Does this final copy follow the guidelines presented in this lesson?

A Lasting Sport

There was a time when football, basketball, and baseball were the only sports Americans cared about. Now soccer has joined the big three as one of the country's most popular sports.

Soccer is already the most popular game in the world. It is also the oldest sport. The Chinese played the

Try Your Skill   Write the answers to these questions about the final copy of a composition.

1. What kind of paper should you use?

2. What three pieces of information are written at the top of the first page?

3. Where is the title written?

4. How should errors be corrected?

5. If you use more than one sheet of paper, where should you put the numbers 2, 3, and so on?

6. How wide a margin should you leave on the left and the right sides of the paper?

Keep This in Mind

· The final copy of your composition should be neat and free of errors.

Now Write   Use the guidelines in this lesson to write a final copy of your composition. Make sure this copy is as free from errors as you can make it. Save your final copy in your folder.

One More Time

Reviewing the Process of Writing

In the following sections, you will be writing many different kinds of compositions. Remember, no matter what kind of composition you write, the process of writing remains the same. Below is a checklist of steps for writing a composition. Refer to this checklist often as you write your compositions.

Guidelines for Writing a Composition

Pre-Writing

- Choose a topic that interests you and that you know something about. Narrow the topic so that you can cover it well in the assigned length of your composition.

- Gather details that you can use to develop the topic.

- Group similar details together around two or three main ideas.

- Organize those details into an order that suits the type of composition you are writing.

Writing the First Draft

- Begin your composition with an interesting introductory paragraph that tells the reader what your composition is ab ut.

- Follow the introduction with the body of your composition. Use your organized details to develop your topic. Each group of details will be a paragraph in the body of your composition.

- Use transitions to lead the reader from one idea to another.

- Add, take out, and reorganize ideas if you need to.
- Finish your composition with a concluding paragraph that sums up your ideas.
- Add an interesting title to your composition.

Revising

- Be sure your composition has an introduction, a body, and a conclusion.
- Check to see that you have included enough details to develop your topic.
- The paragraphs and the ideas within them should be organized logically.
- Each paragraph should have a topic sentence that presents the main idea of that paragraph.
- Use effective transitional words to make your ideas flow smoothly.
- Make sure you have used vivid language.
- Proofread to find and correct errors in grammar, capitalization, punctuation, and spelling.

Final Copy

- Rewrite your composition neatly in ink on white, lined paper.
- Write your name, subject, and the date in the upper right-hand corner of your paper.
- Proofread your final copy one last time. Neatly correct any errors you find.

The Narrative Composition

Get Started

Pre-Writing: Planning a Story

Here's the Idea   Narrative compositions tell stories. Some narratives tell stories about events that really happened. Others tell stories that happened only in the writer's imagination.

Whether real or imaginary, a narrative has to have a point. It is not just a series of events. A narrative should tell a story that the reader can become involved with. The story should tell the reader something about the way people think, feel, and act.

A narrative must also have a setting. The **setting** is where and when a story takes place. The setting may be real or imaginary. The setting may be any time in the past, present, or future. Your story might begin, "As night fell, we were still 3,000 feet from the top of Mount Everest." Describing the setting of your story with specific details will help your readers see what you have imagined.

Narratives must also have **characters.** Your characters can be people or animals. Describe your characters carefully to your readers. What does a character look like? What does his or her voice sound like? How does the character behave?

A good narrative also has an interesting plot. The **plot** of a story is made up of the events that take place. Usually, the plot centers around a conflict. The **conflict** in a story is some problem that a character struggles with. A character might struggle with a fear, such as a fear of the dark. A character might struggle with another character—in a basketball game, for example. A character might also struggle with nature, during a blizzard or alone in a forest.

Finally, like any composition, a narrative has an ending. The **ending** of a narrative brings the story to a close. The conflict is settled, and the reader is satisfied that the story has been brought to a reasonable conclusion.

Check It Out   Look at these pre-writing notes for the plan of a narrative.

Setting	Beech river, an August afternoon
Characters	me and my sister Blanca
Plot	Blanca and I go rafting on the Beech river; my raft overturns, and I nearly drown.
Conflict	me against the icy water and swift currents of the river
Ending	I manage to drag myself to safety along the river-bank.

· Do these pre-writing notes include all of the important parts of a narrative?

Try Your Skill   Along with your classmates, develop a plan for an imaginary story. Where will the story take place? Who will the characters be? What is the plot? What is the conflict? How will the story end?

Keep This in Mind

· A narrative composition tells a story with a point.
· A good narrative has a setting, characters, plot, conflict, and an ending.

Now Write   Think about some stories you would like to tell. These stories may be real or imaginary, serious or humorous. Remember, each story should have a point. It should tell about characters who face and overcome a conflict. Make a list of all your story possibilities and save it in your folder.

Action!

Pre-Writing: Plotting a Story

Here's the Idea Have you ever gone to a movie and then described what happened for some friends who hadn't seen it yet? Whether you realized it or not, you were telling your friends the plot of the story. Plot, as you learned in the last lesson, is all of the events of a story.

Once you have an idea for a narrative composition, you have to plot your story. That is, you have to gather together all of the events that you want to tell about. If you are telling a real story, make notes about everything that happened. Try to remember specific details about each event. These might include names, dates, places, and times. They might also include sensory details. Be sure all of your details are accurate. Plotting an imaginary story calls for the same kind of information. The only difference is that the events and details are not real, but made up.

As you write down the events that tell your story, you must be sure they are arranged in the order that they happened. This is called chronological order. Chronological order makes it easy for the reader to follow the action of your story.

Check It Out Look over these pre-writing notes for a narrative composition.

1. We are camping at Beech river. ⟨ *River Park campground*
   hot August day

2. Blanca and I decide to go rafting.

3. We forget our life jackets back at the camp, but go in anyway.

4. I paddle to middle of river and get carried away by
   current. *Blanca waves her arms at me from shore*

5. I get caught up in a stretch of rapids.

6. Raft overturns—I'm thrown in river. ⟨ *water like icicles*
⟨ *can't catch breath*

7. Rapids tumble me around. ⟨ *I think I'm drowning*
⟨ *My arms feel heavy as lead.*

8. I'm knocked against rock; can't hold on.
⟨ *rocks feel*
slippery

9. I reach for tree branch and hold on.

choking, exhausted
10. I pull myself ashore. ⟨ *Blanca screaming my name in*
distance—too weak to answer

- Are these notes arranged in chronological order?
- Do you notice how the writer added details to the list of events?
- Do you see how the writer has grouped her notes into paragraphs?

Try Your Skill   Practice recalling events and arranging them in the order that they happened. Make a list of everything that you did last Saturday. Remember as many details as you can. Then arrange the items on your list in chronological order.

Keep This in Mind

- Plot is the events that tell a story.
- Arrange the events that make up your plot in chronological order.

Now Write   In the last lesson, **Get Started,** you made up a list of possible stories to tell. Choose the one you like best and make some pre-writing notes about it. Arrange your notes in chronological order. Save your pre-writing notes.

What's Your View?

Pre-Writing: Choosing a Point of View

Here's the Idea   Now you must decide how to tell your story. One thing that affects your story is **point of view.**

In the **first-person point of view,** the story is told through the eyes of one character. This character is identified by the pronoun *I. I* is the narrator, the person who tells the story. The reader knows only what this character knows. Use this point of view when you are writing a story in which you are a character.

A story can also be told from the **third-person point of view.** This point of view uses the pronouns *he* and *she.* There are two types of third-person point of view—limited and omniscient (om·ni′·shunt). In the **third-person limited point of view,** the narrator is not a character in the story. Like a radio announcer at a baseball game, the narrator tells what he or she sees. The narrator never gives his or her opinion about what is happening in the story. The readers never know what the characters are thinking or feeling unless the characters themselves say so. This point of view works well for stories with many characters and much action.

The second type of third-person point of view is called **third-person omniscient.** Omniscient means "all-knowing." Just as in third-person limited, the omniscient narrator is not a character in the story. However, the omniscient narrator knows everything that is going on in the story. The omniscient narrator knows what the characters are thinking and feeling. This point of view allows the writer to choose which details to emphasize and which to keep hidden.

Check It Out   Read the introductions below.

1   Last summer, on a warm August afternoon, my sister Blanca
       and I decided to go rafting on the Beech River. Our family was

camping at River Park. Blanca and I dragged our small rubber rafts a half mile to the river's edge. That's when Blanca realized we had left our life jackets back at camp.

2   Last summer, on a warm August afternoon, Tina and Blanca Vazquez decided to go rafting on the Beech River. Their family was camping at River Park. Tina and Blanca dragged their small rubber rafts a half mile to the river's edge. That's when Blanca realized they had left their life jackets back at camp.

   • What is the point of view of each paragraph?

Try Your Skill   This paragraph uses the third-person limited point of view. Rewrite it twice, once using the first-person point of view, and the second time using the third-person omniscient point of view.

   Steve sat on the stubbly grass surrounding the basketball court. Five other boys his age were playing on the court. They shouted and joked with each other, but paid no attention to Steve. Steve sat stiffly. He never took his eyes off the game.

Keep This in Mind

   • In the first-person point of view, the reader knows only what the main character sees and feels.
   • In the third-person limited point of view, the reader can see and hear only what the narrator describes.
   • In the third-person omniscient point of view, the reader knows everything—thoughts, feelings, and actions.

Now Write   Look over your pre-writing notes from the last lesson, **Action!** Decide which point of view would help you to tell your story best. On the same page with your notes, write the point of view you have chosen. Save your notes.

First Impressions

Writing the First Draft

Here's the Idea A narrative composition has the same parts as any composition. A narrative has an introduction, a body, and a conclusion.

In a narrative composition, the **introduction** usually sets the scene and introduces the characters. The introduction may also present the conflict, although the conflict is often presented in the body. Make your introduction interesting for your readers. Use sensory details to set the scene. Include specific details to describe your characters.

The **body** of a narrative presents the plot of the story. As you write your first draft, use the plot to develop the conflict. Don't simply *tell* your readers that a character is struggling with a problem. *Show* the conflict developing. *Show* how your characters react to it.

In the **conclusion** of a narrative, the conflict is solved, and the story is brought to a close. Be consistent about time sequence, characterization, and point of view. If you have been describing an event in the past, don't leap to the present in your conclusion. If your character has been timid, don't make her or him aggressive. If you've been using the first-person point of view, use it in your conclusion. Make your conclusion interesting. It is the last impression you leave with your reader.

Check It Out Read this introduction.

> It was a fine summer morning in downtown Milwaukee. The breeze off Lake Michigan was cool, and the air was surprisingly clear. Melvin Marvel, the world famous magician, was whistling to himself as he braked for a light. Looking in his rearview mirror, Melvin saw—or thought he saw—an enormous white rabbit sitting in the back seat.

- Does this introduction set the scene?
- Does this introduction introduce the characters?
- What sensory and specific details are included?

Try Your Skill   Read this story in need of a conclusion. Find the conflict in the body. Then write a conclusion for this narrative that solves the conflict and brings the story to a close.

> Jim Allen leaped up the steps and bolted into the house.
> "What is it, Jim?" his mother called.
> Jim moaned, "My telescope has to be mounted and ready for display in the science fair tomorrow morning."
> "You promised to cut the lawn today," his mother said.
> From his room, Jim shouted that he just couldn't do it.
> Jim's mother said that he would have to keep his promise.
> Jim flopped on his bed to think. What should he do? Suddenly the phone rang. Jim ran to answer it. It was his friend Ken.
> Ken was stuck five miles outside of town. He had spent his last quarter on the call. He begged Jim to come and get him.
> Jim tried to explain his own predicament.
> "Please, Jim," Ken interrupted. "I have to be at work soon."
> Jim turned to his mother. He had a difficult decision to make.

Keep This in Mind

- The introduction in a narrative sets the scene and introduces the characters.
- The body of a narrative presents events that tell the story and develop the conflict.
- The conclusion of a narrative solves the conflict and brings the story to a close.

Now Write   Begin writing the first draft of your narrative. Just write the introduction. Be sure to set the scene and introduce the characters. Use specific and sensory details. Try to capture your readers' attention. Save your work in your folder.

She Said, He Said

Writing the First Draft: Using Dialogue

Here's the Idea   Narratives almost always include people, and people like to talk. That is why a narrative often includes dialogue. **Dialogue** is the conversation between characters.

Dialogue is important in a narrative. For example, the things a character says can tell the reader what the character is like. Dialogue can also help the writer to tell the story. Instead of the writer telling the reader what happened, a character can tell the reader through dialogue.

Whenever you write dialogue, try to use language that suits the speaker. If a teenager is speaking, use the kind of words a teen would use. Don't use the same kind of language for the teenager's father. If one of your characters is a bully, be sure he uses a bully's words and way of speaking.

Dialogue always includes words that tell who is speaking, such as *she said* or *Tom said*. Try to use a word other than *said* whenever a different word would suit the speaker. For example, if a character is angry, you might write *She shouted*. If a character is embarrassed, your could write *he mumbled* or *he whispered*.

Always begin a new paragraph whenever a different speaker talks. Be sure to put the quotation marks around the speaker's exact words. To learn more about the correct form for quotation marks, see Handbook Section 16, pages 556–559.

Check It Out   Read this dialogue.

> "We better go back," Blanca said.
> "What?" I said. "You're going to walk all that way for a dumb life jacket?"

"You know what Mom and Dad say," Blanca replied. "They never let any of us go boating without our life jackets."

"Look," I said. "You can swim and so can I. Nothing's going to happen. Let's go."

We paddled close to the shore for a while. Then I decided to head for the middle of the river.

"Be careful," Blanca shouted. "The water looks choppy out there."

- What does this dialogue tell you about Blanca? About her sister?
- How does this dialogue help the writer to tell the story?
- Does the language suit the characters? Give examples.

Try Your Skill Rewrite this narrative using dialogue.

My friend Sammy and I were playing basketball when he said to me that he's never been to the beach at night. I told him that it's great and we should go. Then he said that his parents might not let him. I told him that we could ask them and that my parents would take us. Sammy said that was neat and I said that we should go ask them. We ran off to ask Sammy's parents.

Keep This in Mind

- Dialogue is conversation between characters.
- Dialogue can show what a character is like. It can also help to move the story along.

Now Write Continue writing your first draft. Include dialogue that will help you to tell your story. Save your first draft in your folder.

Go with the Flow

The First Draft: Using Transitions

Here's the Idea   Narratives are usually told in **chronological order**. To make the order clear, you should use transitional words and phrases.

You have used transitional words such as *first, then, next, later, soon,* and *afterwards* within narrative paragraphs. It is also important to use transitional words between paragraphs. These transitional words help your story to flow smoothly from paragraph to paragraph. Examples of paragraph transitions are *later that day, by noon,* and *when I got home.*

Check It Out   Read the body and conclusion of the narrative composition about Blanca and her sister.

> As I neared the middle of the river, the current pushed my small raft faster and faster. I tried to turn back but the current was too strong. I saw Blanca waving her arm at me. She got smaller and smaller as my raft raced down the river.
>
> Soon I heard a low roar ahead. I knew that meant rapids. The rapids weren't very big, but my little rubber raft was no match for them. As soon as I reached the first waves, the raft overturned. I was thrown into the bubbling water.
>
> The river was icy cold. I could barely catch my breath. I tried to swim, but the rapids kept pulling me under. I banged up against big rocks. Once, I grabbed on and almost pulled myself up on a large rock, but the water pulled me back. My strength was almost gone.
>
> Just then I noticed some low hanging tree branches up ahead. If I could grab them, I might be able to pull myself to shore. I reached up and grabbed a branch. The river tried to drag me away, but I held on. Slowly, I dragged myself along the branch toward the shore. Again and again the river tried to snatch me.

Suddenly, I felt solid ground under my feet. Choking, I crawled the last few yards to the shore. In the distance, I heard Blanca screaming my name. But I was too exhausted to answer her. All I could think about was how lucky I was to be alive and how foolish I had been. I had beaten the river this time. I hoped I would never have to try again.

- What transitional words are used between paragraphs?
- What transitional words are used within paragraphs?

Try Your Skill   Rewrite the paragraph below. Arrange the sentences in correct time sequence. Use transitional words and phrases to make the time sequence clear.

I put a sandwich and an orange in a bag for lunch. I woke up too late to eat breakfast. I was so hungry that my stomach growled in class. I saw that I had forgotten my lunch at home. My family was shocked to see how much I ate at dinner.

Keep This in Mind

- Use transitional words to show time order within paragraphs and between paragraphs.

Now Write   Finish writing the first draft of your narrative composition. Remember to include transitional words and phrases to show time order. Be sure your conclusion solves the conflict. Save your first draft in your folder.

A Second Look

Revising Your Narrative Composition

Here's the Idea   You know that your first draft isn't your final composition. You can change it as much as you like until it is just right. The following questions will help you to see where your first draft needs to be changed. Use these questions to help you revise your narrative composition.

1. Does my introduction set the scene and introduce the characters?

2. Have I included all of the events I need to tell my story?

3. Are the events arranged in chronological order?

4. Do the events in the body of my narrative develop the conflict?

5. Have I used the same point of view throughout my story?

6. Have I included dialogue that moves my story along and tells about the characters?

7. Have I used transitional words within paragraphs and between paragraphs to show time order?

8. Does my conclusion solve the conflict and bring the story to a satisfactory close?

Remember to proofread your narrative to find and correct any errors in grammar, capitalization, punctuation, and spelling. Pay special attention to the punctuation you used for dialogue. You can find the correct form for punctuation of dialogue on pages 556–559 in the Handbook.

Check It Out   Read the following paragraph from a narrative.

Alice was not a bit hurt, and she jumped on to her feet in a moment. She looked up, but it was all dark overhead. Before her was another long passage, and the White Rabbit was still in sight, hurrying down it. There was not a moment to be lost. Away went Alice like the wind, and was just in time to hear it say, as it turned a corner, "Oh, my ears and whiskers, how late it's getting!" She was close behind it when she turned the corner, but the Rabbit was no longer to be seen. She found herself in a long, low hall, which was lit up by a row of lamps hanging from the roof.

—LEWIS CARROLL

- What are some of the things that make this a good narrative?

Try Your Skill   Proofread the following dialogue. Find and correct any errors in capitalization and punctuation.

It looks like rain," Bob said.
"Let's hope it holds off" his sister said. "Dad says we've got to get these crops in".
"Dad really loves farming," Bob said.
It's his life, "his sister said, "I guess he hopes it will be ours someday, too.

Keep This in Mind

- Your first draft is not a final copy. Revise your first draft until it is as good as you can make it.

Now Write   Revise your narrative composition. Use the guidelines in this lesson to help you. When you are satisfied with your narrative, make a final copy. Save your narrative composition in your folder.

The Descriptive Composition

It Makes Sense

Pre-Writing: Using Sensory Details

Here's the Idea   A descriptive composition paints a picture with words. Therefore, the first step in planning a descriptive composition is choosing a person, place, or thing that is interesting enough to describe in detail.

Once you have selected a subject, you must begin gathering supporting details. The more vivid and specific your details are, the better your word picture will be. To find vivid details, use each of your senses.

Not every object or scene affects all the senses. Food can be tasted, but it is not often heard. You can see a tree, but you wouldn't taste it. However, you should try to use as many of your senses as possible as you gather details for your description. Here are some questions you might ask for each sense.

Sight: What colors do I see? what shapes? what sizes?

Touch: Is it hot or cold? rough or smooth? dry or oily?

Sound: What sounds do I hear? What words best describe each sound?

Smell: What do I smell? Are the odors strong or weak? pleasant or unpleasant?

Taste: Is the taste pleasant or unpleasant? Is it sweet, sour, salty, spicy, or bitter?

When you have finished making your notes, read them over carefully. Cross out any details that do not seem important to your description. Add new ones as you think of them. Then arrange your details in spatial order. This is the order that you want your reader to notice them.

Look at these pre-writing notes.

Topic   my science lab
science lab, most exciting room in school
odors of gas, strange smelling chemicals
noise: click of brass weights, hum of pump in fish tank
special equipment
classroom: teacher's demonstration table (front)
   supply cabinet (left), tropical fish tank (right)
my table: Bunsen burner (left), test tubes (right)
   sink, chrome faucets (center)
balance: horizontal bar, chains, pans and weights

· What senses have been used in gathering these pre-writing notes?
· How is the writer organizing the details?

Try Your Skill   Make some pre-writing notes for a descriptive composition about the classroom you are in or for any other room in your school. Gather as many sensory details as you can. Then arrange the details in the order that you want the viewers to notice them.

Keep This in Mind

· Gather sensory details to develop your description.
· Arrange your details in the order that you want the viewers to notice them.

Now Write   Choose a person, place, or thing to describe in your descriptive composition. Use your senses to gather details that will make your description vivid. Arrange your details in the order that you want your reader to notice them. Save your organized pre-writing notes in your folder.

Try It Out

Writing the First Draft

Here's the Idea As you write the first draft of your descriptive composition, picture in your mind the person, place, or thing you are describing. This will help you to write a vivid description for your readers.

Remember that your composition must have three parts. The first paragraph is the **introduction.** This paragraph contains a topic sentence. It tells the reader who or what you are describing. The introduction should be interesting. It should make the reader want to read on.

The paragraphs that follow the introduction are called the **body.** The body contains all of the sensory details that develop the description. These details are grouped around two or three main ideas. Each main idea is a paragraph in the body. For example, in the body of a composition that describes a person, one group of details might tell about the person's physical features. Another group might describe the person's clothes.

The final paragraph of your description is the **conclusion.** The conclusion sums up all of the ideas in your composition.

You can make your description clear by using transitional words that tell *where.* Some of these words are *behind, near, beside, in front of, inside, on top of, under,* and *to the left.*

Check It Out Read this introduction.

Our science lab is the most exciting classroom in school. Something is always happening there. As we work, we can smell the chemicals. We hear gas hissing from the compressor in the back closet. Water splashes in the sink near the window. Test tubes clink all around the room. Everywhere in the lab we are busy with special equipment, like Bunsen burners, test tubes, and balances.

- What is the topic sentence in this introduction?
- What transitional words have been used to make the description clear?

Try Your Skill Below are pre-writing notes for an introduction to a descriptive composition. Using these notes, along with details from your imagination, write an introduction.

Topic	our home economics classroom
Introduction	home ec. room—4 superkitchens in 1
	sounds—pots and pans, water, laughing
	mouth-watering smells—blueberry muffins, bread
	good tastes—pizza, apple pie
	stainless steel sinks (along one wall)
	storage cabinets (back)
	wall of windows (to courtyard)
	counter space (wall near door)
	stove—where something good is cooking (?)

Keep This in Mind

- In a descriptive composition, the introduction presents the person, place, or thing being described.
- The body contains sensory details that develop the description.
- The conclusion sums up the description.
- Use transitional words that tell *where* to make your description clear.

Now Write Use your pre-writing notes from the last lesson to write the first draft of your descriptive composition. Be sure your introduction is interesting and has a strong topic sentence. Use transitional words to make your description clear. For now, just write the introduction and the body. Save your first draft in your folder.

In Conclusion

The First Draft: Concluding a Description

Here's the Idea   A descriptive composition should have a strong, clear ending. Your reader should know that the composition is finished.

First, look at the topic sentences for each of the paragraphs in the body of your composition. These are the ideas that you used to develop your topic. Think about how you can pull all of these ideas together to summarize the main idea of your composition. Try to state your ideas in a different way. Don't just copy them.

Second, think about why you are telling the reader about your topic. Why is it interesting or important to you? You can share your feelings in such a way that the reader will feel as close as you do to your subject. In this way, the conclusion will strengthen the main idea of your composition. This main idea was stated in the topic sentence of your introduction.

Sometimes it's possible to end your description on a light or humorous note. Let your attitude about the topic be your guide.

Check It Out   Read the conclusion below.

> Each day in the science lab is a new experience. The sounds and smells are exciting. Working with all the special equipment is challenging. I'm improving my skills every day. Some day I hope to be a research scientist. Then I will be able to work in a lab every day.

- How does the writer feel about the science lab?
- Does the conclusion pull all the main ideas in the composition together?

168

Try Your Skill   Look at the pre-writing notes in **Try Your Skill** on page 167. Use these notes, along with any other details you can imagine, to write a conclusion. Compare your conclusion with those of your classmates.

Now Write   Read the first draft you wrote in the last lesson. Then write a good conclusion to your descriptive composition. Save your first draft in your folder.

Good, Better, Best

Revising Your Descriptive Composition

Here's the Idea   You already know that a descriptive composition paints a word picture. Your goal is to make the person, place, or thing you are describing seem real to your reader. You want your description to be clear and strong. As you read over your first draft, ask yourself if you have achieved your goal. Here are some other questions to help you revise your first draft.

1. Have I collected good sensory details to develop my description? Are all the words and details as specific as I can make them?

2. Have I organized my details in the order that I want my readers to notice them?

3. Have I used transitional words that tell *where*?

4. Is my introduction interesting? Does it contain a topic sentence that presents the person, place, or thing I am describing?

5. Does each paragraph in the body have a strong topic sentence that presents the main idea of that paragraph?

6. Does my conclusion sum up all of the ideas in my composition? Does it tell the reader how I feel about my topic?

When you are satisfied that your ideas and your organization are the best they can be, proofread your composition. Find and correct any errors in grammar, capitalization, punctuation, and spelling. Then make a final copy of your composition, following the guidelines on pages 142–143.

Check It Out   Notice how this paragraph from a descriptive composition has been revised.

Whenever my Dad wants to escape ~~the house~~ he only has to go *retreat*
to the basement. Dad has a place where my brothers and sisters *built special*
and the telephone can't find him. Dad's workroom is his castle. *There, next to the laundry room,* *screaming*
ringing of the

- What types of revisions has the writer made to the ideas in this paragraph? How have these changes improved the description?
- What errors in capitalization, punctuation, or spelling have been corrected?

Try Your Skill Here is more of the rough draft you looked at in **Check It Out**. Continue to revise this descriptive composition. Use the guidelines in this lesson. Remember to proofread for errors in grammar, capitalization, punctuation, and spelling. Compare your revision with those of your classmates.

Dad keeps his tools their, he has his power saw, drill press, and lathe. He has a workbench covered in junk. jars of stuff are on the wall. He always got some project sitting around.

Dad got a chair and hassock in the room. He got our old T.V. there, a lamp and even keeps a refrigerator full of things to eat.

Dad locks the room unless he's there. When hes there he doesn't like to be disturbed. I guess even dad's need a place to go.

Keep This in Mind

- Revise your descriptive composition to make the description vivid, real, and strong.

Now Write Use the guidelines in this lesson to revise the first draft of your composition. When you are pleased with the composition, make a final copy. Save it in your folder.

The Explanatory Composition

Telling *How*

How Is It Done?

Pre-Writing: Listing the Steps

Here's the Idea   An explanatory *how* composition explains the steps in a process. You might explain how to do something, such as how to use a CB radio or how to build a model rocket. You could also explain how something happens, such as how an island is formed. Finally, you might tell how something works, such as an air conditioner. Choose a subject that you know about and could explain well.

When you have chosen a subject, gather supporting details. These details will be all of the steps that make up the process you are explaining. As you gather your details, you will want to be sure you don't leave out any important steps. If you do, your readers won't understand the process. You will also want to be sure that each step in the process is explained simply and clearly.

Check It Out   Read these pre-writing notes.

How To Make Vegetable Soup

select vegetables

firm, fresh
4 or 5 different kinds
different colors, different flavors

preparation

need sharp knife
clean, peel, cut into bite-sized pieces
use cutting board

cooking

vegetables
beef or chicken broth
simmer one hour

season and serve

season to taste
serve with bread and cheese

- What process do these steps explain?
- Have any important steps been left out?
- Is each step worded simply and clearly?

Try Your Skill   Make some pre-writing notes to help you explain how to make a peanut butter and jelly sandwich. Be sure to include *all* of the steps. Each step should be worded simply and clearly. Compare your notes with those of your classmates.

Keep This in Mind

- Explanatory *how* compositions explain the steps in a process. They explain how to do something or how something happens or works.
- List all of the steps that make up the process. Don't leave out any steps.
- Explain each step in the process simply and clearly.

Now Write   Choose a process that you would like to explain. Make a list of all of the important steps in the process. Save your notes in your folder.

One Step at a Time

Pre-Writing: Using Step-By-Step Order

Here's the Idea   A good way to organize an explanatory *how* composition is to follow this plan: introduction, steps in the process, and conclusion.

One sentence of the introduction should serve as the topic sentence for the composition. Suppose that your topic is how to prepare vegetable soup. The topic sentence might be "Vegetable soup is good for you, delicious, and easy to prepare."

In the paragraphs that follow the introduction, give a step-by-step explanation. You might divide the making of vegetable soup into getting the ingredients, preparing the vegetables, and cooking the soup. Each of these steps would become a separate paragraph. You would then develop each paragraph with specific details from your pre-writing notes. Arranging the steps of a process in the order they are supposed to happen is called **step-by-step order.**

You might develop the concluding paragraph from the final step, seasoning and serving the soup. Your concluding paragraph could also be a summary of the process you explained.

Check It Out   Look at these pre-writing notes for an explanatory composition about how a tornado forms.

> time of year—spring
> time of day—usually afternoon or early evening
> temperature—hot, humid
>
> 1. big thunderclouds appear (thunder heard in distance)
> 2. one cloud becomes very dark and dense
> 3. bottom of cloud starts to twist around
> 4. twisting produces a funnel cloud that reaches for ground

5. heavy rain and hail falls—much lightning
6. funnel cloud begins to hiss
7. funnel cloud touches ground—hiss becomes a loud roar
8. funnel cloud stirs up big cloud of dust—begins dancing along ground.

- Do you see how these notes have been arranged in correct step-by-step order?

Try Your Skill   Below is the body of a composition explaining how to take pictures of stars. However, these three steps are not organized correctly. Write them in correct step-by-step order.

Then point your camera at the stars. Center it on the North Star, which appears as the most stable star in the sky. Next, set your camera for a time exposure of one hour or more.

Begin by choosing a clear night for your photography. Find an open field that is away from lights and buildings. When you have a clear view of the stars, mount your camera on the tripod.

During the exposure, sit back and let the camera do its work. Your only job is to avoid bumping or shaking the camera.

Keep This in Mind

- Organize the details of the process you are explaining in correct step-by-step order.

Now Write   Arrange your pre-writing notes from the last lesson, **How Is It Done?**, in step-by-step order. Save your organized notes in your folder.

Say When

Writing the First Draft

Here's the Idea As you write your first draft, be sure to include all of the steps in the process you are explaining. Tell about each step in the correct order. To make the order in your composition as clear as possible, use transitional words and phrases. These are words and phrases that tell *when*. Look at the examples below.

first	the next step	when	before
second	after that	finally	as soon as
then	at the same time	last	afterwards

Transitional words can help make the order of ideas in the paragraph clear. Transitional words can also link paragraphs. They work like a bridge to carry the reader from the main idea of one paragraph to the main idea of the next.

As you write the first draft of your explanatory composition, include transitional words to help make your explanation clear.

Check It Out Review the body of the explanation you corrected in the last lesson. Which transitional words are used within each paragraph? Which ones link the three paragraphs?

Now, read these two paragraphs. They are the introduction and conclusion of a composition on making soup. Notice how they are linked to the body of the composition.

Introduction

What food warms your insides and brings a smile to your face? What tastes great for lunch on a chilly day? Homemade soup. It's everyone's favorite. Vegetable soup is especially nutritious, delicious, and easy to prepare. You can make it by following a few simple steps.

Conclusion

In a short time, the vegetables will become tender and full of flavor. After you have adjusted the seasonings, serve this easy-to-make meal in big bowls. Crusty bread and cheese are good with this soup. Anyone who tastes this hot, hearty, healthful treat will want seconds. People everywhere love vegetable soup.

- What transitional words are used in these two paragraphs?
- Are there any transitional words that link the introduction or the conclusion to the body? What are they?

Try Your Skill   Below is a paragraph about how clouds are formed. There are no transitional words. Copy the paragraph. Make the order in the paragraph clear by adding clear transitional words. Use several different ones.

_____ rain water soaks into the soil. _____ underground water seeps into small streams. _____ the streams empty into rivers. _____ the rivers flow into lakes and oceans. _____ the water from large bodies of water evaporates into the air.

Keep This in Mind

- In an explanatory composition, use transitional words that tell *when*. They help make the step-by-step order clear.
- Transitional words can be used within paragraphs and between paragraphs.

Now Write   Write the first draft of your explanatory *how* composition. Remember to include a strong topic sentence in your introductory paragraph. Use transitional words within and between paragraphs. Be sure the steps in the process you are explaining are simple and specific. Make your explanation as clear as possible. Save your first draft in your folder.

Clearly Correct

Revising Your Explanatory *How* Composition

Here's the Idea When you write the first draft of your explanation, you usually write it very quickly. You don't worry about proper grammar, capitalization, punctuation, or spelling. In your haste you might even forget one of the steps that explain the process to your reader. That is why it is important to revise your explanatory *how* composition. You want to make sure your explanation is clear, complete, and correct.

Here are some questions that can help you to revise the first draft of your explanatory *how* composition.

1. Did I write a strong, clear topic sentence in my introductory paragraph?
2. Did I include *all* of the steps in the process I am explaining?
3. Are my details arranged in step-by-step order? Does each paragraph tell about a different step?
4. Is each step explained simply and clearly?
5. Did I use transitional words that tell *when* to link sentences and paragraphs?
6. Does each paragraph in the body of my composition have a topic sentence?
7. Does my conclusion sum up the process I have been explaining?

After you have used these questions to revise your composition, proofread it. Find and correct any errors in grammar, capitalization, punctuation, and spelling.

Check It Out   Read this paragraph from an explanatory *how* composition.

Do you know how to make raisins? Raisins are dried grapes. Workers pick only grapes that have thick skins. When the grapes have dried out almost completely, they are raisins. They dry easily in the sun. The grapes are picked in August. They are spread on clean paper in the sunshine to dry.

· Does this paragraph need revision? Why?

Try Your Skill   Revise the paragraph in **Check It Out**. Use the guidelines in this lesson to help you. Compare your final copy to those of your classmates.

Keep This in Mind

· When revising your explanatory *how* composition, be sure you have included all of the steps. Also make sure that your explanation is clear.
· Proofread your composition to find and correct any errors in grammar, capitalization, punctuation, and spelling.

Now Write   Using the guidelines in this lesson, revise the first draft of your explanatory *how* composition. When your revision is complete, make a final copy. Save your composition in your folder.

Writing
a Report

Narrow-Minded

Pre-Writing: Choosing a Report Topic

Here's the Idea   A report, like any other composition, is a group of paragraphs about one topic. There are two important differences between a standard composition and a report, however.

First, most compositions include opinions, your feelings about a topic. A report, however, deals only with facts. Facts are statements that can be proven true. To learn more about facts and opinions, read Section 17, **Clear Thinking.**

A second difference is that a report is written from information gathered from outside sources. These outside sources may include encyclopedias, books, and magazine and newspaper articles. The purpose of a report is to use the information you gather from these outside sources to inform your readers about your topic.

The first step in preparing to write a report is choosing a topic. You must be careful to choose a topic that is not too general. You should be able to cover your topic well in the assigned length of your report. A topic such as "The History of Coal" is much too general for a short report. You could easily write a whole book about it. If you wanted to write a report about coal, better topics might be "Inside a Coal Mine" and "How Coal Is Formed."

Check It Out   Read these two paragraphs.

1   The purple martin is a small, sparrow-like bird that lives in eastern Canada and the United States. It is known for its strange nesting behavior. The purple martin nests mainly in birdhouses which people build for it. Biologists and bird-watchers have seen purple martins nesting in trees on rare occasions, but these birds usually depend on people to build houses for them.

2   Miguel looked out his bedroom window and saw the thunderstorm approaching. He was terrified. Huge gray clouds rolled across the sky, throwing shadows over the red tile rooftops of the town. Suddenly, a flash of lightning lit up the sky. Miguel waited nervously for the thunder to follow. When it did, it was as if all the doors in the world had just slammed shut.

- Which paragraph contains information gathered from an outside source?
- Which paragraph is from a report? How can you tell?

Try Your Skill   Below is a list of topics. Write which topics would be good for a report. Remember, a good report topic should not be too general. It must also be a subject that can be explained with facts gathered from outside sources. Discuss your choice with your classmates.

the history of rock music   my favorite television program
the battle of Bunker Hill   magic through the ages
the Civil War   the German shepherd dog
tropical fish   my dog Ralph

Keep This in Mind

- A report is based on information gathered from outside sources.
- A report uses facts to inform the reader.
- A report does not include the writer's feelings or opinions.

Now Write   Think about some possible topics for a report. Write them down as they come to mind. Remember, a good topic is specific. It will be supported with facts that you gather from outside sources. Choose the topic that you most want to write about. Write it down and keep it in your folder.

Just the Facts

Pre-Writing: Gathering Information

Here's the Idea Once you have chosen a topic for your report, you will need to find information about it. A good place to look is an encyclopedia. Other sources are books, magazines, and newspapers. You will find all these sources in your school and community libraries. To learn how to find information in a library, see Section 18, **Using the Library.**

As you research your topic, you will want to copy important facts to use in your report. Use note cards for your notes. Here are some guidelines for making note cards.

1. Use a separate 3 x 5 note card for each fact or idea.
2. Write down where the fact or idea came from. Write down the name of the source and the page number the information was on.
3. Take notes in your own words. **Do not copy sentences directly from your source.** It is not acceptable to use another writer's work word-for-word.
4. Make a separate "source card" for each source you use. On this card, write down the following information for each type of source. You will need this information when you list your sources in Part 6.

Book:	author, title, publisher, date published
Magazine:	author of article (if there is one), title of article, name of magazine, date published, page number of article.
Encyclopedia:	title of article, name of encyclopedia, volume number, page number of article, date published
Newspaper:	author of article (if there is one); title of article; name of newspaper; date published; section, page, and column number of article

Check It Out   Read the information on this note card.

> The skeletons of many
> small ocean creatures
> make up the material
> known as coral.
>   Source — *The World*
> *We Live In*   page 115

- Does the note card include one important fact?
- Does the note card list the source of information?

Try Your Skill   Read the following paragraph. Make two or three note cards to help prepare a report on hamburgers.

The hamburger originated in Russia, where medieval Tartars ate raw meat scraped and shredded with a dull knife and seasoned with salt, pepper, and onion juice. German sailors picked up the dish at Russian ports and brought the recipe back to their home base at Hamburg. Finicky Hamburgers, not used to eating their meat raw, took some of the red out of their tartar steak by broiling the meat. Thus, the hamburger steak was born.

—*The People's Almanac #2* page 956

Keep This in Mind

- As you research your report, write the important information in your own words on note cards.
- Make a source card for each source you use.

Now Write   Go to the library and find two or three sources for your report. Read each source carefully. Make note cards for the important facts and ideas you find. Make source cards, too. Save your cards in your folder.

Order in the Cards

Organizing Notes for a Report

Here's the Idea   You will find it easier to write your report if you have planned it carefully. Organizing your information is an important step in planning your report.

Begin to organize your information by reading through the note cards you have made. You will discover that some of them tell about one main idea and that others tell about a different main idea. Separate the cards into several piles. Each pile should contain cards with information about one main idea.

For example, you might be writing a report about the Pilgrims at Plymouth, Massachusetts. You might find that your note cards had information about three main ideas. These ideas are (1) why the Pilgrims went to Plymouth, (2) how they got there, and (3) how they lived at Plymouth. Each of these main ideas could be a paragraph in your report. You would separate your cards into three piles that match the three main ideas. The cards in the pile about how the Pilgrims lived at Plymouth might include note cards with this information:

1. The Pilgrims found much game to hunt for food.
2. Pilgrims made clothing from the skins of animals they trapped.
3. Indians helped Pilgrims plant corn and other vegetables.

Group your other cards in the same way.

As you organize your information, you may find some cards that do not belong with any others. If this happens, you probably will not want this information in your report.

Check It Out   Each of these sentences describes the main idea of one pile of note cards for a report about the pilgrims at Plymouth. You should write sentences like these to describe the main idea of each group of cards.

1. The Pilgrims left England and sailed to America to escape being put in jail because of their religious beliefs.
2. The Pilgrims sailed across stormy seas, on the *Mayflower*, and landed at Plymouth.
3. The Pilgrims hunted and trapped animals for food and clothing, and farmed with the help of Indians.

- Do you see how each one of these sentences might serve as the topic sentence of a paragraph in a report about the Pilgrims?

Try Your Skill Below are nine facts from note cards on the Pilgrims. Put each fact into one of the following groups: (1) why the Pilgrims went to Plymouth, (2) how the Pilgrims got to Plymouth, and (3) how the Pilgrims lived at Plymouth. Find one fact that does not belong in any group.

- Indians helped the Pilgrims to plant corn and vegetables.
- The *Mayflower* had to cross stormy seas to reach America.
- Most of the Pilgrims refused to belong to the Church of England.
- Many people became seasick on the voyage.
- Pilgrims made clothing from the skins of animals they trapped.
- Plymouth is a popular tourist town today.
- The Pilgrims found much game to hunt for food.
- It took the *Mayflower* sixty-five days to cross the Atlantic.
- The English government arrested people who would not join the Church of England.

Keep This in Mind

- Organize your note cards by grouping together cards that tell about the same main idea.

Now Write Read over your note cards. Organize them into a few main ideas. Write a sentence that describes each main idea. Keep your sentences and your notes in your folder.

Putting It All Together

Writing the First Draft

Here's the Idea   After you have organized your notes, you are ready to begin writing the first draft of your report. The report has three parts—an introduction, a body, and a conclusion. The introduction tells the reader what your report is about. The body develops each main idea of the report with details. The conclusion sums up the important information in the report.

The introduction will be the first paragraph of your report. This paragraph will introduce your subject. Don't begin by saying "In my report I want to tell about . . . " or "My report is about . . . " Instead, write an interesting, informative first sentence. You may want to present some facts from your note cards in the introduction. Notice how the first paragraph in **Check It Out** presents the subject of a report on the Pilgrims.

As you write the paragraph for the body of your report, include topic sentences. You might want to use the topic sentences you wrote when you grouped your note cards in separate piles. Use your cards to add details to each paragraph.

Your report should end with a clearly written conclusion. The conclusion should sum up the information in your report in one brief paragraph.

Check It Out   Read the introduction and first paragraph of the body of a report about the Pilgrims at Plymouth Colony.

> In 1620, a group of colonists left England to search for religious freedom in a new land. They arrived at a point along the shore of Cape Cod Bay in Massachusetts. The colonists named the place Plymouth, after the town of Plymouth in England. They called themselves Pilgrims, a name that refers to people who go on religious journeys.

The Pilgrims left England and sailed to America to escape being jailed because of their religious beliefs. At this time in history, the English government arrested people who would not join the Church of England. Most of the Pilgrims refused to belong to the Church of England. They wanted to live where they could worship in freedom. They decided to leave England and set sail for America.

- Does the introduction tell who this report is about? Is it interesting and informative?
- Are all of the facts in the first paragraph of the body about one main idea? What is that main idea?

Try Your Skill   Go back to the **Try Your Skill** section in the last lesson, **Order in the Cards.** Review the notes you grouped together about the Pilgrims' trip to America. Use these notes to write a second paragraph for the body of the report in **Check It Out** about the Pilgrims at Plymouth Colony.

Keep This in Mind

- A report has an introduction, a body, and a conclusion.
- The introduction tells what your report is about.
- The body develops the topic with facts from your note cards.
- The conclusion sums up the information in your report.

Now Write   Write the first draft of your report. Use your note cards and the topic sentences you wrote in Part 3. Make sure you have a clear introduction, body, and conclusion. Don't worry about spelling, punctuation, or grammar at this point. Just try to present your ideas clearly. Save your first draft in your folder.

The Finish Line

Revising a Report

Here's the Idea   When you have finished the first draft of
your report, you will want to revise it. Take time to read your
report and think about it carefully.

Because a report is written from facts, it is important that
the facts be correct. Also, be sure all of your ideas are clearly
expressed. If a sentence seems unclear, rewrite it.

Be sure that your report is well organized. Make sure the
introduction tells what your report is about. See that the body
develops your topic with good details. Be sure the conclusion
sums up the report.

Proofread your report for errors in grammar, capitalization,
punctuation, and spelling. Neatly copy your report in its final
form. Proofread it for errors one last time.

Check It Out   Read this paragraph. Notice the revisions.

> The pilgrims' first winter at Plymouth was
> a difficult one. ~~It was very cold.~~ The people
> *(They suffered from terrible cold and heavy snowstorms.)*
> had made houses *built* *out of light, wooden boards* that did not keep out
> the cold winds. Their crops failed and
> many people were hungry. By spring,
> nearly half the colony had died
> from sickness.
> *(influenza, pneumonia, and starvation.)*

- Did the writer make this a better paragraph by adding details and improving word choice?
- Did the writer correct all spelling and punctuation errors?

Try Your Skill   Read the following paragraph. Proofread it to find and correct the errors in grammar, capitalization, punctuation, and spelling. Check for sentences that are unclear. If you find one, rewrite it.

Mount Everest is the highest mountan in the world. It is five miles above sea level. The peak is in the Himalaya range, along the boundry's of china and nepal, north of india. Mount Everest was named for Sir George Everest, the Englishman who discovered it:

Keep This in Mind

As you revise your report, ask yourself these questions:
- Is my information accurate?
- Are my ideas stated clearly? Could I add more details or improve my word choice?
- Is my organization logical?
- Is my grammar, usage, spelling, punctuation, and capitalization correct?

Now Write   Use the guidelines in this lesson to revise your report. Check your facts for accuracy. Be sure your ideas are clear. Check your organization. Look for errors in grammar, capitalization, punctuation, and spelling. Make a final copy of your report and proofread it one last time. Neatly correct any errors you find. Save your report in your folder.

Consider the Source

Listing Sources

Here's the Idea Whenever you write a report, you need to tell your readers where you got your information. You must list your sources on a separate page. This list of sources is called a **bibliography**. It tells where to look up more information about your topic. Each source in the bibliography is called an entry.

Look at the source cards you made in Part 2, **Just the Facts**. These cards contain all of the information you need to write a bibliography. Arrange these cards in alphabetical order, according to the author's last name. If no author is mentioned in the source, use the first main word of the title. Now write your bibliography. Here are the correct forms to use.

Book:	Cooke, Alistair. *America*. Alfred A. Knopf, 1973.
Encyclopedia:	"Jupiter." *The World Book Encyclopedia*. Volume 11, pp. 162–164, 1983.
Magazine:	Desauteb, Paul. "Majestic Jewels Find New Setting at Smithsonian." *Smithsonian*. June 1974, pp. 36–43.
Newspaper:	Idaszak, Jerome. "Seeing Yosemite Off the Beaten Trail." *Sun-Times*, 10 January 1984, Sec. A, p. 41, Cols. 1–3.

Check It Out Look at the following bibliography.

Bibliography

Dillon, Frances. *The Pilgrims*. Doubleday, 1973.
"Plymouth Colony." *World Book Encyclopedia*. Volume 15, pp. 518–521, 1967.
Schultz, F. L. "Thanksgiving Pilgrim Style." *American History Illustrated*. Nov. 1982, p. 17.

White, Paul. "Plymouth Revisited." *Chicago Tribune*, 18 September 1984, Sec. B., p. 3, Col. 1.

- Is all of the necessary information included in each entry? Is the information for each entry in the correct order? Are the entries arranged in correct alphabetical order?

Try Your Skill   Write a bibliography entry for each source below. Follow the correct form for each type of source. Then put the entries in correct alphabetical order.

1. an encyclopedia article titled "Mesa Verde" by Herbert E. Kahla in the *World Book Encyclopedia*, 1967, page 344, Volume 13

2. a book titled *A Talent for Detail* by Peter Daniel, published in 1974 by Harmony Books

3. a magazine article titled "Fighting the New Slavery" by Michael Serrill, published on p. 99 of the September 19, 1983 issue of *Time*

4. a newspaper article titled "Shuttle Mission a Success" by Victor Vazquez, in the *Herald Tribune* on Oct 9, 1985, in Section A, page 2, columns 1–4

Keep This in Mind

- The last page of your report should be a list of your outside sources.
- Encyclopedias, books, magazines, and newspapers each have their own form in a bibliography.
- Put your sources in alphabetical order by the author's last name. If no author is mentioned, use the first main word of the title.

Now Write   Make a list of sources for your report. Follow the samples you studied in this lesson. Write your sources in alphabetical order on a separate sheet of paper titled *List of Sources*. Put this page at the end of your report.

Clear Thinking

A Matter of Facts

Learning About Facts and Opinions

Here's the Idea   Facts and opinions are an important part of our lives. We read them in books, magazines, and newspapers. We hear them on radio and television. We exchange them when we talk to family and friends. It is important, therefore, to learn how to use facts and opinions correctly.

The first step in understanding facts and opinions is to learn the difference between them. A **fact** is a statement that can be proved true. Look at the following statements. Each is a fact.

1. The sun rises in the east.
2. In 1543, Copernicus showed that the earth traveled around the sun.
3. President Franklin Roosevelt had polio.

Facts can be proved true in different ways. Statement 1 can be proved true by **personal observation**. You can watch a sunrise and check the direction with a compass. In the same way, if someone says, "It's raining," you can look out a window to see if that statement is true. If it is, the statement is a fact.

Another way to prove that a statement is true is by checking a **reliable source**. An encyclopedia is one reliable source. You can prove that statements 2 and 3 are true by reading what an encyclopedia says about Copernicus and Roosevelt.

Another type of reliable source is a person who has special knowledge about a subject. You could find out if statement 3 is true by asking someone who has studied Roosevelt's life. You could also ask someone who was alive at the same time as Roosevelt and who knew about him.

An **opinion** is different from a fact. Opinions cannot be proved true. An opinion tells what someone believes or feels about something. If you say, "The country is a better place to live than the city," that is just your opinion. It is not a fact.

Check It Out Read the following statements.

1. Mt. Everest is the highest mountain in the world.
2. Basketball is a boring sport.
3. Students should have a long summer vacation because they work so hard during the rest of the year.
4. The state flower of Georgia is the Cherokee rose.

- Which of these statements can be proved true?
- Which of these statements are opinions? How do you know?

Try Your Skill Read each pair of statements. In each pair, which statement is the fact and which is the opinion? Would you use personal observation or a reliable source to prove that each fact is true?

1. Your hair is blond.
   Blond hair is the prettiest type of hair.
2. Winter is the best season.
   Forty inches of snow fell in our city last winter.
3. It rained all day yesterday.
   Rainy days are depressing.
4. Everyone in the world should learn English.
   More people speak Mandarin than any other language.

Keep This in Mind

- A fact is a statement that can be proved true.
- An opinion tells what someone believes or feels. An opinion cannot be proved true or untrue.

Now Write Write down two opinions that you have heard people express about teenagers. Then write down two facts about teenagers. Compare your opinion and facts to those of your classmates. Did anyone confuse an opinion with a fact? Title your paper **A Matter of Facts.** Save it in your folder.

Because I Say So

Supporting Opinions

Here's the Idea   Everyone has the right to state his or her opinions. However, opinions by themselves are not very convincing. An opinion needs support. It should have facts to back it up. Read the following opinion:

> Sudzy Soap is the best detergent for your clothes.

This is the opinion of the makers of Sudzy Soap. It is the way they feel about their product. It is the way they want *you* to feel. By itself, though, this opinion isn't at all convincing. It is not supported by any facts that tell *why* Sudzy Soap is the best. Here's how the makers of Sudzy Soap might back up their opinion to make it more convincing:

Opinion:	Sudzy Soap is the best detergent for your clothes.
Supporting fact:	It has strong ingredients to clean the clothes of active young people.
Supporting fact:	It easily removes grease, food stains, and ground-in dirt.

Remember, the more supporting facts an opinion has, the more convincing it is. Whenever you write an opinion, include facts to back it up. Whenever you read or hear an opinion, look for supporting information that explains *why*.

Check It Out   Read the following discussion.

> "I think that multiple-choice tests are the worst kind," said Jackson.
> "Nope," said Marcia. "It's got to be short-answer tests that are the worst. I hate short-answer tests!"

"You're both wrong," sighed Terry. "Essay tests are the hardest. You have to read the questions so carefully. You have to organize your time. You have to give so many details. Essay tests are definitely the hardest!"

- What is the opinion of each student? Which student supports his or her opinion with facts? What are those facts?

Try Your Skill Look at advertisements in newspapers or magazines. Find advertisements that contain opinions. Try to find two opinions that are supported with facts, then find two that are not well supported. Bring your ads to class and talk about them with your classmates. Are the supported or unsupported opinions more convincing? Why?

Keep This in Mind

- To be convincing, an opinion must be supported by facts.
- The facts that support an opinion should tell *why*.

Now Write Think for a while about some things you believe or feel strongly about. Write several opinions that state your beliefs or feelings. Choose one of your opinions and write a short paragraph about it. State your opinion in the topic sentence. Then support your opinion with facts. Title your paper **Because I Say So**. Save it in your folder.

Using the Library

Part 1 **A Good Place To Go**
How To Use the Library

Part 2 **Pick a Card**
How To Use the Card Catalog

Part 3 **Look Here!**
How To Use an Encyclopedia

A Good Place To Go

How To Use the Library

Here's the Idea   Almost anything you might want to read for pleasure or research is available in your school or public library. Do you know where to find what you want? Do you know how materials are arranged?

The books in the library are divided into two groups, **fiction** and **nonfiction**. Fiction books are arranged alphabetically on the shelves according to the author's last name. For example, *Johnny Tremain*, written by Esther Forbes, would be shelved under **F**.

Most libraries arrange nonfiction books according to the **Dewey Decimal System**. This system puts books into ten general categories. Each category has its own set of numbers. Nonfiction books are arranged numerically on the library shelves by their Dewey Decimal number. The ten categories are listed below.

000–099	**General Works**	(encyclopedias, almanacs)
100–199	**Philosophy**	(conduct, psychology)
200–299	**Religion**	(the Bible, mythology)
300–399	**Social Science**	(economics, law, education, government)
400–499	**Language**	(languages, grammar, dictionaries)
500–599	**Science**	(mathematics, biology, chemistry)
600–699	**Useful Arts**	(farming, cooking, sewing, television, business)
700–799	**Fine Arts**	(music, photography, games, sports)
800–899	**Literature**	(poetry, plays)
900–999	**History**	(biography, travel, geography)

On the spine of each nonfiction book is its **call number.** This number includes the Dewey Decimal number and other information. Look at the example below. Notice the information included in the call number.

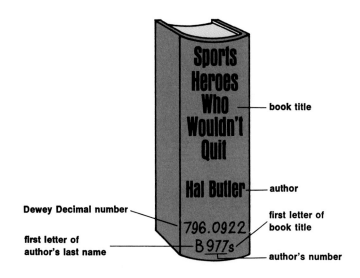

book title
author
Dewey Decimal number
first letter of book title
first letter of author's last name
author's number

Sports Heroes Who Wouldn't Quit
Hal Butler
796.0922
B 977s

Check It Out Look at the spines of the books represented below.

The Contender — Robert Lipsyte

Summer of Fear — Lois Duncan

Soup for President — Robert Newton Peck

The Pinballs — Betsy Byars

The Loon in My Bathtub — Ronald Rood — 591.5 R671ℓ

The Story of Baseball in Words and Pictures — John Durant — 796.35709 D932s

The Birth of the United States — Isaac Asimov — 973 AS1

Your Career If You're Not Going to College — Sarah Splaver — 371.425 Sp51y

- How can you tell if books are fiction or nonfiction?
- What is the general Dewey Decimal category of each nonfiction book?
- How can the call numbers and authors' names on the spines help you find these books?

Try Your Skill   Decide which of the following books are on the fiction shelves and which are on the nonfiction shelves.

1. *May I Cross Your Golden River?* Paige Dixon
2. *Facts About the Presidents,* Joseph Nathan Kane, R973.0992 K131f
3. *Fitzgo: The Wild Dog of Central Park,* Paul Wilkes, 636.7 W652f
4. *Dear Lovey Hart, I'm Desperate,* Ellen Conford
5. *The Cay,* Theodore Taylor
6. *Riders of the Wind: The Story of Ballooning,* 629.13322DW1

Keep This in Mind

- Library books are divided into two groups, fiction and nonfiction.
- Fiction books are filed alphabetically by the author's last name.
- Nonfiction books are classified in ten general categories. Each nonfiction book has its own call number to show where it can be found on the shelves.

Now Write   Go to your school or public library. Find one history book, one science book, and one encyclopedia. Write the name of each book. Also write the author, if there is one. Now write the call number exactly as it appears on the spine of the book. Check the Dewey Decimal numbers on page 204. See if the book has the kind of Dewey Decimal number it should have according to its subject. Save your work in your folder.

Pick a Card

How To Use the Card Catalog

Here's the Idea When you're looking for a book in the library, the **card catalog** is the place to start. Every book in the library is listed there, at least three times.

Every book is recorded on an **author card,** a **title card,** and at least one **subject card.** All three cards give the call number of the book in the upper left corner. The same number appears on the binding of the book. The number determines where the book is located on the shelves.

All three cards contain the same information, but the information is arranged differently on each card. All three cards tell the publisher, the date of publication, and the number of pages in the book. There is also a notation telling whether the book has illustrations. Sometimes, there is a short description of the book or mention of other books on the same topic.

On an **author card,** the author's name is at the top. The author's name is written with the last name first. Author cards are arranged alphabetically by the author's last name.

Author Card

> 793.8 **Rydell, Wendy**
> R972g   The great book of magic: includ-
> ing 150 mystifying tricks you can
> perform/
> by Wendy Rydell, with George
> Gilbert.—New York: H. N.
> Abrams, c. 1976.
>   271 p.: ill. (some col.); 28 cm.
>   Bibliography: p. 264
>
>   ○

On a **title card,** the title comes first. Title cards are alphabetized according to the first word of the title. However, if *A, An,* or *The* is the first word in a title, look for the title card under the first letter of the second word in the title. For example, you would find *The Great Book of Magic* filed under the letter *G.*

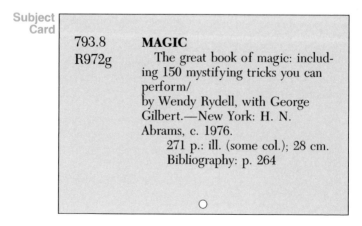

On a **subject card,** the subject is at the top. In the card catalog, the subject card is arranged alphabetically by the first word of the subject. The subject may be written in capital letters or in red.

Check It Out   Look at the three sample cards shown. Answer the following questions.

- Under what letter of the alphabet would each card be filed?
- Where could you look for more books by Wendy Rydell?
- Where would you find more books on magic?

Try Your Skill   Below are the title, author, and call number for a book about magic. On a sheet of paper, draw three rectangles to represent file cards. Use the information below to make an author card, a title card, and a subject card.

The Illustrated History of Magic, by Christopher Milbourne, 793.8 C4666m

Keep This in Mind

- Every book in a library is listed in the card catalog, on at least three different cards—author, title, and subject.
- Each card records the call number, the author, the title, and other important information about the book.

Now Write   Write the name of your favorite fiction author.

Next, think of a subject you're interested in. It might be a hobby, a sport, a person, or an art form. Write it on your paper.

Go to the card catalog in your school or public library. Find two books by the author you have chosen and two books on the subject you have chosen.

On your paper, make a rectangle to look like a file card. Copy the information from one of the cards into the rectangle. Save your work in your folder.

Look Here!

How To Use an Encyclopedia

Here's the Idea   A good way to begin any search for information is to look in an encyclopedia. An **encyclopedia** contains articles on many different subjects. The articles are arranged alphabetically by subject. On the spine of each volume you will find a single letter or guide letters to tell you what subjects are covered in it. Look at the set of encyclopedias arranged below.

If you want to look up *magic*, for instance, first find the volume that contains subjects beginning with *M*. Then, look up the word *magic* in that volume, just as you would in a dictionary. Each page has guide words just as a dictionary does.

A major article in an encyclopedia is often divided into parts. Each part has a subtitle. When you need information on a specific topic, you usually don't have to read every word of the article. Just look under the appropriate heading. For example, you wouldn't need to study an entire article on the United States to find out about the Battle of Gettysburg. You might look in the section on *History* under *The Civil War*.

An article may also tell you where to look for further information, or provide a list of books for further reading.

Different encyclopedias have different reading levels. Read an article in several encyclopedias. Find the one that is easiest for you to understand. Try *Collier's Encyclopedia, Brittanica Junior Encyclopedia,* or *World Book Encyclopedia.*

Check It Out   Look at the sample encyclopedia shown at the left. Answer the following questions.

· In what volume would you find information about New Zealand? Theodore Roosevelt? volcanoes? Mexico?

Try Your Skill   Use the sample encyclopedia pictured in **Here's the Idea.** Write the key word in each question that tells you where to look in the encyclopedia. Next to the key word write the number of the volume in which you would look.

1.   What is the name of the largest crater on the moon?
2.   Was the game of lacrosse invented in North America?
3.   Where does the tradition of Halloween come from?

Keep This in Mind

· An encyclopedia contains articles on many subjects. The articles are arranged alphabetically.
· Use key words to find articles on your topic.

Now Write   Write the same nonfiction subject you chose for the last lesson, **Pick a Card.** Find an encyclopedia article on your subject. List the following information: the name of the encyclopedia, the number and guide letters, the guide words, related articles, and the titles of any recommended books.

Study and Research Skills

The First Step

Understanding the Assignment

Here's the Idea   Your schoolwork presents you with many challenges. You can meet these challenges if you learn good study and research skills. These skills will help you to learn your lessons well and prepare good papers and projects.

The first step in learning to do good schoolwork is understanding the assignments you are given. Whenever you are given an assignment, write it down immediately. Use a special section of your notebook or a separate assignment book. First write the subject. Then write exactly what you are supposed to do. Finally, write the date the assignment is given. Also write the date it is due. Here is an example.

Subject	Assignment	Date Given	Date Due
English	Memorize myths pp. 22-24	10-8	10-11
Math	Review Chapter 8. Do exercises pp. 182 - 183	10-8	10-9
Science	Read Chapter 5 pp. 80-95	10-8	10-12

Before working on the assignment, ask some questions.

1. **What kind of assignment is it?** Will you have to read, study, memorize, write, answer questions or build?
2. **What should the final product be?** Will it be a composition, answers to exercises, a skit, a lab report, or a speech?
3. **What will I need?** Will you have to look at certain books in the library? Will you need any special supplies?
4. **When is the assignment due?** How many days will you have to finish the assignment?

Check It Out   Read the following sample English assignment.

Collect at least five magazine advertisements that include famous people. Paste the ads in your notebook. The notebooks will be due on Friday.

- What two things does the assignment ask you to do?
- What will the final product be?
- What will you need to complete the assignment?
- When is the assignment due?

Try Your Skill   Read the sample math assignment below. What type of assignment is it? What will the final product be? What special supplies will you need?

By Thursday, read the chapter on measurements in your math book. Then measure any two rooms in your house. Use both yards and meters. Write these measurements down in your notebook.

Keep This in Mind

- When you are given an assignment, be sure you understand what kind of assignment it is. Know what the final product should be. Know what supplies you may need. Also know when the assignment is due.
- Enter the details and due dates of your assignments in an assignment notebook.

Now Write   On your paper, draw a page from an assignment book like the one on page 214. Make four columns. Title the columns *Subject, Assignment, Date Given,* and *Date Due.* Look at the two assignments presented in **Check It Out** and **Try Your Skill.** Enter them in your "assignment notebook." Save your work in your folder.

Stop, Look, and Listen

Following Directions

Here's the Idea   Knowing how to follow directions is important whether you are traveling to a new city, learning to work a computer, or doing your homework. In order to understand an assignment completely, you must learn to follow directions carefully. Directions may be spoken or written.

These guidelines will help you follow *spoken* directions:

Listening to Spoken Directions

1. Pay careful attention to what is being said.
2. Notice how many steps there are in the directions. Also notice the order in which the steps should be completed.
3. Listen for the key word in each step, such as *read, answer, write, organize,* or *memorize.*
4. Ask your teacher to explain any step you do not understand.
5. Write down the directions as you hear them.

These guidelines will help you to follow *written* directions:

Reading Written Directions

1. Read *all* of the directions carefully before you begin the assignment.
2. Ask your teacher questions if there is any part of the assignment that you do not understand.
3. Assemble the books and other materials that you will need before you begin.
4. Break down the assignment into steps. Organize these steps in the order that you will complete them.

Read the directions for this sample assignment.

Choose a city in another state or country that you would like to visit. Find a picture of something in that city. Get the pictures from a magazine, or copy a picture out of a book. List three reasons why you would like to visit this city.

- Do you understand exactly what you will need to hand in? Do you know what form the project should be in? If not, what questions could you ask to make these directions clearer?
- How would you break down this assignment into steps?

Try Your Skill   Read and follow this set of directions.

1. Write five words that describe your personality.
2. List three things about yourself that you would like to change.
3. Remember that you should be reading all of the directions completely before beginning. Now ignore directions 1 and 2. Copy the "Reading Written Directions" chart on a piece of paper.

Save your work in your folder.

Keep This in Mind

- Read or listen to *all* of the directions before you begin working.
- Ask questions if there is any part of the directions that you do not understand.

Now Write   Follow this three-step direction:

On a piece of paper first draw a circle. Then draw a square inside the circle. Finally draw a triangle on top of the circle.

Now, make up your own three-part direction about drawing simple shapes. Be prepared to read your directions to your classmates. See how well they follow your directions.

Your Own Space

A Time and a Place To Work

Here's the Idea You plant a vegetable garden in a sunny spot during the spring. You play football in an open field when there's enough light for you to see the ball. Studying also requires a special place and time.

At home you can put a table or a desk in your room or some other quiet place. At school you would use the library or a study hall. At the public library you can usually find a table in a quiet corner. No matter where you find your study space, you should be sure that it meets the following requirements.

Requirements for a Good Study Space

1. **It should be quiet.** You should not be disturbed by TV, radio, the telephone, or other noises.
2. **It should be well lit.** Poor lighting can strain your eyes and give you headaches.
3. **It should be neat and well-organized.** You should not have to search for books, papers, or other materials.
4. **It should be properly equipped.** You should always have a supply of paper, pens, and pencils handy. Your study space should also have a dictionary.

Check It Out Here are six possible study spaces.

1. A desk in a bedroom. There is also a shelf for books and a drawer for pencils, paper, and other study tools.

2. The student cafeteria during lunchtime.

3. A table in the dining room after dinner. Your books and study tools are neatly arranged on this table.

4. The living room floor in front of the television set.

5. A table or desk in the library. The table has enough space for your books and materials.

6. Your bed. The radio is on nearby to relax you.

- Which of these spaces would be good places for studying? Which would not be good places? Explain why you think so.

Try Your Skill   Rate the place where you study by answering the following questions.

1. Do you sit at a table or a desk?
2. Is the light good for studying?
3. What noises can you usually hear?
4. Are your books and supplies neatly organized?
5. Do you have all of the books and other study tools that you need?

Compare your answers to the requirements for a good study space that are listed on the previous page. Rate your place of study as:

A. Excellent (needs no improvement)
B. Fair (needs some improvement)
C. Poor (needs much improvement)

Keep This in Mind

- A study area should be a quiet, well-lit, and neat place.
- A study area should always have paper, pens, pencils, and a dictionary.
- Establish a regular time each day to study.

Now Write   On a clean piece of notebook paper, list four places in your home, in school, or at the public library that are good for studying. Also list the times that these places are available and convenient for you. Then, describe a study place that you think would be ideal. Save your paper in your folder.

Touchdown!

Achieving Goals with a Study Plan

Here's the Idea   If you plan your time carefully you will be able to complete all of your school assignments by their due dates. The best way to plan your time well is to set long-term and short-term goals.

At the end of each day see which assignments are due the next day. These assignments are your **short-term goals.** You should set aside some time every day to complete these assignments.

The assignments that will take longer than one day to complete are your **long-term goals.** Break these assignments down into shorter tasks. Then decide which task needs to be done first, which should be done second, and so on.

Suppose you have to write a report about panda bears. You might break up this long-term goal into the following tasks:

1. Go to the library and find two books.
2. Read the sections on panda bears in these books.
3. Take notes on the important information.
4. Organize the notes into an outline.
5. Write the first draft.
6. Revise the first draft.
7. Make a final copy.

Now you need to develop a study plan. A **study plan** is a schedule of all of your daily activities. It includes your social activities, as well as your school activities and homework. A study plan helps you to schedule your long- and short-term goals around your other daily plans. Make a study plan whenever you have a long-term goal to complete.

Check It Out   Notice how the research report about panda bears has been scheduled in this study plan.

Monday	Tuesday	Wednesday	Thursday	Friday	Saturday	Sunday
Library	Research pandas ___ Guitar lesson	Outline report ___ Swim practice	Write first draft	Dinner, Aunt Nancy's	Revise draft ___ Swim meet	Make final copy of report
Panda report due	Read history chap. 5	Review history chapter	History test ___ Council meeting	Free	Movie with Kevin	Review math problems

- Do you see how the work on this report has been scheduled so that it can be completed on time?
- Did you notice that the student realized there were some nights no work could be done?

Try Your Skill   Break up the following long-term goal into several tasks. Arrange them in the order they need to be done.

Make a notebook that tells about five Greek or Roman myths. Find a book on these myths in the library. Read it and select five myths. Then write your version of the five myths, including a picture for each.

Keep This in Mind

- Set aside a daily block of time for completing short-term goals.
- Break down all long-term goals into small tasks. Then put those tasks in a logical order.
- Make a study plan to schedule your study time.

Now Write   Make a two-week study plan like the one on this page. Show your regular activities. Break down the following assignment into several tasks. Fit them into your schedule. The assignment is to write a paragraph that describes a person from history. Pretend that this was assigned Monday, and is due Friday. Save your work in your folder.

Five Steps

A Way To Study

Here's the Idea   Most of your assignments include reading and studying. You can learn to study more effectively if you use a regular study method. One such method is called **SQ3R**. SQ3R stands for the five steps that make up this study method. The five steps are **s**urvey, **q**uestion, **r**ead, **r**ecite, and **r**eview.

SQ3R	
Survey	Look over the material to get a general idea of what it is about. Read the titles, the subtitles, the introduction, and the summary. Look at any illustrations.
Question	Make a list of questions that you should be able to answer at the end of your reading. These include any questions provided by your teacher or given at the end of the chapter. You can also turn titles, topic sentences, and illustrations into questions.
Read	Identify the main ideas in each section that you read. Try to find the answers to the questions you wrote.
Recite	Recite your answers to the questions. Write brief notes to help you remember these answers. Also take notes on other important ideas.
Review	Quickly read over your notes to review the main ideas of what you read.

Check It Out   Look at the questions that follow these titles.

"Five Steps: A Way to Study"
—What are the five steps?
"Learning to Follow Directions"
—How can I learn to follow directions?
"Croc's and 'Gators: Two Dangerous Reptiles"
—What is dangerous about crocodiles and alligators?

- Do you see how titles can be turned into questions?

Try Your Skill Apply the SQ3R method to the following passage on alligators and crocodiles. Write and answer the questions you think up. Make notes about any other important information.

Croc's and 'Gators: Two Dangerous Reptiles

Alligators and crocodiles are both ugly and dangerous. Crocodiles are more likely to kill humans than are alligators. However, alligators will attack when cornered. Both types of reptiles and their related species are the last living link to the prehistoric dinosaur-like reptiles.

Physical Differences Crocodiles have narrower heads and sharper snouts than alligators. They have two teeth which are always visible. Alligators' teeth cannot be seen when their mouths are closed.

Geographic Differences Crocodiles are found near swamps, rivers, and lakes in Africa, Asia, Australia, Madagascar, and the Americas. Alligators are found in the southeastern United States and in the Yangtze River region of China. Alligators prefer to live near fresh water.

Keep This in Mind

- The five steps of the SQ3R method are survey, question, read, recite, and review.
- Use the SQ3R method to study for all your classes.

Now Write Apply the SQ3R method to the next lesson, **Get It Down.** Write your questions, answers, and notes on notebook paper. Save your work in your folder.

Get It Down

Taking Notes

Here's the Idea Your schoolwork presents you with much new information. One way to learn this information is to take notes. Notes help you to understand what you read and hear. They help you to locate the main ideas in the material. The notes you take can also become a good study guide for later review.

Keep your notes in a notebook. This notebook should be divided into sections for each subject. Write the date and the subject at the top of each page of notes. A good notebook will include the main ideas covered in class. It will also include the notes and questions that you write when you read your textbooks.

When you take notes while someone is talking, you should listen for clues that can tell you what information is important. These clues include phrases like "The main point is . . . ," "Most importantly . . . ," and "To summarize. . . ." Write this important information in your notebook.

When you take notes as you read, you should include all the main ideas, key words, and definitions that you come across. Also, write down the answers to any questions that you think of while you read.

The notes you take do not have to be complete sentences. That would take too much time. Instead, write phrases and key words that will help you remember the main ideas. Use abbreviations whenever you can. You might want to circle or put a star next to the most important information in your notes. Be sure you write your notes neatly and clearly. That way you will have no trouble reading them when it's time to review.

Notice the important ideas in this passage on myth.

Myths are legends that explain things about people and nature. The characters in myths are usually gods and goddesses with special powers. Sometimes they look like humans; sometimes they take the shape of animals. However, they all show human emotions, such as love, hate, and jealousy.

- If you were to take notes on this paragraph, what important ideas would you include?

Try Your Skill Take notes on the following paragraph. Compare your notes with those of your classmates.

There are two basic types of myths. **Creation myths** tell about the beginning of the world and how the different creatures first came to be. **Explanatory myths** try to tell *why* certain things exist or how they began.

Keep This in Mind

- Notes can help you to study and remember information.
- Write your notes in phrases, not sentences.
- Use abbreviations to save time and space.
- Only take notes on the most important facts and ideas.

Now Write Look through an encyclopedia in your school library. Select a one- or two-paragraph passage on a subject that interests you. Take notes on this passage. Follow the suggestions in this lesson for taking good notes. Save your notes in your folder.

Get the Picture

Using Graphic Aids

Here's the Idea   Some of the information you learn in school is presented in words. Other information is presented through illustrations, maps, diagrams, photographs, and tables. These **graphic aids** present information clearly and quickly.

Photographs and illustrations can often show ideas better than words can. Read the captions that appear with these pictures. The captions may contain important information.

Diagrams help you to identify parts of an object. They may also show you how each part is related to the other parts.

Maps are drawings of areas of land and water. A map can give many facts about an area. A map might tell about population or annual rainfall. It could also tell about the height of mountains or the depth of lakes and oceans.

Tables and charts present groups of facts. The information in a table or chart is usually set up in columns.

Graphs are special charts that show how one fact is related to another. To understand a graph, you must first read the title. Next read the key to any symbols in the graph. Finally, read the information inside and along the sides of the graph.

Check It Out   Study these graphic aids. Then ask yourself these questions.

- Which graphic aid is an illustration? a diagram? a map? a table? a graph?
- What is the metal part of a saddle called?
- Which Indian tribe lived in Alberta?
- During which year were the *least* gold records awarded to albums? To singles?

Homelands of Indian Tribes	
Tribe	Homeland
Apache	Arizona, New Mexico
Blackfoot	Montana, Alberta, Saskatchewan
Cherokee	Georgia, North Carolina, South Carolina
Navaho	Arizona, New Mexico
Potawatomi	Illinois, Michigan, Wisconsin

The U.S. Recording Industry—Gold Records
Number of Records Awarded

Prairie Dog

seat, cantle
pommel, skirt, flap, cinch
ENGLISH SADDLE
stirrup strap, stirrup

Apia
UPOLU
WESTERN SAMOA

Try Your Skill   What type of graphic aid would you use to present each type of information listed below? Choose from diagram, map, chart and table, graph, and photograph.

1. The location of the five time zones
2. How to assemble a model airplane
3. How a cumulus cloud differs from a cirrus cloud
4. Attendance at seven football games

Keep This in Mind

- Graphic aids can present information clearly.
- Read the title, abbreviations, and explanations accompanying a graphic aid.

Now Write   Draw a bar graph that displays these facts about the percentage of people who speak different languages around the world: Indo-European, 48%; Siro-Tibetan, 23%; Black African, 7%; Japanese and Korean, 4%. Save your graph.

Be Confident!

Answering Objective Test Questions

Here's the Idea The better you understand what a test is, the easier it will be for you to do well on it. One way to become more confident is to learn about different test questions.

Objective test questions have only one answer. There are three main types of objective test questions. Here are some guidelines to help you answer these types of questions.

Multiple Choice In a multiple choice question, you must choose the best possible answer out of several that you are given. Be sure to read all of the choices before you decide which one is the best answer.

> Which of the following cities is *not* one of the ten windiest cities in the United States?
> (A) Omaha   (B) Chicago   (C) Buffalo   (D) Boston   (E) Dallas

True-False This kind of test question asks you to decide whether a statement is *true* or *false*. Words like "always," "never," "all," or "none" often make a statement false.

> The Taj Mahal was ordered built by an
> Indian ruler as a final resting place for his wife. _____

Matching In a matching question, you are given two lists. You must match items in one list to similar items from the other list. Match those items that you are sure of first. That will make it easier for you to match the items you are unsure of.

Match column A to column B.

Column A	Column B
kangaroo	mollusk
trout	fish
clam	marsupial

Check It Out See how the following questions are answered.

1. True-False questions are always true. _____*F*_____
2. Multiple Choice questions always have:
    (A) one answer that sounds almost right
    (B) one best answer
    (C) all correct answers
3. Match the tests in column A with their types of answers in column B.

A.	**B.**
matching	a circled or written letter
true-false	a line leading to its match
multiple choice	T or F

- Do you see how different types of questions require different types of answers?

Try Your Skill Read an encyclopedia article on a subject that interests you. Use it to make up two examples of each of the following types of questions: true-false and multiple choice. Include the answer to each question.

Keep This in Mind

- Taking tests will be easier if you learn how to recognize and answer different kinds of questions.
- Always read a test question completely before answering it.

Now Write Write an objective test that asks questions about your school. Write three true-false questions and three multiple choice questions. Write a matching question with a list of four academic subjects in one column and four humorous descriptions of the subjects in a second column. Exchange tests with a classmate. See how well you can answer the questions.

Write It Right

Answering Written Test Questions

Here's the Idea   Some test questions require written answers. Study these examples.

Completion or **Fill-in-the-Blank** For this kind of test question, you add the correct word or phrase to an incomplete sentence. If the word or phrase comes at the end of the sentence, add the correct punctuation. If it comes at the beginning of the sentence, capitalize the first letter.

Short Answer A short answer test question asks you to write a one- or two-sentence answer. Answer the questions in complete sentences. Capitalize and punctuate correctly.

Essay An essay test question requires you to write an answer of one or more paragraphs. Before you write, do some prewriting. Find out what the question asks. Words such as "explain" or "describe" are clues. List and organize your ideas on scratch paper. Be sure each paragraph has a good topic sentence.

Check It Out   See how these questions are answered.

1. The earliest examples of cave art have been found in __*France.*__ .

2. What are the two most heavily populated cities in the world?

> *The two most heavily populated cities in the world are Tokyo and Mexico City.*

3. Explain why water is important to the human body.

Water is necessary to the human body. Over fifty percent of all body cells are water. Water dissolves vitamins and carries them throughout the body. Water helps control body temperature.

- Do you see how each of these types of questions should be answered?

Try Your Skill Read an encyclopedia article on a subject that interests you. Use it to make up two examples of completion questions and two examples of short-answer questions. Write the answer to each question. Use the proper form.

Keep This in Mind

- A completion question asks for a word or phrase.
- A short-answer question asks for one or two sentences.
- An essay question asks for one or more paragraphs.

Now Write Answer the following essay test question:

Describe three study and research skills you have learned. Explain why each one is important.

Use correct composition skills in your answer. Capitalize and punctuate correctly. Save your essay in your folder.

Letters and Forms

Hi There!

How To Write a Friendly Letter

Here's the Idea   A **friendly letter** is a letter that you write to someone you know. It should be interesting, neat, and easy to read. A friendly letter should seem as natural as a conversation. Share your feelings. Ask questions. Talk about subjects that interest you. Keep your language lively and specific.

A friendly letter has five main parts: the *heading*, the *salutation* or greeting, the *body* or main part, the *closing*, and the *signature*.

The **heading** appears in the upper right corner of the page. It includes your address and the date.

The **salutation** is the part of the letter where you say "hello." In a friendly letter, the salutation might say "Dear Alec" or "Hi Juan." The salutation begins with a capital letter and is followed by a comma.

The **body,** the main part of the letter, starts on the next line. In the body of the letter you talk to your friend. If the letter is lively, it will make your friend feel as though you were there in person. The first word of the body is indented. Each new paragraph of the body is indented, too.

The **closing** says "goodbye." In a friendly letter the closing might say "Your friend" or "Best wishes." It is written on the line below the last sentence of the body. The closing begins with a capital letter and is followed by a comma.

The **signature** is the last part of your letter. Skip a line after the closing and write your name in line with the first word of the closing. When you are writing a friendly letter to someone you know well, use your first name as your signature. Otherwise, sign your full name.

- What details make this letter interesting?
- Identify the five parts of this letter. Notice when each part appears in the letter.

361 Newton Road
New York, New York 10001
March 11, 19_ _

Hi Juan,

It sure was good to hear from you. I'm glad to hear you are doing so well in math this year. After the trouble you had with it last year, I'm sure you must be feeling relieved. School has been hard for me this year. I have five main subjects, including French.

One bright spot has been the school paper. I have been doing drawings for it this year and am really enjoying it. Who knows, maybe next year I'll have my own comic strip. Keep in touch, and let me know when you're coming to New York again. I'll throw a big party for you when you visit!

Your friend,
Marty

Try Your Skill   Here's a friendly letter that has some problems. Read the letter and decide what's wrong with it. Compare the form of this letter with the letter on page 235. Write a few sentences explaining what should be changed.

27 Whitcomb Street
Price, Utah 84501
January 5, 19__

dear Ronnie,
    Happy New Year. I miss you. I hope you can make it out here this year. School is OK. Not much news to tell. I just wanted to say hello.

Sincerely, Gerry

Now Write   Write **Hi There!** at the top of your paper. Then write a friendly letter to a friend or relative. Be sure you use correct form. Save your letter in your folder.

A Good Send-off

How To Prepare Letters for the Mail

Here's the Idea   Once you've written your letter, fold it neatly. Use an envelope that matches the width of your letter. Carefully insert the letter into the envelope. Seal the envelope.
Follow these steps for preparing your envelope:

1.   Address the envelope. Add your return address.
2.   Double-check all numbers to make sure they are in the proper order.
3.   Include the correct five-number ZIP code. If you do not know the correct ZIP code, look it up in your telephone directory or call your local post office.
4.   Put a stamp on your envelope.

Addressing the envelope accurately will get your letter to the right place. Get in the habit of checking your letters and packages for accuracy. Call your local post office if you need more information.

Check It Out   Look at the envelope below.

Ms. Gwen Linehan
1607 Stratford Street
Big Sky, MT 59716

Dr. Samuel Collins
147 Barnes Road
Farwell, NE 68838

- To whom is the letter being sent? Who sent the letter?
- How could you check to be sure that the state abbreviations and ZIP codes are correct?

Try Your Skill Write each of the addresses below as it should appear on an envelope. Also write a return address.

1. Kate Lawrence, 24 Hampton Road, New Orleans, LA 70118
2. Mr. and Mrs. Peter Donovan, 7318 Skyline Drive, Washington, D.C. 20008
3. Anthony Colelli, 4325 Broadway Boulevard, Apartment 2-C, Oakland, CA 94602
4. Martha Woodworth, 7 Churchill Lane, Durham, NH 03824
5. James O'Shea, 281 Chestnut Street, Phoenix, Arizona 85040

Keep This in Mind

- Prepare your letter correctly. Fold your letter neatly, and use an envelope that matches the width of the letter
- Check addresses for neatness and accuracy. Check abbreviations of states and correct ZIP codes.
- Put your return address on the envelope.

Now Write Take out the friendly letter you wrote in the last lesson, **Hi There!**

On another piece of paper, write the title of this lesson, **A Good Send-off.** Draw a rectangle to represent an envelope. Address it as though you were going to mail it to your friend.

Copy your work onto a real envelope. Fold your letter and put it into the envelope. Put a stamp on the envelope.

Mail your letter. Save your sample envelope in your folder.

Thank You

How To Write Social Notes

Here's the Idea   Invitations and thank-you notes are both short forms of friendly letters. They use the same five parts. The heading may be shortened to include only the date.

An **invitation** should include all the information that the other person needs. Tell what kind of occasion you are inviting him or her to. Tell where and when it will take place. Sometimes you wish to know whether or not the person will attend. Then write *R.S.V.P.* at the bottom of the invitation. *R.S.V.P.* is an abbreviation for a French phrase that means "please reply."

Whenever you receive an invitation, answer as soon as possible. Thank the person for inviting you. Then tell the person whether or not you can accept the invitation. If you can't accept it, express your regrets and give a short explanation.

There are two kinds of **thank-you** notes. One kind of thank-you note is usually written after you have received a present. If a gift was mailed to you, the thank-you note tells the sender that the gift arrived. It also thanks the person for being kind. If you liked the gift, say so. If you didn't like it, you can still thank the sender for her or his thoughtfulness and effort.

Another kind of thank-you note is called a **bread-and-butter** note. This kind of letter thanks someone for his or her hospitality. You would write a bread-and-butter note after you stayed overnight at someone's house.

Both kinds of thank-you letters should show your appreciation for what another person has done for you. Also, both kinds of letters should be written as soon as possible after you receive a gift or someone's hospitality.

239

February 8, 19__

Dear Mr. and Mrs. Cullen,

You were very nice to let me spend last weekend with you. I want you to know how much I appreciate it. I had never been on roller skates before, and that by itself was a great treat.

I hope you get the chance to visit me in Jonesboro sometime. Then your family can stay here, and I can return the hospitality. Thanks for everything.

Sincerely,
Hank Reidell

- What type of social note is this? How is the form of this letter different from the friendly letter shown in **Hi There!** in this section?
- What words and phrases are used to express appreciation in this letter?

Try Your Skill   Read the thank-you note on the next page. Then rewrite it, correcting any errors that you find.

Dear Ms. Bert,

    Thanks for the sweater. It is not really my favorite color, but it's a nice sweater. I guess you didn't know that I don't like blue. Hope everyone is fine at your house.

                Robin

Now Write   Label your paper **Thank You.** Imagine that one of your relatives has sent you a pair of purple sneakers for your birthday. Another has sent you a book by your favorite author. Write a short thank-you note to each relative.

    Save your thank-you notes in your folder.

Get Down to Business

How To Write a Business Letter

Here's the Idea   Many times you will need to write a letter asking for information, ordering a product, or complaining about a product. Such letters are called **business letters.**

Business letters may be written in *modified block form* or *block form.* In the modified block form, the paragraphs are indented, and the closing and signature are in line with the heading, just as in a friendly letter. This form may be used for both handwritten and typed business letters.

The *block* form for a business letter is used only when the letter is typewritten. All the parts of the letter begin at the left margin. The paragraphs are not indented. Instead, there is a double space between paragraphs.

Both forms of a business letter include an inside address. An **inside address** is the name and address of the business or person you are writing to. The inside address is placed above the salutation. It begins at the left margin. If you are writing to a specific person, use *Dear* and the person's name in the salutation. Otherwise, use a general greeting, such as *Dear Sir or Madam.* All salutations begin two lines after the inside address and end with a colon (:).

Always be brief and to the point in a business letter. It's a good idea to make a copy of a business letter for your records. If you make a copy, mail the original.

Check It Out   Look at the business letter on page 243.

- What is the purpose of this business letter?
- Identify the six parts of the letter.
- Is this letter written in block form or modified block form?

39 Hastings Street
Dodge City, Kansas 67801
February 5, 19___

Sales Manager
Old West Nostalgia Shop
4736 Madison Street
Elko, Nevada 89801

Dear Madam or Sir:

My hobby is collecting items related to the American West. My favorite hero is Wild Bill Hickok, who, like me, spent most of his life in Kansas.

Please send me the catalog of your collection called "Heroes of the West." I am enclosing $2.95 for the catalog, plus $1.00 postage.

Yours truly,
Mary Lou Taylor

Try Your Skill   Below are the six parts of a business letter. On your paper, write them in the correct modified block form. Use the correct punctuation.

Heading

14 Boundbrook Road
Nutley, New Jersey 07110
March 13, 19__

Signature

Thomas Presti

Body

Please send me two dozen personalized pencils. Use my full name on each. Enclosed is my check for $6.50 to cover the cost of the pencils, handling, and postage.

Closing

Yours truly

Salutation

Dear Sir or Madam

Inside Address

Sales Manager
Conway Stationery Company
2149 Northern Avenue
East Orange, New Jersey 07019

Keep This in Mind

- Business letters are written to request information, order products, or complain about products. They should be brief and to the point.
- The six parts of a business letter are the *heading,* the *inside address,* the *salutation,* the *body,* the *closing,* and the *signature.*
- *Block* and *modified block* are two forms for a business letter.

Now Write   On your paper, write the title of this lesson, **Get Down to Business.** Choose a company in your city or town. Imagine that you are going to write a business letter to that company. Write the heading and the inside address for such a letter. Be sure to use the proper form. Save your work.

Please Send Me

How To Write a Letter of Request

Here's the Idea   One type of business letter requests information. It should be brief and to the point. The more specific your request is, the easier it will be for the reader to reply. Be sure to include all the necessary information.

Explain *what*. Ask only for the information you need. If you want a timetable for flights between Chicago and Houston, name the two cities. If you also want a list of fares, don't forget to say so.

Explain *when*. If you plan to fly to Houston on June 19, say so.

Explain *why*. Sometimes you may want to tell briefly why you are writing. You might say "I am writing a report on weather forecasting. I need some information from your company to make my report complete."

Always be polite and appreciative. Remember that you are asking someone for help.

Check It Out   Read the letter of request on page 246. Then answer these questions.

- Is this letter of request brief and polite?
- Is all the necessary information requested? Does it explain *what*, *when*, and *why*?

Try Your Skill   On page 247 is a letter of request. It has some problems. First, read the letter carefully. Then rewrite the letter. Use the correct form. Be brief, specific, and polite.

245

76 Linden Lane
Kankakee, Illinois 60901
April 14, 19___

Midwest Airways
188 Lake Towers
Chicago, Illinois 60607

Dear Sir or Madam:

    Please send me your June 1990 timetable for flights between Chicago, Illinois, and Houston, Texas. I also need a listing of all available rates.

    My local travel agency has run out of timetables. They suggested that I contact you directly.

    Thank you for your help.

Yours truly,
Sarah Kaplan

Keep This in Mind

- Business letters of request should be brief, specific, and polite.
- Ask only for the information you need. Include *what*, *when*, and *why*.

Sales Manager
Kelly Flagpole Company
Morristown, New Jersey
07960

13 Ross Way
Prospect, Kentucky 40059
June 25, 19___

Dear Sir,
   Well, we finally did it. We bought a flag
that's too big for our pole. Now we need a
new pole.
   A guy at my V.F.W. post told me you
sell aluminum and wooden poles. He said
your prices were higher than your poles.
How much would a thirty-foot pole cost?
   If I ordered it right away, when could
you guarantee delivery? I'll need it
by the Fourth.
   I'll expect your answer in three days
at the latest, as I don't have much time to
waste.

                    Edgar T. Welsh

Now Write   On your paper, write the title of this lesson,
Please Send Me. Write a letter to your local representative in
Congress. Ask your representative to explain how he or she
feels about an issue that is important to you. You may also want
to ask how he or she voted on key issues. Address an envelope
for your letter and mail it. Save your reply in your folder.

Fill It Up

Filling Out Forms

Here's the Idea   Learning to fill out a form correctly is an important skill. You will be filling out many different forms during your life. For example, you need to fill out a form to get a library card or a social security number. You need a filled out form to go on a school field trip. Study the following guidelines. They will help you to fill out forms correctly.

1. Skim the form. Look it over quickly to learn what kind of information is needed. The form might ask for information that you won't know and will have to find. For instance, a bicycle registration form might ask for the serial number of your bike. It will be helpful for you to have this information on hand before you begin filling out the form.

2. Read the directions carefully. Look for important guidelines. For instance, you may be asked to give your last name first on the form. Or the form may request that you print rather than write.

3. Be sure you have the right kind of writing tool. Most forms request pen and ink. Other forms, however, may require a pencil. Occasionally, you may be asked to type the requested information.

4. Fill out the form line by line. This way, you will be sure that you have completed every item on the form.

5. Proofread the completed form. Have all of the lines been filled in? Is all of the information correct? Are all of the words spelled correctly?

Check It Out   Examine this bicycle registration form.

- Have all the directions been followed?
- Have items on the form been answered completely?
- Has the form been filled in carefully and neatly?

VILLAGE OF SCHAUMBURG, IL   **No.** _____

POLICE 555-3586   (Do not write in this space)

PERMANENT BICYCLE REGISTRATION

(Please print)

FEE $.25   **Serial No.** _JM389170-5_

Licensee _Vasquez   Carmen   A._

          Last name   First name   Middle initial

Address _1407 W. Rose Court, 31044_

School _Sally Ride Elementary_

Phone _914-0273_ _____ **Age** _12_

Make _Schwinn Sportabout_

Special Markings: _Blue with silver lettering_

Signature X _Carmen Vazquez_

For Police use only. Do not write below this line.

Date   **Issued**
Issued _____ **By** _____

Try Your Skill   Copy the form in **Check It Out.** Fill it out as if it were a real form.

> **Keep This in Mind**
>
> - Skim the form before you fill it out. Know what information is needed.
> - Read all instructions carefully. Use the correct writing tools. Proofread the completed form.

Now Write   Get an application form for a library card. Complete this form using the guidelines in this lesson.

Giving a Talk

Hear Ye! Hear Ye!

Formal and Informal Talks

Here's the Idea   Many people get nervous when they have to speak in front of others. Their hands get moist and their mouths go dry. Has this ever happened to you? The best way to overcome this nervousness is to learn good speaking skills.

There are two main types of talks. A **formal** talk covers a subject in some depth. It is usually fairly long. Most formal talks are written out before-hand. An oral report about the causes of the Revolutionary War would be a formal talk. So would a talk explaining why you want to run for a class office. You will learn more about formal talks later in this chapter.

An **informal talk** is much shorter than a formal speech. It is usually used to pass on information quickly. There are four main types of informal talks.

Informal Talks

Type of Talk	Purpose	Examples
Announcements	to tell what has happened or what will happen	telling about a meeting at school inviting people to a party
Directions	to tell how to do something or how to get somewhere	explaining to a friend how to get to the public library
Introductions	to introduce someone	introducing a speaker at the PTA
Demonstrations	to show how to do something	showing someone how to roller skate backwards

Check It Out   Think about each of the following situations.

1. Carly's cousin Michele is coming to visit from another town. Carly has to tell Michele how to get to her house from the airport.

2. The Boy Scouts are having a pancake brunch. They want everyone in the neighborhood to find out about it.

3. Lena is walking with her grandmother when they meet Lena's math teacher.

• Which type of talk should be used in each situation?

Try Your Skill   Which of these situations calls for a formal talk? Which calls for an informal talk? Write your answers.

1. Jessie was asked to give a ten-minute talk to her class. The talk would be about ways students can earn money. She planned to talk about babysitting, delivering newspapers, and doing yard work.

2. The student council from Jefferson Junior High wanted to cut down on bicycle accidents. The council invited one of the city's traffic officers to speak to the school at a special safety assembly.

3. The eighth grade class wanted to decorate a float for the Columbus Day parade. Mr. Pinsker, the art teacher, said he'd show them how.

Keep This in Mind

• A formal talk tells about a subject in some depth. It is usually long and may be written out.

• An informal talk is short. Informal talks include announcements, directions, introductions, and demonstrations.

Now Write   Make a list of situations at school that might require a talk. Try to list at least five situations.

What type of talk would be best for each situation? Write your answers. If an informal talk is called for, tell which kind. Save your list in your folder.

Explain Yourself

Planning an Informal Talk

Here's the Idea   Informal talks are the most common type of talk. You make them every day, both in and out of school. An informal talk is short. However, you must still do some planning if you want it to turn out well.

Announcements. When you make an announcement, you must include *who, what, when, where,* and *why* in your talk. Perhaps you have to announce the next meeting of the ice-skating club. First, find out all the details. Then you might say, "Next Saturday, February 10, the Ice-Skating Club will meet at the Rainbow Ice Rink, 205 Salem Street. The time of the meeting is 1:00 p.m. The members will be treated to a demonstration by Olympic team member Marge Paxson."

Directions. When you give directions, you must give clear, specific information. If someone asks you how to get to the Rainbow Ice Rink for the meeting, first think through the directions. Then you might say, "Take Main Street north to Salem Street. Turn left and walk two blocks. The Rainbow Rink is on the right side of the street, next to the bank."

Introductions. Introductions must be polite and informative. The best way to introduce someone is to talk to that person first. Try to find out some interesting facts about him or her. Suppose that you have to introduce the special guest at the ice-skating club meeting. You talk with her and find out that she won her first figure-skating medal when she was thirteen. You could mention this in your introduction.

Demonstrations. When you give a demonstration, present the steps of the process one at a time. Figure out the steps before you give your talk. Make sure that you don't leave out important information. You may also need to find or to make some props. Suppose that you have been asked to demonstrate a figure eight at the Rainbow Rink. You would probably practice first and then plan what you will say. You might also want to make a diagram to help your audience understand what you are demonstrating.

Check It Out   Read about the following situation.

The student council is trying to raise money to buy books for the junior high school. They decide to have a car wash. The cost will be one dollar per car. The members plan to wash the cars in the school's parking lot. The car wash will be held on Saturday afternoon, October 17, between one and four o'clock. The members announce the car wash at the next PTA meeting.

- What information should be included in the student council's announcement?

Try Your Skill   Plan some directions telling how to get to school from your house. List the directions in step-by-step order. Make sure that you don't leave out any details. Have a friend or relative listen to your directions. Ask whether the information is clear and correct. Rework the directions if they are unclear or incomplete.

Keep This in Mind

- An informal talk requires some background work.
- Gather all of the information you need to make your talk clear and complete.

Now Write   Choose a partner from your class. Get some background information about your partner. Put together an interesting introduction. Make some notes for the introduction. Then introduce your partner to the class. Keep your notes in your folder.

Be Prepared

Preparing a Formal Talk

Here's the Idea If you have given a formal talk in class, you know that this kind of talk calls for a great deal of preparation.

Planning a formal talk is just like planning a composition. You follow the same pre-writing steps. Take the time to prepare properly. If you do, the content of your talk will be better. You will also feel more confident about what you have to say.

Steps for Preparing a Formal Talk

1. Choose an interesting topic. If the topic is interesting to you, it will be easier for you to make it interesting for your audience. Be sure the topic is not too broad or too narrow. You can't talk about the entire history of baseball in five minutes. However, you might be able to discuss some of the qualities that make a winning baseball team.

2. Know your audience. Whom will you be speaking to? How much does your audience know about your topic?

3. Decide on your purpose. What do you want the end result of your speech to be? Do you want your speech to inform, to entertain, or to persuade?

4. Gather your information. The information you need for your speech might come from your experience, or from talking with others. You can also find information by reading. Make sure the information you collect fits your topic, audience, and purpose. Write useful details and ideas on note cards.

5. Organize your information. Put the information on your note cards into a logical order. Choose an order that fits the content and purpose of your talk. Leave out any information that is not important to your main idea.

Gary was gathering information for a talk about hurricanes. His main idea was how hurricanes are formed. He had only five minutes for his talk. His notes included this information:

hurricanes get started over oceans	hurricanes are violent
water must be warm	tropical storms
air pressure must be low	clouds gather around an
hurricanes are given names	"eye"

- Which notes will Gary need for his talk?
- Which notes are not important to Gary's main idea?

Try Your Skill   Choose the topic that would make a good talk for each of the following audiences. Next to each choice, write why you chose that topic for that audience.

Audience	Topic
the Outdoors Club	raising healthy and happy pets
PTA	how to choose good hiking boots
dog owners	school fund-raising techniques

Keep This in Mind

- Plan a formal talk the same way you plan a composition.
- Decide on a topic, purpose and audience.
- Gather necessary information. Take notes.
- Organize your information.

Now Write   Think about some topics that would be good for a formal talk. Choose the one you like the best. Gather the information you need to give an interesting talk. Write that information on note cards. Then arrange the information in a logical order. Save your organized notes in your folder.

It's How You Say It

Making a Good Impression

Here's the Idea "That was a terrific speech!" Have you ever said this? If so, try to remember what made the speech seem so good? Was it just the topic and the arrangement of ideas? Or was it also the *way* the speaker gave the talk?

Whenever you speak, you are not just presenting your ideas. You are also presenting yourself. How you look and how you sound are just as important as what you say. Remember each of the following points:

1. Be sure to look at your audience. This is called **eye contact**. Try to make your audience feel that you are talking to them, not *at* them. Keep your expression pleasant. If you are using notes, look at them only when necessary. Don't bury your face in them.

2. Your **posture** is also important. Don't slouch or let your head hang down. If you stand tall, you will look confident. However, don't stand stiffly. Take a deep breath and relax.

3. Use your **voice** well. The audience wants to hear what you are saying. Be sure your voice is not too loud or too soft. Don't mumble. Speak clearly and slowly. There is no need to rush.

4. Use **gestures** when you speak. Your face and hands can help emphasize important ideas. Smile when you say something funny. Point to stress a fact or detail. Don't fiddle with your hair or play with your notes as you talk. Keep your gestures natural. This will help you appear confident and relaxed.

5. If you use **visual aids** in your talk, use them well. For example, if you use a projector, be sure you know how to run it. If you use a poster, be sure that it is large enough so that everyone can read it.

Check It Out Read the following descriptions:

The announcer introduced Mr. Fred Martin, the candidate for city council. Mr. Martin got up to speak, holding his notes tightly. He looked at the ceiling. He started reading his speech. He talked quickly and softly. The audience grew restless.

Ms. Jackson was presenting the annual report to her company's board of directors. She stood up straight. She looked directly at her audience. She appeared confident. Her voice was clear and easy to understand. She used a large poster to illustrate her talk.

- What did Mr. Martin do wrong? How could he improve his talk?
- Do you think Ms. Jackson's talk was a success? Why?

Try Your Skill Think of something funny that happened to you lately. Tell a friend about it. As you speak, pretend you are giving an informal talk. Look your listener in the eye. Think about the way you are standing. Use natural gestures. Finally, concentrate on speaking slowly and clearly.

Keep This in Mind

- When you present a talk, look at your audience.
- Use good posture, but try to look relaxed.
- Speak slowly in a clear voice.
- Use natural gestures.

Now Write Look over the five guidelines to good speaking discussed in this chapter. Decide how well you could follow each set of guidelines. Do you use your voice well? Do you stand straight? Can you use natural gestures? Write down the areas in which you might need work. Save this list for use in the next part.

Dress Rehearsal

Practicing a Talk

Here's the Idea   Good speakers always practice their talks. This gives them a chance to polish their material. It also helps them become more familiar with it. You should allow time for practice, too. The better you know your speech, the more comfortable you will be with it.

Guidelines for Practicing a Talk

1. Read through your notes several times. This will help you see whether you have all the necessary information. It will also help you to see if your notes are organized properly. You want to be sure that your notes are a good guide for what you want to say.

   As you read your notes, you will also become more familiar with your talk. Then you won't have to depend on your note cards. Remember, you don't have to *memorize* your talk word for word. However, you shouldn't just read it, either.

2. Practice your talk aloud a number of times. First, practice your talk in front of a mirror. Notice your expression and the gestures you use. Check your posture. Do you look relaxed? Are your movements natural?

   Record your speech on a tape recorder, if you can. Does your voice sound pleasant? Do you sound interested in what you are saying? Try to improve the way you speak as you practice.

3. Present your talk to family and friends. Ask them about the way you look and sound. Ask them how you can improve your talk. Use their suggestions to make your talk better. Finally, practice your talk one last time.

Read how this student prepares his talk.

Kim enjoys photography. He decided to give a talk on his hobby for an art project. After Kim gathered and organized his information, he read his notes several times. Then he read them out loud, practicing how he would say them. Next, Kim practiced his talk in front of a mirror. Finally he presented his talk to his parents. After listening to their comments, he decided he was ready to give his talk.

· Do you think Kim's talk will be a success? Why?

Try Your Skill Look over the guidelines for practicing a talk. Then write two more suggestions that would help a student to practice a talk. Discuss your suggestions with your classmates.

Keep This in Mind

· Practice your talk before you give it.
· Work to improve the content of your talk. Also work on the way you deliver it.

Now Speak Use the guidelines in this lesson to practice the talk you prepared in Part 3. When you feel confident, give your talk to the class.

Attention!

Learning To Listen

Here's the Idea   Knowing how to give a talk is an important skill. So is knowing how to listen to one. If you are a good listener, you will get more out of what you hear. You will be able to pick out important ideas and information.

Read the following guidelines. They can help you become a better listener.

Guidelines for Good Listening

1. Find a place where you can easily see and hear the speaker.

2. Give your complete attention to the speaker. Don't whisper to those around you or talk back to the speaker. Don't fidget or cause other distractions.

3. *Show* the speaker that you are listening. Look at the speaker. Keep an alert expression on your face. This will show that you are interested in what the speaker has to say. Take notes if you need to.

4. Listen for the speaker's main ideas. Try to pick out the important information the speaker has to give. Listen for key words and phrases like *first, next, for example, most importantly* and *let me point out.*

Check It Out   Read how one class listens to a talk.

The school assembly had just let out. Mr. Garrett was upset with his class's behavior. He said that they were not good listeners.

"Some people slouched in their seats," he said. "Others booed and hissed when Ms. Lacey said something they didn't like.

"No one sat in the first two rows of seats. Some students were holding their own conversations during the entire talk. And why didn't anyone applaud when the talk was finished?"

- These students were not good listeners. What did they do wrong? What rules of good listening could they have used?

Try Your Skill   As your teacher presents the next lesson, practice your listening skills. Give the teacher your complete attention. Show that you are listening and interested. Try to pick out the main ideas.

Keep This in Mind

- It is important to be a good listener.
- Give your full attention to whomever is speaking. Show that you are interested.
- Listen for the main idea.

Now Speak   Look through the daily newspaper or a news magazine. Find an article you think would be interesting to your class. Read the article to your classmates. Ask them to list the main idea of the article. Have them tell you about the most important details. Were they good listeners? Try your own listening skills as you listen to other students' presentations.

The Verdict, Please

Judging a Talk

Here's the Idea   It is important to be polite when you are part of an audience. As a listener, you may be asked to judge the speaker's talk. To do this, you must listen to *what* is said. This is the **content.** You must also watch for *how* the ideas are said. This is the **presentation.** When you judge a talk, be fair to the speaker.

Guidelines for Judging a Talk

CONTENT

Topic: Did the speaker make the main point of the speech clear?

Purpose: What was the purpose of the speech? Was it to inform, to persuade, or to entertain? Did the speaker succeed in his or her purpose?

Development: Was enough information presented about the subject? Was there any unnecessary information?

Organization: Was the information well organized? Did the ideas flow logically?

PRESENTATION

Eye Contact: Did the speaker look directly at the audience?

Posture: Did the speaker stand up straight? Did he or she appear relaxed?

Voice: Was the speaker's voice easy to hear?

Gestures: Were the speaker's gestures natural?

Preparation: Did the speaker know the talk well?

Check It Out   Read about this student's talk.

LaDonna gave a talk in class about dolphins. Her purpose was to explain how intelligent dolphins are. First she explained how easily dolphins can be trained. Then she told about how dolphins talk to one another. Finally, she mentioned that scientists are trying to learn the dolphins' language so that people can talk to these amazing animals.

As LaDonna talked, she looked right at her audience. She looked at her note cards only a few times. She spoke slowly and clearly. She smiled when she told how some dolphins like to tease their trainers. LaDonna seemed to enjoy her speech as much as her audience did.

- LaDonna's teacher gave her an A in Content and an A in Presentation. What things did LaDonna do right?

Try Your Skill   Judge the presentation of a television newscaster. Use the guidelines on the previous page. Write down the things the newscaster did right and the things he or she did wrong. Give the newscaster's presentation a grade: *good, fair,* or *needs improvement.*

Keep This in Mind

When you judge a talk, listen carefully to the content of the speech. Also notice the speaker's presentation.

Now Write   Make out an evaluation form for judging a speaker. On the top half of your paper write *Content.* Then write the five categories listed in heavy type under *Content* on page 264. Draw a line and write *Presentation.* List the five categories shown under that heading on page 264. When you judge a talk, mark *Good, Fair,* or *Needs Work* next to each category. Save your evaluation form in your folder.

Handbook

A detailed Table of Contents for the Handbook appears in the front of this book.

Learning About Sentences

How would you invite a friend to a picnic? How would you identify yourself on the telephone? How would you ask for the shirt you want at a store?

Without thinking, you would put words together to make sentences. The clearest way to get your ideas across to someone else is to use sentences.

Part 1 What Is a Sentence?

Read the four groups of words below. Each group expresses a complete thought or idea. Each group of words is a sentence. Notice that each sentence begins with a capital letter.

1. Richard made a belt.
2. Greg is a goalie.
3. Laura was handed the trophy.
4. The gym class played volleyball.

A sentence is a group of words that expresses a complete thought.

Sentence Fragments

Read these groups of words. Can you tell whether each group is a sentence?

1. The girls went to the park.
2. Dominic and his brother.
3. Played in the snow.

Maybe you are not sure whether these groups of words are sentences. Here are two questions to help you decide whether a group of words is a sentence:

> *Who or what did something?* Does the group of words tell who or what did something?
> *What happened?* Does the group of words tell what happened?

If a group of words answers both of these questions, it expresses a complete thought. The group of words is a sentence.

If a group of words does not answer both questions, it does not express a complete thought. The group of words is a **fragment.**

Making Sure Sentences Are Complete

Now return to the three groups of words shown earlier and test them for complete thoughts.

Example 1 | The girls went to the park

Who or what did something?	What happened?
The girls	went to the park.

This group of words answers both questions. You know, then, that it is a sentence. It expresses a complete thought.

Example 2 | Dominic and his brother

Who or what did something?	What happened?
Dominic and his brother	

Does this group of words answer both questions? No, it does not. You can see that it is not a sentence. It is a fragment. It tells only part of a thought. You can add words to this fragment to make a whole sentence.

Who or what did something?	What happened?
Dominic and his brother	planted a garden.

Example 3 | Played in the snow

Who or what did something?	What happened?
	Played in the snow

Does this group of words answer both questions? No, it does not. Like Example 2, it is not a sentence. It is a fragment. You can also add words to this fragment to make a sentence.

Who or what did something?	What happened?
The black kitten	played in the snow.

Exercises **Write complete sentences.**

A. For each group of words you must answer the question *What happened?* to make a complete sentence. Write the whole sentence. There are many possible correct answers.

1. The boy with the camera
2. An angry dog
3. My two sisters
4. The TV show
5. Most birds

B. For each group of words you must answer the question *Who or what did something?* to make a complete sentence. Write the whole sentence. There are many possible correct answers.

1. talked on the phone
2. made a spinach salad
3. found an old coin
4. likes football
5. played in the band

C. Number your paper from 1 to 10. Write *Sentence* after each number that stands before a sentence. Write *Fragment* after each number that stands before a fragment.

1. We built a bookshelf
2. The lifeguard
3. An anthill in the yard
4. Our class planned a field trip
5. Carved the turkey
6. Rides a bike to school
7. Our hamster is loose
8. Alice dived into the lake
9. Makes jewelry out of beads
10. The cattle rancher

Part 2 Different Kinds of Sentences

You use sentences for several different reasons. Sometimes you want to tell something. Sometimes you want to ask something. Sometimes you want to tell someone to do something. Sometimes you want to show how strongly you feel about something. There is a different kind of sentence for each of these four purposes. Every sentence that you read or write is one of these four different kinds.

The Declarative Sentence

A declarative sentence tells or states something. Use a period **(.)** at the end of a declarative sentence.

Tomorrow is my birthday.

The Interrogative Sentence

An interrogative sentence asks a question. Use a question mark **(?)** at the end of an interrogative sentence.

Do you enjoy basketball?

The Imperative Sentence

An imperative sentence makes a request or gives directions. Use a period **(.)** at the end of most imperative sentences.

Pass the salt, please.

The Exclamatory Sentence

An exclamatory sentence shows strong feeling. Use an exclamation point **(!)** at the end of every exclamatory sentence.

Our house is on fire!

Exercises   Recognize the four kinds of sentences.

A. Number your paper from 1 to 10. Write *Declarative, Interrogative, Imperative,* or *Exclamatory* to tell what kind of sentence each is.

Example: Are you going shopping Saturday?

Interrogative

1. What good luck you always have!
2. Do you have roller skates?
3. Tom has been taking piano lessons for two years.
4. When will the train arrive?
5. Aim for the center of the target.
6. Tomorrow is my birthday.
7. Are you telling me the truth?
8. Guess the right number.
9. Ouch, that hurt!
10. Hurry up.

B. Number your paper from 1 to 10. Write *Declarative, Interrogative, Imperative,* or *Exclamatory* to tell what kind of sentence each is. Then add the mark of punctuation that belongs at the end of each sentence.

1. The rocket took off on time
2. Have you ever seen the circus
3. What a terrific game it was
4. Ken erased the chalkboards
5. How cold it is today
6. My family took a vacation in Virginia
7. What a mess we made with the paint
8. Have another piece of this delicious bread
9. Where does the bike trail end
10. Watch out

Part 3 Punctuating Sentences

Punctuation marks are important signals in reading and writing. Use the correct signals in your writing. Follow the signals when you read. Remember these rules:

1. **Use a period after a declarative sentence.**

   We will have a school assembly tomorrow.

2. **Use a question mark after an interrogative sentence.**

   Did you enjoy that book?

3. **Use a period after most imperative sentences.** If the imperative sentence expresses strong feeling, use an exclamation point.

   Give me the hot chocolate, please. Don't spill it!

4. **Use an exclamation point after an exclamatory sentence.**

   The Tigers win again!

Exercises **Punctuate sentences correctly.**

A. Copy these sentences. Use the correct punctuation mark at the end of each sentence.

1. How funny the monkey looks
2. What is the name of that movie
3. Turn on the radio, please
4. Are you going on the bike trip
5. Henry, read a story to the class
6. Marcia hit a home run
7. What an exciting game it was
8. What time is it now
9. Our class went to the museum
10. Please open the window

B. Copy these sentences. Use the correct punctuation mark at the end of each sentence.

1. We went to a carnival
2. Can you answer the question
3. Stop it
4. Do you have a ballpoint pen
5. I found a birthday gift for Mother
6. Try the vanilla milkshake
7. Please come to my house after school
8. Does Ellen wear glasses
9. What a surprise this is
10. I watched the baseball game

Part 4   Parts of the Sentence

Every sentence has two parts. One part of the sentence is the **subject.** The subject answers the question *Who or what did something.*

Take another look at these sentences from **Part 1.**

1. Richard made a belt.
2. Greg is a goalie.
3. Laura was handed the trophy.
4. The gym class played volleyball.

Can you find the subject in each of these sentences? Find the answer to the question *Who or what did something* or *What is the sentence about.* Here are the subjects:

1. Richard
2. Greg
3. Laura
4. The gym class

The other part of the sentence is the **predicate.** The predicate tells something about the subject. The predicate tells *What the subject did, What the subject is,* or *What happened to the subject.*

First, see if you can find the predicates in the sample sentences by yourself. Then look at the following chart to find out if you were right.

Subject	Predicate
1. Richard *(who)*	made a belt. *(what the subject did)*
2. Greg *(who)*	is a goalie. *(what the subject is)*
3. Laura *(who)*	was handed the trophy. *(what happened to the subject)*
4. The gym class *(what)*	played volleyball. *(what the subject did)*

The subject of a sentence tells who or what did something, or what the sentence is about.

The predicate of a sentence tells what the subject did, what the subject is, or what happened to the subject.

A group of words is not a sentence unless it has a subject and a predicate.

Here are three new sentences. Which words in each sentence are the subject? Which words are the predicate? Check your answers against the chart that follows.

That big dog is a collie.
My older sister planted the garden.
Dave's math book fell into a puddle.

Subject	Predicate
That big dog	is a collie.
My older sister	planted the garden.
Dave's math book	fell into a puddle.

A. Copy these sentences. Draw a vertical line between the subject and the predicate of each sentence.

Example: The red wagon | makes squeaky noises.

1. My friends went to the beach.
2. The fierce tiger growled in his cage.
3. Don raced on roller skates.
4. Chris is the pitcher.
5. Aunt Beth has many strange plants.
6. The baby reached for her bottle.
7. The first show began at two o'clock.
8. Our neighbors built a treehouse.
9. A baby robin flew from the nest.
10. Susan told a good joke.

B. Copy these sentences. Draw a vertical line between the subject and the predicate of each sentence.

Example: The girls | hiked through the park.

1. The small airplane landed in a field.
2. A team of horses pulled the wagon.
3. My brother's favorite holiday is Halloween.
4. The runners lined up.
5. Our family watched the fireworks from the porch.
6. Ms. Adams did a backflip for the class.
7. Snow fell all day.
8. Mark found a dollar in the hall.
9. My sister makes her own clothes.
10. Doug Henning performed many magic tricks.

Part 5 The Simple Predicate, or Verb

You have learned about the two parts of the sentence. The subject part is called the **complete subject.** The predicate part is called the **complete predicate.**

The complete subject may be short or long. It includes all the words that tell who or what did something.

The complete predicate may also be short or long. It includes all the words that tell what happened.

Complete Subject	Complete Predicate
The girl	played.
The tall girl with glasses	played basketball at the Y.

In each complete predicate, one part is more important than the rest. This part is the **verb.** A verb is a word that can tell of an action. It can also tell that something *is.* Both of the sentences above have the same verb: *played.* The verb is sometimes called the **simple predicate.** In the rest of this book, we will speak of it as the *verb.*

Finding the Verb

The verbs in these sentences are underlined.

The children <u>fell</u> on the ice.
Scott <u>knew</u> the answer.

Some verbs tell of an action you can see.

The quarterback <u>dropped</u> the ball.
The lion <u>jumped through</u> a hoop.

Other verbs tell of an action you cannot see.

> My mother <u>heard</u> the baby's cry.
> I <u>remember</u> all the words of that song.

- Verbs that tell of an action are called **action verbs.**

Another kind of verb tells that something *is*.

> I <u>am</u> a student.   Your desk <u>is</u> new.

- Verbs that tell that something *is* are called **state-of-being verbs.**

Here are some of the most common state-of-being verbs:

| is | am | were | has been | seem |
| are | was | will be | have been | look |

A verb is a word that tells of an action, or that tells that something *is*.

Exercises   Find the verb.

A.   Write the verb in each sentence.

1. Ms. Morgan writes with a quill pen.
2. My uncle is a test pilot.
3. The Apollo spacecraft went to the moon.
4. Margie rested before the race.
5. Three penguins waddled toward the water.
6. The sky looked pink and orange.
7. The zookeeper feeds the lions at noon.
8. The truck took garbage to the dump.
9. Our club planted flowers in the square.
10. Adam hoped for better luck.

B.   Write the verb in each sentence. After the verb, write *Action* or *State-of-Being* to tell what kind of verb it is.

1. That flag is colorful.

2. Valerie's dog performed a new trick.
3. Two girls paddled the canoe.
4. The lizard darted up a tree.
5. Our class published a newspaper.
6. Father seems impatient.
7. Eli used the microphone.
8. The Girl Scouts are at camp.
9. Indians made these beautiful necklaces.
10. The fans were happy about the victory.

Part 6 The Simple Subject, or Subject of the Verb

In each complete subject, one part is more important than the rest. This part is sometimes called the **simple subject.** Another name for it is the **subject of the verb.** The subject of the verb tells *who* or *what* about the verb.

In the examples below, the subject of the verb is printed in *italics*.

Complete Subject	Verb
The *clock*	stopped.
The old *clock* on the shelf	stopped.

Finding the Subject of the Verb

To find the subject of the verb, first find the verb. Then put *who* or *what* before the verb to make a question.

Examples: Monkeys escaped from the zoo.

Verb: *escaped*
Who or what *escaped?*   *monkeys*
Monkeys is the subject of *escaped.*

Three young monkeys escaped from the zoo.
Verb: *escaped*
Who or what *escaped?* *monkeys*
Monkeys is still the subject of the verb.

See if you can find the verb, and then the subject of the verb, in this example.

Students from our class acted in the play.

Did you find the action verb *acted?* The subject tells you *who* acted. What is the subject?

Did you say the *students* acted? *Students* is the subject of the verb *acted.*

In the next example, look for a state-of-being verb. Then find the subject of the verb.

Victor's blue jacket is on the chair.

Did you find the state-of-being verb *is?* The subject tells you *what* is. Did you say the *jacket is?* *Jacket* is the subject of the verb *is.*

Exercises **Find the verb and its simple subject.**

A. Find the verb and its simple subject in each sentence. Write the subject before the verb. Draw a vertical line between them.

Example: The ski slopes were crowded.
slopes | were

1. High waves tipped the sailboat.
2. Juanita added three books to her library.
3. Three jugglers in the main ring tossed hoops into the air.
4. My new gloves are waterproof.
5. Tom Sawyer found a secret hideout.
6. Jocelyn was her sister's bridesmaid.
7. A large group sang carols.

8. Six climbers from Nevada reached the mountaintop.
9. The desert seems endless.
10. Our parrot speaks Spanish.

B. Follow the directions for Exercise A.

1. Outside, hailstones fell.
2. Melinda leaped over the fence.
3. David is sick with the flu.
4. The American flag has fifty stars.
5. The pickers handled the fruit gently.
6. Dr. Mendez taped my wrist.
7. Tomatoes grow in our garden.
8. Today we had a fire drill.
9. A stray dog slept on the back steps.
10. The sweater with yellow and orange stripes is mine.

Part 7 The Subject in Unusual Positions

In most sentences the subject comes before the predicate. Sometimes, though, the subject does not come before the predicate. Where is the subject placed in each of the sentences below?

Example 1   The rocket soared toward the planet Venus.

Verb: *soared*
Who or what *soared?*   the *rocket*

Rocket is the subject of the verb. It is placed before the verb near the beginning of the sentence.

Example 2   Toward the planet Venus the rocket soared.

Rocket is still the subject of the verb. It is still placed before the verb. It is now near the end of the sentence.

Example 3 Toward the planet Venus soared the rocket.

In this sentence, the subject is still *rocket,* but it has been moved again. Now it is placed after the verb.

When you are looking for the subject in sentences like examples 2 and 3, follow the usual steps. First, find the verb. (*What happened?*) Then put *who* or *what* before the verb to make a question.

Example: During the movie we ate some popcorn.

Verb: *ate*

Who or what *ate?* *we* ate

Exercises **Find the subject in unusual positions.**

A. Find the verb and the subject in each sentence. Write the subject before the verb. Draw a vertical line between them.

Example: In the drawer are two pencils.

pencils | are

1. Down the hill ran José.
2. In the early evening, fireflies appeared.
3. On the top branch sat a crow.
4. From the trees fell the colorful leaves.
5. Down came the rain.
6. Into the hall the band marched.
7. Up into the tree sailed the balloon.
8. Into the water fell our money.
9. Out of the dark came a strange sound.
10. Across the range the cowboys rode.

B. Follow the directions for Exercise A.

1. Around the barnyard waddled a goose.
2. Out into the night went the cat.
3. After the storm a rainbow appeared.

4. Into the pond jumped a frog.
5. Over the apple orchard sailed a beautiful kite.
6. In front of the store Mom waited.
7. Through the gate came a hay wagon.
8. Across the snow whisked the sled.
9. Above the clouds the jet soared.
10. At the front of the parade marched the mayor.

Part 8 The Subject in Imperative Sentences

An imperative sentence makes a request, or gives directions or orders. Study these examples of imperative sentences. Look for the subjects.

Switch off the light.	Don't throw the pencil.
Turn left at the gas station.	Finish your test.

In each of these sentences, the subject is not stated. The subject is understood to be *you*. *You* is the person or group being spoken to.

(You) Switch off the light.	*(You)* Don't throw the pencil.
(You) Turn left at the gas station.	*(You)* Finish your test.

Exercises **Find the subject.**

A. Write the subject and the verb in each of the following sentences. If the subject is not given in the sentence, write it in parentheses before the verb.

Example: Wait here for me.
(You) Wait

1. Try it again, please.
2. Taste this soup.

3. Karen took the message.
4. Have a second baked potato.
5. Stay in your seats.
6. I like crisp, sweet apples.
7. Look at that fancy car.
8. Add one cup of flour to the mixture.
9. Read chapter 2 for tomorrow.
10. Those boys need help with the ladder.

B. Follow the directions for Exercise A.

1. Astronomers watch for unusual stars.
2. Bait your hook this way.
3. Speak a little louder, please.
4. Save some money for your bus fare.
5. Careful shoppers compare prices.
6. Do your best.
7. Sing with the music.
8. Rosa entered the science contest.
9. Use fine sandpaper for this job.
10. Buy your tickets at the box office.

Part 9 Compound Subjects

When two or more subjects are used with the same predicate, they are called a **compound subject.** The word *compound* means "having more than one part." Read these two sentences:

Subject	Predicate
Jennifer	played softball.
I	played softball.

Since the predicates are the same, you can join the two sentences. Now the subject has two parts.

Subject	Predicate
Jennifer and I	played softball.

In the new sentence, the word *and* joins the two parts of the subject. The word *or* can also be used to join parts of a subject. (A word that is used to join words or groups of words is called a **conjunction**.)

Look at these sentences with compound subjects:

Carrie and *Jake* left the meeting early.
Sausage or *pepperoni* tastes good on pizza.

When you combine three or more subjects in a compound subject, use commas to separate them. Place the conjunction before the last subject.

Example: Our summer *cottage*, the *dock*, **and** a *rowboat* suffered damage in the hurricane.

Exercises   Find compound subjects.

A.   Find the verb and its compound subject in each of the following sentences. Write the subjects first and then the verb. Draw a line between them.

Example: Dan, Bob, and Ginny came to my house.
Dan, Bob, Ginny │ came

1. The brakes and seat on my bike are new.
2. Suzanne or Richard presents the first speech.
3. Posters and lockers line the hallway.
4. Bacon, lettuce, and tomato make a tasty sandwich.
5. The horse and rider avoided the highway.
6. A chair and a phone were the only props.
7. Karen and Joyce shared a milkshake.
8. The manager and the umpire disagreed on the call.

9. Jenkins, Tortini, and Owens scored runs.
10. Corn, wheat, and soybeans are the main crops of this farm.

B. Follow the directions for Exercise A.

1. Gymnasts and dancers performed at parents' night.
2. The principal and the teachers planned new courses.
3. Rain and winds whipped the countryside.
4. Ponies and cows grazed in the field.
5. Radio, TV, and newspapers reported the crime.
6. Bob or Regina found the books.
7. Colorado, Utah, and Vermont have many ski resorts.
8. The police and paramedics raced to the scene.
9. Palms and ferns need a lot of light.
10. Vic, Al, and Kelly listened to a new album.

Part 10   Compound Predicates

When two or more predicates are used with the same subject, they are called a **compound predicate.** The parts of a compound predicate are joined with a conjunction.

Often you can combine two or more sentences by using a compound predicate.

Subject	Predicate
I	sat at the table.
I	ate my breakfast.

Subject	Predicate
I	sat at the table and ate my breakfast.

When you combine three or more predicates in a compound

predicate, use commas to separate them. Place the conjunction before the last predicate.

> Example: Jean *rehearsed the part, tried out,* **and** *won a role in the class play.*

Exercises   Find compound predicates.

A. Write the compound predicates in each of the following sentences.

1. Laurie watched TV and did her homework.
2. Rob rode the bus and went to the zoo.
3. Ellen dropped the bat and ran to first base.
4. The car skidded on the ice and hit the sign.
5. Our cat caught a mouse and brought it inside.
6. I grabbed my coat and ran to the store.
7. Tina drew a picture and gave it to her mother.
8. Beth raced down the court and shot a basket.
9. Mike read a story and wrote a report.
10. Tony learned a new dance and taught it to us.

B. Follow the directions for Exercise A.

1. The campers pitched their tent and cooked supper.
2. Ed writes folk songs and plays them on his guitar.
3. Jane cut her jeans and made them into shorts.
4. A friend took a brush and painted with me.
5. Joe gets his allowance on Friday and spends it right away.
6. Les took the test and passed it.
7. The tennis instructor explained a serve and demonstrated it.
8. Joanie sorted the mail and delivered it.
9. Terry made a sandwich and cleaned the kitchen.
10. Tom joined the game and played third base.

Sentence Patterns Word Order and Meaning

A sentence is a group of words. However, not every group of words is a sentence. For example, read these word groups. Which one makes sense?

> Pete fast ran.   Pete ran fast.   Ran Pete fast.

The only group that sounds right is the second group. Its words are in the order you are used to hearing. You would say that its words are in the right order for a sentence. A good sentence must have the right word order.

Sometimes a group of words has more than one right order. Read these two sentences. They contain the same words. The words are simply in different order.

> Carrie told Brad.   Brad told Carrie.

Each word order sounds right. Each tells an idea. However, changing the word order changes the idea. The difference in word order makes an important difference in meaning.

Exercise   Change the word order and meaning.

Read each sentence. Then change the order of the words to change the meaning. Write each new sentence on your paper.

1. Herb called Sylvia.
2. The rug hid the dirt.
3. Some dogs chase cats.
4. Bob wrote to my sister.
5. Jeanne called the principal.
6. Tom knows Monica.
7. Julio thanked the coach.
8. The Cubs beat the Mets.
9. Carol heard Dan.
10. The car hit the bus.

ADDITIONAL EXERCISES

Learning About Sentences

A. Recognizing Sentences Number your paper from 1 to 10. Write *Sentence* or *Fragment* for each of the following groups of words to show what each group is.

1. The deer on the highway
2. Maggie slipped
3. Craig borrowed the tape measure
4. Swam across the lake
5. Our rivals from across town
6. Nora filled the wheelbarrow
7. Finished the history assignment
8. John and his three cousins
9. The arrow hit the bull's-eye
10. Ms. Lee directed the play

B. Kinds of Sentences For each of the following sentences, write *Declarative*, *Interrogative*, *Imperative*, or *Exclamatory* to show what kind it is.

1. Have you opened your presents?
2. Try this new dessert.
3. James forgot his social studies book.
4. How deep the snow is!
5. Where did you find that eraser?
6. Two inches of rain fell last night.
7. Take the 4:30 train.
8. Andrew Wyeth did that painting.
9. Don't forget the meeting.
10. What a surprise that was!

C. Punctuating Sentences Copy these sentences. Add the correct punctuation mark to each.

1. Did you meet my brother
2. Wendy packed a picnic lunch
3. Don't forget your watch
4. What is the capital of Maryland
5. How cold it was this morning
6. Dad took us to the zoo
7. Bring your chess game
8. My cousins live on that farm
9. Watch out
10. Where are you going

D. Subjects and Predicates Copy these sentences. Draw a vertical line between the subject and the predicate of each sentence.

1. My cousin plays the violin.
2. Our team uses that locker room.
3. Lou washed the car.
4. Mr. Dickens is the new coach.
5. A coin fell behind the counter.
6. Trisha parachuted from the small plane.
7. Dogs are intelligent animals.
8. The blizzard stopped the air traffic.
9. The campers left at dawn.
10. Dr. O'Connell removed the heavy cast.

E. Verbs Write the verb in each sentence.

1. The jets roared overhead.
2. Laura is the head of the committee.

3. Brad baked apple-raisin bread.
4. Chris painted the garage.
5. The suspect seemed nervous.
6. Ducks swam in the pond.
7. Luis was the president of his class.
8. Bees swarmed around the picnic table.
9. Clay dunked the ball through the hoop.
10. This bread seems stale.

F. Subjects and Verbs   Find the verb and its simple subject in each sentence. Write the subject before the verb. Draw a vertical line between them.

1. Katie made a bookshelf.
2. The store on Saxon Avenue has a sale on T-shirts.
3. Our teacher tells very funny stories.
4. Juanita plays the drums.
5. Grapes are my favorite snack.
6. The carnival was fun.
7. My parents framed the drawing.
8. The new theater opens tomorrow.
9. The trees in the park are maples.
10. Jeff repaired the typewriter.

G. Subjects in Unusual Positions   Find the verb and its subject in each sentence. Write the subject before the verb. Draw a vertical line between them.

1. In the hallways Bob hung posters.
2. Over the mountains the eagle soared.
3. Down the path galloped the horse.
4. In the middle of the gym was a trampoline.
5. Through the grass slithered the snake.

6. During the storm the lights dimmed.
7. Over the roof sailed the baseball.
8. Around the bend a deer appeared.
9. Throughout the night the snow fell.
10. Into the store trotted the beagle.

H. Subjects in Sentences

Find the verb and its subject in each of the following sentences. Write the subject before the verb. Draw a vertical line between them. If the subject is not stated, write it in parentheses.

1. Begin with the third chapter.
2. Marsha drew that picture.
3. Look for a good picnic spot.
4. Try one of these cheese puffs.
5. My father winds this clock every day.
6. Bring your raincoat.
7. Be here at 5:00 P.M.
8. The boys weeded the garden.
9. Water those plants carefully.
10. Larry returned the books.

I. Compound Subjects

Write the compound subjects in each of the following sentences.

1. James or Judy told the principal.
2. The field and bleachers were wet.
3. Marigolds, zinnias, and daisies grew in the garden.
4. Marge and Tony sang a duet.
5. The streets and sidewalks were slippery.
6. Tom, Charlie, and Bill met at the gym.
7. Tennis and golf are his favorite sports.
8. Mushrooms, sausage, and onions covered the pizza.

9. Lisa and Beth wrote the play.
10. Apples, oranges, and bananas filled the basket.

J. Compound Predicates   Write the compound predicates in each of the following sentences.

1. The dog growled at Jeff and snapped at me.
2. Karl washed the windows and dusted the furniture.
3. The club planned the picnic and made the arrangements.
4. Barb made some popcorn and ate it.
5. The vase fell from the ledge and shattered on the floor.
6. Dad washed the walls, painted the ceiling, and vacuumed the carpets.
7. Jill poured the juice and sliced the bread.
8. The audience rose from their seats and applauded the actors.
9. George sealed the letter and mailed it.
10. The player caught the football and ran for a touchdown.

MIXED REVIEW

Learning About Sentences

A. Recognizing fragments and kinds of sentences Read the groups of words below. If a group of words is a fragment, write *Fragment*. If a group of words is a sentence, write *Declarative, Interrogative, Imperative,* or *Exclamatory* to show what kind it is. Punctuate each sentence.

1. Sean and his pet hamster
2. What is the score
3. Gave her report to the class
4. The tall, thin man
5. Darlene opened her locker
6. Giant fir trees lined the road
7. How surprised we were
8. Washed their bikes
9. Close the door, please
10. Is today your birthday

B. Finding subjects, predicates, and verbs Copy the following sentences. Draw a vertical line between each subject and predicate. Then underline each verb.

1. The band played a joyous march.
2. Two trains pulled into the station.
3. Justin rode the elevator.
4. Dad waited in the car.
5. Kelly's umbrella is pink and green.
6. Our parents made the costumes.
7. Ginger looked under her chair.
8. Lightning split the old oak tree.
9. Mr. Jennings is my uncle.
10. Dark clouds hid the sun.

C. Finding the verb and its subject   In some of these sentences, the subject is before the verb. In others, the verb is first. Copy each sentence. Underline the subject once and the verb twice. If a subject is understood, write it in parentheses.

1. Three clowns rode the elephant.
2. After dinner we watched a special on TV.
3. Santa Fe is the capital of New Mexico.
4. Turn the record over.
5. Barbara hit a home run.
6. Down the alley rolled the tennis ball.
7. The boys studied the old map.
8. Across the finish line came the bikes.
9. Listen to this melody.
10. My old brown boots are too small.

D. Finding compound subjects and compound predicates   Label two columns on your paper *Compound Subject* and *Compound Predicate*. Number your paper from 1 to 10. Write the compound subjects and compound predicates from each sentence in the proper columns. Not every sentence will have both.

1. Mary and Tom boarded the plane.
2. We talked and laughed for hours.
3. The pots and pans are washed and dried.
4. Wisconsin, Michigan, and Minnesota have long winters.
5. Kyle shopped for the food and cooked the dinner.
6. Peg found my wallet and returned it.
7. Robins, sparrows, and bluejays visit our birdfeeder.
8. The scouts and their leader hiked into the woods and camped there.
9. The storm raged all night and stopped at dawn.
10. Chip and Molly have birthdays next week.

USING GRAMMAR IN WRITING
Learning About Sentences

A. Imagine that NASA has announced that it will send a young person into space. You are amazed to learn that you have been chosen. Write a letter to NASA, accepting the assignment. Express your excitement at being chosen. Ask any questions you have. Use at least one declarative sentence, one imperative sentence, one interrogative sentence, and one exclamatory sentence. When you are finished, draw a vertical line between the subject and the predicate of each sentence.

B. Following is an imaginary letter that was written to an advice columnist. Rewrite the letter. Correct any sentence fragments that you find. Then pretend you are the columnist and write an answer to the letter. In your answer, include one sentence that has a compound subject. Also include one that has a compound predicate.

> Dear Gabby,
>   Every time I play games or sports. I lose. Even my little sister beats me. At checkers. If I fly a kite. It gets tangled up. In a tree. I even think my dog is smarter than me. I'm crazy. About a pretty red-haired girl, and she couldn't care less. Can you give me some advice?
>   Tired of losing,
>   Charlie Brown

C. There's going to be a party at your house right after school. Some of your classmates will need directions to get to your house. Write a paragraph that tells how to get from your school to your home. Underline each imperative sentence that you use. In parentheses, write the subject of each imperative sentence.

Using Sentences Correctly

You know that a sentence expresses a complete thought.

The papers fell on the floor.

Some groups of words do not express a complete thought. They express only part of a thought. These groups of words are called **sentence fragments.**

Example: The papers on the floor.

Sometimes two or more sentences are written as one sentence. This is called a **run-on sentence.**

Example: The papers fell on the floor some blew away.

See how clear these ideas are when separate sentences are used.

The papers fell on the floor. Some blew away.

Always write sentences carefully. Avoid using fragments and run-ons. In this section, you will be able to practice writing sentences correctly.

Part 1 Avoiding Sentence Fragments

A sentence fragment tells only a part of a thought. For example, a fragment may tell only *who*.

> **Example:** The tall boy in the band

A fragment may tell only *what happened*.

> **Example:** Played the guitar for us

A fragment may tell only *where*.

> **Example:** At the party

Each of these sentence fragments tells only part of an idea. None of these fragments states a complete thought.

A sentence that is written correctly, however, always expresses a complete thought.

> **Examples:** The tall boy in the band played the guitar for us at the party.
> The boy played the guitar.

Exercises **Recognize sentence fragments.**

A. Read each of the following groups of words. Write *Sentence* or *Fragment* to tell what each group is.

1. The film crew built the scenery
2. Took photographs on vacation
3. A terrific hockey game

4. Three books on the library shelves
5. Our class went to the museum
6. Hung from the ceiling
7. Ruby interviewed Steve Garvey
8. Assignments on the blackboard
9. We climbed a rope ladder
10. Margo looks like her older sister

B. Follow the directions for Exercise A.

1. A magazine about cars
2. Several girls won scholarships
3. The bell rang
4. Appeared in a TV series
5. Scientists study animal behavior
6. Predicted rain
7. Carla bought new jeans
8. A stranger peered through the window
9. Only one car in the garage
10. Makes oatmeal cookies with raisins

C. Writing Make sentences from these fragments. Add whatever is needed to make each thought complete. Write each sentence on your paper.

1. ten pages in the math book
2. long, curly hair
3. turned three cartwheels
4. the girls in the chorus
5. an art fair next week
6. the icy streets
7. ate a slice of watermelon
8. pasted photos into a scrapbook
9. one of the new tape recorders
10. the canoe in the water

Part 2 Avoiding Run-on Sentences

A run-on sentence is two or more sentences written as one. These sentences are often joined incorrectly by a comma. Run-ons are confusing because they tell more than one complete thought. See how confusing these examples are:

> The campers sat around a fire they sang songs.
> Dan scrubbed the porch, Marcy weeded the garden.

Now see how clear the ideas are when each sentence expresses just one complete thought:

> The campers sat around a fire. They sang songs.
> Dan scrubbed the porch. Marcy weeded the garden.

Whenever you write, be careful to put just one complete thought in each sentence. End each complete thought with a period, question mark, or exclamation point. Begin each new sentence with a capital letter.

Exercises **Recognize run-on sentences.**

A. Some of the following sentences are run-on sentences. Some are correct sentences. Read each sentence. Write *Correct* or *Run-on* to tell what each one is.

1. Three clowns were riding on one donkey, they pushed each other off.
2. Lillian and Darren raced to the car.
3. I had a piano lesson for one hour then my teacher played a piece for me.
4. Yesterday we played baseball Judy scored three runs.
5. Everyone recited the Pledge of Allegiance.
6. Melvin had tomato soup and a cheese sandwich for lunch.
7. It rained on Labor Day, we had our picnic inside.

8. Jeff answered an ad in the paper he got a guitar.
9. Adelle played chess with her father every night last week.
10. The 4-H Club met Tuesday after school, a speaker told about a contest.

B. Follow the directions for Exercise A.

1. I have two younger brothers, they are twins.
2. Janet delivers papers each morning.
3. My friends from camp exchange letters.
4. My brother catches fireflies he keeps them in a jar.
5. Last year we planted a tree, it's in the back yard.
6. We picked bouquets of tulips and daffodils, we placed them in the dining room.
7. Aunt Meg knits sweaters for everyone in the family.
8. Rick knows the capital city of every state.
9. Luis likes corn and broccoli, he is a good cook.
10. Cassie filled the bookcase with mystery novels.

C. Writing Read each run-on sentence. Then rewrite each one, using correct capitalization and punctuation.

1. Jorge swam twenty laps, he felt tired.
2. Lisa trains animals she is good at it.
3. The Browns have a big family there are ten children.
4. Ms. Lake has a ranch she breeds cattle.
5. The beekeeper was working at the honeycomb he was collecting honey.
6. The cat climbed a tree, we rescued him.
7. The group hiked near the stream they stopped for a swim.
8. Jody paddled the canoe, she traveled downstream.
9. Do sharks swim close to shore have you seen one?
10. The race cars sped down the track, many people watched the race.

ADDITIONAL EXERCISES

Using Sentences Correctly

A. Sentences and Fragments Write *Fragment* or *Sentence* for each of the following groups of words to show what each group is.

1. A strong current pulled our boat.
2. An all-day bike trip.
3. A red notebook with a picture of Charlie Brown on the front.
4. Fans lined up at the gates.
5. Bought fresh orange juice.
6. Cross-country skiing has become popular.
7. A long pass from the forty-yard line.
8. Cathy wore her new clogs to school.
9. The boys made ice cream for the party.
10. Studied the chapters in the science book.

B. Sentences and Run-ons Write *Correct* or *Run-on* for each of the following groups of words to show what each group is.

1. Vera hit a slapshot, it landed in the net.
2. The road with the narrow bridge was flooded.
3. The boys found a cave, they crawled in.
4. The nurse gave me a shot it didn't hurt.
5. The bowling ball is in my locker.
6. TV programs get Emmy awards, movies get Oscars.
7. These windows face the sun.
8. Jenny rode the horse it needed exercise.
9. The drawer was full of photographs.
10. Skaters glided around the rink.

C. Sentences, Fragments, and Run-on Sentences Write *Fragment, Sentence,* or *Run-on* for each of the following groups of words to show what each group is.

1. Carol worked on the engine, she finally fixed it.
2. The jacket hanging in my locker.
3. Van takes piano lessons, George takes voice lessons.
4. Dennis borrowed your bike.
5. A helicopter flew along the shore.
6. The last day of school.
7. The potatoes burned, the fish was too dry.
8. Return these books to the library.
9. Asked several questions about the movie.
10. The sky grew cloudy.

MIXED REVIEW

Using Sentences Correctly

A. Identifying sentences, fragments, and run-on sentences Write *Fragment, Sentence,* or *Run-On* for each of the following groups of words. Then, correct fragments by adding words to make complete sentences. Correct run-ons by using the correct capitalization and punctuation to show where each complete thought begins and ends.

1. The cellar door was left open.
2. My aunt, uncle, and six cousins.
3. We practiced all morning now our act is perfect.
4. Slept until nine o'clock.
5. Don't eat before the race.
6. A scary spy story.
7. Evan's birthday is March 26, he will be thirteen.
8. The movie follows the cartoons.
9. Have you read this book would you like to borrow it?
10. Worked until seven o'clock.
11. Hope recited her poem.
12. Everyone met at Jean's house.
13. Kate collected pine cones, she put them in a basket.
14. The old house on the corner.
15. I need thirty-five cents.

B. Correct fragments and run-on sentences Copy this paragraph. Correct any fragments or run-on sentences.

    Last Saturday night was no ordinary evening for me. My first baby-sitting job. It began at six o'clock. It ended at ten. During that time I fed, chased, and bathed three children and a dog. Also put them to bed. Why is it called baby-*sitting*, I never sat down at all!

USING GRAMMAR IN WRITING
Using Sentences Correctly

A. Imagine that you woke up in the middle of the night. You had just had a vivid dream. You wanted to remember the dream, so you reached for a pencil and pad of paper. In the dark you scribbled down your dream. The next morning, here is what you read:

> I was on a giant roller coaster I got to the top of the highest hill when I looked over I saw next to me Darth Vader was I scared Just then we started downhill we were going so fast I was breathless all I could hear was Darth Vader's loud steady breathing suddenly the car flew off the track and plunged to earth but earth had disappeared I was floating among the stars Darth Vader was laughing a horrible, hollow laugh.

Rewrite your dream. Add the correct punctuation. Be sure you leave no fragments or run-on sentences.

B. Below is a group of sentence fragments. Use at least four of the fragments to write a short paragraph about why it is good to have a sense of humor. Change all of the fragments to complete sentences. You can use the fragments in any order you like.

not always easy	an example
able to laugh	better than complaining
if you're upset	rather than cry
at your own mistakes	a comedian

Using Nouns

Part 1 What Are Nouns?

The words you use to name things are called **nouns.**

Look around you. Who is sitting near you? What is the name of your school? What street or road is it on? What city or town do you live in? The words that you use to name these things are nouns.

Nouns are words that name persons, places, or things. Read these examples:

Persons:	Greg Luzinski, firefighter, pilot, Diana
Places:	frontier, New York City, ranch, playground
Things:	tree, Rocky Mountains, pizza, Frisbee

Some nouns, like those listed on page 308, are names of things that you can see. Other nouns are names of things that you cannot see. Here are some nouns that name things you cannot see.

idea   courage   loneliness   peace

Exercises   Find nouns.

A. Number your paper from 1 to 10. List the nouns in each sentence below.

1. Stacy saw the fireworks last July.
2. A surfer rode a huge wave.
3. A new band performed at the fair.
4. My brother has excellent eyesight.
5. My cousin lives on a farm in Iowa.
6. Jason plays the piano and the trombone.
7. The Dodgers will play in the World Series.
8. Keith has a picture of the Golden Gate Bridge on his notebook.
9. Ms. Mason told a story about the first Thanksgiving.
10. Robert does chores around the house and earns an allowance.

B. Writing This exercise will show you how often nouns are used in writing and in discussion. On your paper, make four lists of nouns according to these directions.

1. Copy the names of five characters from short stories or novels.
2. Copy five nouns from your science book or math book.
3. List five names of foods.
4. List five names of places you have visited or read about.

Part 2 Common Nouns and Proper Nouns

The noun *student* names any person. *Cecilia* names one particular student.

The noun *city* names any place. *San Francisco* names one particular city.

The noun *car* names any thing. *Ford* names one particular car.

A common noun is a general name for a person, place, or thing. A common noun begins with a small letter.

A proper noun names a particular person, place, or thing. A proper noun always begins with a capital letter.

Many proper nouns are made up of two or more words, such as *Atlantic Ocean* and *Grand Canyon National Park*. When the proper noun has several words, capitalize all the important words. You do not have to capitalize *of, on,* or *the.*

Exercise **Find common nouns and proper nouns.**

On your paper, make two columns. Label one column *Common Nouns* and the other column *Proper Nouns*. Write each word below in the appropriate column. Remember to begin every proper noun with a capital letter.

1. person	9. africa	17. dentist
2. city	10. lake superior	18. elm street
3. washington	11. maria	19. cat
4. ms. steele	12. post office	20. the chicago
5. paper	13. england	tribune
6. timothy	14. building	
7. principal	15. mr. ruiz	
8. college	16. chicago	

Part 3   Singular and Plural Nouns

What is the difference between the words in these pairs?

astronaut	cake	idea	town
astronauts	cakes	ideas	towns

You can see that the words are almost the same, but that they have different endings. The bottom word in each pair has an *-s* added. What difference does that *-s* make in the meaning of the words? The *-s* changes the *number* of persons, places, or things that the word names.

A noun that names just one person, place, or thing is called a **singular noun**. A noun that names more than one person, place, or thing is called a **plural noun**. (All the nouns in the top line of the word pairs are *singular*. All the nouns in the bottom line are *plural*.) Changing a word from singular to plural is called forming the plural of the noun.

Here are seven rules for forming the plurals of nouns:

1. To form the plural of most nouns, just add an -s.

stick**s**	cow**s**	bike**s**	drink**s**
stone**s**	dog**s**	skate**s**	snack**s**

2. When the singular noun ends in s, *sh*, *ch*, *x*, or *z*, add -es.

circus**es**	ash**es**	fox**es**
class**es**	lunch**es**	waltz**es**

3. When the singular ends in *o*, add -s.

studio**s**	radio**s**	stereo**s**	banjo**s**

Exceptions: For the following nouns ending in *o*, add *-es*:

echo**es**	hero**es**	tomato**es**	potato**es**

4. When the singular noun ends in *y* with a consonant before it, change the *y* to *i*, and add -es.

fly → fli**es**	penny → penni**es**
pony → poni**es**	candy → candi**es**

5. **For most nouns ending in *f* or *fe*, add -*s*. For some nouns ending in *f* or *fe*, however, change the *f* to *v* and add -*es* or -*s*.**

belief → beliefs	thief → thieves	leaf → leaves
chief → chiefs	knife → knives	half → halves
roof → roofs	wife → wives	shelf → shelves
dwarf → dwarfs	life → lives	elf → elves

6. **Some nouns are the same for both singular and plural.**

deer   trout   sheep   moose   salmon

7. **Some nouns form their plurals in special ways.**

mouse → mice	man → men	tooth → teeth
goose → geese	woman → women	foot → feet
	child → children	

Using a Dictionary To Find Plurals

Here is a dictionary entry for the word *echo*. Notice that the entry shows the plural ending, -*oes*. (The plural noun is *echoes*.) Most dictionaries show the plural form of a noun if the plural is formed in an irregular way. When you are not sure how to form the plural of a noun, look up the noun in a dictionary.

---

ech•o (ek′ō) *n.*, *pl.* **-oes** [< L. < Gr. *ēchō*] **1.** *a*) the repetition of a sound that occurs when sound waves are reflected from a surface *b*) a sound so made **2.** *a*) any repetition or imitation of the words, ideas, etc. of another *b*) a person who repeats or imitates in this way **3.** sympathetic response **4.** a radar wave reflected from an object, appearing as a spot of light on a radarscope —[**E-**] *Gr. Myth.* a nymph who pined away for Narcissus until only her voice remained —*vi.* **-oed, -o•ing 1.** to be filled with echoes [the long hall *echoed* with their laughter] **2.** to be repeated as an echo [his words *echoed* in the valley] —*vt.* **1.** to repeat (the words, ideas, etc.) of (another) **2.** to repeat or reflect (sound) from a surface

---

Form the plurals of nouns.

A.   Number your paper from 1 to 10. Copy each pair of nouns below. Then write the number of the rule that tells how the plural was formed.

1. piano → pianos	6. tooth → teeth
2. roof → roofs	7. tomato → tomatoes
3. doctor doctors	8. life → lives
4. tax → taxes	9. moose → moose
5. party → parties	10. bench → benches

B.   Write the plural form for each of these nouns.

1. woman	6. dwarf	11. trout	16. copy
2. knife	7. radio	12. noise	17. mouse
3. sheep	8. watch	13. half	18. team
4. girl	9. child	14. potato	19. sandwich
5. candy	10. boy	15. gas	20. leaf

Part 4   Making Nouns Show Possession

Study these examples.

> These are my sister's skates.
> (Who owns the skates?)
> Sally's mother called.
> (Whose mother called?)
> This is the boy's hat.
> (Who owns the hat?)

What has been added to the nouns *sister, Sally,* and *boy?* Adding *'s* makes the nouns show ownership, or possession. Words such as *sister's, Sally's,* and *boy's* are **possessive nouns.**

A possessive noun shows possession of the noun that follows.

Making Singular Nouns Show Possession

To make a singular noun show possession, add an apostrophe and s.

Singular Noun	Possessive Noun
mechanic	mechanic's
James	James's
Ms. Roberts	Ms. Roberts's

Making Plural Nouns Show Possession

There are two rules to remember for making a plural noun show possession.

1. If the plural noun ends in s, simply add an apostrophe after the s.

Plural Noun	Possessive Noun
workers	workers'
nurses	nurses'
dentists	dentists'

2. If the plural noun does not end in s, add an apostrophe and an s after the apostrophe.

Plural Noun	Possessive Noun
men	men's
women	women's
children	children's

Adding the Apostrophe

Look at these words. See where the apostrophe is added.

the girl's project	This means a project belonging to one girl.
the girls' project	This means a project belonging to more than one girl.

If you are not sure where to add the apostrophe, write the word by itself first. Then follow the rules.

Exercises   **Make nouns show possession.**

A. Copy the following sentences. Make the underlined words show possession.

1. Rosa team beat Dwayne team yesterday.
2. In my uncle shop they sell men and ladies clothes.
3. Bonnie team won the spelling match.
4. Tammy little sister got lost in the store.
5. Where are the children toys?
6. My two brothers clothes were all over the floor.
7. The girl books fell out of the car.
8. The doctor gently felt the dog paw.
9. I left my sweater at the dentist office.
10. Richard hobby is collecting ballplayers autographs.

B. In each sentence one noun is underlined. Write the noun. Then add an apostrophe or an apostrophe and *s* to make the noun show possession.

1. We found Ramon bike in the basement.
2. There are two girls coats in the closet.
3. One man hat blew into the street.
4. It was "Ladies Day" at Yankee Stadium.
5. The children library closes at five o'clock.
6. We found George mittens.
7. Which department sells babies cribs?
8. Where are the women tickets?
9. I lost my father pen.
10. Pam and Sue were studying Jenny notes.

Sentence Patterns

In an English sentence, words are put together in a certain order to make sense. The word order in most sentences follows a pattern. In this book you will study four **sentence patterns.**

Every sentence has a subject and a verb. The subject is usually a noun. In this chart, *N* stands for the noun in the complete subject. *V* is the verb in the complete predicate.

N	V
Diana	stumbled.
My brother	waited.
This camera	works easily.

The word order in these sentences follows a pattern. That pattern is noun-verb, or N V, and is called the **N V pattern.**

Exercises **Use the N V pattern.**

A. Make a chart like the one above. Label one column *N.* Label the other column *V.* Write these sentences on the chart.

1. Rain fell.
2. Katy bats next.
3. The bus stopped.
4. Scott laughed.
5. The green vase shattered.
6. The train started slowly.

B. Copy this chart. Complete each sentence in the N V pattern.

N	V
1. _____	listened.
2. _____	worked carefully.
3. The sun	_____ .
4. _____	turned around.

C. Write five sentences in the N V pattern.

ADDITIONAL EXERCISES

Using Nouns

A. Recognizing Nouns Write the nouns in each of the following sentences.

1. Mark ate tacos for dinner.
2. That artist shows talent.
3. The boat sailed beneath the bridge.
4. Bob gave Joe two tickets to the performance.
5. The Guggenheim Museum is in New York City.
6. Gerry likes hamburgers with mustard and relish.
7. A colorful glider swooped silently over the crowd.
8. Meg sewed the patches into a quilt.
9. Milwaukee is a city on the shores of Lake Michigan.
10. The music came from the radio in the kitchen.

B. Finding Proper Nouns Write the proper nouns in each of the following sentences. Capitalize them.

1. Leslie and mark play baseball with their friends.
2. Have you crossed the brooklyn bridge in new york?
3. Joan and her family moved from montana to california.
4. In the last game, the pirates beat the cardinals.
5. Mr. lynch drove his plymouth through the mountains.
6. That man crossed the atlantic ocean in a sailboat.
7. The train for atlanta leaves in the morning.
8. Ms. martin explained the long chapter.
9. Her family drove from louisville to chicago.
10. The philippine islands are in the pacific ocean.

C. Forming Plurals Write the plural form of each underlined noun in these sentences.

1. Her brother visited the movie studio.
2. The woman owned the bookstore.

3. Robert searched the library <u>shelf</u> for the book.
4. The chef made the <u>sandwich</u> with rye bread.
5. The <u>baby</u> played with the toys.
6. <u>Salmon</u> swim upstream.
7. The workers repaired the damaged <u>roof</u>.
8. The <u>box</u> of books fell from the rickety table.
9. Bev's <u>mouse</u> ate cheese and crackers.
10. Rick lost his <u>ski</u> on the ski lift.

D. Forming Possessives Write the possessive form of each underlined noun.

1. the <u>teachers</u> meeting
2. <u>Jess</u> part in the play
3. a <u>cartoonist</u> drawings
4. the <u>players</u> pictures in the paper
5. all the <u>boys</u> uniforms
6. the <u>children</u> playground
7. the <u>dog</u> collar
8. <u>Ms. Burns</u> car
9. the <u>cities</u> budget
10. the <u>typist</u> notepad

MIXED REVIEW

Using Nouns

A. Finding nouns and identifying proper nouns Copy the following sentences. Underline all the nouns. If a noun is proper, capitalize it.

1. Amy is moving to hazel crest drive.
2. St. paul is the capital of minnesota.
3. My family drove our camper through the smoky mountains.
4. Donna is studying history at boston college.
5. What foods are eaten during passover?
6. Dale has tickets for the game on saturday.
7. This movie stars clint eastwood.
8. Our library has the new book by beverly cleary.
9. The girls want to play monopoly.
10. The wildlife of africa must be protected.

B. Using plurals and possessives of nouns Copy the following sentences. For each sentence, choose the correct word from the two in parentheses.

1. The principal needs three (copys, copies) of the letter.
2. Two (halfs, halves) make a whole.
3. The (boy's, boys') arm is broken.
4. James has two loose (tooth's, teeth).
5. Ms. Lewis is our (team's, teams) coach.
6. Cheryl lightly touched the (piano's, pianos) keys.
7. The (childrens', children's) department is on the third floor.
8. (Gina's, Ginas') aunt is a doctor at that hospital.
9. That (girl's, girls') hobbies are painting and coin collecting.
10. There are about forty (sheep, sheeps) in that herd.

USING GRAMMAR IN WRITING
Using Nouns

A. Most of our names have a special meaning. For example, the name Debby means "bee" in the Hebrew language. The name Richard originally meant "strong king." What do you know about your name? Try to find out what it means and what language it comes from. Look in the dictionary or in a book about names. Your school or local librarian will help you.

Write a paragraph about your name. Tell what language or country it came from. Also tell what the name means and why it was chosen for you. If there are other forms of your name, write those too.

If you wish, tell whether or not you like your name. If you would rather have another name, what is it, and why? Underline each noun that you use in your paragraph. Underline common nouns once and proper nouns twice.

B. One of your friends has suggested that several of you have a garage sale. At a garage sale, you sell things you don't need anymore. It is a way to make some extra spending money. Make a list of twenty items you would put in the sale. Make your list specific. Include names of games, sports equipment, items of clothing, comics, records, and so on. Underline any proper nouns in your list. Circle any plural nouns. Put a star next to any possessive nouns.

C. Now write an ad about the garage sale that would run in your local newspaper. Give the time, the date, and the location of the sale. Also, mention some of the most interesting items that you have to sell.

Using Verbs

Part 1 What Are Verbs?

Read these sentences. What do the underlined words tell you?

> Roberto <u>hit</u> a home run.   Vera <u>ran</u> to the store.

The underlined words tell what each person did. They tell about action. Words that tell about action are called **action verbs.**

Action Verbs

Some verbs tell about action you can see, such as *hit* and *ran*. Other verbs tell about action you cannot see, as in these examples:

> Sarah <u>worried</u> about the test.   I <u>have</u> two dollars.
> Tony <u>wants</u> a new jacket.   The jury <u>believed</u> the witness.

Find action verbs.

A. Write the action verb in each sentence.

1. The hikers lost their way in the fog.
2. Jennifer agreed with Rick about the plans for the dance.
3. Marty has two younger brothers.
4. Jim wished for a sunny day.
5. Members of Congress make laws.
6. Linda climbed the maple tree.
7. Luis expected a call from his uncle in San Juan.
8. The band marched onto the field at half-time.
9. Jessica traveled through Oregon last summer.
10. The actors painted their faces with makeup.

B. Think of an action verb that will complete each sentence below. Copy the sentences, filling in each blank with an action verb. Many different answers are possible for each sentence.

Example: Toby _____ the ball.
Possible answers: Toby caught the ball.
Toby threw the ball.
Toby held the ball.
Toby hit the ball.

1. The class _____ at the old joke.
2. Aunt Suzanne _____ a new sweater.
3. Several people _____ on the crowded beach.
4. A silver fox _____ over the fence.
5. Gina _____ her new fountain pen.
6. Anita _____ down the hall.
7. The two brothers _____ .
8. The conductor _____ tickets.
9. We _____ for the signal to begin our cheer.
10. The scientists _____ an Arctic expedition.

Verbs That State That Something Is

Not all verbs tell about action. Some verbs state that something *is*. The underlined verbs in these sentences say that something *is*. They are called **state-of-being verbs.**

I <u>am</u> a student.   The girls <u>were</u> happy.
John <u>is</u> my brother.   The weather <u>was</u> bad.
We <u>are</u> late.   We <u>will be</u> on time.

The most common state-of-being verbs are these:

is   am   were   being
are   was   be   been

Other state-of-being verbs include these:

look   seem   become   taste   smell   feel

I <u>feel</u> sick.   The juice <u>tasted</u> good.
Jill <u>became</u> a dancer.   Ed <u>seems</u> surprised.

Verbs are words that tell about an action or state that something *is*.

Exercises   Use action verbs and state-of-being verbs.

A.   Write the verb in each of the following sentences. Some are action verbs, and some are state-of-being verbs.

1. The Dodgers are her heroes.
2. The boys were still hungry.
3. Aaron bought his ticket for the concert.
4. Pam argued with her sister about clothes.
5. The new hardware store opens tomorrow.
6. My cousin is a stunt driver.
7. John and Flo sang together.
8. Lisa climbed the spiral staircase.
9. Dan imagined a trip to Mars.
10. A butterfly sailed in the wind.

B. Number your paper from 1 to 10. Write the verb in each of the following sentences. After the verb, write *Action* or *State-of-Being* to tell what kind of verb it is.

1. Juan plays the drums in the school band.
2. Gino's parents own a toy store.
3. Gloria is the class clown.
4. I made a puppet for my niece.
5. The sparrow injured its wing.
6. The parade is at noon.
7. Max hid in the basement during the thunderstorm.
8. The weather was beautiful.
9. Karen enjoys mystery novels.
10. The basketball landed in the bleachers.

C. Follow the directions for Exercise B.

1. This popcorn tastes too salty.
2. Mike's sister works at the ice cream shop.
3. Your suitcase feels very light.
4. The hotel seems old.
5. George likes country music.
6. Liz chopped wood for the fire.
7. A conch is a large shell.
8. Hutchinson was a fine player.
9. My brother collects arrowheads and fossils.
10. Joey and Maria planned the class trip.

Using Verbs in Sentences

Look at these groups of words. They do not express complete ideas. They are not sentences. What words are missing?

Kevin sick   We the zoo every year

These are not sentences because they do not have verbs.

When you add verbs, you can make sentences like these:

Kevin *was* sick.   We *visit* the zoo every year.

Remember that every sentence must have a verb.

Exercises   Use verbs in sentences.

A. Writing   Read the following groups of words. If a word group is a sentence, write *Sentence*. If it is not a sentence, add a verb. Then write the complete sentence. There are many correct ways to finish each sentence.

1. The quarterback the ball.
2. Heidi a mountain girl.
3. A plane landed on the lake.
4. Rosy a yellow scarf.
5. The elevator stopped.
6. Apples are my favorite fruit.
7. Amy her shoes in the closet.
8. We play soccer in that field.
9. *The Wiz* was a play and a movie.
10. The crowd the national anthem.

B.   Follow the directions for Exercise A.

1. Where the water fountain?
2. Al put posters on the wall.
3. A crabapple sour.
4. The Broncos in the fourth quarter.
5. The girls rode their bikes.
6. My collie sleeps near my bed.
7. The farmer the grain.
8. A tire makes a good swing.
9. Many people turkey on Thanksgiving.
10. The firefighters opened the fire hydrant.

Part 2 Main Verbs and Helping Verbs

Most of the verbs you have studied so far have been just one word: *hit, is, ran,* and *climbed,* for example.

Many verbs are made up of more than one word. Notice the verbs in these sentences.

Betsy *walked* home.
Betsy *is walking* home.
Betsy *has been walking* home.

Steven *called* you.
Steven *was calling* you.
Steven *might have called* you.

When a verb is made up of more than one word, the last word is the **main verb.** The other words are called **helping verbs.**

Helping Verb	+ Main Verb	= Verb
	walked	walked
is	walking	is walking
has been	walking	has been walking
	called	called
was	calling	was calling
might have	called	might have called

The most common helping verbs are forms of *be, have,* and *do:*

be—am, is, are, was, were
have—has, have, had
do—does, do, did

These words can also be used by themselves as main verbs.

Used as Helping Verb

Janet *was visiting.*
Ralph *does like* math.

Used as Main Verb

Janet *was* in Indiana.
Ralph *does* his work.

These are other helping verbs that can be used with main verbs:

be	been	shall	could	would	might
being	can	will	should	may	

A verb may be a single word. A verb may also be a group of words, made up of a main verb and one or more helping verbs.

Exercises **Find main verbs and helping verbs.**

A. Make two columns. Label the first column *Helping Verbs*. Label the second column *Main Verb*. Write the parts of the verb for each of these sentences in the correct column.

Example: That car should have stopped for the bus.

Helping Verbs	**Main Verb**
should have	stopped

1. Ernest has eaten some fudge.
2. Tomorrow we will be going to the museum.
3. One horse was leading the parade.
4. Lorraine is carrying her catcher's mitt.
5. The trip should have ended sooner.
6. Stephanie does like the new apartment.
7. We may wash the car today.
8. They could have arrived on time.
9. Julio has been painting with poster paints.
10. Our teacher had explained the experiment before.

B. Writing Write five sentences. Each sentence should have a main verb and one or more helping verbs. Underline the main verb in each sentence once. Underline the helping verbs twice.

Some Verbs Need Helping Verbs

Read these three sentences:

We *ate* the cheese.
We *eaten* all of the chicken.
We *eating* crackers now.

Something is wrong with the last two sentences. What can you add to make them sound right? You can add helping verbs.

We **have** *eaten* all of the chicken.
We **are** *eating* crackers now.

Four of the verbs that you use very often must be used with helping verbs. They are *been, done, gone,* and *seen.* Verbs with the *-en* ending, like *chosen* or *ridden,* must be used with helping verbs. Verbs with the *-ing* ending, like *sitting* and *talking,* must be used with helping verbs. There are many other verbs that must be used with helping verbs. You will learn more about them in **Section 5.**

Exercises   Add helping verbs.

A.   Read each of these sentences. If the sentence is correct, write *Correct.* If the verb needs a helping verb, write a helping verb and the main verb. There may be more than one right helping verb.

Example: Ms. Lorne waiting at the bus stop.
        was waiting

1. The groundhog seen its shadow.
2. A huge truck has swept the streets.
3. We playing hockey.
4. The vase broken by accident.
5. Superman rescued the miners.
6. Babe Didrikson was a great athlete.

7. A lady walking the tightrope.
8. The girl was running down the alley.
9. We been listening to a Donna Summer album.
10. I using your ruler.

B. Follow the directions for Exercise A.

1. Barb ridden a bronco.
2. Millions of years ago, dinosaurs roamed the earth.
3. The class learning about government.
4. Alec had a strange dream.
5. My sister Carmen chosen the records.
6. A new movie theater opening soon.
7. We leaving for Boston tomorrow.
8. Costumes were stored in a trunk.
9. That dog bitten our mail carrier.
10. Listeners guessing the punch lines.

Separated Parts of the Verb

Sometimes another part of the sentence comes between the helping verb and the main verb.

Ezra **may** not **pitch** today.
Joanne **will** probably **stay** for dinner.
The gate **should**n't **have been locked** last night.

Not and the ending *n't* are never part of the verb, although they do change the meaning of the verb.

In questions, there are usually one or more words between the helping verb and the main verb.

Does this bicycle **need** oil?   **Have** you **been listening?**
Were you **looking** for me?   **Is** Dad **painting** in the garage?

Exercises   Find the separated parts of the verb.

A.   Make two columns on your paper. Label the first column *Helping Verbs*. Label the second column *Main Verb*. Write the parts of the verb for each of these sentences in the correct column.

Example: Joseph didn't see the curb.

Helping Verbs	Main Verb
did	see

1. Our goalie has not blocked any shots.
2. Vicky has never missed a Red Sox game.
3. Would you repeat your answer?
4. The floats were usually awarded prizes.
5. Amanda will probably break the school record in the 100-yard dash.
6. Was the champ resting before the fight?
7. We shouldn't cross the railroad tracks.
8. Leo couldn't believe his eyes.
9. Prisoners have never escaped from that jail.
10. Didn't you bring an umbrella?

B.   Follow the directions for Exercise A.

1. I was only joking about your costume.
2. Will winter ever end?
3. Grandma has never missed my birthday party.
4. Winona could barely reach the swing.
5. Barry has almost finished his homework.
6. Have you ever sung in a choir?
7. When does your library card expire?
8. Can you still smell the fish in the kitchen?
9. I don't understand this assignment.
10. Shouldn't the movie start now?

Part 3   Direct Objects of Verbs

In many sentences, a subject and a verb are enough to express a complete thought.

> The child fell.
> The telephone rang.

In other sentences, the thought is not complete until other words have been added.

> Kirk spilled the **glue.**
> The class thanked **Jean.**

The word that is needed after the verb to complete the action of the verb is the **direct object of the verb.** *Glue* tells what Kirk spilled. *Jean* tells whom the class thanked. *Glue* and *Jean* are the direct objects in these sentences.

The direct object is the word that receives the action of the verb.

Recognizing Direct Objects

To find the direct object in a sentence, first find the verb. Then place *what* or *whom* after the verb to form a question. If a word answers the question formed with *what* or *whom*, it is the direct object.

> Examples: John sharpened his pencil.
> John sharpened *what?*   his *pencil*
> The direct object is *pencil.*
>
> The hockey players cheered their coach.
> The players cheered *whom?*   their *coach*
> The direct object is *coach.*

Direct objects only answer *what* or *whom* after the verb. They do not tell *when* or *where* or *how.* You will see that there are no direct objects in the following sentences.

> Andrew plays in the afternoon.
> His father drove to Tennessee.

However, there are direct objects in these sentences.

> Andrew plays *football* in the afternoon.
> His father drove the *truck* to Tennessee.

Exercises **Find the direct objects.**

A. Copy the following sentences. Underline the verb. Circle the direct object.

> Example: Della was riding her bicycle.

1. Teresa broke her ruler.
2. Tim liked the new coach.
3. The fielder should have caught that ball.
4. The conductor will collect tickets.
5. This computer can solve problems.
6. Did you call your parents?
7. My little brothers made a snowman.
8. Phyllis and Mandy were doing a puzzle.
9. Long ago, Indians hunted buffalo here.
10. Lyndon cut the cake into small pieces.

B. Writing Write ten sentences using the following verbs. Put a direct object in each sentence. Circle each direct object.

1. lost
2. was building
3. dropped
4. will fill
5. likes
6. was writing
7. covered
8. should have read
9. will eat
10. touched

Part 4   Linking Verbs

State-of-being verbs are often called **linking verbs.** Linking verbs connect the subject with a word in the predicate. The word in the predicate tells something about the subject. Read these examples:

Rhonda's dress *was* blue.
The stew *smells* delicious.
Our players *looked* happy.

In the first sentence, *was* connects *blue* with the subject *dress.* What does *blue* tell about *dress?* In the second sentence, *smells* connects *delicious* with the subject *stew.* What does *delicious* tell about *stew?* In the third sentence, *looked* connects *happy* with the subject *players.* What does *happy* tell about *players?*

The most common linking verb is the verb *be. Be* can have many forms:

be	been	is	was
being	am	are	were

The words *seem, look, smell, taste,* and *feel* can also be used as linking verbs.

The words linked to the subject by a linking verb are called **predicate words.** There are *predicate nouns, predicate pronouns,* and *predicate adjectives.* Read these examples:

My mother *is* an **engineer.**   (predicate noun)

This *is* **he.**   (predicate pronoun)

Yuki *seemed* **nervous.**   (predicate adjective)

Find the linking verbs.

A. Make three columns on your paper. Label the first column *Subject*, the second column *Linking Verb*, and the third column *Word Linked to Subject*. Find these three parts in each sentence below. Write them in the proper columns.

Example: The dancers were energetic.

Subject	Linking Verb	Word Linked to Subject
dancers	were	energetic

1. Ansel Adams is a famous photographer.
2. The trail was rough in spots.
3. That comedian is very clever.
4. Everyone seems sorry about the mix-up.
5. That hot vegetable soup smells good.
6. My old winter coat looks shabby.
7. Our flight to Miami was smooth.
8. Larry has been president of the club.
9. Kris is a varsity swimmer.
10. The coach feels confident about the play-offs.

B. Follow the directions for Exercise A.

1. That new cereal tastes soggy.
2. My sister is the class president.
3. The radio is much too loud.
4. Toby felt nervous at rehearsal.
5. The people were tourists from Germany.
6. Logan Beach looks peaceful today.
7. Casey's aunt has been an aide to Senator Mendez.
8. The topics for speeches seem interesting.
9. Lana was curious about the lineup.
10. The stairs to the attic are creaky.

Direct Object or Predicate Word?

What are the differences between these two sentences?

Bob hit a double.   Bob is an outfielder.

You have learned about two kinds of verbs. There are *action verbs* and *linking verbs*. You have also learned about two kinds of words that follow verbs and complete their meaning. There are *direct objects*, and there are *predicate words*.

How can you tell which words are direct objects and which words are predicate words? First, find the verb in a sentence. Is the verb an action verb or a linking verb?

1. If an **action verb** is followed by a noun that tells *what* or *whom*, that noun is a **direct object.**

Examples: Julie studies *Spanish.*   Julie ate *lunch* early.

2. If a **linking verb** is followed by a word that tells about the subject, that word is a **predicate noun,** a **predicate pronoun,** or a **predicate adjective.**

Examples: Julie is a *student.* (predicate noun)
This is *she.* (predicate pronoun)
Julie is *hungry.* (predicate adjective)

Now compare these two examples.

Bob hit a double.
Hit is an action verb. *Double* is a direct object.

Bob is an outfielder.
Is is a linking verb. *Outfielder* is a predicate noun.

Exercises   **Find direct objects and predicate words.**

A.   Write each of the following sentences. If the sentence contains a linking verb, circle the verb and then circle the predicate word that follows it. If the sentence contains an action verb, underline it and then underline its direct object.

1. The girls formed a band.

2. Phil made a metal sculpture.
3. Nicole is a student from France.
4. Roger will design the costumes.
5. *Freaky Friday* is a book by Mary Rodgers.
6. Vanessa is the soprano.
7. This new candy tastes fizzy.
8. My family rented a cabin in the mountains.
9. The weather will be pleasant this spring.
10. That stray dog seems mean.

B. Follow the directions for Exercise A.

1. The dark movie theater was quiet.
2. Blanca's favorite hobby is her computer.
3. We met our cousin for the first time.
4. Kate seems older than her sister.
5. The surrounding farms look prosperous.
6. Josh found his ticket.
7. My brothers built an igloo last winter.
8. Todd feeds his dog every afternoon.
9. Aaron fumbled the pass.
10. After the race, the runners were weary.

Part 5　Verb Tenses

A verb is a time-telling word. It does not just tell what happens or what *is*. It also tells *when* something happens or *is*. By changing its form, a verb can tell whether an action or state of being happened or *was* in the past, is happening or *is* in the present, or will happen or will *be* in the future. The time expressed by a verb is called **tense.**

The **present tense** tells of an action or state of being that is happening now.

I *work* at school.　I *am* a student.

The **past tense** tells of an action or state of being that happened in the past.

> I *worked* all last summer.   I *was* a library aide.

The **future tense** tells of an action or state of being that will happen in the future.

> I *will work* at the pool next year.   I *will be* a lifeguard.

Verbs tell time in three ways:

1. By changing their spelling: I **know** now.
   > I **knew** then.
2. By adding an ending: We **walk** today.
   > We **walked** yesterday.
3. By using helping verbs: She **had decided** last week.
   > She **will decide** next week.

Forming the Tenses

Present Tense. The **present tense** of the verb is the same as the name of the verb: *race, call, do, think* (I *race*, you *call*, they *do*, we *think*). Add *-s* or *-es* to the verb when it is used with a singular noun or a pronoun (a word that takes the place of a noun) such as *he, she,* or *it* (he *races*, she *calls*, it *does*, Sara *thinks*).

Past Tense. The **past tense** of most verbs is formed by adding *-d* or *-ed* to the present tense. Verbs that form the past tense in this way are called **regular verbs.**

> race—race*d*   call—call*ed*

The past tense of some verbs is shown by a change in spelling. Verbs that form the past tense this way are **irregular verbs.**

> do → *did*   think → *thought*

Future Tense. The **future tense** is formed by using the helping verbs *will* or *shall* with the present tense:

> *will* race   *shall* call   *will* do   *shall* think

Recognize and use verb tenses.

A. Write the verb in each of the following sentences. Then write the tense of each verb.

> Example: Superman will stop the runaway train.
> will stop, future tense

1. We always watch the evening news.
2. The crew will build a new gym.
3. At midnight we raided the refrigerator.
4. Julie will have a slumber party on her birthday.
5. Some people dressed in costumes.
6. Ken's watch glows in the dark.
7. The bus will arrive late today.
8. Fresh blueberries taste great on ice cream.
9. Someone painted the lockers orange.
10. Gail tossed the ball to the catcher for the third out.

B. Write each of the following sentences. Use the tense of the verb asked for in each of the following sentences.

> Example: Bill Rodgers (past of *cross*) the finish line first.
> crossed

1. Kara (future of *get*) two free throws.
2. My sister and I (past of *play*) miniature golf.
3. Vicky (present of *mow*) her neighbor's lawn.
4. The jury (future of *decide*) the sentence.
5. Dad (past of *plant*) pumpkins in the garden.
6. I (future of *walk*) to the beach this afternoon.
7. My friends (present of *want*) front-row seats.
8. Carol (present of *pitch*) with her left hand.
9. Steve (past of *joke*) about his haircut.
10. The weather service (past of *warn*) of a tornado.

A sentence in the **N V N pattern** has three parts. The first *N* stands for the subject noun. The *V* stands for the verb. The second *N* stands for the direct object noun. Read the sentences in the following chart. They are in the N V N pattern.

N	V	N
Cora	writes	songs.
Snakes	lay	eggs.
My friends	planned	a party.
The plumber	fixed	the sink.
Donald	likes	his new bike.

Exercises   Use the N V N pattern.

A.   Make a chart like the one above. Write these sentences on the chart.

1. Therese plays the flute.
2. Phyllis called Terry.
3. My dog watches TV.
4. Andy took a bow
5. We cheered our goalie.
6. Saturn has ten moons.
7. An arrow hit the target.
8. Martina rode the train.

B.   Copy this chart. Add words to complete each sentence in the N V N pattern.

N	V	N
1. Angela	pushed	_____ .
2. _____	measured	_____ .
3. James	_____	carrots.
4. _____	answered	the phone.
5. This kitten	chases	_____ .

C.   Make a chart of your own. Write five sentences on your chart in the N V N pattern.

Sentence Patterns

A sentence in the **N LV N pattern** has three parts. The first *N* stands for the subject noun. *LV* stands for a linking verb. (Remember that *linking verb* is another name for a *state-of-being verb*.) The second *N* stands for the noun that follows the linking verb.

N	V	N
Janet	is	an artist.
Ralph	is	her brother.
The best speller	was	Linn.
Cleopatra	is	my kitten.
My skates	were	a birthday present.

Exercises **Use the N LV N pattern.**

A. Make a chart like the one above. Write these sentences on the chart.

1. Tomatoes are fruits.
2. This game is a challenge.
3. Africa is a continent.
4. My partner was Reba.
5. The boys were friends.
6. Larry is a joker.
7. Nutmeg is a spice.
8. These dogs are poodles.

B. Copy this chart. Add words to complete each sentence in the N LV N pattern.

N	LV	N
1. The last batter	was	_____.
2. _____	are	insects.
3. Juan	____	a halfback.
4. _____	was	_____.
5. _____	is	a good sport.

C. Make a chart of your own. Label the columns *N*, *LV*, and *N*. Write five sentences on your chart in the N LV N pattern.

Sentences in the **N LV Adj pattern** have three parts. The *N* stands for the subject noun. *LV* stands for the linking verb. *Adj* stands for adjective that follows the linking verb. The sentences in the following chart are in the N LV Adj pattern.

N	LV	Adj
The classroom	is	quiet.
Lemons	taste	sour.
Chris	was	fearless.
This record	sounds	scratchy.
These new boots	look	large.

Exercises   **Use the N LV Adj pattern.**

A.   Make a chart like the one above. Write these sentences on the chart.

1. Connie looks happy.
2. These roads are narrow.
3. Your sweater feels soft.
4. Tacos are tasty.
5. The radio sounds loud.
6. The mail was late.
7. The oranges were ripe.
8. This radish tastes bitter.

B.   Copy this chart. Add words to complete each sentence in the N LV Adj pattern.

N	LV	Adj
1. _____	is	funny.
2. _____	looks	sad.
3. Sandpaper	feels	_____.
4. The Halls	_____	friendly.
5. _____	was	_____.

C.   Make a chart of your own. Label the columns *N*, *LV*, and *Adj*. Write five sentences on your chart in the N LV Adj pattern.

ADDITIONAL EXERCISES

Using Verbs

A.   Action Verbs and State-of-Being Verbs   Write the verb in each of the following sentences. Beside the verb, write *Action* or *State-of-Being* to show what kind it is.

1. That classroom was a lunchroom last year.
2. Carly made a bowl out of clay.
3. Walt Disney was the creator of Mickey Mouse.
4. The doctor put a cast on Mandy's arm.
5. The science experiment was a failure.
6. Alex wrote his report in the library.
7. During the ride, Carl closed his eyes.
8. Nora is the best player on our team.
9. We hung the wallpaper with a thick paste.
10. The tennis courts are wet.

B.   Main Verbs and Helping Verbs   Write the helping verbs and the main verbs in the following sentences. Underline the helping verbs once and the main verbs twice.

1. The Bears are practicing for the first game.
2. Someone should have called the police.
3. Cindy may visit her grandmother in Minneapolis.
4. Tony was immediately sent to the nurse's office.
5. Ruthie has always liked sports.
6. Carlos is concentrating on his homework.
7. The vice-president didn't attend the meeting.
8. Our team should win this game.
9. Were you reading that magazine?
10. The comedian will be appearing nightly.

C.   Verbs and Direct Objects   Copy each of the following sentences. Underline each verb. Circle each direct object.

1. The quarterback passed the football.

2. Martin shoveled the driveway.
3. The Pep Club will sponsor a carnival.
4. Can you play the piano?
5. Roberto made chili for dinner.
6. The pirate walked the plank.
7. You can peel the potatoes.
8. The divers recovered some Roman coins.
9. Larry has memorized the poem.
10. The gardener planted the flowers.

D. Linking Verbs Make three columns. Label the first *Subject*, the second *Linking Verb*, and the third *Word Linked to Subject*. Write these parts in the proper columns.

1. The horses became restless.
2. Margaret was the winner of the contest.
3. This spoon feels greasy.
4. Claude was the goalie.
5. Mr. Cruz will be the new mayor.
6. Those koala bears seem shy.
7. Your desk looks messy.
8. Louise Nevelson is an artist.
9. Keith was happy about the victory.
10. Your projects have always been successful.

E. Verb Tenses Write each verb and its tense.

1. The aquarium displays many types of fish.
2. Mr. Vito will change the date of the play.
3. Each cast member worked hard.
4. Jan always plays the guitar for her friends.
5. Larry asked for a different book.
6. An usher will take you to your seat.
7. Meg brought lemonade to the beach.
8. Ms. Brown conducted the band.
9. Tony works evenings and weekends.
10. I changed my mind.

MIXED REVIEW

Using Verbs

A. Finding action verbs and state-of-being verbs, and identifying tenses   Write the verb from each sentence. After it write *Action* or *State-of-Being* to show what kind it is. Then write whether the verb is present, past, or future tense.

1. Hannah plays first base.
2. Maria is from Mexico City.
3. The tall clown was Jack.
4. My brother will drive us to the concert.
5. Ben will see that movie tomorrow.
6. Kim and he are twins.
7. The rabbits ate the lettuce and the marigolds.
8. Wayne and Lou were the best pitchers this season.
9. We will be late for the parade.
10. Beth caught the first fish.

B. Finding helping verbs, main verbs, and direct objects   Make three columns. Label the first *Helping Verbs,* the second *Main Verbs,* and the third *Direct Objects.* Write the verbs and direct objects in the proper columns. Not every sentence will have a helping verb or a direct object.

1. Tim and Darcy are decorating the cake.
2. The Olympic gymnast is practicing his routine.
3. Have you ever crossed the Brooklyn Bridge?
4. Kathryn is painting the porch.
5. Drifts of snow covered the cars.
6. Mrs. Kelly has been teaching violin for seven years.
7. Does this store sell wallpaper?
8. The flock of pigeons flew away.
9. I will be taking Spanish next year.
10. Josh will attend a computer camp this summer.

C. Identifying linking verbs and predicate words, and action verbs and direct objects Write the verb in each of the following sentences. Label it *AV* if it is an action verb and *LV* if it is a linking verb. If the verb is an action verb, write its object and label it *DO*. If the verb is a linking verb, write the predicate word and label it *PW*.

1. Ocean water tastes salty.
2. This hat is too big for me.
3. Ants carried crumbs from our picnic.
4. This book about dinosaurs is excellent.
5. Sally Ride is a famous astronaut.
6. The weather has been rainy all week.
7. Fred made a mobile for his room.
8. My brother sailed the boat out of the harbor.
9. In the kitchen we smelled vegetable soup.
10. The building on Oak Street is the new library.

D. Using sentence patterns Write two sentences for each of the following sentence patterns.

1. N V
2. N V N
3. N LV N
4. N LV Adj

USING GRAMMAR IN WRITING
Using Verbs

A. What is your favorite TV show? Is it a situation comedy? Is it a detective show or an exciting police series? Imagine that a friend of yours has never seen the show. Pick an episode that you saw recently. Tell your friend what happened in that story. Use strong action verbs to show how exciting it was. Underline all the main verbs once. Underline all helping verbs twice.

B. A company that makes electronic games put this classified ad in the paper:

WANTED

Ideas for new video games. Send us your idea. Describe the game in a paragraph. We will pay $100 for any idea we can use.

You have what you consider a winning idea. Write about it in a paragraph. At least two sentences should contain direct objects. When you are finished, underline all the verbs. Then circle the direct objects.

C. Imagine that your aunt is a skywriter. She writes messages in the sky using the smoke from her plane. Companies hire her to advertise their products. A breakfast cereal company has hired your aunt. She has asked you to help her write the ad. She asks you to write four sentences that would tell about the breakfast cereal. Use linking verbs in your sentences. Underline the linking verbs.

Using Irregular Verbs

Part 1 Principal Parts of Verbs

Every verb has many forms. Here are some forms the verb *talk* can have:

talk	talked	will talk
was talking	had talked	have been talking

All of these forms of *talk* are made from the three basic parts of a verb. These three basic parts are called the **principal parts** of a verb. The principal parts of a verb are the **present,** the **past,** and the **past participle.**

Here are some examples:

Present	Past	Past Participle
call	called	(have) called
hurry	hurried	(have) hurried
look	looked	(have) looked
paste	pasted	(have) pasted
stop	stopped	(have) stopped
walk	walked	(have) walked

The *present* part of the verb is used to form the present tense. Add *-s* or *-es* to the verb when it is used with a singular noun or *he, she,* or *it.*

Will or *shall* added to the present part forms the future tense.

The *past* part of the verb is used to form the past tense.

The *past participle* is used with helping verbs to make other forms of the verb. Some of these helping verbs are *has, have, had, will have,* and *shall have.* Here are some examples:

The storms **have stopped.**
Bob **had stopped** at the library.
The team **will have stopped** practicing by then.

Part 2   Regular Verbs

The verbs given in the list of principal parts above are called **regular verbs.** Every verb that is *regular* forms its past tense by adding *-ed* (*called*) or *-d* (*pasted*) to the present part. The past participle of a regular verb is the same as the past part and is always used with a helping verb. Most English verbs are regular.

Exercises   **Use principal parts of verbs.**

A.   Write the verb form indicated for the following regular verbs. Use helping verbs with each past participle.

1. like (past)
2. notice (past participle)
3. arrange (present)
4. watch (past participle)
5. snow (past)

6. smell (present)
7. listen (past participle)
8. rock (past participle)
9. use (past)
10. explain (past)

B. Writing   Write a sentence for each of the verbs below. Use the verb form indicated.

1. turn (past participle)
2. paint (past)
3. chase (past participle)
4. juggle (present)
5. open (past)

6. weigh (present)
7. pound (past)
8. struggle (present)
9. help (present)
10. order (past participle)

Part 3   Irregular Verbs

Some verbs do not form their pasts and past participles in the regular way. These five verbs are examples:

Present	Past	Past Participle
feel	felt	(have) felt
go	went	(have) gone
know	knew	(have) known
see	saw	(have) seen
think	thought	(have) thought

These verbs are not regular verbs. They are **irregular verbs.** There are only about sixty irregular verbs in the English language. They are important because many of them are verbs you use frequently.

In order to use irregular verbs correctly, you must know their correct past forms and past participles. The best way to learn to use irregular verbs correctly is to memorize as many of these verb forms as possible. A list of the most commonly used irregular verbs is given on page 351.

When you are using irregular verbs, you should remember these two rules:

1. The past form is always used by itself, *without* a helping verb.
   We *went* to the library last Saturday.
2. The past participle is always used *with* a helping verb.
   We *have gone* to the library every Saturday this month.

Helping Verbs

Forms of *be* and *have* are the helping verbs most often used with past participles. Here are the forms of *be* and *have*.

Be		Present	Past
Singular	I	am	was
	you	are	were
	he, she, it	is	was
Plural	we	are	were
	you	are	were
	they	are	were

Have		Present	Past
Singular	I	have	had
	you	have	had
	he, she, it	has	had
Plural	we	have	had
	you	have	had
	they	have	had

The forms *be, been,* and *being* are helping verbs that must be used with other helping verbs.

He *should be* arriving soon.
Ginny *has been* looking for a job.
They *were being* helped.

Principal Parts of Common Irregular Verbs

Present	Past	Past Participle
begin	began	(have) begun
break	broke	(have) broken
bring	brought	(have) brought
choose	chose	(have) chosen
come	came	(have) come
do	did	(have) done
drink	drank	(have) drunk
eat	ate	(have) eaten
fall	fell	(have) fallen
freeze	froze	(have) frozen
give	gave	(have) given
go	went	(have) gone
grow	grew	(have) grown
know	knew	(have) known
ride	rode	(have) ridden
ring	rang	(have) rung
rise	rose	(have) risen
run	ran	(have) run
say	said	(have) said
see	saw	(have) seen
sing	sang	(have) sung
sit	sat	(have) sat
speak	spoke	(have) spoken
steal	stole	(have) stolen
swim	swam	(have) swum
take	took	(have) taken
teach	taught	(have) taught
throw	threw	(have) thrown
wear	wore	(have) worn
write	wrote	(have) written

Using a Dictionary To Find Principal Parts

If you are not sure about a verb form, look it up in a dictionary. If the verb is regular, only one form will usually be listed.

If the verb is irregular, the dictionary will give the irregular forms. It will give two forms if the past and past participle are the same: *say, said.* It will give all three principal parts if they are all different: *sing, sang, sung.*

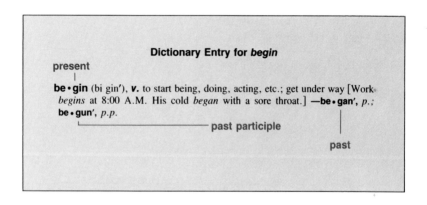

Dictionary Entry for *begin*

present

be•gin (bi gin′), *v.* to start being, doing, acting, etc.; get under way [Work *begins* at 8:00 A.M. His cold *began* with a sore throat.] —**be•gan′,** *p.;* **be•gun′,** *p.p.*

past participle

past

Part 4 Practice Pages on Irregular Verbs

A few irregular verbs are especially troublesome. They cause problems in writing and in speaking. Many people get confused about which form is used alone to mean the past, and which form is used with helping verbs.

On pages 354–366, you will find practice sentences for irregular verbs that are used often. To find out which verbs are difficult for you, do the following exercise.

If the exercise shows that you do know these verbs, you may only have to review this section.

If the exercise shows that you need more practice with certain verbs, turn to the pages with exercises for verbs. For each verb there are many sentences that will help you to "say it right," "hear it right," and "write it right."

Exercise **Use irregular verbs.**

Number your paper from 1 to 20. For each sentence, write the correct verb form from the two given in the parentheses.

1. A relief pitcher has (began, begun) to warm up.
2. That driver has (broke, broken) the law.
3. Joan has (took, taken) her books with her.
4. I have never (saw, seen) a funnier movie.
5. Has Bert (done, did) what he promised?
6. It (took, taken) a long time to find the right house.
7. Christopher has (ate, eaten) a whole pint of blueberries.
8. Jake has (rode, ridden) his bike to the park.
9. Jennifer has (wrote, written) some exciting stories.
10. My brother (ran, run) to catch his bus this morning.
11. Dolores has (gave, given) an excellent report.
12. The Johnsons have (gone, went) on vacation.
13. The sunflower has (grew, grown) five feet high.
14. Barry (knew, known) the rules of the game.
15. The ranch hand (rode, ridden) a wild horse.
16. The students have (took, taken) two tests this week.
17. Your teammates have (ran, run) as fast as you.
18. I (seen, saw) you at the mall.
19. Jan (grew, grown) to like her new school.
20. The fog (began, begun) to clear last night.

Say It Right   Hear It Right

Say these sentences until the correct use of the verbs sounds natural to you.

1. The little boy *began* to cry.
2. Suddenly the airplane *began* flying in a circle.
3. My mother *has begun* her new job.
4. We *began* by washing the kitchen windows.
5. Alex *had* just *begun* packing for the trip.
6. *Have* you *begun* your social studies report?
7. Many forest fires *are begun* by careless campers.
8. I *have* finally *begun* to get along with my sister.
9. The film *began* with an eerie scene.
10. We *should have begun* the decorations sooner.

Write It Right

Write the correct verb from the two forms given. Check your answer by saying the complete sentence to yourself.

1. We have (began, begun) a new unit in science class.
2. My father (began, begun) cooking lessons last month.
3. By evening the hurricane had (began, begun) to lose force.
4. The next day people (began, begun) returning home.
5. I have (began, begun) to think about a career.
6. Mr. Jansen, have you (began, begun) to correct our tests?
7. Eight people (began, begun) the race, but only three finished.
8. The mayor (began, begun) her speech with a joke.
9. While we set up the tent, it (began, begun) to rain.
10. The hamburgers were ready, so we (began, begun) eating.

Say It Right   Hear It Right

Say these sentences until the correct use of the verbs sounds natural to you.

1. What *broke* in the kitchen?
2. Paula *has broken* a plate.
3. My bike *broke* down on the way home.
4. Have you ever *broken* a leg?
5. I once *broke* a finger.
6. The clock radio is *broken*.
7. Ms. Berger *broke* up the argument in the hall.
8. Lorne *had* already *broken* his promise.
9. Carly *broke* the high jump record.
10. What *have* you *broken*?

Write It Right

Write the correct verb from the two forms given. Check your answer by saying the complete sentence to yourself.

1. The chick has (broke, broken) out of the shell.
2. My pencil (broke, broken) again.
3. The sand dollars on the beach are all (broke, broken).
4. The lamp was (broke, broken) into a hundred pieces.
5. His glasses (broke, broken) when he fell.
6. Mitch has finally (broke, broken) in his new hiking boots.
7. The second bus must have (broke, broken) down.
8. All the plates in this box are (broke, broken).
9. We (broke, broken) open the coconut with a hammer.
10. Jim (broke, broken) the eggs into the frying pan.

Use the Right Word

Say It Right   Hear It Right

Say these sentences until the correct use of the verbs sounds natural to you.

1. I *did* my homework before dinner.
2. Gerry *had* never *done* any woodworking before.
3. Denise *did* everything she could to help.
4. Who *has*n't *done* the assignment?
5. The cast *did* an extra show.
6. *Have* you ever *done* needlepoint?
7. The cleanup crew *did* a great job.
8. What *was done* about the leaky faucet?
9. Cheryl's science project *has* never *been done* before.
10. Kate *did* her best on the balance beam.

Write It Right

Write the correct verb from the two forms given. Check your answer by saying the complete sentence to yourself.

1. I (did, done) all I could to pass my test.
2. What have you (did, done) with your report card?
3. Those pictures were (did, done) by Carlos.
4. Mary (did, done) the shoveling by herself.
5. I haven't (did, done) a thing about the broken window.
6. We (did, done) most of the work ourselves.
7. Has Mike (did, done) his homework?
8. I should have (did, done) better on my painting.
9. Jack (did, done) more push-ups than anyone else.
10. Faith (did, done) an excellent science project.

Say It Right   Hear It Right

Say these sentences until the correct use of the verbs sounds natural to you.

1. What *have* you *eaten* for breakfast?
2. I *ate* eggs and toast this morning.
3. Skip *has eaten* all of the salad.
4. Paula *ate* a delicious slice of watermelon.
5. Johnny *had* never *eaten* oysters before.
6. Hot peppers *are eaten* in Mexico.
7. We *ate* a small lunch before the race.
8. *Haven't* you *eaten* yet?
9. Snails *are eaten* with butter and garlic.
10. Wendy *ate* four apples.

Write It Right

Write the correct verb from the two forms given. Check your answer by saying the complete sentence to yourself.

1. The squirrels have (ate, eaten) all the crumbs.
2. Teddy has (ate, eaten) the last piece of bread.
3. Shelly (ate, eaten) dinner with us last night.
4. Al had just (ate, eaten) breakfast when the phone rang.
5. We should have (ate, eaten) our lunch in a shady spot.
6. Tim has (ate, eaten) the rest of the popcorn.
7. By morning, the raccoons had (ate, eaten) all of our food.
8. Kevin has (ate, eaten) his lunch in a hurry.
9. Why haven't you (ate, eaten) your breakfast?
10. Ruth must have (ate, eaten) one of my sandwiches.

Say It Right   Hear It Right

Say these sentences until the correct use of the verbs sounds natural to you.

1. Who *gave* you that book?
2. The roller coaster *has given* me a stomachache.
3. Kim *gave* John some tips on ice skating.
4. The conductor *had given* me the wrong change.
5. Tom *gave* me a ride home yesterday.
6. *Haven't* you *given* your report yet?
7. Our team *gave* a cheer for Coach Long.
8. Ellen *has given* me her new address.
9. Only Susan *had given* the correct answer.
10. Bob *gave* the dog a shampoo.

Write It Right

Write the correct verb from the two forms given. Check your answer by saying the complete sentence to yourself.

1. My mother has (gave, given) me a dollar to buy lunch.
2. Officer Wendell (gave, given) a talk on traffic safety.
3. Calculators were (gave, given) as door prizes.
4. The manager (gave, given) my sister a raise.
5. Linda (gave, given) me a piece of cranberry bread.
6. I was (gave, given) a bike for my birthday.
7. Eric may have (gave, given) the book to Ms. Coleman.
8. The class (gave, given) Sandy a going-away party.
9. I have (gave, given) Bobby my best model car.
10. Has Lois (gave, given) you a copy of the contest rules?

Say It Right   Hear It Right

Say these sentences until the correct use of the verbs sounds natural to you.

1. Why *has* Laurie *gone* home early?
2. She *went* home sick.
3. My notebook *is gone* again.
4. Gilbert *went* to the band concert with his cousin.
5. I *had* never *gone* sailing before.
6. Everyone but Pete *went* to the picnic.
7. *Have* you ever *gone* to Missouri?
8. Nina *went* on an errand.
9. Betty *must have gone* fishing in the motorboat.
10. Jeff *went* for a ride on his bike.

Write It Right

Write the correct verb from the two forms given. Check your answer by saying the complete sentence to yourself.

1. Do you know where Ken's family (went, gone)?
2. They have (went, gone) camping again.
3. Fortunately, the hurricane had (went, gone) out to sea.
4. Has Julie (went, gone) already?
5. We haven't (went, gone) to a basketball game lately.
6. Ms. Jamison (went, gone) to the Smoky Mountains last year.
7. My family has always (went, gone) away for Christmas.
8. Last year, we (went, gone) to Washington.
9. The entire class has (went, gone) on a field trip.
10. When we looked, the deer had (went, gone).

Say It Right   Hear It Right

Say these sentences until the correct use of the verbs sounds natural to you.

1. Hank's puppy *has* really *grown.*
2. The injured starfish *grew* a new leg.
3. *Have* you ever *grown* a cactus?
4. The farmer *grew* all sorts of vegetables.
5. The lioness *had grown* too old to hunt.
6. Delicious strawberries *are grown* in Michigan.
7. The noisy crowd *grew* louder and louder.
8. The tomatoes *have grown* rapidly.
9. Terry *grew* pleased with his new school.
10. Country music *has grown* in popularity.

Write It Right

Write the correct verb from the two forms given. Check your answer by saying the complete sentence to yourself.

1. The climbers had (grown, grew) too tired to continue.
2. Mom has (grew, grown) impatient with Larry's practical jokes.
3. The thunder (grew, grown) louder as the storm continued.
4. I have (grew, grown) much closer to my dad.
5. Thick, green ivy has (grew, grown) all over the old house.
6. Rita had finally (grew, grown) tall enough to play basketball.
7. The pollution problem has (grew, grown) even larger.
8. I (grew, grown) weary of reading and fell asleep.
9. Some pineapples are (grew, grown) in Puerto Rico.
10. Palm trees have (grew, grown) all over the island.

Say It Right   Hear It Right

Say these sentences until the correct use of the verbs sounds natural to you.

1. Judy *knew* that she had passed the test.
2. Our family *has known* the O'Neills for years.
3. *Had* you *known* that Kurt was worried?
4. North Carolina *is known* for its beauty.
5. We *knew* that the snow would melt by morning.
6. I always *knew* about Frank's talent for painting.
7. How long *have* you *known* Susan?
8. Dogs *are known* for their loyalty.
9. The sportscaster *should have known* the score.
10. Everyone *knew* that the suspect was lying.

Write It Right

Write the correct verb from the two forms given. Check your answer by saying the complete sentence to yourself.

1. Only Gail (knew, known) how to repair the bicycle.
2. John Galvani is (knew, known) as Jackie to his friends.
3. I have never (knew, known) anyone as stubborn as Debra.
4. No one could have (knew, known) that answer.
5. Steve and Carlos have (knew, known) him for years.
6. Our cat Eleanor would have (knew, known) how to protect herself.
7. Dad never (knew, known) his cousin Rosemary very well.
8. If only I had (knew, known) you were home!
9. Everyone had (knew, known) that the work would not be easy.
10. I have always (knew, known) when I could do better.

Say It Right   Hear It Right

Say these sentences until the correct use of the verbs sounds natural to you.

1. *Have* you ever *ridden* a horse?
2. The surfer *rode* the waves.
3. We *should have ridden* to school on the bus.
4. Mom's new car *rode* well.
5. The cowboy *has ridden* back to the ranch.
6. The posse *rode* their horses to the badlands.
7. Five people *have ridden* together on this sled.
8. Keith *rode* a train across the country.
9. At night we *rode* with lights on our bikes.
10. In London, horses *are ridden* by some police officers.

Write It Right

Write the correct verb from the two forms given. Check your answer by saying the complete sentence to yourself.

1. The executive (rode, ridden) in the first-class section.
2. Janet (rode, ridden) her bike on the nature trail.
3. Bo (rode, ridden) in his uncle's sailplane.
4. Even the cat (rode, ridden) along on the trip.
5. Ramon has (rode, ridden) the bronco.
6. Portia has (rode, ridden) the roller coaster.
7. Horses were (rode, ridden) by Pony Express carriers.
8. Some people in the parade (rode, ridden) unicycles.
9. The sailors had (rode, ridden) out the storm.
10. The clowns had (rode, ridden) elephants around the ring.

Say It Right   Hear It Right

Say these sentences until the correct use of the verbs sounds natural to you.

1. The meeting *ran* late.
2. The grocery store *has run* out of milk.
3. Michelle *ran* for class president.
4. *Have* you ever *run* a mile?
5. We think our cat *ran* away.
6. The old car *hadn't run* for years.
7. Who *ran* up the stairs?
8. Marathon races *are run* in many cities.
9. Mary *ran* into an old friend from school.
10. The quarterback *should have run* with the ball.

Write It Right

Write the correct verb from the two forms given. Check your answer by saying the complete sentence to yourself.

1. I have never (ran, run) a lawnmower before.
2. Mom stopped baking because she had (ran, run) out of flour.
3. Our gym class hasn't (ran, run) the fifty-yard dash yet.
4. Bicycle races are (ran, run) on a bowl-shaped track.
5. Paul (ran, run) the carousel at the school carnival.
6. The team had (ran, run) out of energy.
7. Cara (ran, run) every morning last summer.
8. The stalled truck must have (ran, run) out of gas.
9. Franklin D. Roosevelt (ran, run) for President four times.
10. Anita will (ran, run) with the track team.

Say It Right   Hear It Right

Say these sentences until the correct use of the verbs sounds natural to you.

1. *Have* you *seen* Billy?
2. I *saw* him in the gym an hour ago.
3. Angelina *has seen* three plays.
4. We *saw* a mysterious looking man.
5. I thought I *had seen* him somewhere before.
6. Darin *saw* him, too.
7. The suspect *was* last *seen* this morning.
8. Who *has seen* Cindy's gloves?
9. Astronomers *have seen* Mars through their telescopes.
10. Loretta *saw* her mistake in the math problem.

Write It Right

Write the correct verb from the two forms given. Check your answer by saying the complete sentence to yourself.

1. Joey says he once (saw, seen) a UFO.
2. Lana (saw, seen) the tennis match.
3. I have already (saw, seen) that movie.
4. We had (saw, seen) that card trick before.
5. Connie (saw, seen) deer and wild turkey on the island.
6. The Patriots game wasn't (saw, seen) on local TV.
7. Have you ever (saw, seen) the President in person?
8. Terry (saw, seen) her guests to the door.
9. Has anyone (saw, seen) my pencil?
10. No one (saw, seen) Vincent run out the back door.

Say It Right   Hear It Right

Say these sentences until the correct use of the verbs sounds natural to you.

1. Kevin *took* the twins to the movies.
2. *Have* you *taken* your vitamins?
3. Tim *took* his sled to Squirrel Hill.
4. This seat *is taken.*
5. What *took* you so long?
6. Ginger *has taken* her sister to school.
7. I *took* first prize in the art fair.
8. Betty *had* often *taken* a taxi before.
9. The prisoner *was taken* to a cell.
10. Lee *took* a course in woodworking.

Write It Right

Write the correct verb from the two forms given. Check your answer by saying the complete sentence to yourself.

1. Shouldn't we have (took, taken) the Taylor Road bus?
2. Keith has (took, taken) out a book about tennis.
3. It has (took, taken) me an hour to get home.
4. Good friends are sometimes (took, taken) for granted.
5. Aunt Charlene (took, taken) me to a double-header.
6. Who could have (took, taken) the clothes to the cleaners?
7. It has (took, taken) you long enough to get ready.
8. Lucy (took, taken) many pictures on her trip.
9. Peter has (took, taken) the baby for a walk.
10. The injured boy was (took, taken) to the nurse's office.

Use the Right Word

Say It Right   Hear It Right

Say these sentences until the correct use of the verbs sounds natural to you.

1. Janie *wrote* the note in green ink.
2. *Has* anyone *written* to Uncle George?
3. I *wrote* to him the other day.
4. The report *was written* neatly.
5. *Have* you *written* your name on your paper?
6. Donna *wrote* another story about her brother.
7. Louis *had* never *written* a poem before.
8. Alexis *wrote* her name in the guest book.
9. The message *is written* in code.
10. Mr. Johnson *wrote* the instructions on the board.

Write It Right

Write the correct verb from the two forms given. Check your answer by saying the complete sentence to yourself.

1. I like the poems that you (wrote, written).
2. Everyone has (wrote, written) his or her name on my cast.
3. Lupé's letter was (wrote, written) in Spanish.
4. My neighbor has (wrote, written) a mystery story.
5. Ms. Jacobson (wrote, written) the year in Roman numerals.
6. Haven't you (wrote, written) to your pen pal?
7. Geraldo should have (wrote, written) in ink.
8. I had (wrote, written) so much that my hand hurt.
9. Have you ever (wrote, written) to a newspaper?
10. I must have (wrote, written) five letters to Sally.

ADDITIONAL EXERCISES

Using Irregular Verbs

Irregular Verbs   Write the correct verb from the two forms given. Check your answer by reading the sentence to yourself.

1. A loud cheer (began, begun) the pep rally.
2. A thief has (broke, broken) into the safe.
3. Our class (wrote, written) a letter to the mayor.
4. Sherry (gave, given) away the ending of the movie.
5. Bart (did, done) a flip off the diving board.
6. The Davis family (went, gone) on a camping trip last summer.
7. Grandpa could have (ate, eaten) the whole salad.
8. Carrie and Jill (knew, known) how to plant the garden.
9. The usher has (took, taken) our tickets.
10. Kirk (ate, eaten) the rest of the grapes for lunch.
11. The commander (gave, given) an order to the troops.
12. The team has (gone, went) into a huddle.
13. Margie's sunburn (grew, grown) painful.
14. Cindy (knew, known) the magician's secret.
15. The sheik (rode, ridden) a white stallion.
16. Ed has (began, begun) to read an exciting book.
17. All the children have (ran, run) to the ice cream truck.
18. We (saw, seen) the movie at the drive-in.
19. Susan (did, done) a lot of work for the school play.
20. C.S. Lewis has (wrote, written) good science fiction.
21. The glass (broke, broken) in the dishwasher.
22. That avocado pit has (grew, grown) into a plant.
23. Haven't you (rode, ridden) a bicycle?
24. The horses should have (ran, run) around the track.
25. Cliff (saw, seen) that movie on television.

MIXED REVIEW

Using Irregular Verbs

A. Identifying irregular verbs Write the correct form of the verb from those given in parentheses. After each verb, write *Present, Past,* or *Past Participle.*

1. Dad has (given, gave) me money for the tickets.
2. I (known, know) the answer.
3. Patti has (took, taken) French for two years.
4. The chorus (sang, sung) songs by Stephen Sondheim.
5. The storm (damaged, damage) many houses.
6. I (seen, saw) Roger at the library.
7. The plant has (outgrown, outgrew) its pot.
8. The sparrow's eggs were (stolen, stole) from the nest.
9. Laura (gone, went) to camp last summer.
10. I have (chose, chosen) an album by Men at Work.
11. Brad (writes, written) to his grandparents every week.
12. We (watch, watched) the fireworks last night.
13. Emily has (swam, swum) in two oceans.

B. Using irregular verbs Write each of the following sentences, using the form given in parentheses.

1. Carol (past of *give*) us a hand.
2. The lake has (past participle of *freeze*).
3. Terry (past of *run*) all the way home.
4. Shelly (present of *speak*) English and Spanish.
5. The baby robins have (past participle of *fly*) away.
6. The runners (past of *drink*) two quarts of lemonade.
7. The children have (past participle of *go*) to bed.
8. I have (past participle of *wear*) this jacket before.
9. Doug often (present of *steal*) second base.
10. The movie (past of *begin*) on time.

USING GRAMMAR IN WRITING
Using Irregular Verbs

A. Have you ever bought something and been sorry about it later? Was it a record, a game, or some item of clothing? Was it a ticket to a concert or a movie? Write a short paragraph about what you bought and why it was a mistake. In your paragraph use several of the following irregular verbs. Be sure to use the correct form of each verb.

buy	begin	take
give	see	teach
speak	have	throw
break	ride	wear
do	say	grow

B. Imagine that you just got home from one of the best parties ever. Before you go to sleep, you want to write about it in your journal. Use the past or the past participle form of five or six of the following verbs in your journal entry:

go	swim	take
dance	choose	wear
eat	bring	ride
sing	know	have

C. You have a new cat. Someone has asked why you named your pet "Trouble." Explain why in a paragraph. Use each of the following verbs, in the form shown. Remember to use helping verbs with past participles.

spill (past)   *chase* (past)
drink (past participle)   *break* (present)
scratch (past participle)   *run* (past participle)

Using Troublesome Verbs Correctly

There are some verbs that people find troublesome to use correctly. You have studied irregular verbs. In this section, you will learn about other verbs that cause problems. You will then be able to use these verbs correctly, too.

> We was waiting for you.
> Here is some cookies.
> Rodney set down to watch TV.
> The Burtons don't have no pets.

Can you find the trouble spots?

Part 1 Using the Right Form of *Be*

You have already learned that the verb *be* has many forms:

is	was	am	being
are	were	be	been

Some of these forms may be used alone or as helping verbs. Others may be used only *with* helping verbs.

Here are five important rules to remember when using the forms of the verb *be*. Each rule is followed by example sentences. Read each of the sentences aloud. When you hear the verbs used correctly, you will be able to remember the rules more easily.

1. If the subject names one person, place, or thing, use the forms *is* and *was*.

Christine *is* here.   She *is sitting* near me.
Teddy *was* here.   He *was called* away.

2. If the subject names more than one person, place, or thing, use the forms *are* and *were*.

The children *are* late.   They *are riding* their bikes.
The cookies *were* on that plate.   They *were eaten* at lunch.

3. When the subject is *you*, use the forms *are* and *were*.

You *are* my best friend.   *Are* you *coming* with me?
You *were* the fastest swimmer.   You *were doing* a good job.

4. When the subject is *I*, use the forms *am* and *was*.

I *am* here.   I *am studying* English.
I *was* at home.   I *was sleeping* in bed.

5. Use a helping verb before the forms *be*, *being*, and *been*.

Do not use one of these forms alone or as the only helping verb before a main verb.

Karen *will be* here later.
The patient *was being taken* to surgery.
Jeff *has been looking* for you.
These directions *have been* hard to follow.

Exercises   **Use the right form of *be*.**

A.   Number your paper from 1 to 10. Write the correct form of *be* from the two given in parentheses.

1. George and Eileen (is, are) my neighbors.
2. I (is, am) a forward on the basketball team.
3. (Is, Are) you the team captain?
4. The TV (been, has been) on for several hours.
5. You (was, were) blocking my view.
6. (Was, Were) Craig and Janet going roller skating?
7. The Great Dane (being, was being) playful.
8. Your backpack (is, are) loaded with books.
9. Nancy (be, is) a figure skater.
10. The boys (been, were) practicing for the band concert.

B.   Follow the directions for Exercise A.

1. Tammy and I (is, are) building a bird feeder.
2. I (am, is) just guessing his age.
3. (Is, Are) you a good sport when you lose?
4. Jorge (be, is) feeding the fish in the science lab.
5. I (am, be) helping by cooking dinner tonight.
6. Eric and Sam (been, have been) at the beach.
7. The haunted house (was, were) torn down.
8. They (was, were) building a fort in the snow.
9. You (was being, were being) silly.
10. (Is, Are) the passengers boarding the plane?

Part 2 Using the Right Verb After *There, Here,* and *Where*

Many sentences begin with the words *There is* or *There are.* How can you tell when to use each?

First find the subject of the sentence. The word *there* is never the subject. When a sentence begins with *there,* the subject usually comes after the verb.

> There is a squirrel in the tree. (*Squirrel* is the subject)
> There are the boats. (*Boats* is the subject)

Next, find out whether the subject names one person, place, or thing, or more than one. Then follow the rules for the forms of the verb *be.*

Can you decide which form to use in each of these sentences?

> There (is, are) a motor in that boat.
> There (is, are) papers on the floor.

The subject in the first sentence is *motor.* The subject names one thing. You should have chosen *is.* The subject in the second sentence is *papers.* Since this names more than one thing, you should have chosen *are.*

The words *here* and *where* are also used to begin sentences. They cause the same problem as *there.* When should you say *Here is* or *Where is?* When should you say *Here are* or *Where are?*

You can tell by finding the subject. *Here* and *where* are never the subject. In sentences beginning with *here* or *where,* the subject comes after the verb. If the subject names one thing, use *is.* If the subject names more than one thing, use *are.*

> Here *is* the *trail.* (*Trail* is the subject of the verb *is.*)
> Where *is* the *door?* (*Door* is the subject of the verb *is.*)
> Here *are* the *pens.* (*Pens* is the subject of the verb *are.*)
> Where *are* the *books?* (*Books* is the subject of the verb *are.*)

Use the right verb after *There, Here,* and *Where.*

A. Copy these sentences, using the correct form of *be.*

1. Where (is, are) your friends?
2. There (is, are) five magazines on the table.
3. Where (is, are) the two broken bicycles?
4. There (is, are) a strong wind from the west.
5. Here (is, are) the oldest trees in the park.
6. There (was, were) a letter for Rick in the mailbox.
7. There (is, are) several students in the library.
8. Where (is, are) the Big Dipper?
9. (Was, Were) there any more apples on the tree?
10. Here (is, are) the computer program you need.

B. Follow the directions for Exercise A.

1. Where (is, are) my math book?
2. There (is, are) six tomatoes left.
3. Here (is, are) several old photographs.
4. Where (is, are) the keys for the car?
5. Here (is, are) a box of your old clothes.
6. There (is, are) a good reason for my mistake.
7. Here (is, are) the tracks of a big animal.
8. Where (is, are) my old blue jeans?
9. Here (is, are) the folder of papers you lost.
10. There (is, are) my two best friends.

Part 3 Some Confusing Pairs of Verbs

Some pairs of verbs cause trouble because they are alike in meaning. In this section you will learn how to use these verbs.

Learn and *Teach*

Learn means "to understand" or "to gain knowledge."

Everyone should *learn* to swim.

Teach means "to show how" or "to explain."

Can you *teach* me how to swim?

The principal parts of these verbs are:

learn, learned, learned   teach, taught, taught

Say these sentences until they sound correct and natural.

Learn

Present: The students *learn* new words by reading.
Past: Britt *learned* to read a compass.
Past Participle: I *have learned* some of the customs of India.

Teach

Present: Trained instructors *teach* diving.
Past: Ms. Voss *taught* us science last year.
Past Participle: My sister *has taught* me how to play Scrabble.

Exercise   **Use *learn* and *teach* correctly.**

Write the correct verb from the two given in parentheses.

1. Will you (teach, learn) me to play chess?
2. Ms. Casey (teaches, learns) eighth-graders.
3. I have (taught, learned) to operate our school's computer.
4. Mr. Dior (teaches, learns) ballet classes at his studio.
5. My sister has (taught, learned) me to ride a horse.
6. Beginners can (teach, learn) the game by watching.
7. By reading, Al has (taught, learned) about other lands.
8. Your parents (taught, learned) you good manners.
9. Ms. Fairbanks (taught, learned) our class about the birth of the solar system.
10. These students have (taught, learned) about programming.

Let and Leave

Let means "to permit."

> *Will* you *let* me borrow a pencil?

Leave means "to go away from."

> The bus *will leave* in an hour.

The principal parts of these verbs are:

let, let, let   leave, left, left

Say these sentences until they sound correct and natural.

Let

Present: *Let* me go!
Past: Tracy *let* her dog jump into the icy water.
Past Participle: My parents *have let* me decide that myself.

Leave

Present: *Leave* me alone.
Past: Kerry *left* the house in a hurry.
Past Participle: The girls *have left* us with the clean-up chores.

Exercise   Use *let* and *leave* correctly.

Write the correct verb from the two given in parentheses. Check by reading each sentence to yourself.

1. Don't (let, leave) the toast burn.
2. Our guests will (let, leave) soon.
3. Sometimes Dad has (left, let) me win at backgammon.
4. (Let, Leave) your suggestions in the box.
5. Have you (let, left) your gym shoes at school?
6. (Let, Leave) Earl choose the music for our videotape.
7. Will you (let, leave) your brother help us?
8. (Let, Leave) my books in the classroom.
9. Will Mom (let, leave) you attend camp this summer?
10. Ben and Molly have (let, left) their bikes in the yard.

May and Can

May refers to permission, or to something that is possible. *Might* is another form of *may*. There are no principal parts. Both *may* and *might* are used only as helping verbs.

> You *may* go to the beach.   We *might* see Frank there.

Can means "to be able to do something." *Could* is another form of *can*. There are no principal parts. *Can* and *could* are usually used as helping verbs.

> Tim *could* have done better.   I *can* speak Spanish.

Say these sentences until they sound correct and natural.

May

You *may* check out only five books.
May we use the gym after school?
Might I help?

Can

This ladder *can* reach the roof.
The dolphins *could* jump through hoops.
That librarian *could* have helped Al.

Exercise **Use *may* and *can* correctly.**

Write the correct verb from the two given in parentheses.

1. (May, Can) I borrow your ruler?
2. Magnets (may, can) attract metals.
3. Most magicians (may, can) make things disappear.
4. Lionel (may, can) fix anything.
5. Yes, you (may, can) have some dessert now.
6. Cats (may, can) see in the dark.
7. (Can, May) you tell me what time it is?
8. You (may, can) try my new camera.
9. No one (may, can) shout in the library.
10. (May, Can) we please feed the animals?

Set and Sit

Set means "to place something somewhere."

> *Set* the grocery bags on the counter.

Sit means "to rest in one place."

> I usually *sit* in the front seat.

The principal parts of these verbs are:

set, set, set   **sit, sat, sat**

Say these sentences until they sound correct and natural.

Set

> Present: The machine *sets* the crates on end.
> Past: Chuck *set* his books on the desk.
> Past Participle: The stage crew *has set* the props in place.

Sit

> Present: Kyle *sits* in the back row.
> Past: Connie *sat* in an inner tube.
> Past Participle: The girls *have sat* by the fireplace all evening.

Exercise   **Use *set* and *sit* correctly.**

Write the correct verb from the two given in parentheses. Check by reading each sentence to yourself.

1. I will (set, sit) the plates on the table.
2. Please (set, sit) in this chair.
3. We (set, sat) in the front row.
4. (Set, Sit) that heavy carton on the counter.
5. In music class we (set, sit) in small groups.
6. Margie (set, sat) the vase on the piano.
7. My dog will (set, sit) by my side.
8. Don't (set, sit) the ice cream on the stove.
9. Anne will (set, sit) under the hairdryer.
10. Did the old man (set, sit) his hat down?

Write the correct verb from the two given in parentheses. Check your answer by reading the sentence to yourself.

1. (May, Can) whales live underwater?
2. We will (let, leave) the campgrounds tomorrow.
3. (Set, Sit) your cards in front of you.
4. Beth has (taught, learned) me the words to the song.
5. (May, Can) we please open the gifts now?
6. Don't (let, leave) the water run.
7. Tall people should have (set, sat) in back.
8. Nobody (teaches, learns) babies to talk.
9. Sarah (may, can) stand on her head without help.
10. The coach will (let, leave) us rest now.
11. (May, Can) I see your new bike?
12. You should never have (let, left) your parrot out of its cage.
13. Henry (taught, learned) us the rules for basketball.
14. The movers will (set, sit) the furniture in place.
15. (Teach, Learn) me that card trick, Raoul.

Part 4   Using Contractions

Sometimes a verb is combined with another word to make one word. These shortened forms are called **contractions.** Here are some examples:

is not = isn't	that is, that has	=	that's
were not = weren't	will not	=	won't
I have = I've	where is, where has	=	where's
she would = she'd	can not	=	can't

When you write a contraction, use an **apostrophe** to show where letters have been left out.

Make contractions correctly.

A. Copy each contraction below. Place the apostrophe where it belongs.

1. Ive	5. theres	9. thats
2. well	6. arent	10. Im
3. theyve	7. dont	11. heres
4. cant	8. hes	12. isnt

B. Writing Copy the following sentences. Make a contraction of the underlined words in each sentence.

1. You are the first to arrive.
2. Francis has not eaten lunch yet.
3. They are all ready to go to the beach.
4. We are on Debra's softball team.
5. I will help you carry these books.
6. What has happened here?
7. I think she would like to go.
8. Beth will not go near snakes.
9. Where is the bike pump?
10. It is Bill's football.

Part 5 Using Negatives Correctly

Some contractions are made by joining *not* with certain verbs, like this: *is + not = isn't.*

The **apostrophe (')** takes the place of the *o* in *not*. These contractions are called *not*-words.

have + not = haven't			is + not = isn't	
were + not = weren't			do + not = don't	
would + not = wouldn't			could + not = couldn't	

380

The *no*-words are different. You can see *no* in all but one:

no   nobody   none   never
no one   nothing   nowhere

Together, the *not*-words and the *no*-words are called **negatives.**

Two negatives used together make what is called a **double negative.** Do not ever use double negatives. They are always incorrect.

Wrong: Melvin does**n't** do **nothing.**

Correct: Melvin does**n't** do anything.

or

Correct: Melvin does **nothing.**

The sentences below show the right way to use negatives. Read the sentences aloud until they sound correct and natural to you:

There is**n't** any flour left.
There is **no** flour left.

Do**n't** ever do that again!
Never do that again!

We have**n't** gone anywhere this week.
We have gone **nowhere** this week.

Have**n't** you ever ridden in a plane?.
Have you **never** ridden in a plane?

Exercises   Use negatives correctly.

A.   Copy these sentences. Choose the correct word from the two given in parentheses. Then read the completed sentence to yourself.

1. Doesn't (nobody, anybody) want to play tennis?
2. Don't those boys have (anything, nothing) to do?
3. Haven't you (never, ever) been to the ocean?

4. There isn't (none, any) of the stew left for us.
5. Adam doesn't go (nowhere, anywhere).
6. Isn't there (no one, anyone) we could ask?
7. There weren't (any, no) prizes left for Jason and her.
8. I guess no one (is, isn't) coming.
9. (Does, Doesn't) nobody want to sing along?
10. (Weren't, Were) none of you at the picnic?

B. Write the correct word from the two given in parentheses. Check your answer by reading the sentence to yourself.

1. There won't be (anything, nothing) left for lunch.
2. Those girls don't do (nothing, anything) wrong.
3. Nothing was (never, ever) said about the broken window.
4. We didn't hear (anybody, nobody) crying.
5. Doesn't (nothing, anything) ever go wrong at camp?
6. We don't want (any, no) trouble.
7. I couldn't see (nothing, anything) on the stage.
8. Isn't there (any, no) milk left in the carton?
9. The bus didn't have (no, any) empty seats.
10. Manuel's glasses (were, weren't) nowhere to be found.

ADDITIONAL EXERCISES

Using Troublesome Verbs Correctly

A. The Right Form of *Be*   Write the correct form of *be* from the two given in parentheses.

1. Lois (is, be) in the library.
2. Gregg and Jan (is, are) the goalies.
3. (Was, Were) you late for class?
4. The tomatoes (is, are) on the windowsill.
5. You (is, are) the first one here.
6. I (was, were) waiting for you.
7. Sue (be, has been) studying for the test.
8. The twins (was, were) absent today.
9. I (is, am) working tonight.
10. The cat (be, is) chasing the mouse.

B. The Right Verb After *There, Here,* and *Where*   Write the correct form of *be* from the two given in parentheses.

1. There (is, are) two reasons for our delay.
2. Here (is, are) the best map of the area.
3. Where (was, were) the children hiding?
4. There (was, were) no commercials on that station.
5. Here (is, are) the scripts for the show.
6. There (was, were) a message for you.
7. Here (is, are) the ambulance.
8. Where (is, are) the jello salad?
9. There (is, are) seven candles on the table.
10. Where (is, are) the jars of paste?

C. Confusing Pairs of Verbs   Write the correct verb.

1. Will you (learn, teach) me the school song?
2. Barb (let, left) her gym shoes in her locker.

3. (May, Can) we please take the subway downtown?
4. Bev and Gloria (set, sat) together on the bus.
5. Ms. Barnes (let, left) us choose our project topics.
6. (Let, Leave) Grace help herself.
7. You (may, can) have some cheese.
8. Eric (set, sat) his tray on the table.
9. Chuck (taught, learned) me how to drive the boat.
10. You (may, can) be excused now.

D. Contractions   Make a contraction of the underlined words.

1. We are writing a news article.
2. Roberto has not watered that plant for days.
3. I will never trust Freddie again.
4. What has been discussed in student council?
5. Dad said he would take us bowling.
6. Maria does not want dessert.
7. They have already left.
8. I could not eat the squid.
9. Steve should not have gone.
10. I have caught a cold.

E. Negatives   Write the correct word.

1. The curtain hasn't (never, ever) gone up on time.
2. I have (any, no) money left.
3. (Does, Doesn't) no one recycle aluminum cans here?
4. Report cards show (nothing, anything) but grades.
5. Haven't you (never, ever) attended a play?
6. We can't go (anywhere, nowhere) without a car.
7. (Weren't, Were) none of you listening?
8. Isn't (anybody, nobody) leaving soon?
9. There isn't (no one, anyone) on the stage.
10. Don't buy (no, any) more of these pens.

MIXED REVIEW

Using Troublesome Verbs Correctly

A. Using the right form of *be* after *there*, *here*, and *where* Make two columns on your paper. Label one *Subject* and the other *Verb*. Write the subject of each sentence below in the *Subject* column. Then choose the correct form of the verb given in parentheses and write it in the *Verb* column.

1. Here (is, are) your photographs.
2. Where (is, are) the library?
3. There (was, were) ten people in line.
4. Where (is, are) my track shoes?
5. Here (is, are) the list of names.
6. There (was, were) a flock of geese over the lake.
7. Here (is, are) the notes for my report.
8. There (is, are) a new program at school for children.
9. Where (is, are) the buried treasure?
10. Here (is, are) the answer to the problem.

B. Using the correct verb Write the correct verb for each sentence below.

1. (Learn, Teach) me that new dance.
2. Let's (set, sit) down and rest.
3. (May, Can) I borrow your pen?
4. We should (leave, let) Jay work by himself.
5. Don't (set, sit) your glass on this table.
6. Carrie (let, left) her bike out in the rain.
7. I (may, can) need your help.
8. My cousin (learned, taught) me to speak German last summer.
9. Please (let, leave) your boots outside the door.
10. Our class (set, sat) in the balcony.

C. Using contractions and negatives correctly Copy each of the following sentences. Write the underlined words as a contraction. Choose the correct word of the two in parentheses.

1. Erin <u>did not</u> do (anything, nothing) wrong.
2. I <u>have not</u> (never, ever) used Dad's camera.
3. Chuck <u>could not</u> think of (anything, nothing) to write.
4. We <u>can not</u> find (anybody, nobody) to play shortstop.
5. This desert <u>does not</u> get (no, any) rain.
6. She <u>is not</u> doing (anything, nothing) this evening.
7. <u>Do not</u> (never, ever) play with fire.
8. The king <u>will not</u> listen to (anyone, no one).
9. There <u>were not</u> (no, any) empty seats in the theater.
10. <u>Does not</u> (anybody, nobody) want another taco?

D. Using verbs correctly Six of the following sentences contain errors in the use of verbs. If a sentence contains an error, rewrite it correctly. If a sentence is already correct, write *Correct.*

1. We set near the water.
2. Karen learned me the magic trick.
3. Mr. Fisher taught the lesson well.
4. Where is my keys?
5. I be tired from swimming.
6. The bus left without Leon.
7. There were many questions about the assignment.
8. Here are another bag of plums.
9. Can I please look at your map?
10. Dan let me borrow his bike.

USING GRAMMAR IN WRITING
Using Troublesome Verbs Correctly

A. Do you ever feel that there are disadvantages to being a teenager? Write a paragraph telling about two or three things that are hard about being your age. Begin two sentences with the words *There is* or *There are,* and *Here is* or *Here are.* In the other sentences, include at least two of the following verbs. Use the correct form of each verb.

> learn—teach   let—leave—left   may—can

B. The following story was turned in to the sports editor of your school paper. The editor was too busy to rewrite it. She has asked you to do the job. She wants you to change any verbs followed by negative words into contractions. Be sure all other contractions are punctuated correctly. She also wants you to make sure there are no double negatives.

> Friday's game was not the best I have ever seen. Our basketball team was not in peak form. No one couldn't score. None of our opponents missed a shot. That isn't no exaggeration, either.
>
> Three of our best players were not playing because they had the flu. That is not the worst part. Forward "Ace" Green sprained his ankle. There wasnt no replacement for him.
>
> We haven't never played so badly. I hope we will not repeat the performance neither.

Using Pronouns

Part 1 Substituting Pronouns for Nouns

Read the two paragraphs below. Which paragraph sounds more natural?

Ned and *Carla* wanted to earn money to buy an aquarium. *Ned* and *Carla* asked *Ned* and *Carla's* mother for a job. *Ned* and *Carla's* mother told *Ned* and *Carla* that *Ned* and *Carla* could paint the garage. *Ned* and *Carla* worked hard. *Ned* and *Carla* earned enough money for the aquarium.

Ned and *Carla* wanted to earn money to buy an aquarium. *They* asked *their* mother for a job. *She* told *them* that *they* could paint the garage. *Ned* and *Carla* worked hard. *They* earned enough money for the aquarium.

Did you decide that the second paragraph sounds more natural? How did the second paragraph avoid using the names *Ned* and *Carla* too often? Try to find the places where the following words were used instead of those names: *they, their, them.* Can you find where *she* was used instead of *Ned and Carla's mother?*

The words *they, their, them,* and *she* are **pronouns.** Using pronouns in the second paragraph did not change the meaning of the paragraph, but it did improve the sound.

A pronoun is a word used in place of a noun.

You use pronouns to do three things.

1. To refer to yourself.
   I asked *my* mother to give *me* a ride.
2. To refer to the person you are talking to:
   Did *you* bring *your* camera?
3. To refer to other persons, places, or things:
   The people ran from the lion. *They* were afraid of *it.*

Like nouns, pronouns can be singular or plural. Study this chart:

The Forms of Pronouns

Singular Pronouns			
Person Speaking:	I	me	my, mine
Person Spoken To:	you	you	your, yours
Other Persons, Places, and Things:	he	him	his
	she	her	her, hers
	it	it	its
Plural Pronouns			
Persons Speaking:	we	us	our, ours
Persons Spoken To:	you	you	your, yours
Other Persons, Places, and Things:	they	them	their, theirs

Find the pronouns.

A. Write the pronouns used in each sentence below.

> Example: He gave me a new watch.
>
> He, me

1. I wore my new boots today.
2. Katy displayed her model ships in our classroom.
3. Steve, do you read comic books?
4. Dad brought me to the roller rink.
5. The horse tugged at its reins.
6. Roger told us a secret.
7. She took the rock and skipped it across the water.
8. The waitress asked them for their order.
9. Carrie threw snowballs at him and me.
10. We rubbed our hands to keep them warm.

B. Copy the sentences below. Use pronouns instead of nouns where they will make the sentences sound better.

> Example: Geno was riding Geno's bike.
>
> Geno was riding his bike.

1. Ted ran in the 50-yard dash. Ted was the winner.
2. Maria likes baseball, and Maria plays every Saturday.
3. The building is closed. The building is very old.
4. The men saw Jim walking down the road. The men waited for Jim.
5. Betty brought Betty's new book to school.
6. Tom and I are neighbors. Tom and I walk to school together.
7. The boys wore the boys' best suits for the program.
8. Sam is Lisa's brother. Sam is two years older than Lisa.
9. We ate the fruit. The fruit was cold and sweet.
10. Toni, would Toni lend me Toni's pencil, please?

Part 2 Using Pronouns as Subjects

You remember that the subject of a sentence tells who or what does something. Find the subject in each of these sentences:

> I visited my uncle.   He has a motorcycle.
> We drove along River Road.

Did you find that the subjects were the pronouns *I, he,* and *we?* These are three of the pronouns often used as subjects. Four others are *you, she, it,* and *they.*

Usually you will have no trouble using these pronouns as subjects. However, when the subject is compound, sometimes you may get confused.

Which of these sentences is correct?

> Rita and *she* played together.
> *or*
> Rita and *her* played together.

To decide which pronoun to use in a compound subject, use this simple test. Try each pronoun separately with the verb.

> She played.   Her played.

You can hear that *she* is the correct pronoun. So the correct sentence is *Rita and she played together.*

Use the same test when there are two pronouns in the subject.

> **Example:** (She, Her) and (I, me) took piano lessons.
> **Try:** *She* took piano lessons.   *Her* took piano lessons.
> **Try:** *I* took piano lessons.   *Me* took piano lessons.

Now you know the correct pronouns:

> *She* and *I* took piano lessons.

Here are two important rules for using pronouns as the subject of a sentence.

1. Only these pronouns may be used as the subject:

Subject Pronouns	
I	we
you	you
he, she, it	they

2. If the pronoun *I* is used with one or more nouns or pronouns as the subject of a sentence, put *I* last.

Robert and I were in Boston.   *He and I* saw the marathon.

Exercises Use pronouns as subjects.

A. Choose the correct words from those in parentheses.

1. Frances and (I, me) are going to a party.
2. Jane and (her, she) will be there.
3. Donald and (them, they) visit me often.
4. Philip and (he, him) went to the circus.
5. (Juan and I, I and Juan) ate the oranges.
6. You and (I, me) make a good team.
7. Ms. Coburn and (we, us) saw a movie yesterday.
8. Eva and (me, I) will finish the work.
9. (He, Him) and his mother painted his room.
10. (I and Donna, Donna and I) watched the parade.

B. Follow the directions for Exercise A.

1. Lydia and (I, me) started arguing.
2. Rusty and (them, they) don't play fairly.
3. Elena and (she, her) demonstrated a cartwheel.
4. Someday you and (me, I) will play on the varsity team.
5. (Me and Joanne, Joanne and I) apologized to Kim.
6. My parents, my teachers, and (I, me) had a meeting.
7. Uncle Jerry and (we, us) ate dinner at Ruth's house.
8. Alex and (he, him) are best friends.
9. Julie and (they, them) raced for the front seat.
10. (She, Her) and Carl caught two trout.

Part 3   Using Pronouns After Linking Verbs

Read these two sentences:

The doctor is *she.*   *She* is the doctor.

These sentences mean the same thing. As you can see, the pronoun following the linking verb *is* can be used as the subject without changing the meaning of the sentence.

Pronouns used after linking verbs are called predicate pronouns. Predicate pronouns are the same as those pronouns used as subjects. Read these sentences.

The best player was he.
He was the best player.

The semifinalists were Dan and I.
Dan and I were the semifinalists.

The newest members are she and Chris.
She and Chris are the newest members.

Remember to use only these pronouns after linking verbs:

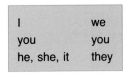

I	we
you	you
he, she, it	they

Exercises   Use pronouns after linking verbs.

A.   Write the correct pronoun from the two given in parentheses.

1. The new library aides are Darla and (he, him).
2. Tim's closest neighbors are Lee and (I, me).
3. The family's best golfers are (her, she) and Dad.
4. The only shoppers left were (them, they).

5. Your biggest fans are Deena and (me, I).
6. The lifeguards are Melissa and (I, me).
7. The first people in line were (her, she) and Rose's brother.
8. The co-captains are Stewart and (I, me).
9. The cooks for the banquet are Candy and (him, he).
10. My dad's bosses are (she, her) and Mr. Jones.

B. Follow the directions for Exercise A.

1. Kim's ski instructors were (her, she) and Tim.
2. The newest teachers are Mr. Reynolds and (she, her).
3. The fastest runners are (he, him) and Tony.
4. The newspaper's editor is (her, she).
5. The crossing guards are Vanessa and (he, him).
6. One of the disc jockeys is (her, she).
7. Our biggest rivals are (they, them).
8. Judith's lab partners are Jon and (he, him).
9. My favorite comedians are (she, her) and Bill Cosby.
10. The most reliable bus drivers are Curt and (her, she).

Part 4 Using Pronouns as Objects

Which pronoun should be used in each of these sentences?

1. The cat scratched (they, them).
2. Eddie asked Rachel and (she, her) a question.
3. Divide the candy among (we, us) now.

If you are not sure which pronoun to use in a sentence, first decide whether the missing pronoun is the subject or follows a state-of-being, or linking, verb. You know that if the pronoun is the subject or follows a linking verb, you use, *I, you, he, she, it, we, you,* and *they.*

If a pronoun is not used as the subject or as a predicate pronoun, use *me, you, him, her, it, us, you,* and *them.* These pronouns are called the **object pronouns.** Notice that the pronouns *you* and *it* stay the same as subject or object pronouns.

Object Pronouns	
me	us
you	you
him, her, it	them

In Example 1, the subject is *cat.* Since the missing pronoun is not the subject, you cannot use *they.* The correct sentence is: *The cat scratched* **them.**

In Example 2, what is the subject? Is the missing pronoun the subject? Since the missing pronoun is not the subject, you cannot use *she.* The correct sentence is: *Eddie asked Rachel and* **her** *a question.*

In Example 3, *you* is the understood subject. The missing pronoun is not the subject. Which pronoun did you choose? The correct sentence is *Divide the candy among* **us** *now.*

Exercises **Use pronouns as objects.**

A. Write the correct pronoun from the two given in parentheses. Then read the sentence to yourself.

1. Eduardo's mother called (him, he) and his brother.
2. The baseball coach called Bill and (I, me).
3. Would you like to visit Pete and (we, us)?
4. Sue chose Brian and (she, her) for the team.
5. Mort made dinner for Hal and (she, her).
6. Louella finally found Marion and (they, them).
7. Telephone Mike and (I, me) after the game.
8. Jan saw Mary Lou and (me, I) at the store.

9. Did you see Ann and (I, me) at the track meet?
10. Can you give Arlene and (she, her) your address?

B. Follow the directions for Exercise A.

1. The letter surprised Joan and (us, we).
2. Jody's father sent (he, him) a postcard from Kansas City.
3. My sister helped Ellen and (she, her) with the work.
4. Did you meet Valerie and (she, her) at the park?
5. I made hamburgers for (them, they) and me.
6. A loud crash frightened Angelo and (we, us).
7. The officer handcuffed Mills and (he, him).
8. Hit some fly balls to Emily and (me, I).
9. Mrs. Johnson settled the argument between Jason and (I, me).
10. Show Roberto and (she, her) to their seats.

Part 5   Using *We* and *Us*

Read each pair of sentences. In each pair, which sentence is correct?

1. We boys are going hiking.
   or
   Us boys are going hiking.

2. Have you ever seen us girls in a hockey game?
   or
   Have you ever seen we girls in a hockey game?

Read the sentences without the word *boys* or the word *girls*. You will see that in the first example the pronoun is part of the subject. *We* is the correct pronoun. The correct sentence is: *We* boys are going hiking.

In the second example, the pronoun is part of the object. *Us* is the correct choice. The sentence is: Have you ever seen *us* girls in a hockey game?

Whenever you have trouble choosing pronouns, try each pronoun alone in the sentence.

Exercises   **Use *we* and *us* correctly.**

A.   Write the correct pronoun for each sentence below. Check by reading each sentence to yourself.

1. (We, Us) girls went to the gym.
2. Mother sent (we, us) boys to the grocery store.
3. (We, Us) cyclists took our lunch with us.
4. In the woods (we, us) hikers saw a deer.
5. The new band costumes are for (we, us) two.
6. After lunch, (we, us) gardeners rested for a long time.
7. The coach praised (we, us) girls for our victory.
8. Terence told (we, us) Scouts about his climb.
9. The food was divided among (we, us) four.
10. Mr. Scott, this present is from (we, us) students.

B.   Follow the directions for Exercise A.

1. (We, Us) girls took the bus downtown.
2. The gentle pony nuzzles (we, us) visitors.
3. (We, Us) boys had a tug-of-war.
4. Finally, Jamie spotted (we, us) wanderers.
5. (We, Us) six planned a farewell party.
6. A net fell on top of (we, us) girls.
7. The child asked (we, us) bystanders for help.
8. The girls challenged (we, us) boys.
9. Together (we, us) swimmers pulled the boat to shore.
10. An acrobat performed for (we, us) boys.

Part 6 Possessive Pronouns

To make the possessive form of a noun, you add an apostrophe or an apostrophe and *s* to the noun. Pronouns have special possessive forms. These forms do not use apostrophes at all.

Here are the possessive pronouns.

Possessive Pronouns	
my, mine	our, ours
your, yours	your, yours
his, her, hers, its	their, theirs

Now read these sentences that use possessive pronouns:

This is *my* coat.   We have *our* tickets.
The coat is *mine.*   These tickets are *ours.*

Is that *your* hat?   Are those *your* books?
Is that *yours?*   Are those *yours?*

Here is *his* dog.   Do you like *their* pets?
The dog is *his.*   The pets are *theirs.*

Where is *her* cat?
This cat is *hers.*

Its and *It's*

The major problem most people have with possessive pronouns is confusing the possessive *its* with the contraction *it's*. **Its** (without the apostrophe) is the possessive form of *it*.

Example: That book is missing *its* cover.
(The cover belongs to the book)

It's (with the apostrophe) means *it is* or *it has*.

Example: *It's* a library book.
(*It is* a library book.)

Exercises   **Use possessive pronouns and *it's*.**

A. Copy these sentences. Include a possessive pronoun according to the information in the parentheses.

> Example: I found _____ notebook. (The notebook belongs to him.)
>
> I found his notebook.

1. _____ handwriting can be read easily. (The handwriting belongs to me.)
2. Did you see _____ faces? (The faces belong to them.)
3. Those keys are _____ . (The keys belong to you.)
4. Next comes _____ turn. (The turn belongs to him.)
5. The error is _____ . (The error was made by her.)
6. The reward is _____ . (The reward belongs to us.)
7. This is _____ chance. (The chance belongs to us.)
8. That was _____ mistake. (The mistake was made by me.)
9. The fingerprints are _____ . (The fingerprints belong to him.)
10. The pictures are _____ . (The pictures belong to them.)

B. Copy the following sentences. Insert apostrophes where they are needed.

1. Its a home run!
2. Its been raining for two days.
3. The leopard chased its prey through the tall grass.
4. What is its title?
5. The puppy wagged its tail when we came home.
6. My mother makes bread, and its delicious.
7. The railroad stopped its service to Clinton.
8. Our school has its own hockey team.
9. Grandpa has a beard. Its white and thick.
10. Its too early to buy tickets for the game.

ADDITIONAL EXERCISES

Using Pronouns

A. Recognizing Pronouns Write the pronouns in the following sentences.

1. Have you seen my algebra book?
2. Do you want to watch the football game with us?
3. Paul watered their plants while they were away.
4. Coach Ryan gave her a special award.
5. She and I have earned our lifesaving badges.
6. Cheryl showed me her stamp collection.
7. Our skating club meets Wednesday at 3:00.
8. Your brother, Darren, found it for me.
9. His handwriting is similar to mine.
10. Chris and he share a locker.

B. Subject Pronouns Write the correct pronouns.

1. Cora and (I, me) babysat for the triplets.
2. (Him, He) and his brother traded baseball cards.
3. (Her, She) and her sister work as cashiers.
4. The other team and (we, us) lined up for the kickoff.
5. Suzanne and (me, I) agreed on a plan.
6. You and (I, me) are on the same team.
7. Mark and (he, him) painted the garage.
8. Jill and (they, them) split the prize.
9. The horse and (she, her) walked around the ring.
10. (Clark and I, I and Clark) play in the jazz band.

C. Pronouns After Linking Verbs Write the correct pronouns.

1. The men in uniform were (him, he) and Dad.
2. Our school's nurse is (her, she).

3. The best dancers were George and (she, her).
4. The co-pilots are Jackie Miller and (he, him).
5. The only people in the audience were (us, we).
6. The leaders are Sara and (I, me).
7. The dance contest winners are (they, them).
8. Two new students are (she, her) and Joyce.
9. The masked pirates were Dennis and (he, him).
10. Our best runner is (she, her).

D. Object Pronouns Write the correct pronouns.

1. Geraldo gave directions to (they, them).
2. Francie invited (we, us) to her party.
3. Cathy split a banana with (me, I).
4. Brooke showed Mark and (her, she) the ballet steps.
5. A taxi took Diane and (he, him) to the airport.
6. The bus driver gave Adele and (I, me) directions.
7. Mom brought Lill and (she, her) to the movie theater.
8. The kangaroo punched (they, them) several times.
9. Give John and (I, me) some popcorn, please.
10. Craig lent the book to Gary and (he, him).

E. Using *We* and *Us* Write the correct pronoun for each sentence. Check by reading each sentence to yourself.

1. (We, Us) runners must train every day.
2. Ms. Stevens gave (we, us) students a special assignment.
3. (We, Us) three built a model of Sears Tower.
4. The pilot spoke to (we, us) passengers.
5. Without the map, (we, us) hikers would have been lost.
6. The tourists asked (we, us) guides for information.
7. Together (we, us) girls can move these desks.

8. Next year, (we, us) band members will have new uniforms.

9. The gym was decorated by (we, us) art students.

10. The platform will not hold all of (we, us) boys.

F. Possessive Pronouns Copy the following sentences. Where there is a blank, write the correct possessive pronoun.

1. Bill injured _____ ankle. (The ankle belongs to Bill.)

2. The company hires _____ own guards. (The guards belong to the company.)

3. The sketches are _____ . (The sketches belong to her.)

4. The car has kept _____ shine. (The shine belongs to the car.)

5. All of the ideas were _____ . (The ideas belong to them.)

6. That backpack is _____ . (The backpack belongs to me.)

7. Those are _____ new books. (The books belong to you.)

8. This garage is _____ . (The garage belongs to us.)

9. Marcy completed _____ report. (The report belongs to Marcy.)

10. Alex stapled _____ papers together. (The papers belong to Alex.)

MIXED REVIEW

Using Pronouns

A.   Using pronouns as subjects and objects   Write the correct pronoun from those given in parentheses. After each answer write *S* if the pronoun is used as a subject or *O* if the pronoun is used as an object.

1. (He, Him) babysits on Friday nights.
2. The coach gave (she, her) the trophy.
3. Ben and (I, me) painted the fence.
4. You and (she, her) are tied for first place.
5. Joel brought (I, me) the newspaper.
6. (He, Him) and I are tennis partners.
7. I will ride with (they, them).
8. (We, Us) live in the same building.
9. The stage manager showed (we, us) the dressing rooms.
10. Karla got a birthday card from Liz and (she, her).

B.   Using pronouns correctly   Write the correct pronoun from those given in parentheses.

1. The sound scared (they, them) and me.
2. Ms. McAllister and (they, them) chose the script.
3. The teachers were proud of (we, us) students.
4. You and (she, her) sang well together.
5. The winners are Christy and (I, me).
6. (We, Us) girls can play soccer on the south field.
7. We found (she, her) in the library.
8. Two members of the committee were Sandy and (he, him).
9. The stray dog followed Tim and (I, me) home.
10. I'll cheer for (they, them) at the game.

C. Using subject, object, and possessive pronouns
Change the underlined nouns to pronouns in the following sentences. After each new pronoun you write, write S (Subject), O (Object), or P (Possessive) to show what kind it is.

1. Carla is my younger sister.
2. Rob and Sam are finished with their project.
3. Sue and Katy are happy in their new home.
4. Jeff and I found it under your bed.
5. Jack gave his tickets to Rick and Tom.
6. It is Rita's turn to bat.
7. Greg showed me Greg's coin collection.
8. Paul told us about Paul's vacation.
9. Did you lend John and Kelly your books?
10. I bought it for Nancy.

D. Using possessive pronouns correctly   Six of the following sentences use possessive pronouns incorrectly. Rewrite those six sentences correctly. If a sentence is already correct, write *Correct.*

1. Its time for lunch.
2. The musical instruments are their's.
3. His dog and our cat got into a fight.
4. It's too late to call.
5. Are these records your's?
6. The raccoon dipped its food in the water.
7. Its their anniversary today.
8. The store closes its doors at six o'clock.
9. The video recorder is our's.
10. Its a very funny movie.

USING GRAMMAR IN WRITING
Using Pronouns

A. Almost everyone likes going to the zoo to watch the animals. Have you ever wondered how the animals feel? Imagine that you are an animal at the zoo. You might be a monkey. Perhaps you're an elephant, or a penguin. If you could talk, what would you say about the *people* you see at the zoo? Write a paragraph about what you would say. Use a number of different pronouns in your sentences. Underline each pronoun that you use.

B. You may have heard the saying, "You can't judge a book by its cover." This means our first impressions of something or someone may be wrong. For example, once you may have met someone that you didn't like at first. Later, he or she may have become a good friend. Write about an experience like this. In some sentences use a pronoun as the subject. In other sentences, use a pronoun as a direct or an indirect object. Use at least one possessive pronoun in your paragraph.

C. Imagine that you are running for president of your class. Write a short speech explaining why the students should vote for you. Mention the changes you would make in your school. Use at least four subject pronouns in your paragraph. Underline all the pronouns you use.

D. Imagine that after reaching your destination by airplane you and two friends can't find your luggage. You walk to the baggage claim booth to ask about your luggage and the luggage of the others in your group. Write the conversation that takes place. Use a possessive pronoun in each sentence.

Using Adjectives

Part 1   What Are Adjectives?

What do you see in your mind when you read this sentence?

I saw dogs.

The sentence expresses a complete idea, but it does not make the idea clear. It needs words to describe *dogs* more exactly. Here are four ways the sentence could be made clearer. What do you see when you read these sentences?

I saw huge, furry dogs.   I saw vicious, wild dogs.
I saw small, playful dogs.   I saw four lovable dogs.

The words *huge, furry, small, playful, vicious, wild, four,* and *lovable* tell more about *dogs*. They make the meaning of the word more exact. These words are called **adjectives.**

Adjectives are used with nouns and pronouns. They may come before the noun or pronoun they describe.

I saw *brown* and *black* dogs.

They may also come after the word they describe. Sometimes adjectives follow a linking verb and describe the subject.

The dogs were *friendly*.   They were *restless*.

Notice how differently the word *dogs* is described in these two sentences:

I saw small, playful dogs.
I saw vicious, wild dogs.

You can see that adjectives change, or *modify*, the meaning of the word they describe. For this reason, adjectives are called **modifiers**.

An adjective is a word that modifies a noun or pronoun.

Usually, when you use two or more adjectives together, you separate them with commas. Adjectives that tell *how many* do not have to follow this rule.

The *friendly, lovable* dogs belonged to *two young* children.
Several dangerous alligators lived in the *warm, murky* pond.

Exercise   Find the adjectives.

In each of the following pairs of sentences, only the adjectives have been changed. For each pair of sentences, list the nouns that are modified. After each noun, write the adjectives that modify it.

Example: a. The short *man* lifted the heavy *box*.
b. The strong *man* lifted the huge *box*.

man—short, strong   *box*—heavy, huge

1. a. The small girl ran through the grassy field.
b. The careless girl ran through the muddy field.

2. a. Twenty clowns wore colorful costumes.
   b. Wacky clowns wore silly costumes.
3. a. Many children won different prizes.
   b. Lucky children won valuable prizes.
4. a. Soft music played on an old radio.
   b. Classical music played on a new radio.
5. a. The large vase was filled with red flowers.
   b. The silver vase was filled with fresh flowers.

Some Adjectives Tell *What Kind*

Most of the adjectives used so far in this section describe *what kind*. Here are some adjectives used so far to tell *what kind*:

huge	brown	furry	vicious	playful
small	black	murky	dangerous	lovable
wild	warm	young	friendly	restless

In the last three columns, you can see five endings often found on adjectives: *-y, -ous, -ful, -able,* and *-less.*

Exercises **Use adjectives that tell *what kind.***

A. Read each sentence. Write each adjective that tells *what kind.*

1. Joyful shouts came from the stands.
2. Mr. Chalmers is a capable carpenter.
3. Jed wore his warm, red parka.
4. We sang funny songs on the long trip.
5. Marguerite threw out the old, dirty sneakers.
6. Cecilia put a large poster on the blank wall.
7. The spare room is a hopeless mess.
8. Max drew furry, monstrous creatures.
9. Long, colorful streamers hung from the ceiling.
10. A beautiful sunset lit the rosy sky.

B. Writing In this exercise, you will write your own sentences using adjectives that tell *what kind*. The following list gives ten nouns with an adjective modifying each noun. Write at least five sentences. Use two of the adjective-noun combinations in each of your sentences. You may add some adjective-noun combinations of your own in any of your sentences.

fearless captain	loud music
spicy pizza	helpful doctor
dark room	silky shirt
rocky ground	poisonous air
friendly face	thoughtful friend

Some Adjectives Tell *How Many*

Some adjectives tell *how many*. Here are examples of adjectives that tell *how many:*

six animals	*many* birds	*several* people
three stores	*few* lions	*more* insects

Exercises **Find adjectives that tell *how many*.**

A. Read each sentence. Write the adjectives that tell *how many*.

1. Two jets power the plane.
2. Eight children raced past our house.
3. A trainer groomed four horses.
4. We waited for the bus for forty minutes.
5. Curt read several books about China.
6. Lucinda put nine daisies in one vase.
7. The question has many answers.
8. The girls made a dozen candles.
9. Jupiter has many moons.
10. Few people knew the song.

B. For each sentence below, write the adjectives that tell *how many*.

1. Both eggs hatched.
2. The program lasts thirty minutes.
3. We picked three bushels of apples.
4. Mother bought a dozen doughnuts.
5. Ken did twenty push-ups.
6. Seven cars were damaged in the accident.
7. Few people were at the movie.
8. I have six dollars in my wallet.
9. Dee had one scoop of strawberry ice cream.
10. There are thirty students and only twenty-five desks.

Some Adjectives Tell *Which Ones*

Some adjectives tell *which one* or *which ones*. Here are four adjectives in this group that are used often:

> *this* team   *these* mitts
> *that* field   *those* players

Adjectives that point to persons, places, and things always come before the words they point to.

Exercise   **Find the adjectives that tell *which ones*.**

For each sentence below, write the adjective that tells *which ones*. Then write the noun that it modifies.

1. These jackets have pockets.
2. Those colors are my favorites.
3. This house has nine rooms.
4. Will this salad serve six people?
5. This book has many pages.
6. Several sandwiches are in that bag.
7. This record player has three speeds.

8. That octopus in the picture has only seven arms.
9. We bought sourdough bread at that bakery.
10. Some swans swim on that pond.

You have learned that adjectives modify nouns and pronouns. You have also learned that adjectives tell three different things about the nouns and pronouns they modify. Study this chart. It will help you to recognize adjectives and to use them correctly.

An adjective tells

what kind
how many
which one

**about the noun or pronoun
it modifies.**

Exercises Recognize adjectives.

A. Write each adjective and the noun it modifies.

1. Put these three blue boxes on that empty shelf.
2. We had several sheets of green paper.
3. Many young people crowded into one tiny room.
4. Look at that silver tray of delicious sandwiches.

B. Follow the directions for Exercise A.

1. Does that noisy dog herd this flock of sheep?
2. This tall lighthouse warns stray ships of dangerous rocks.
3. Hand me that old purple sweatshirt with long sleeves.
4. Two stocky men with dark beards rescued the weary campers.

Part 2 Articles

The words *a*, *an*, and *the* are called **articles.** Since they always modify nouns, they are also adjectives.

You may use the word *the* before singular or plural nouns beginning with any letter.

the alphabet   *the* sentences   *the* onion   *the* record

You may use the words *a* and *an* before singular nouns only. Follow these rules in choosing the correct article:

1. Use *a* before words beginning with consonant sounds:

   a person   *a* fresh egg   *a* story   *a* black olive

2. Use *an* before words beginning with vowel sounds:

   an average person   *an* egg   *an* impossible story

Some words begin with a silent *h*. In these words, you do not say the *h* sound. Instead, you begin the word with a vowel sound. Therefore, you follow the second rule, and use *an*.

an hour   *an* honor   *an* honest child

Exercises   **Use articles.**

A.   Copy these sentences. Fill in the blanks with *a* or *an*.

1. Do you keep _____ diary?
2. Judge Rogers is _____ honorable judge.
3. Sarah held _____ brush and _____ comb.
4. Gordon got _____ haircut.
5. The train left _____ hour ago.
6. _____ dachshund has _____ long body.
7. Diana tossed _____ horseshoe.
8. _____ old woman opened _____ umbrella.
9. I had _____ nightmare last night.
10. The forester carried _____ ax and _____ saw.

B. Writing There are eight nouns below. Write eight sentences, using one noun in each sentence. Place an article (*a*, *an*, or *the*) and another adjective before each noun.

1. wolf   3. movie   5. book   7. idea
2. lunch   4. team   6. sister   8. friend

Part 3 Predicate Adjectives

When an adjective follows a linking verb like *is* or *feels*, it is part of the predicate. However, it often modifies a noun or pronoun in the subject. Look at these examples:

The slopes looked *icy*.   Jill is *right*.
The patient seems *upset*.   They were *rude*.

When an adjective follows a linking verb and modifies the subject, it is called a **predicate adjective.**

Exercises **Use predicate adjectives.**

A. Writing Copy these sentences. Put a predicate adjective in each blank. Draw an arrow from the predicate adjective to the word it modifies.

1. Joel seemed _____ yesterday.
2. The buzzer on my alarm clock is too _____.
3. Our gym is _____ and spacious.
4. The strings on this tennis racket are _____.
5. This album is _____.
6. This country road is very _____.
7. A swan dive looks _____.
8. The sky was _____ and gray.
9. The price of those skis is too _____.
10. The berries on that tree are _____.

B. Write the predicate adjective in each sentence below.

1. Unless we hurry, we will be late.
2. That film is scary.
3. I will be nervous on stage.
4. CB radios are popular with truckers.
5. The food in the cafeteria tastes spicy.
6. The fruit on the tree looked ripe.
7. After dinner, Megan felt better.
8. Several of the records seem unbeatable.
9. The new fashions look weird.
10. The TV picture looks hazy.

Part 4 Proper Adjectives

In this section, you have already used many adjectives formed from common nouns: *furry, playful, lovable.* **Proper adjectives** are adjectives formed from proper nouns.

You know that a proper noun names a particular person, place, or thing. By adding adjective endings to some proper nouns, you change them into proper adjectives. Here are some examples:

Proper Noun	Proper Adjective + Noun Modified
Spain	Spanish music
China	Chinese food
Mexico	Mexican jewelry
Bible	Biblical verse

Very often a proper name is used as an adjective without the addition of an adjective ending. Here are some examples of the second kind of proper adjective:

Ford engine	Cinderella story
Hitchcock thriller	Beethoven symphony

A proper adjective is an adjective that has been made from a proper noun.

A proper adjective begins with a capital letter.

Use proper adjectives.

A. Write each proper adjective that you find in these sentences. Capitalize the proper adjectives.

1. Ms. Ames wears french perfume.
2. Jonathan asked for swiss cheese on rye.
3. Grandpa sent us a bushel of florida oranges and california avocados.
4. Scientists studied the martian soil.
5. We purchased a bushel of idaho potatoes to make german potato salad.
6. Paula wears italian shoes.
7. Do you enjoy mexican food?
8. Sue prefers dannon yogurt.
9. Nadia's brother has a dodge truck.
10. Two british ships docked in the harbor.

B. Follow the directions for Exercise A.

1. Carol sang an english folk song.
2. The french soldiers marched in long lines.
3. Some african countries export oil.
4. Are there guards at the canadian border?
5. Have you ever eaten german chocolate cake?
6. Some indian jewelry is made from turquoise and silver.
7. Drew is training for the olympic track team.
8. Many hollywood actors make commercials.
9. Craig's brother has a honda motorcycle.
10. The democratic candidate won the election.

Part 5 Using Adjectives Correctly

Four adjectives that tell *which one* or *which ones* are *this, that, these,* and *those.* When they modify nouns and pronouns, they point out specific things.

> *This* book is more interesting than *that* one.
> *These* pencils are sharper than *those* pencils.

Using *Them* and *Those*

Look at these sentences carefully.

> I saw *those* men on the airplane.
> Jeanie saw *them,* too.

The word *those* is an adjective. It tells *which* men. The word *them* is not an adjective. It is never used to point to a noun. *Them* is a pronoun. It is used *in place of a noun.*

> We found *those books* in the pack.
> Someone left *them* there.

Using *This Kind* and *That Kind*

The word *kind* sometimes causes problems. It means just *one kind.* If you want to speak of more than one kind, say *kinds.*

When you use an adjective to point to *kind,* use *this* or *that.* Never say "those kind" or "them kind."

When you use an adjective to point to *kinds,* use *these* or *those.*

Study the sentences below to see how these words are used.

> I like *this kind* of bicycle.
> I wore *that kind* of hat last year.
> *Those kinds* of tapes are the best.
> I like *those kinds* of books.

Choose the right word.

A. Write the correct word for each sentence. Check your choice by reading the sentence to yourself.

1. We like (them, those) plaid shirts best.
2. Do you have any of (those, them) magazines?
3. (This, Them, These) kind of tire is safest.
4. (Them, These) kinds of problems are very hard.
5. I use (that, those, them) kind of pen at school.
6. We read (those, them) books last summer.
7. (This, Them, These) kind of story appeals to me.
8. Will you take (those, them) packages to the office?
9. Where can I see (them, those) kinds of monkeys?
10. (Them, Those) clothes must be washed.

B. Follow the directions for Exercise A.

1. (Those, Them) firecrackers exploded.
2. (That, Those) kind of apple is tart.
3. Do (them, those) gloves keep you warm?
4. Audrey always makes (this, these) kind of tennis shot.
5. I am allergic to (that, them, those) kind of fruit.
6. (Those, Them) reins control the horse.
7. Queen Elizabeth wore (them, those) jewels.
8. Terry likes (this, these) kinds of projects.
9. Many farmers in the U.S. grow (them, those) grains.
10. Marietta builds (that, those) kind of model airplane.

Part 6 Making Comparisons with Adjectives

You often use adjectives to compare people, places, and things. The adjectives used to describe must be changed slightly when they are used to compare.

For example, you could describe two students with these sentences:

Marilyn is *tall*.
Frank is *tall*.

What if you want to compare the two, and to say that they are not the same size? You would use one of these sentences:

Marilyn is *taller* than Frank.
Frank is *taller* than Marilyn.

Now, suppose you want to compare a third student with Frank and Marilyn. Charles is taller than Frank, and taller than Marilyn. What would you say?

You probably gave this sentence:

Charles is the *tallest*.

Here are the rules for using short adjectives in comparisons:

1. When you compare two people, places, or things, you usually add -*er* to the adjective.

tall + er = taller   happy + er = happier
large + er = larger   funny + er = funnier

If the adjective ends in *e*, drop the *e* before adding -*er*. If the adjective ends in *y* following a consonant, change the *y* to *i* before adding -*er*.

2. When you compare more than two people, places, or things, you usually add -*est* to the adjective.

tall + est = tallest   happy + est = happiest
large + est = largest   funny + est = funniest

If the adjective ends in *e*, drop the *e* before adding -*est*. If the adjective ends in *y* following a consonant, change the *y* to *i* before adding -*est*.

Using *More* and *Most* in Comparisons

You do not always add *-er* or *-est* to make comparisons. If the adjective is a long one, use *more* and *most* instead of adding *-er* and *-est*.

Ted has been *more careful* since the accident.
Barbara was the *most careful* of the three girls.

My puzzle is *more difficult* than yours.
This is the *most difficult* dive of all.

Here are the rules for using long adjectives in comparisons:

1. Use *more* when comparing two persons, places, or things.

more difficult   more terrible   more dangerous

2. Use *most* when comparing more than two persons, places, or things.

most difficult   most terrible   most dangerous

Use only one form of comparison at a time. If you use *-er* or *-est*, do not use *more* or *most* in the same comparison. You would not say, "my brother is *more bigger* than I am." Instead, you would say, "My brother is *bigger* than I am." You would not say, "Our dog is the *most smartest* dog on the block." You would say, "Our dog is the *smartest* dog on the block."

The Forms of *Good* and *Bad*

A few adjectives change to become completely new words when they are used in comparisons. Here are two important adjectives of this kind:

good	better	best
bad	worse	worst

Read these examples:

> My father is a *good* bowler.
> Doug is a *better* pitcher than Dan.
> Is Patty the *best* swimmer in the class?

> The weather is *bad* today.
> Will tomorrow's storm be *worse* than this?
> The blizzard in Chicago was the *worst* storm this year.

Exercises   Make comparisons with adjectives.

A.   Some of the following adjectives add -*er* and -*est* when they are used in comparisons. Others are used with *more* and *most*. Copy each adjective. Then write the two forms it uses in comparisons.

> Examples: slow
> slow, slower, slowest
> colorful
> colorful, more colorful, most colorful

1. helpful	6. intelligent
2. dark	7. wonderful
3. dangerous	8. silly
4. pretty	9. curious
5. hard	10. great

B.   Write the correct adjective form for each sentence below. Check your choice by reading each sentence to yourself.

1. The cheetah is the (most fastest, fastest) animal of all.
2. A whale is (larger, more large) than an elephant.
3. Laura is the (most happy, happiest) baby I've seen.
4. This map is (more useful, usefuller) than the globe.
5. Pat is (carefuller, more careful) than Tom.
6. Darren is the (fastest, most fast) runner of all.

7. The lake is (more clean, cleaner) than it was last year.
8. Your house is (more large, larger) than ours.
9. The last math problem was also the (most hard, hardest).
10. This is the (most delicious, deliciousest) salmon I have ever eaten.

C. Follow the directions for Exercise B.

1. Which of the two pails is (larger, largest)?
2. I picked the (smaller, smallest) of the three packages.
3. This piece of cloth is the (biggest, bigger) of the two.
4. In our dance class, who is the (more graceful, most graceful)?
5. Was Harry's the (worse, worst) injury of the race?
6. I read the (longer, longest) of the three books.
7. Of the thirty flavors, which is (better, best)?
8. The (bigger, biggest) of the two packages was mine.
9. Which of the two ponies is (gentler, gentlest)?
10. In Jane's family, her mother is the (better, best) athlete.

ADDITIONAL EXERCISES

Using Adjectives

A. **Recognizing Adjectives** Write the adjectives in the following sentences. Beside each adjective, write the noun it modifies. Put the noun in parentheses. Ignore *a, an,* and *the.*

> Example: The young skater won two medals.
>
> young (skater), two (medals)

1. The teacher spoke in a quiet voice.
2. Jessica paints with vivid colors.
3. Those four magazines are for young people.
4. A large, muddy dog bounded into the full classroom.
5. David made a special sauce for the raw vegetables.
6. The new committee had several foolish plans.
7. That dentist uses modern equipment.
8. Many tall buildings line those elegant streets.
9. That boy has curly blond hair.
10. Jean wore one bracelet and four rings.

B. **Articles** Number your paper from 1 to 10. Write the correct article for each sentence.

1. The committee made (a, an) announcement about the art contest.
2. Susan found (a, an) unusual old coin.
3. Has anyone ever seen (a, an) live dinosaur?
4. (A, An) elevator is sometimes called a lift.
5. I'll be back in about (a, an) hour.
6. Our cat discovered (a, an) mouse in the basement.
7. The squirrel buried (a, an) acorn near its nest.
8. (A, An) taxi will cost too much.

9. The bride carried (a, an) bouquet of white flowers.
10. Beth has grown (a, an) inch this year.

C. Predicate Adjectives   Write the predicate adjective in each sentence.

1. That style of jacket is popular.
2. Our victory over the Wildcats was lucky.
3. The crowd in the street seems orderly.
4. The winners were grateful.
5. Everyone in class looked happy.
6. Is the sidewalk slippery?
7. These turnips taste bitter.
8. That book was enjoyable.
9. These shoes are tight.
10. The battery in the car is new.

D. Proper Adjectives   Write the proper adjectives in the following sentences. Capitalize them correctly.

1. The bread was made with california raisins.
2. Danny's favorite candy is english toffee.
3. The orchestra played music by german composers.
4. Todd prefers american cheese to swiss cheese.
5. A russian ballet company performed at the auditorium.
6. The museum has a display of american folk art.
7. Her songs have a nashville sound.
8. Please pass the french bread.
9. Honey and nuts covered the greek pastries.
10. The plane crashed in the brazilian jungle.

E. Using Adjectives Correctly   Write the correct word from those given for each of the following sentences.

1. Read (them, those) reports immediately.
2. (This, Them, These) kind of cloth is waterproof.

3. (Those, Them) kinds of flowers are hardy.
4. Look at (them, those) ducks on the pond.
5. Matt usually wears (this, these, them) kind of jacket.
6. Kelly saw (those, them) shoes on sale.
7. Aunt Julia likes (that, them, those) kind of soup.
8. Do you like (these, them) kinds of flowers?
9. (This, Them, Those) kind of knife is for cleaning fish.
10. Who has (those, them) newspaper articles?

F. Adjectives in Comparisons Write the correct form of the adjective from the two given.

1. Of the four questions, this one is (harder, hardest).
2. The sun seems (hotter, more hot) today than yesterday.
3. That measurement is (accuratest, most accurate).
4. This licorice is the (chewier, chewiest) I've ever had.
5. Is Sally (younger, youngest) than Ray?
6. Which of the two photographs is (older, oldest)?
7. The loss was their (worse, worst) defeat in three years.
8. Ron is the (better, best) speaker in our class.
9. That ladder is (sturdier, more sturdy) than this one.
10. That clown has the (saddest, most saddest) face of all!

MIXED REVIEW

Using Adjectives

A. Using articles and predicate adjectives Copy these sentences. Choose the correct word from the two given in parentheses. Write an adjective where the blank space is.

1. (A, An) owl is _____ .
2. (A, An) rainy day feels _____ .
3. (A, An) costume can be _____ .
4. (A, An) old friend is _____ .
5. (A, An) taco tastes _____ .
6. (A, An) igloo must be _____ .
7. (A, An) haunted house seems _____ .
8. (A, An) ocean breeze feels _____ .
9. (A, An) game of basketball is _____ .
10. (A, An) spy story is _____ .

B. Using adjectives that tell *how many, which ones* and *what kind* Make four columns on your paper. Label them *How Many*, *Which Ones*, *What Kind*, and *Noun Modified*. Write the adjectives from the following sentences in the correct columns. Write the noun that each adjective modifies on the same line as that adjective.

1. Several good players were injured in that game.
2. Dad will hang yellow and white wallpaper in the large bedroom.
3. This old sled has rusty runners.
4. Many customers complained about the slow service.
5. Jill used five quarts of blue paint.
6. He ordered two large glasses of orange juice.
7. I haven't seen that movie for several years.
8. Those girls weren't frightened by the big green bug.

9. The new mayor won by a few thousand votes.
10. Did you make these colorful pillows?

C. Using adjectives correctly For each sentence, write the correct adjective from the two given in parentheses. After each adjective, write the noun it modifies.

1. Darren's handwriting is the (better, best) in the class.
2. I like (them, those) grey mittens.
3. (This, These) kinds of flowers grow wild here.
4. A shark is (more dangerous, dangerouser) than a barracuda.
5. (This, These) box is heavier than (that, those) box.
6. What is the (most useful, usefulest) tool for this job?
7. These are the (worse, worst) strawberries I have ever eaten.
8. Jenny bought (those, this) kind of sweater.
9. George's score was (worse, badder) than mine.
10. Who is the (faster, fastest) player on the team?

USING GRAMMAR IN WRITING
Using Adjectives

A. You have just heard about a contest, called "I Scream for Ice Cream!" The sponsor, a dairy, is looking for a new flavor that everyone will "scream" for. Write a description of your new ice cream flavor. Tell why it's better than other flavors. Use as many vivid adjectives as you can. Use at least two adjectives in the comparative form. Underline all the adjectives. Circle any articles you use.

B. Imagine that you have been given permission to design and decorate a room of your own at home. What colors would the room be? What kind of furniture would it have? Would it contain any special equipment? Be creative. Write a paragraph to describe your wonderful new room. Include at least two predicate adjectives. Underline all the adjectives in your description. Draw an arrow from each adjective to the noun it modifies.

C. Your next door neighbor is a science fiction writer. Yesterday she told you that she is fresh out of ideas. She asked you to help her. She wants you to write about an imaginary planet for her next book. You will have to describe any forms of life on the planet. Include adjectives that tell *what kind, how many,* and *which ones.* Underline all the adjectives you use.

D. Make a proper adjective from each of the following proper nouns. Look in a dictionary if you need help with the spelling. Then use each proper adjective in a sentence: *Italy, Texas, Germany, Midwest, Japan.*

Using Adverbs

Part 1 What Are Adverbs?

In **Section 8,** you learned that adjectives are modifiers that tell *what kind, how many,* or *which ones* about nouns and pronouns.

There is another kind of modifier called an **adverb.** Study the examples below.

> The students worked **quietly.**
> The pigeons flew **away.**
> My train leaves **soon.**
> The clerk was **very** helpful.

Adverbs tell *how, where, when,* or *to what extent.* Adverbs can modify verbs, adjectives, or other adverbs.

Adverbs Modify Verbs

The baby crawled.

How? The baby crawled *quickly.*

Where? The baby crawled *everywhere.*

When? The baby *sometimes* crawled.

Adverbs Modify Adjectives

That box is heavy.

How heavy? That box is *terribly* heavy.

This is an interesting book.

How interesting? This is an *extremely* interesting book.

Adverbs Modify Other Adverbs

Dale eats hamburgers often.

How often? Dale eats hamburgers *very* often.

He never eats pizza.

To what extent? He *almost* never eats pizza.

An adverb modifies a verb, an adjective, or another adverb.

It tells *how, where, when,* or *to what extent.*

Many adverbs are formed by adding *-ly* to an adjective, as in these examples:

quick—quickly	happy—happily	powerful—powerfully
slow—slowly	sad—sadly	careless—carelessly

Here are some other examples of words often used as adverbs:

How?	well, hard, fast, much
Where?	here, there, everywhere
When?	now, never, always, often
To what extent?	very, too, quite, almost

If you are not sure whether a word is an adverb, ask yourself two questions. Does the word modify a verb, an adjective, or another adverb? Does it tell *how, where, when,* or *to what extent?* If you can answer *yes* to these questions, the word is an adverb.

Study this chart to help you recognize adverbs and to use them correctly.

> **An adverb tells**
>
> how
> when
> where
> to what extent
>
> **about a verb, an adjective, or another adverb.**

Exercises   **Use adverbs.**

A.   In these sentences the words in *italics* are adverbs. Find the verb that each adverb modifies.

1. Trigger whined *sadly,* but Luke left him behind.
2. Luke started *slowly* up the mountain.
3. He *carefully* watched where to put his feet.
4. One of the rocks slipped *suddenly.*
5. Luke scrambled *wildly* for a footing.
6. Then blackness surrounded him *completely.*
7. When he awoke, his head throbbed *painfully.*
8. He moved *slowly* in the darkness.
9. A cold nose touched his cheek *lightly.* It was Trigger!
10. Trigger barked *happily.*

B.   Write every adverb used in each sentence.

1. The bikers were hopelessly lost.
2. The hunters never found the deer.
3. This watch is always wrong.
4. The new hobby store opens tomorrow.

5. The driver instantly stopped the car.
6. Debbie tugged quite hard on the rope.
7. Leroy outgrew his clothes very quickly.
8. My canteen is almost empty.
9. The bus nearly hit the sign.
10. Merle peered timidly around the corner.

Part 2 Making Comparisons with Adverbs

Adverbs, like adjectives, can be used in comparisons.

John Henry worked *harder* than the steam engine.
He worked the *hardest* of all the drillers.

There are three ways adverbs change to show comparisons.

1. Some short adverbs add -*er* when two persons or things are being compared. They add -*est* when more than two are compared.

hard	harder	hardest	early	earlier	earliest
fast	faster	fastest	soon	sooner	soonest

2. Most adverbs that end in -*ly* use the word *more* in comparing two persons or things. They use *most* in comparing more than two.

carelessly	more carelessly	most carelessly
quickly	more quickly	most quickly

3. Some adverbs change their forms completely when they are used in comparisons.

well	better	best
badly	worse	worst
much	more	most
little	less	least

Exercises **Make comparisons with adverbs.**

A. Copy each adverb below. Then write the two forms it uses in comparisons. Use the guidelines on page 431 to help you.

1. rapidly
2. little
3. happily
4. naturally
5. fast
6. carefully
7. brightly
8. badly
9. loudly
10. well

B. For each sentence below, write the correct adverb form from the two given in parentheses.

1. Please wake me (earlier, more early) tomorrow.
2. Louise pushed (hardest, harder) than Dan.
3. The squirrel came (more near, nearer) to Jan than to Rob.
4. The new toaster works (more well, better) than the old one.
5. Of the two girls, Anna jumped (higher, highest).
6. Colin runs (faster, more fast) than I can.
7. Jess swam (better, best) today than yesterday.
8. The team played (best, bestest) in the finals.
9. Of the three cereals, I like Wheaties (least, littlest).
10. The large fish ate (most greedily, more greedily) of all.

C. Follow the directions for Exercise B.

1. Anna writes (neatlier, more neatly) than I do.
2. This sailboat finished the race (sooner, soonest) than that one.
3. Sequoias grow (taller, more tall) than other trees.
4. The swift flies (fastest, most fast) of all birds.
5. The fog spread (lower, more low) over the city.
6. This train rides (more smoothly, smoother) than any other.

7. Which of the two movies ends (most happily, more happily)?
8. Of the two girls, Donna was dressed (more warmly, most warmly).
9. Trish draws (better, best) of all the artists.
10. Train travel costs (less, least) than air travel.

Part 3   Adjective or Adverb?

Adjectives tell about nouns and pronouns. Adverbs tell about verbs, adjectives, and other adverbs. Sometimes it is hard to tell which modifier to use. This confusion happens because many adverbs and adjectives look alike.

Many adverbs are made by adding *-ly* to an adjective. See how this works:

> **Adjective:**   The *loud* music bothered me.
>
> **Adverb:**   We sang *loudly*.
>
> **Adjective:**   Traffic was *slow* tonight.
>
> **Adverb:**   Traffic moved *slowly* tonight.

Now look at this sentence:

> My brother Jim drives (*careful, carefully*).

Would you use *careful* or *carefully* in the sentence?

To find the answer, ask what you are trying to say. Are you trying to say:

> *how many* Jim drives?
> *which one* Jim drives?
> *what kind* Jim drives?

Or are you trying to say:

> *how* Jim drives?

You are trying to say *how*. The kind of word that tells how something happened or how something was done is an adverb.

This adverb modifies the verb *drives*. You would use the adverb *carefully* in this sentence.

My brother Jim drives *carefully*.

When you are choosing the correct modifier, ask yourself:

1. Which word does the modifier tell about?
2. What does the modifier tell?

This chart will help you to answer these questions.

An adverb tells	An adjective tells
how	what kind
when	how many
where	which one
to what extent	
about a verb, an adjective, or another adverb.	**about a noun or pronoun.**

Exercises **Choose the right modifier.**

A. Copy each sentence below. Choose the correct modifier from the two given in parentheses. Draw an arrow from the modifier to the word it modifies. Then write *Adjective* or *Adverb* to show how the modifier is used.

Examples: The batter hit the ball (solid, solidly).

The batter hit the ball *solidly*. Adverb

Carol was (hopeful, hopefully) about the test.

Carol was *hopeful* about the test. Adjective

1. I see (perfect, perfectly) without glasses.
2. Ramon ran (quick, quickly) to the corner.
3. Janet was (eager, eagerly) for the play to begin.
4. My father handles his tools (careful, carefully).
5. Harriet won the game (fair, fairly).

6. The sky was (clear, clearly).
7. Faith decorated the room (colorful, colorfully).
8. The old turtle moved (slow, slowly) through the grass.
9. The sun shone (bright, brightly).
10. A group of students talked (quiet, quietly) in class.

B. Follow the directions for Exercise A.

1. The younger children ran (noisy, noisily) to the gym.
2. The dinner smells (deliciously, delicious)!
3. The tractor moved (slowly, slow) across the field.
4. Dale spoke (soft, softly) on the phone.
5. The racer turned the corner (sharp, sharply).
6. The prospector made a (careful, carefully) search of the area.
7. Your serve is (near, nearly) perfect.
8. To their trainer, the animals seemed (hungry, hungrily).
9. Paul was (shy, shyly) with the strangers.
10. Lance stitched the seam (perfect, perfectly).

Using *Good* and *Bad,* and *Well* and *Badly*

You will have no trouble with the words *good* and *bad* if you follow this rule:

Use *good* and *bad* to describe nouns or pronouns. These words are adjectives.

> Examples: Jane has a good clarinet.   (what kind)
>
> Jim has a bad cold.   (what kind)

Follow this rule for using *well* and *badly:*

Well and *badly* are used with verbs to tell how something is done. When used in this way, these words are adverbs.

> Examples: Jane plays the clarinet *well*.   (*how* she plays)
>
> Jim behaved *badly*.   (*how* he behaved)

Well can also be used after a linking verb to mean "in good health." In this case, *well* is a predicate adjective.

I feel *well* today.

Exercises   **Use *good* and *bad*, and *well* and *badly*.**

A. Copy each sentence. Draw an arrow from each under-lined modifier to the word it modifies. Then write *Adjective* or *Adverb* to tell how each modifier is used.

Example: You are good at spelling.

You are good at spelling.   Adjective

1. Dark clouds are a bad sign.
2. Tina has good news.
3. Hank draws very well.
4. The ferris wheel is a good ride.
5. Rosa is good at playing comic roles.
6. That bike is in bad shape.
7. John feels well despite a nagging cold.
8. A bad storm delayed the shuttle launch for hours.
9. Last spring Matt had the worst cold ever.
10. Marva performs well on the balance beam.

B. Follow the directions for Exercise A.
1. The other team played badly.
2. Did you eat a good breakfast?
3. We planned the party well.
4. Tony has a bad temper.
5. My friend writes good letters.
6. The old car rattles badly.
7. A bad drought plagued the Midwest.
8. Jeff skated badly after he sprained his ankle.
9. Tim decided the rainbow was a good sign.
10. Rick felt well after a restful night.

ADDITIONAL EXERCISES

Using Adverbs

A. Recognizing Adverbs Copy each sentence. Circle the adverb. Draw an arrow from the adverb to the word it modifies.

> Example: Paint spilled everywhere.
>
> Paint spilled (everywhere.)

1. The cards were hidden somewhere.
2. The fly ball landed far in the outfield.
3. A new movie opened yesterday.
4. A snow plow slowly cleared the streets.
5. Grease from the pan splattered everywhere.
6. Our friends called later.
7. We arrived too late for the movie.
8. Janice almost forgot her club dues.
9. Brian practices the piano often.
10. Marla completed the puzzle quickly.

B. Adverbs in Comparisons Write the correct form of the adverb.

1. One actor spoke (more softly, most softly) than the other.
2. Jake walks the dog (more often, most often) than Beth does.
3. The train leaves (earlier, more early) on Tuesdays than on Mondays.
4. Of the three shirts, this one fits (better, best).
5. A helicopter flies (lower, lowest) than a jet.
6. Sue guessed the song title (faster, fastest) than I did.
7. Norman prints (more neatly, neatlier) than he writes.

8. The teachers dressed (more formally, most formally) than the students.
9. Of all the movies I've seen, that is my (least favorite, less favorite).
10. My bike stops (faster, more fast) than yours.

C. Adjective or Adverb? Write the correct modifier for each.

1. The police followed the suspect (close, closely).
2. Todd read that mystery (quick, quickly).
3. The accident happened quite (sudden, suddenly).
4. Last night's snowfall seems (light, lightly).
5. The downhill slope looked (dangerous, dangerously).
6. The scientist measured the chemicals (careful, carefully).
7. All of the contestants looked (nervous, nervously).
8. The pickles tasted (bitter, bitterly).
9. Ms. Rogers was (grateful, gratefully) for the help.
10. The pilot landed the jet (smooth, smoothly).

D. Using *Good* and *Bad*, and *Well* and *Badly* Write the correct modifier for each.

1. Marta has a (good, well) ten-speed bike.
2. She rides the bike (good, well).
3. Larry's bike has (bad, badly) brakes.
4. This radio sounds (bad, badly).
5. Vicky rides a horse very (good, well).
6. Mark has a (bad, badly) bruise on his arm.
7. Grandmother isn't feeling (good, well) today.
8. That cafe serves (good, well) food.
9. The new antenna works (good, well).
10. Rehearsal today went (bad, badly).

MIXED REVIEW

Using Adverbs

A. Finding and using adverbs Write the adverbs used in the following sentences. After each adverb, write the words it modifies. Write *how, where, when,* or *to what extent* to show what each adverb tells. Two sentences have two adverbs.

1. The swimmer glided easily through the water.
2. Do you always shop here?
3. We searched everywhere for the ring.
4. Karen was quite honest about her mistake.
5. Ted often forgets his homework.
6. The crew landed the aircraft smoothly.
7. Clara eats too fast.
8. I never saw the first Superman movie.
9. Paula quickly read the instructions.
10. Write your name here.

B. Making comparisons with adverbs Read each sentence below. Write the correct modifier from the two given in parentheses. Tell whether the modifier is an adjective or an adverb. Then write the word it modifies.

1. Julie knows (more, most) about computers than Ray.
2. Of the three dogs, Patch behaves (better, best).
3. Lynn runs (faster, more fast) than anyone on the team.
4. Of the planets, Venus shines (most brightly, brightliest).
5. Which animal is the (most smart, smartest)?
6. The good news spread (more quickly, quicklier) through Rob's class than Marilyn's.
7. Amy reads (better, best) than I do.
8. No one was hurt (bad, badly) in the accident.
9. Of all the players, Skip plays the (hardest, most hard).
10. Steve did his swan dive (perfectly, perfect).

USING GRAMMAR IN WRITING
Using Adverbs

A.   Following are two mini-poems. Notice that the subjects and verbs in each are the same. It is the adverbs that make the big difference in meaning. They tell how the action was done.

I	II
Softly I walked,	**Boldly** I walked,
Slowly I talked,	**Loudly** I talked,
Finally I stopped.	**Suddenly** I stopped.

Now write two mini-poems of your own. Use the subjects and verbs below in each poem. Put an adverb in front of each subject and verb. Then change the adverbs in the second poem. Make the two poems as different as possible. Do not use any of the adverbs that were used in the two poems above.

_____ I ran
_____ I leaped
_____ I danced
_____ I tripped
_____ I fell

B.   It's Saturday afternoon, and you have to take care of your neighbor's two children. You take them to the park. They love to swing, to play on the slide, to ride the merry-go-round and the see-saw, and to climb on the jungle gym. Describe the children as they play. Use adverbs that tell *when, where, how,* and *to what extent* an action happened. Include one or more adverbs in the comparative form. Also include at least one sentence in which you use *good* or *well.* Include another sentence that uses *bad* or *badly.*

Using Prepositions and Conjunctions

In this section you will learn about prepositions and conjunctions. These are words that have little meaning in themselves. They are used to connect words and groups of words. They are also used to show how one word in a sentence is related to another. Prepositions and conjunctions are important because they show relationships and combine ideas.

Part 1 What Are Prepositions?

Prepositions are words that show relationships. A preposition stands before its object. It shows how the object is related to another word in the sentence. Read this sentence:

The jet flew over Mexico.

In this sentence, *over* is the preposition. It stands before its object, *Mexico*. *Over* relates *Mexico* to *flew*.

The following prepositions are in italics. Find the object of each preposition and the word the object is related to.

Melanie walked *across* the playground.
Harry studied *before* the test.

In the first sentence, the preposition is *across*. Its object is *playground*. *Across* relates *playground* to *walked*.

In the second sentence, the preposition is *before*. Its object is *test*. *Before* relates *test* to *studied*.

A preposition is a word that relates its object to some other word in the sentence. It may show time, location, or people and things in special relationships.

Words Often Used as Prepositions

about	behind	except	on	to
above	below	for	onto	toward
across	beneath	from	out	under
after	beside	in	outside	until
against	between	inside	over	up
along	beyond	into	past	upon
among	but (*except*)	like	since	with
around	by	near	through	within
at	down	of	throughout	without
before	during	off		

Find the prepositions and their objects.

A. Number your paper from 1 to 10. Write the preposition and its object in each of the following sentences.

1. There is gum on my shoe.
2. Jeff opened his book to the index.
3. Our team can't compete under the new rules.
4. This portrait of George Washington is two hundred years old.
5. Louisa May Alcott wrote about her own times.
6. The cans on this shelf are dented.
7. We went bowling with my cousins.
8. The Plains Indians depended upon the buffalo.
9. The pinch hitter rifled the ball into left field.
10. Everybody in my family has blue eyes.

B. Writing Read each sentence. How many different prepositions can you find that fit each blank space? Refer to the list on page 442 to help you choose. Write at least two prepositions for each sentence.

> Example: Put the bench _____ the table.
>
> near, under, beside, behind

1. B. J.'s dog was playing _____ the house.
2. Cornelia heard a strange noise _____ the hall.
3. A flock of birds flew _____ the river.
4. Who put the butter _____ the oven?
5. An American flag flew _____ the house.
6. We found these coins _____ the bookcase.
7. The pen _____ the desk is mine.
8. The winners of the contest will travel _____ Alaska.
9. You'll find the sugar bowl on the shelf _____ the sink.
10. The clown jumped _____ the platform.

Using Prepositional Phrases

The group of words that includes a preposition and its object is called a **prepositional phrase.** All the words that modify the object are also part of the phrase.

> Example: We rode *in the bus.*
> We rode *in an old, broken-down bus.*
>
> Gail was waiting *for dessert.*
> Gail was waiting *for the special chocolate dessert.*

If a preposition has more than one object, all the parts of the object are included in the prepositional phrase.

> Example: Weeds grew *in the lawn, the flower garden, and the vegetable garden.*

Some sentences have more than one prepositional phrase.

> Bob works in the cafeteria with his friends.
> Every member of the team will play during the game.

Exercises **Find the prepositional phrases.**

A. Write the prepositional phrase or phrases that you find in each of the following sentences.

> Example: The yarn was stuck to the paper with glue.
>
> to the paper
> with glue

1. Everybody in the classroom saw the accident.
2. The doll beside the teddy bear has eyes made of black buttons.
3. We found a good spot for our picnic.
4. Maureen and her little brother played on the swings for hours.
5. Donald plays clarinet in the orchestra at school.

6. The acrobat balanced on the tightrope stretched between two buildings.
7. Mary Ann waited near the school until four o'clock.
8. Put the keys on the hook in the hall.
9. The apartment across the hall has been empty for a month.
10. Mother hung a clock with a flower design above the door.

B. Follow the directions for Exercise A.

1. During its journey, the space probe will travel past Venus.
2. Rosa tied a ribbon around the present for her cousin.
3. The puppy slept on a rug in the corner.
4. Janet finished her painting of the willow trees along the river.
5. Tell me about the characters in that story.
6. After the hurricane, the river spilled over its banks.
7. A squirrel ran up the maple tree outside my window.
8. You may choose among the last three items on the menu.
9. Dave shopped at the drugstore beside the new restaurant.
10. The team from El Paso plays against us before Thanksgiving.

Part 2 Objects of Prepositions

Using Nouns as Objects of Prepositions

You have seen that nouns may be used as subjects or objects of verbs. Nouns also are used as objects of prepositions. Here are some examples of objects of prepositions:

The campers pitched their tents *near the* **river.**
Mickey left his gym shoes *in his* **locker.**
The winning run was scored *by* **Bonita.**
The movie showed the arrival *of* **aliens** *on* **earth.**

Exercise **Find nouns used as objects of prepositions.**

Number your paper from 1 to 10. For each sentence, write each prepositional phrase and underline the noun that is the object of the preposition.

1. We all cleared the dishes from the table.
2. These Civil War photographs are by Matthew Brady.
3. Nobody in that movie is well known.
4. Elizabeth Blackwell began the study of medicine here.
5. The new computer will be delivered before Friday.
6. The temperature went below zero last night.
7. The lid on this jar won't budge.
8. When was gold discovered in California?
9. Around the Christmas tree were piled many presents.
10. The football sailed over the goal posts and into the stands.

Using Pronouns as Objects of Prepositions

When a pronoun is used as the object of a preposition, its object form must be used. The object forms are these:

Object Pronouns	
me	us
you	you
him, her, it	them

Examples: The prize was awarded *to us.*
Was there a message *for me?*
Laura's mother was looking *for her.*

Using Pronouns in Compound Objects of Prepositions

Usually you make few mistakes in using the object form of a pronoun as the object of a preposition. However, you may become confused when the object of a preposition is compound. Read the examples to yourself.

Simple Object	Compound Object
I talked *with* **her.**	I talked *with* **Darren** *and* **her.**
We stood *near* **him.**	We stood *near* **Jackie** *and* **him.**
Give that *to* **me.**	Give that *to* **her** *and* **me.**

If you are not sure which form to use, say the sentence with the pronoun alone following the preposition. Then say the complete sentence.

Example: We're waiting for James and (she, her).
We're waiting for *her.*
We're waiting *for James and her.*

Using *Between* and *Among*

Often people use the prepositions *between* and *among* as if there were no difference between them. There is a difference that you should know, so that you can use them correctly.

Use *between* to speak of two persons or things or two groups of persons or things.

Choose **between** *these two programs.*
The next game is **between** *the Jefferson High team and our team.*

Use *among* to speak of more than two. Here are examples:

We will divide the jobs **among** *Nancy, you, and me.*
There was a three-way tie **among** *the Yankees, the Red Sox, and the Indians.*

Exercises   Use pronouns as objects of prepositions.

A.   Choose the correct pronoun from the two given in parentheses. Write the complete prepositional phrase.

> Example: The villain shot at Superman and (he, him).
> at Superman and him

1. The coach called on Leo and (I, me).
2. The roof over Marcia and (them, they) started to leak.
3. Carrie lives near Juan and (she, her).
4. Will you sit beside your mother and (me, I)?
5. The car behind Beverly and (us, we) broke down.
6. A firecracker exploded near Timothy and (we, us).
7. My advice to Norita and (him, he) was ignored.
8. The wolves howled at Thompson and (they, them).
9. The album by James Taylor and (her, she) went on sale today.
10. The rivalry between Ohio State and (them, they) started years ago.

B.   Follow the directions for Exercise A.

1. On your cue, turn toward Ms. Bennett and (she, her).
2. As Paula hurried past Brian and (him, he), she waved.
3. Mr. Washington was looking at Jason and (I, me).
4. The puppy's high-pitched whine went right through Ginny and (we, us).
5. Terrence's kite flew above the boys and (he, him).
6. That car almost bumped into Gayle and (they, them).
7. I ordered a cheese and mushroom pizza for Susan and (her, she).
8. Everyone but Peter and (us, we) has had a turn.
9. The paper carried an article about (they, them) and the marching band.
10. My pet duck waddles after my friends and (I, me).

Part 3   Preposition or Adverb?

Several words used as prepositions are also used as adverbs.

Example: We looked *up.*   (adverb)
We looked *up the chimney.*   (preposition)

If you aren't sure whether a word is an adverb or a preposition, study the way it is used in the sentence. If it begins a phrase and has an object, it is probably a preposition. If it is used alone, it is probably an adverb.

Exercises   Find prepositions and adverbs.

A.   The word in italics is used both as an adverb and as a preposition. Number your paper from 1 to 10. After each number, write *a.* and *b.* After each letter, write *Preposition* or *Adverb* depending on which you find in that sentence.

Example: a. Look *out!*   b. Look *out* the window.
a. Adverb   b. Preposition

1. a. There was litter all *around* the store.   b. There was litter all *around.*
2. a. Don't come *near!*   b. Don't come *near* the cliff!
3. a. Can you get *past* the barrier?   b. Can that big Cadillac get *past?*
4. a. Those cans should be stored *underneath* the cabinet.   b. Those cans should be stored *underneath.*
5. a. Miguel will soon be coming *along.*   b. Miguel is coming *along* the path.
6. a. Please stand *by.*   b. Please stand *by* the window.
7. a. *Above* the fog, the lights glowed.   b. *Above,* the lights glowed.
8. a. A hiker climbed *up.*   b. A hiker climbed *up* the hill.
9. a. We've met *before* today.   b. We've met *before.*
10. a. Puffs of white smoke drifted *up.*   b. White smoke drifted *up* the chimney.

B. Follow the directions for Exercise A.

1. a. Agatha took her coat *off.*   b. Agatha took her coat *off* the hanger.
2. a. Many children walked *behind* the parade.   b. Many children walked *behind.*
3. a. *Beyond,* the sea stretched to the horizon.
   b. *Beyond* the rocky shore, the sea stretched to the horizon.
4. a. Cut the cake into layers and spread the filling *between.*   b. Spread the filling *between* the layers.
5. a. My friends are waiting *outside* the house.   b. My friends are waiting outside.
6. a. A DC-10 flew *over.*   b. A DC-10 flew *over* the playground.
7. a. The stuntman fell *down* the chute.   b. The stuntman fell *down.*
8. a. Don't just stand *around!*   b. Don't just stand *around* the kitchen!
9. a. Abigail opened the freezer and put the meat *inside.*   b. Abigail put the meat *inside* the freezer.
10. a. When the light changes, you can get *across.*
    b. When the light changes, you can get *across* the intersection.

Part 4   Using Prepositional Phrases in the Right Places

Some prepositional phrases may be moved from one position in a sentence to another without changing the meaning of the sentence. Here is an example:

We visited Meramec Cavern <u>during our vacation.</u>

<u>During our vacation</u> we visited Meramec Cavern.

To give your writing variety, begin a sentence with a prepositional phrase now and then. However, always placing a prepositional phrase at the beginning of a sentence can become boring. Try to begin sentences in a variety of ways.

Some prepositional phrases do not move easily from one position in a sentence to another. The position of the phrase can make a great deal of difference in the meaning of the sentence.

> **Example:** Walter touched the flower <u>with purple petals</u>.
>
> <u>With purple petals</u>, Walter touched the flower.

The second sentence suggests that Walter used purple petals to touch the flower. This prepositional phrase should not be moved away from flower, the word it describes.

> **Example:** Gerri called the dog <u>with a loud voice</u>.
>
> <u>With a loud voice</u>, Gerri called the dog.

The second sentence puts the prepositional phrase where it belongs, next to *Gerri*. This position makes the meaning much clearer. A prepositional phrase should be placed as close as possible to the word it tells about.

Exercises   **Use prepositional phrases correctly.**

A. The following sentences are confusing. By changing the position of one prepositional phrase in each sentence, you can make the meaning clear. Rewrite each sentence to make it clear.

1. Bill put the bowl on the table of potato chips.
2. The clock has Roman numerals over the mantel.
3. On the roof Marian spotted a squirrel.
4. Do you have the keys with you to the house?
5. Everybody signed Lisa's photo on the team.
6. With a torn cover, Gordon found an old math book.

7. On the clothesline, Thelma saw a chickadee.
8. The book isn't mine in my locker.
9. The pencils should be sharp on my desk.
10. From her aunt, Jennifer put away the hat.

B. Follow the directions for Exercise A.

1. A painting hung on the wall of a sunset.
2. Under the car, Dorothy noticed the softball.
3. Penelope made a puzzle in her room of the United States.
4. Albert wrote a story for the class about his cat.
5. With a curly red wig, Mr. Morgan watched the clown.
6. I have buttons on my dress of gold.
7. There is a beautiful carved mask in the museum of an Indian chief.
8. People for breakfast eat lots of eggs.
9. The special effects deserve a prize in that movie.
10. The crew in the distance sighted a whale.

Part 5 What Are Conjunctions?

You have learned that prepositions show relationships between words in a sentence. Relationships are also shown by another kind of word: a **conjunction.**

How is the word *and* used in each of these sentences?

> *Tracy* **and** *Deborah* went to the movie.
> The class *wrote* **and** *performed* the play.
> Allen's puppy *broke his leash* **and** *ran away.*
> Yastrzemski hit a *double* **and** two *singles* in the game.

Do you see that in each sentence, *and* connects words or groups of words of the same type? In the first example, *and* joins two subjects. In the second example, *and* joins two verbs.

In the third example, *and* connects two predicates. In the last example, *and* connects two direct objects. The word *and* is a conjunction.

A conjunction is a word that connects words or groups of words.

Two other conjunctions you use often are *but* and *or.* Like *and,* they may be used to connect sentence parts.

Andrew *or* **Ginny** will bring the potato chips.
   (compound subject)

Our forward **shot** *but* **missed.**
   (compound verb)

The class **could see a movie** *or* **study the science chapter.**
   (compound predicate)

Please buy **bread** *or* **rolls.**
   (compound direct object)

The package was **bulky** *but* **light.**
   (compound predicate adjective)

The orchestra performed for the **faculty** *and* **parents.**
   (compound object of a preposition)

Exercises   Use conjunctions correctly.

A.   For each of the following sentences, write the compound sentence parts and their conjunction. Circle the conjunction. Tell what kind of compound words you found. Write *Compound Subject, Compound Verb, Compound Predicate, Compound Direct Object,* or *Compound Object of a Preposition.*

Example: The Mets survived that season but finished last.

survived that season (but) finished last

compound predicate

1. The snow and ice made the roads impassable.
2. For breakfast, Lorraine likes eggs or oatmeal.

3. The wind shook the windows and whistled down the chimney.
4. I wrote a message on the box and the card.
5. Our television and stereo were stolen last night.
6. Gerald takes piano lessons but doesn't practice.
7. The puppy yawned and stretched.
8. Football and soccer are Lennie's favorite sports.
9. Trudy accidentally splashed Doug and me with her paint.
10. Tecumseh and his brother led their forces against the U.S. Army.

B. Write sentences with compound subjects, verbs, predicates, direct objects or objects of a preposition as the directions state. Use *and, but,* or *or.*

> Example: Compound direct object. Use a noun and a pronoun.
>
> Please take **Amy** *and* **me** to the library.

1. Compound subject. Use a noun and a pronoun.
2. Compound verb.
3. Compound direct object. Use two nouns.
4. Compound object of a preposition. Use two nouns.
5. Compound predicate.

ADDITIONAL EXERCISES

Using Prepositions and Conjunctions

A. Prepositional Phrases Write the prepositional phrases in each of the following sentences. Circle each object of the preposition. Some sentences have more than one prepositional phrase.

1. My birthday is in September.
2. Eddie found these shells on the beach.
3. There is a telephone call for Nerissa.
4. Jessica volunteers at the hospital during the summer.
5. When will *Star Wars* be on television?
6. Laina wants mint sherbet with raspberries.
7. We shone the flashlights into the cave.
8. Are you going to the sale on Saturday?
9. In California, winters are mild.
10. After lunch, we shopped for a gift.

B. Pronouns as Objects of Prepositions Choose the correct pronoun from the two given. Write the complete prepositional phrase.

1. The taxi splashed water onto Joan and (I, me).
2. Two FBI agents explained their work to (us, we).
3. A tall man sat in front of Chris and (I, me).
4. The scenery was designed by Lee and (she, her).
5. The play-offs are between the Tigers and (us, we).
6. The surprise party for (they, them) was postponed.
7. Clyde shares his locker with Brian and (he, him).
8. The messages were for Helen and (they, them).
9. Give your entry blank to Ms. Lee or (she, her).
10. The gift is from my brother and (I, me).

1. The runners jumped over the hurdles.
2. Below the deck the crew was working.
3. The Dodgers fell behind.
4. A light breeze rippled across the countryside.
5. We sang the national anthem and sat down.
6. The cats played outside.
7. Come in and relax.
8. The parakeet flew around the room.
9. The little girl blew the candles out.
10. Oil spilled onto the floor.

D. **Placement of Prepositional Phrases** The following sentences are confusing. By changing the position of one phrase in each sentence, you can make the meaning clear. Rewrite each sentence to make it clear.

1. In the pot, Paul placed the vegetables and the chicken broth.
2. The locket has my initials engraved in silver on it around my neck.
3. With a wagging tail, Lance saw the dog.
4. Myra bought the towel at the bazaar for her grandmother.
5. The crack is widening in the sidewalk.
6. Mr. Klein told a story to the students with a surprise ending.
7. Jesse in the wishing well saw a silver dollar.
8. Everybody sent a card to Joan in the class on her birthday.
9. From the teakettle Martin saw steam rising.
10. There is a model in the gift shop of the Sears Tower.

E. Conjunctions and Compound Sentence Parts Write each compound sentence part with its conjunction. Circle the conjunction.

1. This game requires skill and practice.
2. Cheryl or Denny will help me.
3. An omelette should be light and fluffy.
4. Carter read the paper but skipped the comics.
5. Ben dashed outside without a hat or gloves.
6. Meg can play the piano and the violin.
7. Band members and chorus members will be excused early.
8. The airline offered chicken or lasagne on the noon flight.
9. We mowed the lawn and weeded the garden.
10. Is the letter from Jenny or Sue?

MIXED REVIEW

Using Prepositions and Conjunctions

A. Finding prepositions and objects of prepositions
Make two columns on your paper. Label one *Prepositions* and the other *Objects of Prepositions*. For each sentence, write the preposition and its object in the correct columns. Some sentences have more than one preposition and object.

1. The cash register on the counter is made of brass.
2. For hot-air balloons, races are tests of accuracy.
3. The jockey on Daredevil wiped mud from his eyes.
4. There is a mass of wires behind the TV screen.
5. A wagon drawn by horses plodded through the snow.
6. Into the spotlight stepped the master of ceremonies.
7. Mom placed a bag of ice on my sprained ankle.
8. The sailboat glided under the bridge and into the harbor.
9. The box of old clothes is on the shelf in that closet.
10. The blimp flew over the stadium during the game.

B. Finding adverbs and prepositional phrases Make one column on your paper and label it *Adverbs*. Make a second column and label it *Prepositional Phrases*. Write each adverb and prepositional phrase that you find in the following sentences in the correct column. Every sentence does not have one of each.

1. You can sit beside me.
2. The flock of gulls flew away.
3. We drove past Independence Hall.
4. The skater fell down.
5. Walk carefully near those thorny bushes.
6. We stayed inside during the storm.
7. The movie was over at nine o'clock.

8. Tanya wished upon a star.
9. Keith hid behind an old locomotive in the station.
10. Did you let the cat out?

C. Using prepositional phrases correctly Nine of the following sentences do not use prepositional phrases correctly. In some, the prepositional phrase is in the wrong place. In others, the pronoun used as the object of the preposition is in the wrong form. Correctly rewrite any sentences containing errors. If a sentence is already correct, write *Correct*.

1. There's a robin's nest under the eaves.
2. The money is for the delivery person in the drawer.
3. We discussed our plans with Mr. Jacobs and they.
4. The mechanic crawled under the car.
5. Lisa told us about her trip to California at lunch.
6. David spread on the hot dog catsup and mustard.
7. Several students visited our school from Germany.
8. Don't leave without an umbrella.
9. I saw a bird with yellow wings.
10. In the file drawer Mrs. Dobbs neatly arranged the papers.
11. Jeannie sat in the bleachers with Paul and I.
12. I got a birthday card from her.
13. Without Eric and he, our team can't play.
14. We enjoyed the cool breeze from the lake.
15. The books are mysteries on this shelf.

D. Finding conjunctions and compound sentence parts
Write any compound subjects, compound verbs, compound predicates, compound direct objects, or compound objects of prepositions from the following sentences. Label each one. Underline the conjunction that connects the parts of each compound.

1. Jeff climbed the mountain and enjoyed the view.

2. Street vendors sell hot dogs and pretzels in the city.
3. The girls made their own Chinese kite and flew it.
4. These bushes provide food for birds and squirrels.
5. Ben or Molly will represent our class in the meet.
6. The wild horse pranced and reared.
7. Wendy found a fossil and an old coin among the ruins.
8. My mother and I made this quilt from scraps of old clothing.
9. The audience cheered and applauded.
10. Sylvia took the test and passed it.
11. Rosa borrowed my skateboard but did not return it.
12. We planted a lilac bush between the porch and the garage.

USING GRAMMAR IN WRITING
Prepositions and Conjunctions

A. It is your job to plan a treasure hunt to take place in your classroom. You are to write five clues. Each clue should contain one prepositional phrase. Use some of these prepositions:

above	behind	by	in	near
against	below	down	down	of
among	beneath	over	inside	off
around	beside	through	into	onto
upon	between	under	to	outside

Don't make your clues too easy. When you finish your sentences, write one more sentence that tells what the treasure is and where you hid it.

B. You have a whole day off from school. You can spend it as you like. Will you go to the shopping mall? Will you take a hike or a bike ride? Perhaps you will just stay home and listen to records. Tell about your day off. Use at least five prepositional phrases as you describe it. Underline each preposition you use. Circle the object of each preposition.

C. Describe two people in your class. You may first want to ask them some questions to get information. In your description, use most of the following conjunctions: *and, but, or, both-and, either-or, neither-nor.*

Using the Parts of Speech

Part 1 The Parts of Speech

You have studied verbs, nouns, pronouns, adjectives, adverbs, prepositions, and conjunctions. You have been learning to recognize these kinds of words and to use them correctly in sentences. The name used for these groups of words is **parts of speech.** There are eight parts of speech. In this section, you will review the parts of speech you have studied. You will also learn about another part of speech called **interjections.**

What Are Interjections?

In addition to the seven parts of speech you have studied, there is another part of speech called **interjections.**

An interjection is a word or short group of words used to express strong feeling.

An interjection may express surprise, joy, anger, or sadness. An interjection is often followed by an exclamation mark (!).
Look at these examples of interjections:

No way! I'm not singing by myself.
Congratulations!
Ouch! That hurts.
Great!

Now you have learned about all eight parts of speech.

The Parts of Speech			
nouns	verbs	adverbs	conjunctions
pronouns	adjectives	prepositions	interjections

A word fits into one of these groups because of the way it is used in a sentence.

Exercises **Recognize the parts of speech.**

A. Write each underlined word. Beside each word, write what part of speech it is.

1. Hamburgers were cooking on the grill.
2. Gail keeps her jewelry in a blue box.
3. I need a ride to town.
4. Luis smiled warmly at his friends.
5. Never! I wouldn't jump from here!
6. Tracy and Chuck can't keep secrets.
7. Vinnie peered at the sky through a telescope.

8. *The Farmer's Almanac* predicts the <u>weather</u>.

9. The tiger moved <u>suddenly</u> into sight.

10. Our group climbed sand <u>dunes</u> all morning.

B. Follow the directions for Exercise A.

1. <u>Oh, no</u>! It's raining.

2. Do <u>you</u> remember your dreams?

3. Hans is worried <u>about</u> the math test.

4. <u>Later</u> we will have a sing-along.

5. Too many <u>people</u> crowded onto the bus.

6. <u>These</u> lights warn of approaching trains.

7. Lisa's birthday cake had <u>twelve</u> candles.

8. You can get candy <u>or</u> gum from the machine.

9. The arrow <u>hit</u> the bullseye.

10. A water snake skimmed <u>across</u> the pond.

Part 2 Using Words as Different Parts of Speech

You cannot tell what part of speech a word is until you see how the word is used in a sentence. Many words can be used as different parts of speech.

In **Section 10,** you learned that the same word could be used as either an adverb or a preposition. Read this pair of sentences:

> Climb <u>up</u>.
>   (In this sentence, *up* is an adverb. It modifies the verb *climb*.)
> Climb <u>up</u> the ladder.
>   (Here, *up* is a preposition. Its object is the noun *ladder*.)

Other words may be used as different parts of speech. Here are more examples for you to study.

Please clear the table.
> (Here, *clear* is used as a verb.)

The day was clear and sunny.
> (And here, *clear* is used as a predicate adjective. It follows the linking verb *was* and it describes the noun *day*.)

Farmers plant wheat in the spring.
> (In this sentence, *plant* is used as a verb.)

This plant grows best in light, sandy soil.
> (In this sentence, *plant* is used as a noun.)

My father is a plant foreman.
> (Here, *plant* is used as an adjective. It describes the noun *foreman*.)

I feel very well.
> (Here, *well* is used as a predicate adjective. It follows the linking verb *feel* and describes the pronoun *I*.)

You skate very well.
> (In this sentence, *well* is an adverb. It describes the action verb *skate* by telling *how*.)

When a word is used as a certain part of speech, it follows the rules for that part of speech. For example, when you use *plant* as a noun, you form the plural by adding -*s: plants*. When you use it as a verb, you form the past tense by adding -*ed: planted*.

There is only one sure way to decide what part of speech a word is. Check to see how the word is used in the sentence.

Exercises **Recognize the part of speech.**

A. In each pair of sentences that follows, one word is used as two different parts of speech. Number your paper from 1 to 10. After each number, write *a*. and *b*. After each letter, write the word in italics and tell how it is used. It may be a noun, a verb, an adjective, an adverb, or a preposition.

1. a. I *brush* my hair.   b. This *brush* is plastic.
2. a. *Name* your favorite foods.   b. What's your *name*?
3. a. The bus turned *around*.   b. Joggers run *around* the block.

4. a. The store is *open*.　b. *Open* this box.
5. a. *Place* the book on the desk.　b. Where is a quiet *place?*
6. a. She must take the *late* bus.　b. The speaker arrived *late.*
7. a. Carol fixed a *light* snack.　b. Turn on the *light.*
8. a. Hold your arms *high.*　b. *High* waves hit the ship.
9. a. A motorbike zoomed *past.*　b. I rode *past* your house.
10. a. *Flag* down that car.　b. Which *flag* is blue and green?

B. Follow the directions for Exercise A.

1. a. We have a *color* TV.　b. What *color* is this?
2. a. The *last* act is best.　b. Which float comes *last?*
3. a. Rita has a new *watch.*　b. I *watch* the news every night.
4. a. Sunday was a *fine* day.　b. Does the judge *fine* people?
5. a. It's time for a *rest.*　b. Horses *rested* in the stable.
6. a. I asked for *more* milk.　b. Jody practices *more* often than Ed.
7. a. The young boys dashed *off.*　b. Randy flipped *off* the balance beam.
8. a. The ship *sails* soon.　b. One *sail* was ripped.
9. a. We followed a *dirt* path.　b. *Dirt* covered the floors.
10. a. A small cart trailed *behind.*　b. The cat lay *behind* a bush.

ADDITIONAL EXERCISES

The Parts of Speech

Parts of Speech Read each sentence. Write the underlined words. Then write what part of speech each of those words is.

1. Rena stuffed her notebook into a backpack.
2. Our entire class flew kites on the beach.
3. That movie was the true story of the discovery of radium.
4. The treasure was hidden underwater.
5. Three trees were uprooted during the tornado.
6. Allen found his friends at the baseball park.
7. Adam learned to type when he was ten.
8. We can reach the island by plane or ferry.
9. Hooray! School's out for the summer!
10. That campground has been closed since the dam burst.
11. Help! This boat is sinking!
12. Maggie removed the horse's saddle.
13. Did anybody bring the hot dog buns?
14. The cowhand finally roped the steer.
15. A hot-air balloon drifted slowly above the countryside.
16. The boat sailed away.
17. The newsstand sells magazines and comic books.
18. What are the key issues in the campaign?
19. Finally, the storm blew over.
20. Jamie tossed a pillow at her brother.
21. Give this letter to Mr. Scott.
22. Can we help them with their work?
23. You left the car door open.
24. They attended a music festival.
25. Do you shop at the new mall in Hazeltown?

MIXED REVIEW

The Parts of Speech

Identifying the parts of speech Write the underlined word or words in each of the following sentences. Then write its part of speech.

1. She climbed cautiously up the stairs to the dark attic.
2. Mom caught three rainbow trout.
3. No way! I washed the dishes last night.
4. Scott can swim under water for two minutes.
5. These jeans are too short for me.
6. Karla has brown eyes and wavy black hair.
7. They are going to Tennessee and Kentucky during their vacation.
8. He can sit in the back with his friends.
9. Marc planted twenty tulip bulbs last fall.
10. Kit's bike needs a new chain.
11. The runner slid into third base.
12. We met them after the concert.
13. The store will reopen in September or October.
14. All the water leaked out.
15. We were lost without a map.
16. Patti is fourteen years old.
17. Liz can only babysit during the day.
18. Wow! I can't wait until Saturday.
19. She hurried but missed the bus.
20. Dad refinished this old rocking chair.

USING GRAMMAR IN WRITING
Using Parts of Speech

A. Read the following advertisement. Notice the underlined words in it. Make a list of those words and write the part of speech of each word as it is used in the advertisement.

> You will <u>love</u> the new Mighty Bike! Its <u>design</u> is outstanding. Its <u>wheels</u> grip the hills. It <u>climbs</u> faster and performs <u>better</u> than any other dirt bike. Mighty Bike has <u>power</u>, <u>speed</u>, and <u>control</u>. Stop in today at your nearest bike <u>shop</u> to test drive it!

Now, choose any five words from the list. Use each word in a sentence.

B. Many people, especially poets, enjoy playing with words. They like to rhyme words. They also like to use words in different ways—as different parts of speech, for example. Here are two lists of rhyming words. Choose one of the lists and write a four-line poem. Each line should end with one of the rhyming words. Write the part of speech of each rhyming word you use.

Now, write one sentence for each of the rhyming words you used. Write what part of speech each rhyming word is used as in each sentence.

brick	glow
kick	slow
trick	hoe
pick	low
sick	row
tick	show

CUMULATIVE REVIEW
The Parts of Speech

A. Identifying parts of speech There are twenty under-lined words in the following paragraph. Decide what part of speech each word is used as. Number your paper from 1 to 20. Write *Noun, Verb, Pronoun, Adjective, Adverb, Preposition,* or *Conjunction* for each word. Be sure to check *how* the word is used in the sentence.

A new water <u>event</u> was introduced <u>at</u> the 1984 Summer Olympics <u>in</u> Los Angeles. This exciting sport
is <u>called</u> boardsailing. A <u>small</u>, colorful sail is attached
to an <u>ordinary</u> surfboard. The <u>boardsailor</u> must hold
the <u>sail</u>, control her direction, and stay <u>up</u>. Wind and
water <u>provide</u> the <u>fun</u> and challenge. Boardsailing is
not <u>very</u> difficult to learn, <u>but</u> <u>it</u> is necessary to have
an <u>instructor</u>. Anyone who <u>weighs</u> sixty-five pounds <u>or</u>
more can learn this sport. If <u>you</u> are interested, be
prepared for many dunkings. Boardsailors say you
<u>must fall</u> five hundred times before you master <u>the</u>
technique!

B. Recognizing how words are used Each of the follow-ing sentences contains an underlined word. Decide how that word is used. Number your paper from 1 to 15. Write *Subject, Verb, Direct Object, Object of the Preposition, Predicate Noun,* or *Predicate Adjective* to show what each word is.

1. Patti asked a difficult <u>question</u>.

2. After the party, the cleanup committee began its work.
3. Ron performed several card tricks.
4. Sandra's hair becomes lighter in the sun.
5. Jenna's dog is a Shelty.
6. Our class found several fossils in the rock.
7. Has your film been developed yet?
8. The trees behind the barn are silver maples.
9. We visited the Okefenokee swamp.
10. The farmers are hoping for more rain.
11. Ms. Beck showed us a film about first aid.
12. The river looks clean and clear.
13. The hurricane raged for five days.
14. Todd is usually tired after hockey practice.
15. Nicola is Luke's sister.

Making Subjects and Verbs Agree

Do these sentences sound correct to you?

The ham sandwich are good.
One star shine in the sky.
My friends is coming with me.
Many families goes on vacations.

If you listen carefully, these four sentences should sound incorrect to you. Each one of them breaks a basic rule of English grammar: The subject and verb in a sentence must agree.

Part 1 Rules for Making the Subject and Verb Agree

When a noun or pronoun names one thing, it is **singular** in number.

friend   bus   country   he

When a noun or pronoun names more than one thing, it is **plural** in number.

friends   buses   countries   they

Verbs, too, can be singular or plural in number. An *s* at the end of a verb shows that the verb is singular in number.

sings   crawls   speaks

If there is no *s* at the end of the verb, the verb is plural in number.

sing   crawl   speak

When a subject noun or pronoun in a sentence is singular, the verb in that sentence must also be singular. If the subject noun or pronoun is plural, the verb must be plural. When the subject and the verb in a sentence are both singular or both plural, the subject and verb are said to **agree in number**.

Read these examples:

Singular	Plural
Jane sings in the choir.	Some **girls sing** alto parts.
The **baby crawls** everywhere.	Most **babies crawl.**
Al speaks Spanish.	Those **boys speak** French.

Remember these rules:

1. The subject and verb in a sentence must agree in number.
2. If the subject is singular, use the singular form of the verb.
3. If the subject is plural, use the plural form of the verb.

Prepositional Phrases After the Subject

Be careful with prepositional phrases that come between the subject and the verb. Remember, the verb must agree in number *only* with the subject. The subject of the verb is never found in a prepositional phrase.

Read this sentence. Which verb would you choose?

The members of the team (practices, practice) every day.

In this sentence, *members* is the subject of the verb. *Of the team* is just a prepositional phrase describing *members*. Because *members* is plural in number, the verb must also be plural in number. *Practice* is the correct verb for this sentence.

The members of the team *practice* every day.

Here's another example. Which verb would you choose?

A flock of geese (visits, visit) this lake each spring.

In this sentence, *flock* is the subject of the verb. *Of geese* is just a prepositional phrase describing *flock*. Because *flock* is singular in number, the verb must also be singular in number. *Visits* is the correct verb for this sentence.

A flock of geese *visits* this lake each spring.

Exercises   **Recognize singular and plural forms.**

A.   On your paper, write the subjects listed below. After each subject, write *Singular* or *Plural* to tell whether it will take the singular or the plural form of the verb.

1. typewriter
2. kittens
3. ambulance
4. ravens
5. fingers
6. lesson
7. menu
8. members
9. teachers
10. treehouse

B. Write the subject and verb in each sentence. Write whether they are singular or plural.

1. The movie shows a strange creature.
2. This truck rides well over dirt roads.
3. Today's newspaper contains a good editorial.
4. The books on the bookcase fell.
5. A box of apples sits in the corner.
6. The nurses in the hospital work hard.
7. One package of raisins lasts all week.
8. Monica's parents camp frequently in Yellowstone.
9. The girls on our block play basketball after school.
10. A string of firecrackers makes a loud noise.

Special Forms of Certain Verbs

A few verbs have special forms that you should keep in mind.

Is, Was, Are, Were. The verb forms *is* and *was* are singular. The forms *are* and *were* are plural.

> Singular: The bus *is* here.   The bus *was* here.
> Plural: Our buses *are* here.   Our buses *were* here.

Has, Have. The verb form *has* is singular. *Have* is plural.

> Singular: Paula *has* a plan.
> Plural: They *have* a plan.

Does, Do. The verb form *does* is singular. *Do* is plural.

> Singular: Joe *does* the cooking.
> Plural: They *do* the cooking.

Exercises   Use the correct verb.

A. Write the correct verb from the two given.

1. New York City (has, have) a large population.
2. Every Sunday my family (have, has) a big breakfast.
3. The travelers (has, have) a lot of luggage.

4. Notre Dame (was, were) ahead at the half.
5. Franklin (does, do) his homework after school.
6. This ice-cream shop (has, have) twenty flavors.
7. Jan's left leg (is, are) in a cast.
8. These carpenters (does, do) a good job.
9. (Is, Are) calculators always right?
10. The winners of the tournament (is, are) proud.

B. Follow the directions for Exercise A.
1. Runners usually (does, do) warm-up exercises.
2. (Does, Do) the gymnasts use the rings?
3. Jerry (does, do) a great Eddie Murphy imitation.
4. The crate of oranges (is, are) heavy.
5. The waves in the Pacific (is, are) best for surfing.
6. This stack of letters (has, have) no addresses.
7. The bags by the door (has, have) gifts inside.
8. The dogs (is, are) in the kennel.
9. This batch of brownies (does, do) taste good.
10. Those pinball machines (was, were) fun to play.

Part 2 Special Problems with Subjects

Sometimes making subjects and verbs agree can be a little difficult. Some subjects are tricky to use. You can learn to use these tricky subjects with the correct verbs.

Certain Pronouns

The words listed below are singular pronouns. Each is used with a singular verb form.

each	either	everyone	anyone
one	neither	everybody	nobody

Read these sentences several times until they sound correct and natural to you.

> *Each* of my sisters *sings* well.
> *One* of the gymnasts *is practicing.*
> *Is either* of you *coming?*
> *Neither* of the stories *is* long.
> *Everyone does* homework.
> *Is anyone* home?
> *Nobody leaves* early.

Be especially careful when a singular pronoun is used as a subject followed by a prepositional phrase. If the object of the preposition is plural, don't make the mistake of using a plural verb form. Remember, the verb must agree *only* with the subject.

> Neither of the cars (is, are) new.
>   What is the complete subject? *Neither of the cars*
>   What is the prepositional phrase? *of the cars*
>   What is the subject? *Neither*
>   *Neither* is singular, so the verb must be singular.
> *Neither* of the cars *is* new.

Exercises Use the right verb form.

A. Copy these sentences, choosing the right form of the verb from the two given in parentheses. Circle the prepositional phrase that comes between the subject and the verb.

> Example: Neither of the movies (were, was) good.
>   Neither (of the movies) was good.

1. Neither of the bikes (works, work) well.
2. One of the library books (are, is) overdue.
3. Either of those routes (is, are) fast.
4. Each of the pets (need, needs) special care.
5. Everyone in our class (like, likes) a good joke.

6. Either of these radios (works, work) well.
7. Neither of the magazines (has, have) poetry.
8. One of the clues (leads, lead) to the treasure.
9. Everyone on the horses (ride, rides) well.
10. Each of the players (try, tries) hard.

B. Choose the right form of the verb for each sentence and write it.

1. Everybody on the bus (get, gets) off at Maple Avenue.
2. One of the phones (is, are) always busy.
3. Everyone in the cafeteria (eat, eats) with friends.
4. Each of the speed-skaters (deserve, deserves) to win.
5. Each of the boys (carve, carves) wooden figures.
6. Either of the computers (prints, print) out responses.
7. Everybody in the art studio (studies, study) drawing.
8. Neither of the squad cars (patrol, patrols) this area.
9. Everybody in the stands (cheers, cheer) loudly.
10. Neither of the radios (have, has) a powerful sound.

There Is, Where Is, Here Is

Many sentences begin with *There, Where,* or *Here.* These words are never subjects. In sentences beginning with these words, the subject usually comes after the verb.

Before you can choose the right verb form, you have to know what the subject is. You have to know whether it is singular or plural.

> There are your parents.   (*Parents* is the subject; the plural form *are* is correct.)
> Here is the trail.   (*Trail* is the subject; the singular form *is* is correct.)
> Where do the dishes belong?   (*Dishes* is the subject; the plural form *do belong* is correct.)

A.   Write the correct form of the verb from the two given.

1. There (is, are) no rules for this game.
2. Where (does, do) the ticket line start?
3. Here (is, are) the dugout for the players.
4. There (was, were) no boots in my size.
5. Here (is, are) my fishing license.
6. Where (is, are) the nearest phone?
7. There (is, are) scratches on that antique desk.
8. Here (is, are) the pizzas we ordered.
9. Where (is, are) the chess pieces?
10. Here (is, are) the girls' lockers.

B.   Follow the directions for Exercise A.

1. Where (has, have) the salespeople gone?
2. Here (is, are) the relief pitcher.
3. There (is, are) poster paints for the project.
4. Where (does, do) your parents work?
5. Where (was, were) the President's bodyguards?
6. Where (is, are) the road to Springfield?
7. Here (is, are) the sandwiches you ordered.
8. Where (is, are) the batteries for the flashlight?
9. There (is, are) a club for model airplane buffs.
10. Here (is, are) the thief's fingerprints.

Compound Subjects

When the parts of a compound subject are joined by the conjunction *and,* use the plural form of the verb.

The *judge* and the *lawyers* **were** in a meeting.
Are my *hat* and *coat* upstairs?

479

When the parts are joined by *or, either—or,* or *neither—nor,* use the form of the verb that agrees in number with the subject noun or pronoun nearer to it.

Tom or *Dick* **is driving.**
Neither Aunt Ginny nor my *cousins* **are** here.
Either ten pencils or one *pen* **costs** a dollar.

Exercises **Use the right verb form.**

A. Write each sentence, choosing the right form of the verb from the two given in parentheses. If a conjunction with *or* or *nor* is used in the subject, circle the part of the compound subject nearer the verb you chose.

1. Neither Kelly nor Jason (plays, play) soccer.
2. Either the roast or the potatoes (is, are) burning.
3. Neither Lee nor her sisters (wants, want) that dress.
4. Martha and her brother (speaks, speak) Norwegian.
5. Both the costumes and sets (is, are) Ben's creations.
6. Either milk or fruit juice (is, are) available.
7. Neither the stadium nor the park (holds, hold) enough fans for the championship game.
8. Either the books or the shelf (is, are) labeled wrong.
9. (Is, Are) Hal's bike and my scooter missing?
10. Neither he nor his brothers (likes, like) that program.

B. Follow the directions for Exercise A.

1. (Is, Are) the snow and ice melting?
2. Neither my dog nor my other pets (eats, eat) much.
3. Either the Scouts or another club (is, are) selling cookies.
4. Either the stereo or the records (is, are) damaged.
5. Neither the park nor the back lot (has, have) a baseball diamond.
6. Chess and checkers (is, are) similar in some ways.

7. Either Bob or his sister (has, have) the keys to the bike shed.
8. Either the head lifeguard or her assistant (sits, sit) here.
9. Neither our clothes nor our furniture (has, have) been delivered.
10. (Is, Are) candy or flowers the usual Valentine's Day gift?

Using *I*

Although *I* stands for a single person, it does not usually take a singular verb form. The only singular verb forms used with it are *am* and *was*.

> I **am** the shortstop.   I **was** in our garage.

Otherwise, the verb form used with *I* is the same as the plural form.

> I **do** the dishes every day.   I **have** a friend in Mexico.

Using *You*

The word *you* can stand for one person or for several persons. It may be either singular or plural. Whether it is singular or plural, always use the plural verb form with the pronoun *you*.

> You **were** the only *person* with a bike.
> You **were** the only *students* in the hall.

Exercises **Use the right verb form.**

A. Write the correct verb form from those given.

1. You (was, were) the biggest vote-getter.
2. I (is, are, am) watching a TV special on China.

3. I (makes, make) candles and paper flowers in craft class.
4. (Was, Were) you courteous to all of the customers?
5. (Has, Have) you tried bagels and cream cheese?
6. After everyone left, I (was, were) lonely.
7. You (was, were) nervous before the exam on Monday.
8. You (has, have) a fine stamp collection.
9. I (was, were) sad when my best friend moved away.
10. I (draws, draw) cartoons for the school paper.

B. Follow the directions for Exercise A.

1. I (was, were) a crossing guard last year.
2. (Is, Are) you hungry after our long hike?
3. You (makes, make) delicious fudge.
4. I (am, is) cold after shoveling all that snow.
5. (Has, Have) you read *Johnny Tremain?*
6. With that hat on, you (looks, look) silly.
7. Greg, you always (loses, lose) your ticket.
8. On Mondays I (takes, take) the train into the city.
9. I (am, is, are) using my new hockey stick.
10. During the last game, you (was, were) the dealer.

ADDITIONAL EXERCISES

Making Subjects and Verbs Agree

A. Making Subjects and Verbs Agree Write the correct form of the verb for each sentence.

1. Our albums (contains, contain) many photos.
2. TV detectives always (solves, solve) the crime.
3. This sports story (quotes, quote) our coach.
4. The hand brakes on my bike (sticks, stick).
5. This bunch of wildflowers (comes, come) from the woods.
6. The booth for refreshments (stands, stand) behind the fence.
7. The lions at the zoo (is, are) fed at two o'clock.
8. A swarm of ants (has, have) raided our picnic.
9. (Does, Do) this book of ghost stories scare you?
10. This pair of skates (does, do) not fit.

B. Using Problem Subjects Write the correct form of the verb for each subject.

1. Each of my shirts (is, are) dirty.
2. Neither of the skis (has, have) been waxed.
3. Everybody in the cast (likes, like) the director.
4. There (is, are) several days of vacation this month.
5. Here (is, are) the deepest snowdrifts.
6. Coffee and some colas (contains, contain) caffeine.
7. Neither the showers nor the pool (is, are) heated.
8. Either rain or high winds (has, have) delayed the flight.
9. I (believes, believe) that flying saucers do exist.
10. You (was, were) the strongest hitter on the team.

MIXED REVIEW

Making Subjects and Verbs Agree

Making subjects and verbs agree Copy each of the following sentences. Choose the correct form of the verb from the two in parentheses. Underline the subject once and the verb twice.

1. The plants in that windowbox (need, needs) water.
2. One of my best friends (is, are) captain of the rugby team.
3. This bag of plums (weigh, weighs) one pound.
4. Everyone in my family (has, have) brown eyes.
5. Joe's cousins (live, lives) in Austin, Texas.
6. The dishes in the dishwasher (is, are) clean.
7. Nobody in our class (understand, understands) the assignment.
8. This book (has, have) less than two hundred pages.
9. Here (is, are) my medical forms.
10. My cousin and I (has, have) a secret code.
11. I (is, am) the best candidate for the office.
12. Where (is, are) your nearest neighbors?
13. (Has, Have) you seen today's headlines?
14. The girl in the yellow sweater (look, looks) like you.
15. Neither of these dresses (fits, fit) me.
16. There (is, are) some talented students in our class.
17. I (has, have) an identical twin brother.
18. You (keep, keeps) your room very neat.
19. Luis or Tony (are, is) the best qualified candidate.
20. Neither Beth nor Sara (has, have) arrived yet.

USING GRAMMAR IN WRITING
Making Subject and Verbs Agree

A. Everyone has had experiences that are embarrassing. Often those experiences seem very funny a day or a week later. Think of a time when you were embarrassed. Then see if you can remember what seemed funny about it later. Write about your experience. Use *I* to tell the story, and be sure to make all subjects and verbs agree. Then write the story again, but pretend it happened to someone else. Use *He* or *She* instead of *I*. Remember, when you change the subject of a sentence, the form of the verb may change.

B. Think of two people you know. They may be relatives, friends, or even characters in a TV series. Think about the ways they are alike and the ways they are different. Write about their similarities and differences. Use at least five of the following words as subjects. Be sure that the verb agrees with its subject in each sentence.

Each	She/He	Everyone
Both	One	The other
Neither	Nobody	They
Either	No one	Anybody

C. Write six sentences about the last day of school. Use the following words and phrases as subjects of sentences. Then label each subject and verb as either singular or plural.

1. the last day of school
2. students
3. principal
4. books of the entire class
5. school assembly
6. all of the lockers

CUMULATIVE REVIEW
Usage

A. Choosing the correct word Write the correct word from the two given in parentheses.

1. Lemonade tastes (good, well) on a hot summer day.
2. (Leave, Let) the bird go when (its, it's) wing has healed.
3. You speak French very (good, well).
4. (May, Can) I use (your, you're) eraser?
5. (Their, They're) team lost a close game last Sunday.
6. This is a (good, well) day to (lie, lay) in the sun.
7. (Them, Those) kinds of books are my favorite.
8. (Its, It's) too late to call Amy.
9. (Their, They're) working on (their, they're) oral pre-sentation.
10. The situation looked (bad, badly).

B. Using words correctly Twenty words are underlined in the following paragraph. Ten of the underlined words contain errors in the use of verbs, nouns, pronouns, adverbs, and adjectives. Ten of the words are correct. Rewrite, correcting the errors.

Martha looked sad at her rusty old bike. Wouldn't anyone never buy it from she? Ads in the paper hadn't worked. Neither had notes posted on her school's bulletin board's, reading "Bike for Sale—Handywoman's Delight." It were not possible to trade it in for a newest model. Al, the bike shop's owner, only excepted bikes in working condition. Martha's bike looked badly. It needed a fresh coat of paint, a chain, and a new seat. She decided then and there to get them things fixed. She sanded the front fender and plan her next ad: "Bike for Sale—Completely Remodeled".

Using Compound Sentences

Part 1 A Review of the Sentence

Throughout this book you have been studying sentences. Now is a good time to review what you have learned.

A **sentence** has two basic parts, a subject and a predicate.

Subject	Predicate
Girls	hike.
Those four girls	hike.
Those four girls	hike every summer.
Those girls from Atlanta	hike in the forest every summer.

The **subject** of a sentence tells *who* or *what* the sentence says something about. The **predicate** tells *what the subject did, what the subject is,* or *what happened to the subject.*

Compound Parts of the Sentence

You have also learned that all parts of the sentence may be **compound**. That is, all the parts of the sentence may have more than one part.

Compound Subject:

> *Carla* and *Dave* sit closest to the teacher.

Compound Verb:

> Lena *has read* and *studied* all morning.

Compound Predicate:

> The Earth *has one moon* and *revolves around the sun.*

Compound Direct Object:

> The principal asked *Rob* and *Laura* to the meeting.

Compound Object of a Preposition:

> Settlers drove the wagons across *prairies* and *deserts.*

A Definition of the Sentence

You can see that each of these example sentences expresses one main idea. These sentences, like all of those you have been studying, are called **simple sentences.**

A simple sentence is a sentence with two basic parts, subject and predicate. The subject and the predicate, or any part of the subject and predicate, may be compound.

Exercises   Review simple sentences.

A. Write each sentence. Draw a vertical line between the subject and the predicate.

1. The planet Jupiter has many moons.
2. The roller rink rents skates.
3. The rings in a tree trunk tell its age.
4. Roberto and Ken are bowling this evening.
5. The dentist cleans teeth and fills cavities.
6. The mice escaped from the cage in the biology lab.
7. The people of Mexico are proud of their culture.
8. Athena and Diana are goddesses in Greek mythology.
9. The door to the hallway slammed shut.
10. The school is much larger than the library.

B. Follow the directions for Exercise A.

1. The lumberjack cuts down trees for the sawmill.
2. Corn, tomatoes, and spinach grow in our garden.
3. A blizzard stopped traffic and closed the airport.
4. The space shuttle glided to a smooth landing.
5. Yesterday's game had two overtimes.
6. Some trains travel over one hundred miles an hour.
7. The roads were slippery and dangerous after the ice storm.
8. Charles Dickens wrote stories for magazines.
9. Ellen raked the leaves and bagged them for the trash collectors.
10. The gymnast did flips and cartwheels on the mat.

Part 2 What Are Compound Sentences?

Sometimes two sentences are so closely related in thought that you join them together. You can join them by using the conjunctions *and, but,* and *or.* Then you have a different kind of sentence. You have a sentence with two closely related main ideas. Each main idea has its own subject and predicate. This is called a **compound sentence.**

Ernie Banks was elected to the Baseball Hall of Fame **and** he was thrilled.

My family arrived at the airport on time, **but** the storm delayed our flight.

The bread must be baked for one hour, **or** it will be soggy.

Now look at the parts of these compound sentences:

Subject	Verb	Conjunction	Subject	Verb
Ernie Banks	was elected	and	he	was
family	arrived	but	storm	delayed
bread	must be baked	or	it	will be

A compound sentence consists of two or more simple sentences joined together.

Why Write Compound Sentences?

Why would you want to write compound sentences? Why not use only simple sentences? You will know the answer as soon as you read this paragraph.

I tried to water-ski last summer. I put on the water-skis. They fell off. Finally, I found the proper skis. The boat stalled. We had to get a different boat. I jumped into the water. I tried to get up on the skis. I tried at least twenty-five times. Each time I fell. At last, I succeeded. Skimming the water felt terrific. All the effort was worthwhile.

You can see that these sentences are very short and sound choppy when you read them. Many of these sentences are closely related in thought. Combined into compound sentences, they read much more smoothly.

I tried to water-ski last summer. I put on the water-skis, but they fell off. Finally, I found the proper skis, but then the boat stalled. We had to get a different boat. I jumped into the water, and I tried to get up on the skis. I tried at least twenty-five times, but each time I fell. At last, I succeeded. Skimming the water felt terrific, and all the effort was worthwhile.

Use compound sentences.

A. Make three columns on your paper. Label them *Subject/Verb, Conjunction,* and *Subject/Verb.* Fill in the columns with the correct words from each of the following sentences.

Example: Dana went to the movie, but I stayed home.

Subject / Verb	Conjunction	Subject / Verb
Dana went	but	I stayed

1. Lori got new shoes, but they hurt her.
2. Last summer Mom grew vegetables, and we picked them daily.
3. The forest is very dry, and everyone worries about fires.
4. Tracy pumped water, and we drank it immediately.
5. The food must be eaten, or it will spoil.
6. A dog barked loudly, and it scared us away.
7. The rocket roared into life, and the flight to the moon was underway.
8. Jo Ellen used the water wings, and Kate had the inner tube.
9. Connie went to the doctor, and she had allergy tests.
10. These tickets were expensive, but the seats are terrible.

B. Follow the directions for Exercise A.

1. Wendy made the team, but she is on the second string.
2. The game was tough, and it ended in a tie.
3. Do you like hamburgers, or would you prefer a pizza?
4. Linda is very friendly, and she is always cheerful.
5. Two boats capsized, but the others reached the shore.
6. The defense is strong, but the offense is weak.
7. Katy had braces, and now her teeth are straight.

8. Keith is a good actor, but he didn't get the part.
9. Do you bring your lunch, or do you buy it at school?
10. Tom rolled the bowling ball, and he scored a strike.

Punctuating Compound Sentences

Because compound sentences contain more than one idea, they can be confusing. To help the reader keep the closely related thoughts clear, put a **comma** before the conjunction in a compound sentence. The comma alerts the reader to the end of the first idea, and it prepares the reader for the second idea.

I hit the ball and my brother fielded it.
I hit the ball, *and* my brother fielded it.

You may leave out the comma only when the two sentences that you join are very short.

Dinner was served and we ate.
The sun shone and the birds sang.

Exercises **Punctuate compound sentences.**

A. Copy the following compound sentences. Add a comma wherever one is needed. Circle the conjunction that joins the parts of the sentence.

1. You must hold the lid or the popcorn will pop out.
2. The math test is tomorrow but I haven't studied yet.
3. The sun was hot but the breeze was refreshing.
4. Carol climbed the snowbank and Julie followed her.
5. Down jackets are warm and they are lightweight, too.
6. Pam met her friends in the cafeteria and they ate together.
7. Sue lost her shoe but she finished the race.
8. Dan shot for the goal but he missed it by a foot.
9. Kim sawed and I hammered.
10. Did you make that glider or did you buy it?

B. Follow the directions for Exercise A.

1. The sky was hazy but I got a sunburn anyway.
2. Doors slammed and windows shook.
3. Sarah shaped the clay and then she fired it in the kiln.
4. Mom selected the lumber and she made the bookcase.
5. The helicopter landed and three people got out.
6. Brad enjoys math but science is his favorite subject.
7. Is Gilda in the hospital or has she recovered?
8. Two outfielders ran for the ball but neither caught it.
9. Jeff walks to school and Ramona rides her bike.
10. Candy learned some magic tricks and she does them well.

C. Writing   Write a paragraph about a pet. Use three compound sentences in your paragraph. Underline the subject once and the verb twice in each part of each compound sentence. Circle the conjunction that joins both parts of the sentence. Be sure to use a comma.

ADDITIONAL EXERCISES

Using Compound Sentences

A. Simple Sentences Write the subjects and verbs in these simple sentences. Some parts may be compound.

1. Once again, Emily searched for the book.
2. Don and Liz made vases with the clay.
3. The baby squirmed and cried in the highchair.
4. Cathy played well at her piano recital.
5. Elliot closed his locker and hurried to class.

B. Compound Sentences Copy each sentence. For both parts of the compound sentence, underline the subject once and the verb twice. Then add the punctuation needed to make the sentence correct.

1. Bill subscribes to *Tennis Monthly* and he reads every article.
2. Sandy lives in the city but she likes the country better.
3. One station plays jazz but the rest play rock music.
4. Are you hungry or have you eaten dinner?
5. The TV set is on but nobody is watching it.
6. Dad has a moustache and Uncle Joe has a beard.
7. First the swimmers warm up and then they race.
8. The house is empty but eerie sounds come from it.
9. Rain fell for days and the rivers overflowed.
10. Hal plays chess often but he always loses.
11. I start crossword puzzles and my sister finishes them.
12. Have you missed practice or was it canceled?
13. The train stopped and we got off.
14. This horse is gentle but she runs very fast.
15. The pitcher threw a curve ball and the batter doubled.

MIXED REVIEW

Using Compound Sentences

A. Recognizing simple and compound sentences   Copy each of the following sentences. If a sentence is simple, write *S*. If it is compound, write *C*. Underline the subjects once and the verbs twice. If a sentence is compound, be sure to underline both sets of subjects and verbs.

1. Do you walk to school, or do you take the bus?
2. After dinner, we all washed and dried the dishes.
3. Chris needs plywood and wire for his project.
4. Mom cut the flowers, and we arranged them in vases.
5. Vera addressed the envelopes, but I mailed them.
6. Bob sings and plays the guitar in a rock group.
7. This weather is beautiful, but we need rain.
8. Rick walks but Liz rides.
9. Dana and Keith learned sign language.
10. Kristen applied for a paper route and got one.

B. Combining sentences   Combine the following pairs of simple sentences into compound sentences. Use the conjunctions *and, but,* or *or.* Punctuate them correctly.

1. Gail served the ball. I returned it.
2. Eric likes cats. He is allergic to them.
3. You can borrow my book. You can get one from the library.
4. Dennis dusted the furniture. Larry vacuumed the rug.
5. Sally might buy that dress. She might make one just like it.
6. I enjoy music. I have no talent.
7. We gave Jan a surprise party. She wasn't surprised.
8. Juan entered the photo contest. He won second prize.
9. Do you just watch sports? Do you participate?
10. These records are old. They are in good condition.

USING GRAMMAR IN WRITING
Using Compound Sentences

A. Do you sometimes wish you had special powers like Superman or Superwoman? If you had special abilities, how would you use them? Write about what you would do. In your paragraph, include at least one sentence with a compound subject. Include at least one with a compound verb. Underline each compound subject once. Underline each compound verb twice.

B. You work at a Chinese fortune cookie factory. It is your job to compose the fortunes. Fortunes tell what will happen in the future. They tell about life, love, fame, fortune, health, happiness, and friendship. You must write six fortunes. Each fortune must be a compound sentence. Use *and, but,* and *or* to connect the parts of the compound sentences.

> Example: You will find a great treasure, *but* you will lose it through carelessness.

C. Imagine that you have volunteered for a scientific experiment. You will be able to travel through time. You can choose where you would like to go. You could go hurtling into the future or spinning back in time. Write about the choice you make. Tell what you saw and did during your day in the past or the future. One sentence should contain a compound subject and one a compound verb. Include two compound sentences.

CUMULATIVE REVIEW
The Sentence

A. Identifying kinds of sentences Copy the following sentences. Insert the correct punctuation. After each sentence, write *D* for declarative, *INT* for interrogative, *IMP* for imperative, or *E* for exclamatory. Underline each subject once and each verb twice.

1. Has the mayor arrived yet
2. Water is pouring into the basement
3. This flat tire cannot be repaired
4. Fasten your seat belt
5. The choir sang beautifully
6. Did you lock the bikes securely
7. What an unusual fish you caught
8. Mark designed and built that birdhouse
9. Read the directions on the box
10. There's a bear outside our tent

B. Understanding agreement in sentences Number your paper from 1 to 15. Write the correct word from the two given in parentheses.

1. The milk in these cartons (is, are) leaking out.
2. The apartments in our building (was, were) remodeled last year.
3. Each of the students had (his or her, their) picture taken for the yearbook.
4. Here (is, are) the plates and napkins.
5. Books about history (interest, interests) Ted.
6. One of my best friends (is, are) moving to Arizona.
7. Either Sam or his brothers (knows, know) how to fix your bike.

8. They (don't, doesn't) understand Spanish.
9. Each of the girls chooses (her, their) own position on the team.
10. Most of Roger's poems (describe, describes) nature.
11. The squirrels buried (its, their) acorns near this tree.
12. Where (is, are) the tools for the job?
13. Have the robins returned to (their, its) nest?
14. The rose and the petunias (need, needs) more water.
15. You (is, are) the first guest here.

C. Correcting fragments and run-on sentences   The following paragraph contains fragments and run-on sentences. Rewrite the paragraph. Use capitalization and punctuation to correct the fragments and run-ons. Do not add or change any words.

It seems strange to me that so many people ski. For fun and relaxation. It snows all the time. In my state. I use my skis to run errands and to deliver the newspapers on my route I also use them to get to school. The history of this sport. Proves that I am not alone. In the past, skis have been used by messengers, mail carriers, and even armies, skiing as a sport came much later. What do I do? For fun and relaxation? I sit by a blazing fire and read about warmer climates.

D. Writing good sentences   Rewrite each of the following sentences. Follow the directions in the parentheses.

1. Kevin writes stories for young children. (Add the prepositional phrase *about talking animals.*)
2. Lynn will play on the hockey team. She will join the basketball team. (Combine these two simple sentences into a compound sentence using **, or.**)
3. Marcella found her ring. (Add the prepositional phrase *near third base.*)

4. The carpenters built the new deck. (Add the prepositional phrase *on Thursday*.)
5. Maurice Sendak wrote that book. He illustrated it. (Combine these two simple sentences into one with a compound verb.)
6. Grant studied the code. He couldn't understand it. (Combine these two simple sentences into a compound sentence using **, but**.)
7. Karen is a friendly girl. (Change this N LV N sentence into one with a N LV ADJ pattern.)
8. Anita tried to catch the ball. Scott tried, too. (Combine these two simple sentences into one with a compound subject.)
9. The cocoa is too hot to drink. (Add the prepositional phrase *in that pot*.)
10. Sylvia cleaned yesterday. (Change this NV sentence to one with a NVN pattern.)

Diagraming the Sentence

Part 1 What Is Diagraming?

A **diagram** of a sentence is a picture of the parts of a sentence. A diagram shows how the parts of a sentence work together and how they are related.

When you make diagrams, you follow patterns. It is important to follow the patterns exactly. You will need to put words in the right places. You will need to make vertical lines, horizontal lines, and slanted lines. Copy words exactly as they appear in a sentence, with capital letters or without them. Do not copy any punctuation marks except the apostrophes within a word.

In this section, you will be learning how to diagram sentences. Diagraming can help you to see how the parts of a sentence work together to express an idea.

Part 2 Diagraming Verbs and Their Subjects

A sentence diagram always begins on a horizontal line. A vertical line cuts the horizontal line in two. It separates the subject from the verb. The subject is placed to the left of the line. The verb is placed to the right side of the line.

Roosters crow.

Dorothy Taylor sang.

Exercise   **Diagram verbs and their subjects.**

Diagram the verb and its simple subject in each of the following sentences. (Ignore all other words.)

1. The jet climbed.
2. Rhonda hesitated.
3. The fireworks exploded.
4. Penguins waddle.
5. The candle drips.
6. A rainbow appeared.
7. The room darkened.
8. The bus swerved.
9. JoAnn went to the door.
10. My book dropped into the mud.

Part 3 Diagraming Subjects in Unusual Order

In some sentences, the subject and verb are in an unusual order. Their position on a diagram, however, does not change.

Down our street came the parade.

High above our heads flew the kites.

Exercise **Diagram subjects in unusual order.**

Diagram the subjects and verbs in the following sentences. (Ignore all other words.)

1. Around the curve came the cars.
2. Under the car hid the kitten.
3. In the field grazed some cows.
4. Onto the floor tumbled the tomatoes.
5. Over the beach flew the helicopter.
6. Into the pool dove Sandra.
7. From the woods came a deer.
8. Through the yard raced a rabbit.
9. Down the street zoomed a motorcycle.
10. Around in circles went the Tilt-a-Whirl.

Part 4　Diagraming Questions

When you diagram a question, put the subject and verb in normal order. Remember that you capitalize only the words that are capitalized in the sentence.

Have you heard the news?

Does Jim help with the chores?

Exercise　**Diagram questions.**

Diagram the subject and verb in each of the following questions. (Ignore all other words.)

1. Does the snake bite?
2. Should we feed the cat?
3. Did Mary lock the gate?
4. Did you solve the mystery?
5. When did the fire begin?
6. Have you ever seen a ghost?
7. Do you babysit at night?
8. Has the aquarium arrived?
9. Where are volcanos located?
10. Will the runner steal third base?

Part 5 Diagraming Imperative Sentences

When the subject of an imperative sentence is understood, show it on your diagram by writing (*you*).

Fold your paper in half.

Put this gift under the tree.

Exercise Diagram imperative sentences.

Diagram the subjects and verbs in the following imperative sentences. (Ignore all other words.)

1. Explain this problem.
2. Keep that smile on your face.
3. Find some more clues.
4. Read at your own pace.
5. Have a good time.
6. Open that old trunk.
7. Whisper in the library.
8. Ride your bike on the street.
9. Try a new approach.
10. Enter through the side door.

Part 6 Diagraming Sentences with *There*

There is often just an "extra" word. It is placed on a separate line above the subject in a sentence diagram.

There are twenty students in this class.

Were there many people at the dance?

Exercise   **Diagram sentences with *there*.**

Diagram the subjects and verbs in the following sentences with *there*.

1. Is there a chance of rain?
2. There are only seven ducks on the pond.
3. Are there new rules for this game?
4. There are two good programs on TV tonight.
5. There is a purpose for each lesson.
6. Were there footprints by the window?
7. There were several leaks in the ceiling.
8. There was a thunderstorm last night.
9. Are there any books on that subject?
10. Is there time for another tennis match?

Part 7 Diagraming Compound Subjects and Verbs

To diagram the two or more parts of a compound subject, split the subject line. Put the conjunction on a connecting dotted line.

Jill and her father sailed the boat.

To diagram the two or more parts of a compound verb, split the predicate line. Put the conjunction on a connecting dotted line.

Sam swept, washed, and waxed the floor.

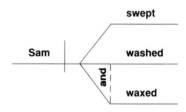

Exercise **Diagram compound subjects and verbs.**

Diagram the compound subjects and verbs.

1. Tara designed and built a small table.
2. Smoke and fumes pollute the air.
3. Chris waters, feeds, and prunes her plants.
4. The newscaster and sports reporter gave their reports.
5. Have Steve and Lisa visited the museum?
6. The wild animals gathered and drank at the stream.
7. There are sandwiches and fruit in the picnic basket.
8. We fished from the riverbank and caught three fish.

9. Toward the finish line dashed Judy and Carmen.
10. Rangers survey the forest and watch for danger.

Part 8 Diagraming Sentences Containing Direct Objects

When you diagram a sentence, place a direct object on the horizontal line following the verb. Separate it from the action verb by a vertical line that does not cut through the subject-verb line.

My parents bought a new car.

For compound direct objects, continue the horizontal line a little way beyond the verb and then split it. Make as many parallel direct-object lines as you need. Put the vertical line before the split, to show that all the words that follow are direct objects.

We met Laura, Dawn, and Billy at the bus stop.

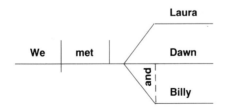

Exercise **Diagram sentences containing direct objects.**

Diagram the subjects, action verbs, and direct objects in these sentences. (Some direct objects may be compound.)

1. The puppy took a nap.

2. He made a beautiful drawing.
3. We recycle bottles, cans, and newspapers.
4. Get a subscription to this magazine.
5. Ernest collects stamps and coins.
6. The hikers ate lunch on a hilltop.
7. Did the class plan a party?
8. Beth and Rochelle played Scrabble.
9. We bought apples, plums, and strawberries.
10. The magician hypnotized two people in the audience.

Part 9 Diagraming Sentences Containing Predicate Nouns

The diagram for a sentence containing a predicate noun is different from that for a sentence containing a direct object.

Dr. Sarah Powers is our dentist.

Notice that the predicate noun is on the horizontal line in the same position as the direct object. But the line that separates the predicate noun from the linking verb slants back toward the subject. This is to show its close relationship to the subject.

For sentences containing **compound predicate nouns,** use parallel lines. Put the slanting line after the verb and before the main line is split.

Duke was a good pet but a poor watchdog.

Diagram sentences containing predicate nouns.

Diagram the subjects, linking verbs, and predicate nouns in the following sentences.

1. The Pizza Palace is a new restaurant.
2. A tandem is a bicycle for two people.
3. Is Buddy the pitcher today?
4. Dolphins are mammals.
5. Are Sam and Dick best friends?
6. Spaghetti is an Italian dish.
7. Three string instruments are the violin, the cello, and the bass.
8. Two useful knots are the half-hitch and the butterfly.
9. Gwendolyn Brooks is a famous poet.
10. Ben Franklin was a writer, an inventor, and a statesman.

Part 10 Diagraming Sentences Containing Predicate Adjectives

You show predicate adjectives on diagrams just as you show predicate nouns. Place them on the horizontal line following the linking verb, and separate them from the verb by a line slanting back toward the subject.

That platform seems unsafe.

For sentences with compound predicate adjectives, use parallel lines. Put the slanting line after the verb and before the main line is split.

The hikers were cold and tired.

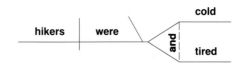

Exercise **Diagram sentences containing predicate adjectives.**

Diagram the subjects, linking verbs, and predicate adjectives in the following sentences.

1. The races were fun.
2. Diamonds are extremely hard.
3. Computers are quick and accurate.
4. Be careful.
5. My backpack is empty.
6. That watermelon is ripe, sweet, and juicy.
7. The moon is full tonight.
8. These tomatoes and cucumbers are very fresh.
9. Soccer is fast and rough.
10. Is Sherry happy in her new neighborhood?

Part 11 Diagraming Sentences Containing Adjectives

On a diagram, an adjective is shown on a line that slants down from the noun or pronoun it modifies. (Articles are shown the same way.)

That new cook made a thick, lumpy gravy.

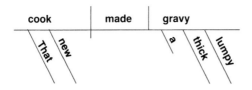

Mrs. Holmes is a patient, friendly teacher.

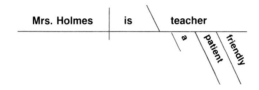

Exercise   **Diagram sentences containing adjectives.**

Diagram the subjects, verbs, articles, and adjectives in the following sentences. Also diagram any direct objects, predicate nouns, or predicate adjectives.

1. Kirstin heard strange, squeaky noises.
2. The large group sang patriotic songs.
3. That antique clock is beautiful and accurate.
4. Kathleen wrote those short, humorous poems.
5. The hefty weightlifter raised the heavy barbell.
6. Does this album contain old snapshots?
7. Ten acrobats walked the high tightrope.
8. The politician made an angry, forceful speech.
9. The lemon is a small, yellow, sour fruit.
10. An alert neighbor spotted the dangerous sparks.

Part 12   Diagraming Sentences Containing Possessive Nouns

Possessive nouns are diagramed in the same way that adjectives are. They are written on lines slanting down from the nouns with which they are used.

These are Ellen's books.

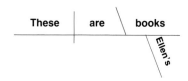

We heard the minister's sermon.

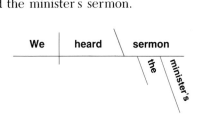

Exercise   **Diagram sentences containing possessive nouns.**

Diagram the subjects, verbs, and possessive nouns in the following sentences. Also diagram any direct objects, predicate nouns or predicate adjectives, articles, and adjectives.

1. The Riveras' black cat followed me.
2. Kendra's mother is an excellent pianist.
3. Bruce's serve is strong and fast.
4. Read Jack London's stories.
5. Cathy's dog found Dad's brown slippers.
6. The girls' chorus sang Andy's original songs.
7. Ms. Mason's class toured museums and historic places.
8. Did Douglas borrow Elena's new album?

9. The town's mayor proposed several laws.

10. The siren's shrill wail filled the air.

Part 13 Diagraming Sentences Containing Adverbs

Adverbs, like adjectives, are shown on diagrams on slanting lines attached to the words they modify. The following diagram shows an adverb modifying a verb.

Finally, the shy boy raised his hand.

The next diagram shows one adverb modifying a verb, another modifying an adjective, and a third modifying another adverb.

Some fairly young children play musical instruments very well.

Notice how *fairly* is attached to *young.* Notice how *very* is attached to *well.*

Exercise **Diagram sentences containing adverbs.**

Diagram the subjects, verbs, and adverbs in the following sentences. Also diagram adjectives, articles, predicate adjectives or predicate nouns, and direct objects.

1. The climber moved upward quickly.
2. Finally, the police caught the suspect.
3. Fans wildly cheered the team's victory.
4. The butcher rapidly trimmed the steaks.
5. Tomorrow Al will referee the hockey game.
6. This train is too noisy.
7. This yellow is an extremely vivid color.
8. Did most students study hard?
9. They usually ride their bikes.
10. Very few stations play classical music.

Part 14   Diagraming Compound Sentences

It is not difficult to diagram compound sentences if you can already diagram simple sentences. A compound sentence is just two or more simple sentences joined together. First, you draw the diagram for the first simple sentence. Then you draw a dotted line "step" for the conjunction. Finally, draw the diagram for the second simple sentence.

> Daniel slept soundly, but the other campers didn't close their eyes.

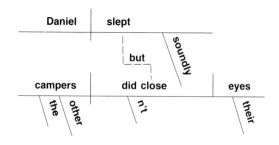

Sally is a strong swimmer, and she has won many races.

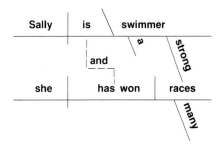

Diagram compound sentences.

Diagram the following compound sentences. Diagram each part of the sentence. Then join the parts.

1. Winston hid Heather's mittens, but she found them.
2. The flowers are growing, but the weeds are growing faster.
3. Stacey arrived late, and she left early.
4. Did Dan walk, or did he ride his bike?
5. The door opened, but nobody entered.
6. Hop aboard, or you will miss the train.
7. Noah is a fair player, but he is tough.
8. Jan found a shiny silver ring, and he kept it.
9. Liz always takes out the garbage, but she never dries the dishes.
10. Badminton and volleyball are outdoor sports, but they are also played indoors.

ADDITIONAL EXERCISES

Diagraming the Sentence

A. Diagraming Subjects and Verbs Diagram the subjects and verbs in the following sentences. Ignore any other words.

1. Elizabeth answered.
2. Over the roof flew the robin.
3. Can the baby walk?
4. Try harder.
5. There is a squirrel in the attic.
6. Cars and trucks blocked the entrance.
7. The builders sawed and hammered.
8. Did our team win?
9. I swept, washed, and waxed the floor.
10. Watch the screen.

B. Diagraming Direct Objects and Predicate Words Diagram the subjects, verbs, direct objects, and predicate words in each of the following sentences.

1. Karen, Dennis, and Juan organized the picnic.
2. Yolanda brought food, a blanket, and a radio.
3. Tanya is our candidate.
4. Don't forget your boots and umbrella.
5. Is Mr. Holmes your teacher?
6. The wrestlers were breathless and weak.
7. Two popular evergreens are pine and spruce.
8. Does this book seem mysterious?
9. Rebecca is a fine dancer.
10. Lou entered the math competition.

C. Diagraming Modifiers Diagram the subjects, verbs, direct objects, predicate words, and modifiers in the following sentences.

1. Choose a bright, cheerful card.
2. Can the farmer's heavy tractor plow this rocky field?
3. Randi washed Evan's shaggy dog.
4. Very few people play this complex game correctly.
5. A fierce, hot wind swept the plains.
6. Everyone enjoyed Karen's funny story.
7. They never heard the final score.
8. We ate crisp, buttery popcorn.
9. Tony read the latest report very carefully.
10. The wooden raft drifted lazily downstream.

D. Diagraming Compound Sentences Diagram the following sentences.

1. Nancy Lopez is a golfer, and she has won many prizes.
2. Will you call, or will you write?
3. We roasted the corn, and we ate it hungrily.
4. Is that lovely fruit real, or is it wax?
5. The clouds are dark, and it will rain soon.
6. Ted missed the movie, but he can see it tomorrow.
7. The porch is wide, and the windows are large.
8. Sue planted beans, and Jerry planted squash.
9. We caught three trout, and Dad grilled them.
10. Did Gary and Elsa ride horses, or did they take their bikes?

MIXED REVIEW

Diagraming the Sentence

Diagraming sentences   Diagram the following sentences.

1. The ten campers wore bright red shirts.
2. The audience cheered and applauded wildly.
3. There aren't enough plates.
4. The boys rented a canoe.
5. The bacon sizzled and the coffee perked.
6. Are you the new captain?
7. Did Abby finish that difficult puzzle?
8. Williamsburg is an old, historic city.
9. Carol and Ben wrote the play, and our class performed it.
10. The kitten ran and hid.
11. Did Lennie believe your story?
12. Call again later.
13. The church choir sang Handel's *Messiah.*
14. Lawrence saw a UFO, and he reported it.
15. Jamie collects coins, stamps, and postcards.
16. We could hardly hear the lovely music.
17. Our cellar is cool and damp.
18. The coals are still hot, but we have eaten all the marshmallows.
19. Beverly Cleary is my favorite author.
20. Debbie walks, but her friends take the bus.

USING GRAMMAR IN WRITING
Diagraming the Sentence

A. Your friend has written you a message. She didn't want her nosey younger brother to read it, so she put the message in "code." She wrote it entirely in sentence diagrams. To find out what she said, you must "de-code" the diagrams.

1.

2.

3.

4.

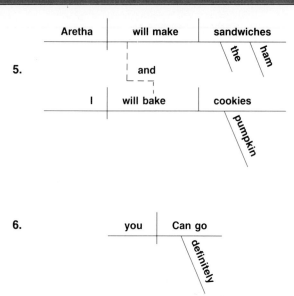

5.

Aretha | will make | sandwiches
the / ham /

and

I | will bake | cookies
pumpkin /

6.

you | Can go
definitely /

B. After you decode the message in *A*, answer it in three or four sentences. Put your answer in diagram code like your friend's message.

Capitalization

The use of capital letters is called **capitalization.** When you use a capital letter at the beginning of a word, you *capitalize* the word.

Capital letters are used to call attention to the beginnings of sentences and to certain special words. Using capital letters makes everything easier to read.

In this section you will be learning rules for capitalization. Study the rules and their examples. Refer to them whenever you have a question about capitalization.

Proper Nouns and Proper Adjectives

A **common noun** is a general name for a person, place, or thing.

>   hero   country   planet

A **proper noun** is the name of one particular person, place, or thing.

>   Hercules   Switzerland   Mars

Begin every proper noun with a capital letter.

The words below are proper nouns. Some of them are made up of two words. Both words are parts of the proper noun. Both begin with capital letters.

>   Independence Day   South America   February
>   Exton Mall   Lake Erie   Mary Shelley

A **proper adjective** is an adjective made from a proper noun.

>   *Herculean* strength   *Swiss* cheese   *Martian* atmosphere
>   (from *Hercules*)   (from *Switzerland*)   (from *Mars*)

Begin every proper adjective with a capital letter. Proper adjectives are often used with common nouns. Do not capitalize the common noun.

Proper Noun	Proper Adjective	Adjective and Noun
England	English	English language
Rome	Roman	Roman numerals
Canada	Canadian	Canadian mountains
Indian	Indian	Indian corn

Most pronouns are treated like common nouns and are not capitalized. The pronoun *I*, however, is always capitalized.

Use capital letters.

Number your paper from 1 to 15. Copy each word below, changing small letters to capitals where necessary. After each word, write the group that the word belongs to: *Common Noun, Proper Noun,* or *Proper Adjective.* Some words can belong to more than one category.

1. boston	9. park
2. city	10. actress
3. french	11. los angeles
4. mississippi river	12. woman
5. kentucky	13. disney world
6. pete rose	14. carrie fisher
7. texan	15. school
8. singer	

Names and Initials

Capitalize the names of people and pets.

Carla   Michael   Snoopy

Begin every word in a person's name with a capital letter.

Dan Rather   Sandra Day O'Connor   Martin Luther King, Jr.

Capitalize an initial and follow it with a period. An **initial** is the first letter of a name. An initial stands for a name.

Susan B. Anthony   S. F. B. Morse
P. T. Barnum   O. J. Simpson

Capitalize words for family relations when they are used as names of specific people.

Father	Mother	Aunt Em
Dad	Mom	Uncle Henry
Pa	Ma	Grandma

However, if you use a possessive noun or pronoun before the word stating a relationship, do not capitalize the word.

Meet **A**unt **K**ate.   *but* Meet Sally's aunt.
Today **D**ad took the bus.   *but* Today my dad took the bus.

Titles and Their Abbreviations

You may have noticed that many people have special words before their names. Your dentist has the word *Doctor* before his or her name. So has your doctor. These special words are titles. Titles that are followed by names are capitalized. Titles used by themselves are not capitalized.

Doctor Rosen will see you   *but*   The doctor will see
now.   you now.
Marcia wrote to **G**overnor   *but*   Marcia wrote to the
Happ.   governor.

Many titles have short forms. A shortened form of a word is an **abbreviation.** Abbreviations for titles are capitalized and followed by a period. Never use an abbreviation unless you follow it with a name.

Doctor = **D**r. Brown   Governor = **G**ov. Johnson
Reverend = **R**ev. Clements

Always capitalize the titles *Mr.*, *Mrs.*, *Ms.*, and *Miss.* Be aware that *Ms.* has no long form and that *Miss* has no short form.

Capitalize titles and their abbreviations when you use them with names. Follow an abbreviation with a period.

Exercises   **Use capital letters correctly.**

A.   Copy the following sentences. Change small letters to capital letters wherever necessary.

1. We live next door to dr. l. e. brown.
2. My brother luis met superintendent julia f. jones.

3. The mayor presented an award to miss allen.
4. My father knows judge mercedes blake and senator steven thomas.
5. Last Thursday senator phyllis r. grimes and professor a. e. ames visited our school.
6. The writer charles lutwidge dodgson used the pen name lewis carroll.
7. Perhaps i'll name my new puppies pepper and salt.
8. The best players on rhonda's team are rhonda and i.
9. Some famous indian leaders were chief joseph, sitting bull, and cochise.
10. At the convention, clara and her cousin b. j. met governor ridge.

B. Follow the directions for Exercise A.

1. Katy moran's mom produces a television show.
2. Yes, aunt aretha and i met dr. cooley.
3. My neighbor, mrs. avellini, repairs cars.
4. A dog named benji adopted us.
5. Did you see the program with steve martin?
6. One champion golfer is judy rankin.
7. The bill was introduced by senator hernandez.
8. "Stamp out forest fires," smokey tells us.
9. Yesterday, grandma and my brother jeremy made soup.
10. Timothy bottoms and joseph bottoms are brothers.

Months, Days, and Holidays

Capitalize the names of months, days, and holidays.

Do not capitalize names of seasons, such as spring and summer.

My birthday is **S**eptember 1.
We observe **L**incoln's **B**irthday on **F**ebruary 12.
Next **F**riday is the first day of summer.

Particular Places and Things

Capitalize the names of cities, states, and countries.

Did you live in **K**ansas **C**ity, **K**ansas, or **K**ansas **C**ity, **M**issouri?
The **U**nited **S**tates shares borders with **M**exico and **C**anada.

Capitalize both letters of the two-letter abbreviations for states, used in addresses on all mail.

California = **CA**   Maine = **ME**   Wisconsin = **WI**

Capitalize the names of streets, bridges, and buildings, such as schools.

Chambers **E**lementary **S**chool is on **S**haw **A**venue.
The **O**akland **B**ay **B**ridge was being repainted.

Capitalize geographical names.

Also capitalize such words as *north, south, east,* and *west* when they refer to a section of the country. Do not capitalize them when they are used as directions.

The explorers traveled *south* along the **M**ississippi **R**iver.
The **W**est is beautiful country.
The storm is moving *east* over the **A**tlantic **O**cean.

Exercises   **Use capital letters correctly.**

A.   Copy the following sentences. Change small letters to capital letters wherever necessary.

1. Cactus grows in the southwest.
2. Vacation begins on tuesday.
3. The danube river flows into the black sea.
4. My friend miya osaka has relatives in japan.

5. On may 5, harper school will hold a carnival.
6. A time for picnics is independence day, july 4.
7. The international peace bridge connects canada and the united states.
8. Norman's little sister, linda, wrote to big bird at 123 sesame street, new york, new york.
9. Last saturday terry and i saw a ball game at comiskey park.
10. The aleutian islands are southwest of alaska.

B. Follow the directions for Exercise A.

1. The swedish ship passed through the panama canal.
2. Huge tortoises live on the galapagos islands.
3. The pentagon is the world's largest building.
4. The first monday in september is labor day.
5. Ms. e. e. stefano is the librarian at the carver public library.
6. Did you know that elm street is made of bricks?
7. On may 5, 1961, alan shepard became the first american to travel in space.
8. Last summer dad and i crossed the golden gate bridge.
9. The paddlewheel boat toured the missouri river.
10. Union troops were led by general u. s. grant of illinois.

Religions, Nationalities, and Languages

Capitalize the names of religions, nationalities, and languages.

Three major faiths are Christianity, Judaism, and Islam.
Many Mexicans speak both Spanish and English.

Clubs, Organizations, Businesses

Capitalize the names of clubs, organizations, and businesses.

Mary Ann belongs to the Junior Photographers' Club.
The Campfire Girls took a tour of the Bell Telephone Company offices downtown.

Exercises **Use capital letters correctly.**

A. Copy these sentences, using correct capitalization.

1. Did o. j. simpson play for the buffalo bills?
2. Last december russian dancers performed here.
3. Juan martinez speaks spanish at home and english at school.
4. The national geographic society has a fascinating magazine.
5. Yes, uncle tony, schwinn builds ten-speed bicycles.
6. Did you see the beautiful indian cloth and jewelry?
7. A store called go fly a kite at 1434 third avenue sells kites.
8. Many chinese people practice buddhism.
9. Jeb and i read about the israeli leader golda meir.
10. The sierra club holds nature outings each summer.

B. Follow the directions for Exercise A.

1. My sister jeannine has posters of british monarchs.
2. The polish scientist madame curie discovered radium.
3. In october, logan school started the snowflake club.
4. Cathy stover has folk dolls from portugal and brazil.
5. The springfield bicycle league held a race on august 5.
6. The museum is open from october to june.
7. During the christmas season, f.a.o. schwarz is a busy store.
8. The spanish explorer balboa discovered the pacific ocean.
9. The white house is at 1600 pennsylvania avenue.
10. Last spring mom and i flew a delta jet to atlanta.

C. Writing Copy this paragraph, using correct capitalization.

Our teacher, ms. abbott, told us about woodrow wilson the other day. At princeton university, professor wilson taught politics. He later became president of princeton university. Then he was known as doctor wilson. In 1912, the people elected him to the presidency of the united states. After that he was called president wilson.

First Words

Any word is capitalized if it appears in certain places in written work.

Sentences

Capital letters are important sentence signals. They tell when a new sentence begins.

Capitalize the first word of every sentence.

My brother likes mushrooms on his pizza.
Does February have twenty-nine days this year?
Look out!

Direct Quotations

When you write the exact words somebody else said, you are **quoting** that person. The words are a **direct quotation.**

Capitalize the first word of a direct quotation.

"Today we can expect two inches of snow," said the forecaster.

Usually, when you are writing what a person has said, you use explaining words like *he said* or *she asked*, before or after the direct quotation. If these explaining words come before the direct quotation, capitalize the first explaining words. Then capitalize the first word of the direct quotation.

"It's raining," my brother said.
My mother asked, "Is the cake still in the oven?"

Exercises **Use capital letters correctly.**

A. Copy these sentences using correct capitalization.

1. giant reptiles roamed the earth in prehistoric times.
2. "a robot has no brain," mr. rodriguez said.
3. maria asked, "may i use the microscope?"
4. "would you like to take a bike trip?" roosevelt asked.
5. wildflowers grow in the forest.
6. i explained, "a spaceship has landed on the surface of mars."
7. a kayak is similar to a canoe.
8. mother reminded me, "your fish must be fed."
9. mona asked, "have you seen my sweater?"
10. the teacher said, "admiral byrd was the first person to fly over the south pole."

B. Writing These sentences belong in one paragraph. Write them as a paragraph. Indent the first line. Use correct capitalization.

many years ago lanterns were used to light the streets of big cities.
candles were used in the lanterns.
the people in each house had to hang out a lantern.
in paris, in 1666, nearly three thousand lanterns gleamed in the streets.
isn't it strange to think of a city street lighted by candlelight?

Poetry

Capitalize the first word in most lines of poetry.

Cats sleep fat and walk thin.
Cats, when they sleep, slump;
When they wake, pull in—
And where the plump's been
There's skin.
Cats walk thin.

—ROSALIE MOORE, from "Catalogue"

Sometimes, the lines of a poem do not begin with capital letters.

Foghorns

The foghorns moaned
   in the bay last night
  so sad
  so deep
I thought I heard the city
   crying in its sleep.

—LILIAN MOORE

Outlines

Capitalize the first word of each line of an outline.

The major ideas of an outline are marked with Roman numerals (I, II, III). The secondary ideas are marked with capital letters (A, B, C).

Systems of Measurement

  I. The British system
     A. Inch, foot, yard, mile
     B. Ounce, pound, ton
     C. Cup, pint, quart, gallon

  II. The metric system
     A. Meter
     B. Gram
     C. Liter

Letters

Capitalize the greeting and the first word of the closing of a letter.

Dear **S**ir: **D**ear **L**ucy,   **S**incerely,   **Y**our friend,

Exercises   **Use capitals correctly.**

A. Capitalize the following poem, outline, and letter.

1. (poem)   **The Steam Shovel**

the steam digger
is much bigger
than the biggest beast i know.
he snorts and roars
like the dinosaurs
that lived long years ago.

—ROWENA BENNETT

2. (outline)   The Lewis and Clark Expedition

I. why it was needed
  a. the Louisiana Purchase of 1803
  b. lack of good maps

II. why Lewis and Clark were chosen
  a. achievements of Meriwether Lewis
  b. achievements of William Clark

3. (letter)
euclid park school
cleveland, ohio 44112
march 17, 19__

dear ms. lopez,
   we enjoyed your lesson about how to use a videotape camera. it was fun to see ourselves on television. in the future we will be able to videotape plays and other activities in our classroom.

sincerely yours,

william hodges

B. Follow the directions for Exercise A.

1. (poem)

How To Tell the Top of a Hill

the top of a hill
is not until
the bottom is below.
and you have to stop
when you reach the top
for there's no more UP to go.

—JOHN CIARDI

2. (outline)

Planning a Vegetable Garden

   I. choose a good spot
     a. enough sunshine
     b. good soil
     c. proper drainage

  II. choose your crops
     a. tasty vegetables
     b. easily grown vegetables

 III. draw a garden plan

3. (letter)

november 2, 19__

dear sarah,
    i am sending you a photo i took of my newest pet. panda is a beagle and a very playful puppy. by next summer she should be ready to go on our long hikes. whatever we do at the lake, panda will do, too. i know you'll like her.

your friend,

marie

Capitalizing Titles

Capitalize the first word and all important words in chapter titles, titles of magazine articles, titles of short stories or single poems, and titles of songs.

Use quotation marks for these titles.

Chapter:	Chapter 3, "Our Solar System"
Magazine article:	"Safety on Skateboards"
Short story:	"The Legend of Sleepy Hollow"
Poem:	"Catalog"
Song:	"America the Beautiful"

Capitalize the first word and all important words in titles of books, newspapers, magazines, movies, and television programs.

Underline these titles. (When these titles are printed, they are *italicized.*)

Book:	*Abe Lincoln Grows Up*
Newspaper:	*Chicago Tribune*
Magazine:	*National Geographic*
Movie:	*King Kong*
Television program:	*Nova*

Do not capitalize words such as *the, in, for, from, by, at, a,* or *an,* unless they come first or last in a title.

Exercises **Use capital letters correctly.**

A. Copy the following titles. Capitalize them correctly.

1. *i am the cheese* (book)
2. "east of the sun and west of the moon" (story)
3. *little house on the prairie* (book)
4. *and now miguel* (book)
5. "the lady or the tiger?" (short story)

6. "the life of the pioneers"   (chapter title)
7. "the top ten on television"   (magazine article)
8. *creative computing*   (magazine)
9. "the horses of the sea"   (poem)
10. *willie wonka and the chocolate factory*   (book and movie)

B.   Follow the directions for Exercise A.

1. *m.c. higgins, the great*   (book)
2. *wall street journal*   (newspaper)
3. "a visit from st. nicholas"   (poem)
4. *the lord of the rings*   (book and movie)
5. "the highwayman"   (poem)
6. "building better kites"   (magazine article)
7. *wild, wild world of animals*   (television program)
8. "the star-spangled banner"   (song)
9. *freedom train*   (book)
10. "casey at the bat"   (poem)

ADDITIONAL EXERCISES

Capitalization

A. Proper Nouns and Proper Adjectives Copy each of the following sentences. Change small letters to capital letters wherever necessary.

1. Do wesley and craig phillips live on cherry street?
2. Last summer aunt rhoda studied mexican art.
3. Lloyd j. curtis sails his yacht on lake michigan.
4. Last tuesday governor scott was re-elected.
5. My teacher, mr. olsen, rides a bike to school.
6. The first day of spring is march 21.
7. This wednesday, february 14, is valentine's day.
8. Last may the mason family moved to georgia.
9. Alicia plays the french horn in our school orchestra.
10. The principal of skiles middle school is ms. j. e. clark.
11. Is salt lake city west of the rocky mountains?
12. The boys clubs of america sponsor service projects.
13. The founder of buddhism was a teacher from india.
14. We buy spanish magazines at books galore on oak street.
15. Does the colorado river flow through arizona?
16. Last summer i took the train to minneapolis, minnesota.
17. The bill from dr. bates arrived on tuesday.
18. An important jewish holiday is yom kippur.
19. Beth speaks english, russian, and italian.
20. Our tour began at the united nations building in manhattan.

B. First Words and Titles Copy each of the following items. Change small letters to capital letters when necessary.

1. terry asked, "has the bell rung?"

2. "estes national park is terrific!" jenny said.
3. he has a heart of gold beneath
   but the lion just can't trust his teeth.
   —JOHN CIARDI, from "Why Nobody Pets the Lion at the Zoo"
4. *the jungle book* was written by rudyard kipling.
5. one very popular movie was *return of the jedi.*
6. mr. grant asked, "where are those reports?"
7. kinds of business ownership
      I. corporation
        a. privately held
        b. publicly held
     II. partnership
    III. individual ownership
8. ms. irwin assigned the book *the chocolate war.*
9. laura memorized the poem "mending wall" by robert frost.
10. dear sharon,
       meet me in the library at 4:00. i found the book you need for your report.

              your friend,
              nancy
11. watch out! there's a pothole in the street.
12. jim said, "let's try out for the diving team."
13. "what is that sculpture supposed to be?" asked ted.
14.   **the termite**

    some primal termite knocked on wood
    and tasted it, and found it good,
    and that is why your cousin May
    fell through the parlor floor today.
              —OGDEN NASH
15. mr. johnson announced, "we will see the movie *the red pony* tomorrow."

MIXED REVIEW

Capitalization

A. Using capital letters correctly Copy the following sentences. Change small letters to capital letters wherever necessary.

1. the ancient romans spoke latin.
2. dad and i will visit the san diego zoo this summer.
3. when walking in a tiny rain
   across a vacant lot,
   a pup's a good companion—
   if a pup you've got.
   —GWENDOLYN BROOKS, from "Vern"
4. orphan annie has a dog named sandy.
5. "did you read *sounder*?" asked marge.
6. john lennon was a rock singer from england.
7. the students at lincoln school will celebrate chinese new year this tuesday.
8. have you ever attended a hawaiian luau?
9. president ronald reagan was once the governor of california.
10. nathan asked, "are you going to los angeles this friday?"
11. Have you read the article "don't be shy" in *scholastic* magazine?
12. The beck family canoed down the eagle river.
13. the chorus sang "what do the simple folk do?" from the play *camelot*.
14. "oh, yes! we'd love to go sledding!" exclaimed the children.
15. my uncle enjoys watching *masterpiece theatre* each week.

16. dear sir:
    enclosed is a donation for the american heart asso-
    ciation.

    sincerely,

    jerry lipke

17. "do you have the july, 1981, issue of *national geo-
    graphic?*" asked mike.
18. i am in the seventh grade at tuley junior high.
19. "we're going to aunt jane's house for thanksgiving,"
    said mother.
20. are you going to try out for the tiger's pom-pom club?

B. Using capital letters correctly in proofreading
Proofread the following letter. Rewrite it, changing small letters to capital letters where necessary.

december 31, 19_ _

Hi brad,
    greetings from the north. I remember the great
send-off i received from my friends at prairie school
when I left Kansas. It helped me to get through my
first minnesota winter. i think snow was invented just
for Minneapolis. cross-country skiing around Lake
nikomas keeps me in shape the way running did in
kansas city. my family is planning a return visit for
memorial day weekend. Say hello to pat, terry, and the
rest of the gang for me.

see you in may,

marc

USING MECHANICS IN WRITING
Capitalization

A. Your pen pal in another country is very interested in popular American music. He or she has written a letter asking what songs, singers, and groups you enjoy most. Write to your pen pal about the music you like. Include at least two names of groups, two performers, and three album titles. Tell what new song is your favorite. Be sure to use capital letters correctly.

B. Think about a country you would like to visit. Look up that country in an encyclopedia. Write down the names of the country's capital and its major cities. Also write the names of major rivers, lakes, mountain ranges, or other geographic features. Write a paragraph telling some facts about this country. Remember to use capital letters correctly.

C. Choose five interesting places in your city or town. These places could include streets, buildings, museums, and parks. Write a paragraph about these places. In your paragraph, tell where each place is and why it is interesting. Remember to capitalize all of the proper nouns you use.

D. Make a list of your three favorite books. Write the author of each book. Then make a list of your three favorite TV shows. Include the names of the characters.
   Then write two paragraphs. One paragraph should tell about your favorite books. Tell who wrote them and why you like them. The second paragraph should be about your favorite TV shows. Explain why they are your favorites. Tell who stars in them. Use capital letters correctly.

Punctuation

Punctuation marks are signals. They signal the ends of sentences. They also signal pauses inside sentences. A punctuation mark can signal a direct quotation, a question, or an exclamation. Punctuation helps you to write clearly. It helps your readers understand what you have written.

In this section, you will learn rules for punctuating correctly. Study the rules and their examples. Whenever you are writing, use this section to make sure you are using punctuation marks correctly.

Using the Period

When you write, you use a **period (.)** for different purposes. Here are four uses of the period.

The Period at the End of a Sentence

A period is used at the end of a declarative sentence and at the end of an imperative sentence. The period is a signal that the sentence has ended. When you are reading aloud, the period tells you to drop your voice.

Declarative: Navaho Indians built homes called hogans.

Imperative: Help me find my sweater.

Use a period at the end of a declarative sentence and at the end of an imperative sentence.

The Period After an Initial

An **initial** is the first letter of a name. An initial is always capitalized and followed by a period.

Nancy L. Kassebaum   John F. Kennedy

Use a period after an initial.

The Period After an Abbreviation

An **abbreviation** is a short form of a word. An abbreviation is usually followed by a period.

Here are abbreviations for the days of the week.

Sun.   Mon.   Tues.   Wed.   Thurs.   Fri.   Sat.

Here are abbreviations for months of the year:

Jan.   Feb.   Mar.   Apr.   Aug.   Sept.   Oct.   Nov.   Dec.

What three months are left out? Why? A word that is short in its regular form does not usually have an abbreviation.

Some abbreviations stand for more than one word and have more than one period.

D.C.
District of Columbia

A.M. (*ante meridiem*)
means before noon

P.M. (*post meridiem*)
means after noon

P.O.
Post Office

B.C.
Before Christ

A.D. (*Anno Domini*)
means in the year of the Lord

Below is a list of common abbreviations.

Titles

Mr.   Mrs.   Ms.
Mister   Mistress   (no long form)

Dr.   Rev.
Doctor   Reverend

Geographic Terms

Rd.   Ave.   U.S.A.
Road   Avenue   United States of America

Blvd.   St.
Boulevard   Street

English Measure

oz.   lb.   in.   doz.
ounce(s)   pound(s)   inch(es)   dozen

yd.   mi.   ft.
yard   mile   foot (or feet)

Not all abbreviations use periods. Here are some examples:

mph   UN   ZIP
miles per hour   United Nations   Zone Improvement
                                    Plan

Use a period after most abbreviations.

Using Abbreviations Correctly

Abbreviations may be used in lists, addresses, arithmetic problems, or other special forms of writing. You should not use abbreviations in sentences, paragraphs, and compositions. For example, on an application for a library card, or on an envelope, you may write your address in this way:

2176 So. Taylor Rd.

In a sentence, you should write this:

I live at 2176 South Taylor Road.

As a general rule, the only abbreviations you should use in sentences are *A.M.* and *P.M.*, *B.C.* and *A.D.*, and titles with names, such as *Dr. Perez.*

The Period After Each Numeral or Letter in an Outline

Use a period after each numeral or letter that shows a division of an outline.

How the Months Got Their Names

I. Months named for real people

A. July

B. August

II. Months named for gods

A. January

B. March

C. May

D. June

III. Other months

544

Exercises

A. Copy these sentences, using periods where needed.

1. The Rev Lydia Marshall spoke at our church
2. Capt James Cook sailed across the ocean
3. Ms Sue Schneider refereed the game
4. J Fred Muggs was a famous chimpanzee
5. Ask Dr Jean Casey for an appointment
6. Be sure to bring warm mittens
7. Capt B J Hunnicutt talked to Gen Sherman Potter
8. Make yourself comfortable
9. Send your questions to Mr Thomas N Sane
10. Author P L Travers wrote about Mary Poppins

B. Copy the following, putting periods where necessary.

1. 1301 Ridge Ave
2. 260 B C
3. 4:15 P M
4. 4 Pond St Winthrop, MA 02152
5. PO Box 253
6. Dec 15, 1985
7. 20 lb
8. Dr C G Opaskar
9. 5 ft 7 in
10. 55 mi

C. Copy this outline, putting periods where necessary.

Abraham Lincoln

I Before becoming President
  A Childhood
  B Early career
II As President
  A Civil War
  B Emancipation Proclamation

Using the Question Mark

A **question mark (?)** is used at the end of every interrogative sentence. It is a signal that a question has been asked. When you are reading aloud, the question mark tells you to raise the pitch of your voice.

Are you ready to go? What did you say?

Use a question mark at the end of every interrogative sentence.

Exercises **Use question marks correctly.**

A. Copy these sentences. Use either a period or a question mark at the end of each sentence.

1. I built a bookshelf in shop class
2. Does Jason collect stamps
3. Look at that printing press
4. What is batik
5. Can you grow a plant from orange seeds
6. How does this camera work
7. Mom made the costumes for our play
8. Do all of the problems on this page
9. When was the Battle of Gettysburg fought
10. Do you have this album

B. Follow the directions for Exercise A.

1. Sam plays the saxaphone
2. Are you babysitting for the Mayberry children
3. Measure the length and width of the room
4. I make animals and flowers from paper scraps
5. Can you tie a half-hitch knot
6. Come and join our softball game
7. Have you ever made granola

8. Recycle glass bottles to save natural resources
9. What is that sound in the engine
10. The motor is racing

Using the Exclamation Point

An **exclamation point (!)** is used at the end of an exclamatory sentence and after words or phrases that show strong feeling. An exclamation point tells the reader that the sentence or words should be read with strong feeling. The exclamation point signals surprise, joy, fear, excitement, or shock.

Don't open that door!

Help! Fire!

Good grief!

Use an exclamation point at the end of an exclamatory sentence or word.

Exercises **Use the exclamation point correctly.**

A. Copy these sentences. Use a period, a question mark, or an exclamation point where it is needed.

1. Do you have a sweet tooth
2. Hooray We won
3. Oh, no The bus has gone
4. When does the dance begin
5. Where is your prize
6. We went to the new house
7. Let's play these records
8. May I use the shovel
9. Start with a simple project
10. Halt

Example: *Event*—I received a 10-speed bicycle.
Exclamation—This is just what I wanted!

Using the Comma

The **comma (,)** generally signals a pause in a sentence, or a separation between related ideas. When you are reading aloud, the comma tells you to pause briefly.

There are eight uses of the comma that you should know.

Use a comma to separate the day of the month from the year.

Thomas Jefferson died on July 4, 1826.

The stock market crashed on October 29, 1929.

If the date appears in the middle of the sentence, place a comma after the year, also.

Peace came on November 11, 1918, to the nations of Europe.

On August 9, 1974, President Nixon resigned.

Use a comma to separate the name of a city from the state or country in which it is located.

Toronto, Canada   Detroit, Michigan

Miami, Florida   Tokyo, Japan

If the name appears in the middle of a sentence, place a comma after the state or country.

We lived in Cherry Valley, Ohio, for several years.

Every year in Rutland, Vermont, there is a county fair.

Use a comma to set off the name of a person spoken to.

Will you close the door, Juan?

Miss Bristol, may I leave early today?

I think, Nancy, that I'll be late today.

Use a comma after introductory words, such as *yes* and *no*.

No, planets are not stars.

Yes, we will meet you before the game.

Use a comma to set apart words or names in a series.

Two words or names are not a series. There are always more than two in a series.

We had watermelon and sherbet for dessert. (no series)

We had apples, pears, and cheese for dessert. (series)

Read and punctuate a series carefully.
How many girls are named in each sentence below?

I invited Mary, Louise, Sue, Ann, and Jean.

I invited Mary Louise, Sue Ann, and Jean.

You see that changing the number of commas changes the number of girls from five to three.

Use a comma before or after a direct quotation.

The crowd shouted, "Run to third base!"

"I like swimming best," Ted replied.

Use a comma after the greeting of a friendly letter and the closing of any letter.

Dear Joseph,   Yours truly,

549

Use a comma in a compound sentence.

Place the comma before the conjunction.

Casey struck out, and the game was over.

The cookies burned, but we ate them anyway.

Exercises **Use commas correctly.**

A. Copy the following sentences. Put in commas where they are needed. Be ready to explain the reason for each comma you put in.

1. Dad where did you find my gloves?
2. Julie answer this riddle.
3. The Declaration of Independence was signed on July 4 1776.
4. Amelia Earhart was born in Atchison Kansas on July 24 1898.
5. Yes you may have another glass of apple juice.
6. A Kentucky Derby winner must be bold fast and strong.
7. Do you always stop look and listen at crossings?
8. "You'll feel better after a rest" the nurse said.
9. The birdcage fell and my parakeet screeched.
10. Courtney said "Pick a card."

B. Follow the directions for Exercise A.

1. No I'd rather have soup.
2. Stacey said "Try this magic trick."
3. The Astrodome is in Houston Texas.
4. This lake is cool deep and clear.
5. The guide arrived early but the tour began late.
6. Debbie did you see the seahorse?
7. "I'll be outside" Larry said.
8. We had planned a picnic but it rained all day.

9. The fielder caught dropped and recovered the ball.

10. Sputnik was launched on October 4 1957.

C. Writing Copy the following note, using necessary commas.

Dear Kate

Yes my parents said that I may visit you and your family in Little Rock on the weekend of July 4. I am so excited! I cannot wait to see you Kate. I will be arriving by bus on July 2 at 2:30 P.M. Be sure to give my best to Jodie Sara Maggie and your parents.

Your friend
Ginny

Using the Apostrophe

The **apostrophe (')** is used for two different purposes. When you are reading aloud, it has no effect on how you say the word in which it appears.

The Apostrophe To Show Possession

A **possessive** is a word that shows that someone or something owns something else.

To form the possessive of a singular noun, add an apostrophe and an s.

The tent that belongs to James is James's tent.

The car that belongs to his mother is his mother's car.

To form the possessive of a plural noun that does not end in s, add an apostrophe and an s.

The toys of the children are the children's toys.

The hats that belong to men are men's hats.

To form the possessive of a plural noun that ends in s, add only an apostrophe.

The cages of the tigers are the tigers' cages.

The costumes of the actresses are the actresses' costumes.

Exercises **Use apostrophes to show possession.**

A. Write the possessive form of these words.

1. Maria	5. boss	9. the Smiths
2. our class	6. woman	10. tribe
3. people	7. workers	11. ranchers
4. puppies	8. Chris	12. hostess

B. Copy the groups of words below. Make the underlined word in each group show possession.

1. the <u>kittens</u> mother
2. the <u>catcher</u> mitt
3. bus <u>drivers</u> uniforms
4. <u>Ann</u> cousin
5. the <u>children</u> library
6. your <u>grandparents</u> house
7. the <u>captain</u> orders
8. the <u>woman</u> office
9. <u>Geraldo</u> uncle
10. the <u>canary</u> cage

The Apostrophe in Contractions

Do you often use the word *don't*? It is a short way of saying *do not*. The apostrophe shows that a letter has been left out.

A word made up of two words combined into one by leaving out one or more letters is called a **contraction**.

Common Contractions

is not = isn't		it is = it's	
does not = doesn't		I will = I'll	
do not = don't		I am = I'm	
cannot = can't		they are = they're	
will not = won't		we are = we're	
have not = haven't		you have = you've	
would not = wouldn't		I would or I had = I'd	

Use an apostrophe in a contraction, to show where one or more letters have been omitted.

Be especially careful with *it's* and *its*. Remember:

It's (with an apostrophe) always means *it is* or *it has*.
It's time for lunch.

Its (without the apostrophe) is the possessive of *it*.
The kitten played with *its* rubber mouse.

Remember also that no apostrophe is used with the possessive pronouns *hers, yours, ours,* and *theirs*.

This guitar is *hers*.	*Ours* is the best team.
That one is *yours*.	*Theirs* is losing now.

Here are some contractions and other words that are often confused.

Who's means *who is* or *who has*.
Who's been eating my porridge?

Whose is the possessive of *who*.
Whose coat is this?

You're means *you are*.
You're the first person to give the right answer.

Your is the possessive of *you*.
I'll put *your* paper on the bulletin board.

They're means *they are*.
They're on the plane to Oregon now.

Their is the possessive form of *they*.
The band members played *their* instruments well.

There means a place, or it is used to begin sentences.
I am going *there* later.   *There* is someone at the door.

A. Write each pair of words. Beside each pair, write its contraction.

1. have not	5. would not	9. are not
2. does not	6. were not	10. had not
3. it is	7. I am	11. you are
4. was not	8. did not	12. she would

B. Copy the following sentences, inserting apostrophes where they are needed.

1. Isnt that racket yours?
2. Whos building the fire?
3. I cant play chess.
4. Doesnt your city have a childrens museum?
5. Youll enjoy Lisas new records.
6. Vics house is full of pets.
7. Its a picture of a lions den.
8. The kittens are Mandys and hers.
9. Theyre in Mr. Baxters art class.
10. The box wont fit on this shelf.

Using the Hyphen

Often when you are writing you run out of space at the end of a line and cannot fit in all of the next word. When this happens, you write part of the word, followed by a **hyphen (-),** on that line. You write the rest of the word at the beginning of the next line.

Use a hyphen to divide a word at the end of a line.

In prehistoric times, the dinosaur roamed the earth.

Only words of two or more syllables can be divided at the end of a line. Never divide words of one syllable, such as *pound* or *might*. If you are in doubt about dividing a word, look it up in a dictionary.

A single letter must not be left at the end of a line. For example, this division would be wrong: *a-part*. A single letter must not appear at the beginning of a line either. It would be wrong to divide *dictionary* like this: *dictionar-y*.

Exercises **Use the hyphen.**

A. Decide whether you can divide each of these words into two parts. Each part should have more than one letter. Check the word in a dictionary to be sure. If a word can be divided, write it as you would if the word occurred at the end of a line. Add the necessary hyphen. If the word can be divided into two parts in more than one way, show both ways. If the word cannot be divided, just copy it.

Examples: a. arithmetic   b. able
arith- or arithme-   able
metic   tic

1. bury	5. owl	9. live
2. adventure	6. copy	10. honest
3. sail	7. groceries	11. together
4. music	8. marbles	12. hungry

B. Follow the directions for Exercise A.

1. banner	5. equal	9. body
2. collection	6. history	10. measure
3. strange	7. sketch	11. neighborhood
4. pony	8. amazing	12. crafts

Using Quotation Marks

When you write the exact words that someone said, you are quoting that person. The person's exact words are called a direct quotation. **Quotation marks (" ")** are the sign that someone is being quoted exactly.

Use quotation marks before and after the words of every direct quotation.

Read this sentence carefully:

Molly called, "The game starts in ten minutes."

Notice these things about the sentence above:

1. There is a comma (,) before the quotation.
2. Only the speaker's exact words are placed inside the quotation marks.
3. The quotation begins with a capital letter.
4. The punctuation at the end of the sentence is placed *inside* the quotation marks.

Study each of these sentences. See how each one follows the four rules.

Kenneth yelled, "There is a fire in the kitchen!"

Della asked, "Did anybody find a red glove?"

The director insisted, "Speak slowly and clearly."

A Quotation at the Beginning of a Sentence

Sometimes a quotation is placed at the beginning of a sentence.

"This plant needs water," Mr. Crockett said.

Notice that the comma ending the quotation is placed inside the quotation marks. Notice that the punctuation ending each of the following quotations is also placed inside the quotation marks. Notice, too, the punctuation at the end of each sentence.

"There is a fire in the kitchen!" yelled Kenneth.

"Did anybody find a red glove?" Della asked.

"Speak slowly and clearly," the director insisted.

Exercises **Punctuate quotations correctly.**

A. Copy these sentences. Punctuate them correctly.

1. Make up your mind Dennis urged.
2. I finished the puzzle he announced.
3. JoAnn asked Is that a sparrow?
4. The zookeeper warned Don't disturb the panda.
5. Where is the North Star she asked.
6. What causes a storm Lauren asked.
7. Mom raises bees said Jeff.
8. A chameleon changes color Terri noted.
9. Dad asked Where are your gloves?
10. Mr. Owens said Sing that verse again.

B. Follow the directions for Exercise A.

1. What happened to my room Caroline asked.
2. The doctor shouted I need a bandage!
3. Put your feet in the stirrups she said.
4. Here's the entrance Kyle yelled.
5. Charlene asked What's your favorite color?
6. The monarch is a butterfly Alonzo explained.
7. Steve shouted My kite string broke!
8. Emily said I have a Venus' flytrap.
9. I asked Have you read the comic strips?
10. Where is the Nancy Drew book Alison asked.

C. Writing Each of these five sentences has one mistake in it. Write the sentences correctly.

1. "Mary said, I will be home soon."
2. "Do you deliver the newspaper" Ms. Conklin asked the girl on the bicycle.
3. Jeff yelled, "look out for the car!"
4. Lydia said, "You may use my skateboard".
5. "My watch broke, Spencer" complained.

Divided Quotations

Sometimes a quotation is divided by explaining words. These are words like *she said* or *he asked* that come in the middle of the quotation.

"After three hamburgers," Vic said, "pie would be too much."

Divided quotations follow the same capitalization and punctuation rules that you have already studied. Here are three more rules for divided quotations:

1. Use two sets of quotation marks.

2. Use a comma or a period after the explaining words. Use a comma if the second part of the quotation does not begin a new sentence. Use a period if the second part of the quotation is a new sentence.

"Did you know," Katherine asked, "that mammoths once lived here?"

"Turn off the TV," Larry suggested. "Nothing good is on now."

3. If the second part of the quotation begins a new sentence, capitalize the first word. This was done in the second example above. Otherwise, do not capitalize the first word.

A. Copy these divided quotations. Add punctuation and capital letters where they are needed.

1. Some people Josh noted don't laugh much.
2. I'm tired Suzanne said let's rest.
3. After you move Jeff asked will you write to me?
4. During the summer Amy said we make ice cream.
5. What's cooking I asked it smells good.
6. We're late Mom said the show has started.
7. When does camp start Sonia asked I'm ready.
8. I have a layout Bill said for a model railroad.
9. For my project Tom said I made soap sculptures.
10. We've looked at stars Lynn said we used a telescope.

B. Follow the directions for Exercise A.

1. My favorite ballplayer Kelly said is Pete Rose.
2. Drop the anchor Sandra called we'll fish here.
3. The space shuttle *Columbia* Marilyn reported has been reused many times.
4. Drumbeats our guide noted are a way of sending messages.
5. Thread the needle Dad said then make a knot.
6. Eric made a film I explained of our science project.
7. Try this sauce my sister said it's very good.
8. Throw the boomerang Judith said it will return.
9. What's a tangram Joe asked is it a puzzle?
10. What asked Elena can we learn from fossils?

Using Quotation Marks for Titles

Use quotation marks to enclose chapter titles, titles of magazine articles, titles of short stories or single poems, and titles of songs.

Chapter:	Chapter 7, "The Civil War"
Magazine article:	"Finding Summer Jobs"
Short story:	"The Tell-Tale Heart"
Poem:	"How To Eat a Poem"
Song:	"The Battle Hymn of the Republic"

Underlining

When you are writing or typing, underline the titles of books, newspapers, magazines, movies, and television programs.

<u>The Incredible Journey</u>   <u>Kansas City Star</u>
<u>Rocky</u>   <u>Sports Illustrated</u>

When these titles are printed, they are printed in *italics*, rather than underlined.

Book:	*The Incredible Journey*
Newspaper:	*Kansas City Star*
Magazine:	*Sports Illustrated*
Movie:	*Rocky*
Television program:	*Good Morning, America*

Exercise   Punctuate titles correctly.

Copy the following titles. Use quotation marks or underlining to make each title correct.

1. Babe, the Blue Ox   (short story)
2. The Moonspinners   (movie)
3. How To Train Your Dog   (magazine article)
4. Hot Rod   (magazine)
5. Karen   (book)
6. Seattle Times   (newspaper)
7. Women in America   (chapter title)
8. You Are My Sunshine   (song)
9. Nightline   (TV program)
10. Annabel Lee   (poem)

ADDITIONAL EXERCISES

Punctuation

A. The Period Write the following items, adding periods where they are needed.

1. E B White wrote several famous children's books
2. The bus will leave Washington, D C at 4:30 P M
3. Write me at P O Box 640, Ada, Ohio, after June 1
4. Ms K L Waverly visited the UN building
5. The Battle of Hastings was fought in A D 1066
6. Dr F T Richards
   800 Austin St
   Evanston, IL 60202
7. Salads
   I Fruit salads
     A Waldorf salad
     B Hawaiian salad
   II Vegetable salads
8. Mr John J Lynk works for Data Control, Inc
9. The note read, "Meet me at 9:00 A M , Thurs , Jan 28"
10. Gen George S Patton lead U S Army troops during World War II

B. The Period, the Question Mark; and the Exclamation Point Copy these sentences. Put either a period, a question mark, or an exclamation point where it is needed.

1. When does the play begin
2. Transplant this rosebush to the back yard
3. Oh no The kitten has climbed a tree
4. Joseph mailed the basket of fruit and cheese to Aunt Evelyn
5. Where is my ski cap
6. How are pearls formed

7. Julie practiced the piano after school
8. Ouch I burned my finger
9. Cliff scored sixteen points in the basketball game
10. Congratulations You won the race

C. The Comma Write the following sentences or phrases, adding commas where they are needed.

1. On June 28 1919 the treaty was signed in Versailles.
2. No Sharla I've never been to Toledo Ohio.
3. The interviewer asked "Mr. Cassidy what are your plans?"
4. Yes they sell blueberry raspberry and strawberry yogurt.
5. Dad made apple pancakes and they were terrific.
6. Well Ms. Baker John plays the tuba and I play the saxophone.
7. "This car needs a battery tires and a paint job" said the mechanic.
8. Craig are you going to visit Springfield Illinois or Springfield Massachusetts?
9. The chef said "The recipe calls for fresh tomatoes green peppers and onions."
10. Dear Roger
   I will arrive at the airport in Atlanta Georgia at 8:00 P.M. on June 13 1990. Let me know if you can meet me.

   Your friend
   Jeff

D. The Apostrophe Write each sentence, adding an apostrophe where it is needed.

1. Jamess brother built a model of a space station.
2. This theaters prices have increased again.
3. Arent the boys lockers just like ours?

4. Whos the womens diving champion?
5. Im surprised that youre here.
6. Doesnt the childrens matinee begin at 2:00 P.M.?
7. Cant you go, or dont you want to?
8. Claires cousin couldnt attend the meeting.
9. Its the pilots voice on the intercom.
10. Were going to the Taylors house.

E. The Hyphen Decide whether you can divide each of these words into two parts. Each part should have more than one letter. If a word can be divided, write it as you would if the word occurred at the end of a line. Add the necessary hyphen. If the word can be divided into two parts in more than one way, show both ways. If the word cannot be divided, just copy it. Use a dictionary to check your work.

1. hobby
2. candle
3. razor
4. misbehave
5. pillow
6. plate
7. library
8. cactus
9. sofa
10. drafty

F. Quotation Marks Write each sentence, adding quotation marks where they are needed.

1. Jessica asked, How are pickles made?
2. The next holiday is Halloween, Maria said.
3. We had a picnic, Olivia said, beside a lake.
4. That tunnel goes through the mountains, Steven said.
5. Eve Merriam wrote the poem called Cheers.
6. Who wants pepperoni, asked Vic, and who wants mushrooms?
7. Mr. Barker remarked, The traffic is heavy today.
8. Hold that line! shouted the cheerleaders.
9. At midnight the band played Good Night, Ladies.
10. Give me two burgers, ordered the waiter, but no fries.

MIXED REVIEW

Punctuation

A. **Using punctuation correctly** Copy the following sentences, adding periods, question marks, exclamation points, apostrophes and commas where necessary.

1. Did you read the book *Extra Cash for Kids* before starting your business
2. Yes I visited EPCOT Center in March 1984
3. The baby played in the mud the sand and the water
4. On July 8 1990 we will move to Mobile Alabama
5. The Smithsonian Institution is in Washington D C
6. Susan B Anthony worked for womens rights
7. I looked said Ray but I cant find the hamster
8. Dr Kramer will see you at 10:00 A M said Gail
9. Im cheering for the Giants said Alison I hope they win
10. Jeff isnt this your notebook I asked

B. **Using punctuation correctly in letters** Copy the following letter. Add the punctuation that is needed.

Camp We-Ha-Kee
Winter WI 53714
July 20 19_ _

Dear Molly
   You were right Im so busy with my activities here that I hardly have time to miss you and the folks Archery sailing and riding are my favorites Our drama group will be performing The Princess and the Pea for Parents Weekend Are you coming too I hope youre keeping my side of the room clean Molly

Your sister

Jennifer

C. Proofreading for correct punctuation Proofread the following paragraph. Most of the punctuation in it is missing. Rewrite the paragraph, adding the correct punctuation.

Throughout history, people have built many amazing things The Great Wall of China is one of them The Great Wall of China was built more than 2,000 years ago. Its almost 4,000 miles long and it is the only structure on earth that astronauts in outer space can see The Great Wall was built to protect the Chinese people against invaders Wouldnt you like to visit this wonder of the world Prof Hsang from the university will lead a tour starting July 1985. The tour will depart from Chicago Illinois You can read more about the Great Wall in the article Chinas Amazing Wall in this month's *Adventure* magazine.

USING MECHANICS IN WRITING
Punctuation

A.   Imagine that you are out riding your bike one day. A blinding white light suddenly appears. Then the light disappears. On the ground is a glowing object. As you look closer, you see that it is an electronic message. The words are in English, but there is no punctuation. You must punctuate it in order to make sense out of it.

> Hello earthlings We are friendly beings from another galaxy We know your language but we are not sure you know ours Thats why we are writing in English We are curious about life on your planet How interesting it seems We want to learn more about you and we are eager to tell you about life on our planet Polaria Would you like to communicate If so write your name age and address on this scroll We will come for it at 830 Mon Nov 12 in front of Lincolns statue in the park Don't be afraid

B.   You dialed the phone number of your best friend. For some reason, you got the Twilight Zone instead. A famous person from history answers the phone. Write down the unusual conversation you have with this person. Use quotation marks correctly in recording your dialogue.

Spelling

When you speak, you never have to think about how a word is spelled. When you write, however, correct spelling is absolutely necessary. Because you want your writing to make sense, you want to be a good speller.

You can become a better speller by developing a few good habits and understanding a few basic rules. These habits and rules will help you to write clearly. In this section you will learn the most important habits and rules of good spelling.

Plan Your Study of Spelling

There may always be a few words that you will have trouble spelling. However, you will be able to master most words quickly if you work at developing the following habits.

Habits for Improving Your Spelling

1. Make a habit of looking at words carefully.

When you come to a new word, be sure you know its meaning. If you are not certain, look up the word in a dictionary.

Practice seeing every letter. Many people see a word again and again but don't really look at it. When you see a new word, or a tricky word, like *government*, look at all the letters. To help you remember them, write the word several times.

2. When you speak, pronounce words carefully.

Some people spell words wrong just because they do not pronounce them right. If you leave out certain sounds, you will have a hard time spelling words correctly.

Here is a list of words that cause trouble because they are often pronounced wrong. The letters in dark print are the letters that are often left out in spelling because they are left out in pronouncing the words.

February	dif**fe**rent	gover**n**ment
lib**r**ary	groc**e**ry	family
hund**r**ed	hist**o**ry	proba**b**ly
sev**e**ral	fun**e**ral	ever**y**body

3. Find out your own spelling enemies and attack them.

Look over your papers and make a list of the misspelled words. Also keep a list of new words that are difficult for you. Study these words until you can spell them correctly and easily.

4. Find memory devices to help with problem spellings.

Some words are difficult to remember. In these cases, a memory device may help you. A memory device is a trick, or a catchy sentence about the word, that you can remember easily. The device tells you how to spell the word. Here are two examples:

> **friend** *I* will be your fr*iend* to the *end.*
> **believe** There is a *lie* in be*lie*ve.

5. Proofread what you write.

To make sure that you have spelled all words correctly, reread your work. Examine it carefully, word for word. Don't let your eyes race over the page and miss incorrectly spelled words.

6. Use a dictionary.

You don't have to know how to spell every word. No one spells everything correctly all the time. A good dictionary can help you to be a better speller. Use a dictionary whenever you need help with your spelling.

7. Study the few important spelling rules given in this section.

Steps for Mastering Specific Words

When you notice that you are having trouble with a certain word, take a few minutes to study it carefully. Give it all your attention. If you spend the time and energy to learn it correctly once, you will save yourself all the trouble of correcting it many times.

Follow these steps to master a specific word.

Steps for Mastering Specific Words

1. Look at the word and say it to yourself.
Pronounce it carefully. If it has two or more syllables, say it again, one syllable at a time. Look at each syllable as you say it.

2. Look at the letters and say each one.
If the word has two or more syllables, pause between syllables as you say the letters.

3. Without looking at the word, write it.

4. Now look at your book or list to see if you have spelled the word correctly.
If you have, write it once more. Compare it with the correct spelling again. For best results, repeat the process once more.

5. If you have misspelled the word, notice where the error was.
Then repeat steps 3 and 4 until you have spelled the word correctly three times in a row.

Exercises   Develop good habits.

A.   Here are some words that are often pronounced carelessly and then misspelled. Look at each letter of every word. Pronounce the words correctly to yourself. Write the words in alphabetical order.

1. regular	4. ruin	7. diamond	9. violet
2. Saturday	5. police	8. poem	10. finally
3. general	6. different		

B. **Writing** Write five of the words listed in Exercise A in good sentences. Check your spelling when you write the words.

C. Read through some of your recent papers to find words you have misspelled. Make a list of five to ten of your personal spelling enemies. Then study them, following the **Steps for Mastering Specific Words.**

Rules for Spelling

Many words in our language follow certain spelling patterns. Studying the following rules should help you with these words.

Spelling Words with *ie* and *ei*

Many students find it hard to tell whether *i* comes before or after *e* in spelling certain words. When the sound is long *e* (*ē*), the following rhyme provides some rules which will help you.

> *I* before *e*
> Except after *c*,
> Or when sounded like *a*
> As in n*ei*ghbor or w*ei*gh.

This rhyme does help. Look at the words below. Decide which lines of the rhyme work for each of these words.

believe	receive	weigh
niece	conceit	weight
relief	ceiling	eight

The rule will help you with most words. But you will have to study and remember these four words. They do not follow the rule. They are **exceptions** to the rule.

either	neither	seize	weird

Write words with *ie* and *ei*.

Writing   Write ten sentences using words with *ie* or *ei*. (You may use more than one such word in each sentence.) Underline each of the *ie* or *ei* words you use.

Example: My *niece received eight* presents.

Adding Prefixes

A **prefix** is a syllable or group of syllables that is added to the beginning of a word to change its meaning. Here are some common prefixes and examples of their use:

Prefix	Base Word	New Word
re- (again)	+ write	= rewrite (write again)
dis- (not)	+ approve	= disapprove (not approve)
un- (not)	+ able	= unable(not able)
in- (not)	+ formal	= informal (not formal)
im- (not)	+ possible	= impossible (not possible)
counter- (against)	+ act	= counteract (act against)
pre- (before)	+ view	= preview (see before)
mis- (incorrectly)	+ spell	= misspell (spell incorrectly)

When a prefix is added to a word, the spelling of the word stays the same.

Adding the Suffixes *-ly* and *-ness*

A **suffix** is a letter or syllable added to the end of a word to change its meaning. For example, the suffix *-s* is added to a singular noun to make it plural. The suffix *-ed* is added to a verb to change the action to the past. Adding a suffix sometimes adds a spelling problem to a word.

The suffix *-ly* added to an adjective changes it to an adverb.

Adjective	Adverb
The *total* price is ten dollars.	The car was *totally* ruined.
This puzzle is a *real* challenge.	This puzzle is *really* difficult.
My mother is a *careful* driver.	My mother drives *carefully*.

When the suffix -*ly* is added to a word ending with *l*, both *l*'s are kept.

The suffix -*ness* added to an adjective changes it to a noun.

Adjective	Noun
Kirk is *open* and honest.	I admire Kirk's *openness*.
Meat with little fat is called *lean*.	Look for *leanness* when you buy bacon.

When the suffix -*ness* is added to a word ending with *n*, both *n*'s are kept.

Exercise   Add prefixes and suffixes.

Find the misspelled word in each of these sentences and spell it correctly.

1. I liked the eveness of Tammy's haircut.
2. Spencer thoughtfuly brought a gift to the graduation party.
3. A dog is unnable to climb a tree.
4. Winding this watch is unecessary.
5. The thiness of this pencil makes it hard to hold.
6. Some people misstrust cats.
7. We admired the salesperson's openess.
8. Those hints were awfuly misleading.
9. Holmes uncovered a totaly new clue.
10. We usualy see movie previews.

Adding Suffixes to Words Ending in Silent e

Notice what happens when you add suffixes beginning with vowels to words that end in silent *e*.

hope + ing = hoping   fame + ous = famous
refuse + al = refusal   pale + er = paler
expense + ive = expensive   like + able = likable

When a suffix beginning with a vowel is added to a word ending in silent e, the e is usually dropped.

Now see what happens when you add suffixes beginning with consonants to words that end in silent *e*.

care + ful = careful   move + ment = movement
lone + ly = lonely   same + ness = sameness
score + less = scoreless   bore + dom = boredom

When a suffix beginning with a consonant is added to a word ending in silent e, the e is usually kept.

The following words are exceptions to these two rules:

truly   argument   ninth   wholly

Exercise   Add suffixes correctly.

Add the suffix given for each word. Write each new word correctly.

1. place + ing
2. use + able
3. sure + ly
4. confuse + ion
5. hope + ful
6. come + ing
7. make + er
8. safe + ty
9. like + ly
10. save + ing
11. desire + able
12. remove + al

Adding Suffixes to Words Ending in y

See what happens when you add suffixes to words that end in *y* following a consonant.

baby + es = babies   lazy + ness = laziness
empty + er = emptier   carry + ed = carried
happy + ly = happily   story + es = stories

When a suffix is added to a word that ends with _y_ following a consonant, the _y_ is usually changed to _i_.

However, the _y_ is not changed when the suffix -_ing_ is added.

empty + ing = emptying   carry + ing = carrying
fly + ing = flying   apply + ing = applying

Notice too, what happens when you add suffixes to words that end in _y_ following a vowel.

boy + s = boys   play + ed = played
buy + er = buyer   stay + ing = staying

When a suffix is added to a word that ends with _y_ following a vowel, the _y_ usually is not changed.

The following words are exceptions: _paid, said._

Exercise   Add suffixes correctly.

Add the suffix given for each word. Write each new word correctly.

1. hurry + ing   6. play + er   11. carry + ed
2. story + es   7. fly + ing   12. happy + ness
3. heavy + est   8. sky + es   13. early + est
4. fly + er   9. ready + ness   14. toy + s
5. enjoy + ed   10. easy + ly   15. cry + ing

Doubling the Final Consonant

What happens to these words when you add suffixes?

spin + ing = spinning   fat + er = fatter
hot + est = hottest   scrub + ed = scrubbed

You can see that the last letter is doubled when suffixes beginning with a vowel are added to these words.

In words of one syllable that end with a consonant following one vowel, double the final consonant before adding -*ing*, -*ed*, -*en*, -*er*, or -*est*.

The final consonant is **not** doubled when it follows two vowels.

trail + er = trailer	shout + ed = shouted
steam + ing = steaming	float + er = floater
peel + ed = peeled	shoot + ing = shooting

Exercise   Double the final consonant.

Decide whether or not the final consonant should be doubled. Add the suffix as shown. Write the new word correctly.

1. fat + est
2. stop + ed
3. sad + er
4. hear + ing
5. pat + ed

6. bit + en
7. soon + est
8. get + ing
9. plan + ed
10. big + est

11. put + ing
12. hot + er
13. leak + ed
14. rot + en
15. hop + ed

Review Exercises   Use the spelling rules.

A.   Find the misspelled words in these sentences and spell them correctly. (In some of the sentences, more than one word is misspelled.)

1. The surface of this desk is very iregular.
2. The wagons moved into the openess of the plains.
3. Beth recieved a carefuly wrapped gift.
4. Mom ordered a birthday cake especialy for Terry's party.
5. I copied the poem on a clean peice of paper.
6. I beleive I hear a mysteryous sound.

7. The theif opened the safe easyly.
8. Shopers spoted the bargains.
9. We're geting excited about the upcomeing play.
10. Hikeing and bikeing are two camp activities.

B. Add the suffix given for each word below and write the new word.

1. bite + ing	8. enjoy + s	15. hope + ful
2. stay + ed	9. waste + ing	16. fat + en
3. play + ing	10. fry + ed	17. stumble + ing
4. try + ed	11. hope + ing	18. live + able
5. heat + er	12. tiny + est	19. worry + ing
6. shop + ed	13. sit + ing	20. run + ing
7. make + ing	14. big + er	

Homonyms and Other Words Often Confused

Sometimes while you are writing, you may get confused by words that look almost the same. It is not always easy to know which word to use.

Much of this confusion is caused by homonyms. **Homonyms** are words that sound the same, or nearly the same, but that are spelled differently and have different meanings. Here are some examples of homonyms:

> **by** The parade passed *by* my house.
> **buy** I want to *buy* that game.

> **meat** Pork, beef, and lamb are kinds of *meat*.
> **meet** Cara wants to *meet* her new neighbors.

> **threw** Bob *threw* the ball to the shortstop.
> **through** The laser burned a hole *through* the wood panel.

Before you can use homonyms correctly, you must know what each one means. You cannot depend on spelling rules to help you. The best approach is to memorize which spelling goes with which meaning.

Following is a list of homonyms and other words that are frequently confused. Study the sets of words. Try to connect each word with its correct meaning. Refer to the list if you have further problems with these words.

accept means to agree to something or to receive something willingly.

>Ms. Daly will not *accept* excuses.

except means to leave out, or leaving out.

>Everyone *except* Carl won a prize.

all ready means completely prepared.

>The party decorations are *all ready*.

already means previously or before.

>The hikers have *already* returned.

capital means chief or important. It also means the city or town that is the official seat of government of a state or nation.

>Begin every sentence with a *capital* letter.
>Lincoln is the *capital* of Nebraska.

capitol is the building where a state legislature meets.

>The *capitol* in Lincoln is a new building.

the Capitol is the building in Washington, D.C. in which the United States Congress meets. This *Capitol* is always capitalized.

>The nation's lawmakers meet at the *Capitol*.

hear means to listen to.

>I *hear* a drumbeat.

here means in this place.

>Drop your fishing line *here*.

its shows ownership or possession.

We studied Mexico and *its* people.

it's is the contraction for *it is* or *it has*.

We visited Calico. *It's* a ghost town.

knew means understood or was familiar with.

Sherry *knew* many card tricks.

new is the opposite of old and means fresh or recent.

The horse has a *new* saddle.

know means to understand or to be familiar with.

The pilots *know* their flight patterns.

no is a negative word meaning *not* or *not any*.

This snowman has *no* hat.

lead (lĕd) is a heavy, gray metal.

The pipes were made of *lead*.

lead (lēd) means to go first, to guide.

The general will *lead* his army.

led (lĕd) is the past form of lead (lēd).

Pioneers *led* the way west.

loose means free or not tight.

My brother pulled his *loose* tooth.

lose means to mislay or suffer the loss of something.

If you leave, you will *lose* your place in line.

peace is calm or stillness or the absence of disagreement.

The rival tribes enjoyed a time of *peace*.

piece means a portion or part.

Liz molded the *piece* of clay.

plain means clear or simple. It also means an expanse of land.

> Trish put a decal on the *plain* T-shirt.
> Horses roamed across the *plain*.

plane refers to a woodworking tool. It also is the short form of *airplane*.

> A *plane* is useful in carpentry.
> The small *plane* landed in a field.

principal means first or most important. It also refers to the head of a school.

> The *principal* purpose of TV is to entertain.
> Our school *principal* talked to parents.

principle is a rule, truth, or belief.

> Superman's *principle* is justice for all.

quiet means free from noise or disturbance.

> The rabbit is a *quiet* pet.

quite means truly or almost completely.

> Those acrobats are *quite* daring.

right means proper or correct. It also means the opposite of left. A third meaning refers to a fair claim.

> Maria found the *right* key for the safe.
> Hebrew is read from *right* to left.
> The colonists felt freedom was their *right*.

write refers to forming words with a pen or pencil.

> We must *write* a thank-you note.

their means belonging to them.

> The children took *their* rafts to the beach.

there means at that place.

> Plant the tomato seeds *there*.

they're is the contraction for *they are*.

> *They're* taking the train to Cleveland.

to means in the direction of.

> Snowflakes drifted *to* the ground.

too means also or very.

> My sister wants to come, *too*.

two is the whole number between one and three.

> The moose had *two* huge antlers.

weather is the state of the atmosphere, referring to wind, moisture, temperature, and other such conditions.

> Tornadoes usually occur during warm *weather*.

whether indicates a choice or alternative.

> Jon asked *whether* wood sinks or floats.

who's is the contraction for *who is* or *who has*.

> *Who's* throwing those snowballs?

whose is the possessive form of *who*.

> *Whose* house is closest to school?

your is the possessive form of *you*.

> Did *your* wish come true?

you're is the contraction for *you are*.

> *You're* looking at a haunted house.

Exercises **Use homonyms and other confusing words correctly.**

A. Write the correct word from those given in parentheses.

1. A dog can (hear, here) high-pitched sounds.
2. There are (know, no) lifeboats on this ship.

3. Did you (loose, lose) your library card?
4. (Their, There, They're) making stained glass.
5. Who knows the (right, write) answer?
6. This church is cool and (quiet, quite).
7. (Who's, Whose) banging those cymbals?
8. Penny has (all ready, already) finished her drawing.
9. No one (accept, except) Ramón had seen the bear.
10. Gravity is a (principal, principle) of science.

B. Follow the directions for Exercise A.

1. The bike trail begins (hear, here).
2. A giraffe raised (its, it's) head.
3. The collectors (knew, new) about foreign stamps.
4. An elephant (lead, led) the circus parade.
5. Our cabin has (to, too, two) portholes.
6. The runners are (all ready, already) for the race.
7. I borrowed (your, you're) radio.
8. The artist started with a (plain, plane) white canvas.
9. Which city is the (capital, capitol, Capitol) of Texas?
10. Joe tied the rowboat with a (peace, piece) of rope.

C. Choose the correct homonym from the two or three in parentheses. If you are not sure which word is correct, look up each homonym in the dictionary. Then write the correct word.

1. What is the (some, sum) of five plus seven?
2. The dog followed the (heard, herd) of cattle.
3. May I borrow a (pair, pare, pear) of scissors?
4. The carnation is the state (flour, flower) of Ohio.
5. How do you control the (brakes, breaks) on the bike?
6. Rhea hates to (waist, waste) time waiting for people.
7. For this macramé project, I tied a special (knot, not).
8. When Kenny fell, he complained of the (pain, pane).
9. The snowmobiles (road, rode) over the frozen marsh.
10. Gum is stuck to the (heal, heel) of my left shoe.

ADDITIONAL EXERCISES

Spelling

A. Spelling Look at each sentence carefully. Find the misspelled words. Write each word correctly.

1. Pat recieved many Valentines.
2. My neice is actualy older than I am.
3. It is immpossible to reset this watch.
4. We noticed the eveness of Fred's writing.
5. This new ink is realy eraseable.
6. A furyous bull charged into the field.
7. Whistleing happyly, Carlos finished his project.
8. Jason hurryed to the nearest phone.
9. Kelly's bating average is amazeing.
10. Jenny riped the letter and tosed it into the garbage.

B. Homonyms and Words Often Confused Write the correct word from the two words in parentheses.

1. Jody Turner (accepted, excepted) the nomination.
2. I (hear, here) the music starting.
3. The plant lost (its, it's) leaves.
4. This parade has (know, no) end!
5. How did you (loose, lose) your voice?
6. Please have a (peace, piece) of cake.
7. The horses tossed (their, they're) heads.
8. Lyle wondered (weather, whether) the team had won or lost.
9. (Who's, Whose) speech is next?
10. (Your, You're) garden is filled with weeds.

MIXED REVIEW

Spelling

A. Spelling words correctly Pick out the words that are spelled incorrectly in the following sentences. Write them correctly. Some sentences have more than one misspelled word.

1. Everyone at the party recieved a prize.
2. Dad tryed an unusual recipe.
3. His meaness made him unpopular.
4. Our forth bater struck out.
5. Is cleanlyness important to you?
6. The bicycle seat is to lose.
7. The stale bread is still useable.
8. The butcher is triming the meet.
9. Carolyn wrote the sillyest limerick.
10. Don't go swiming buy yourself.

B. Proofreading for correct spelling Proofread the following paragraph. It contains twelve spelling errors. Rewrite the paragraph, spelling all the words correctly.

I enjoy going to the libary and reading storys about famous explorers. Last Saturday I red about the British explorer Captain James Cook. During the 1770's, Cook led three voyages in the South Pacific. He discovered and explord many islandes that Europeans did not no about. These included the Cook Islands, New Zealand, and Hawaii. During one voyage, Cook searched for a knew continent. Geographers beleived it was south of Australia. The whether was bitter, and icebergs towered over Cook's boat. Dense fog and harsh winds made sailing immpossible. Finaly, the explorers had to give up there search. It wasn't until 1840 that Charles Wilkes discovered this continent— Antarctica.

USING MECHANICS IN WRITING
Spelling

A. The English language is full of spelling demons. Spelling demons are words that are tricky to spell. Try to outwit the demons in this writing assignment. Remember the spelling rules and hints you have learned. Also remember the exceptions!

Here are fifteen words. Seven of them are misspelled. Correct the misspelled words. Then write a story using any ten of the fifteen words. The story can be funny or serious.

confusion	steaming	cieling	Febuary
hurrying	fameous	police	funeral
flying	immpossible	diffrent	totaly
realy	believe	seize	

B. Mr. Spellright taught English for thirty years. His students remembered him for one thing: he always drilled them on homonyms. He would get quite upset when a student wrote *hear* for *here*, or *too* for *to*.

When Mr. Spellright died, his students sent a wreath of flowers. On it they wrote, "Rest in Piece, Deer Mr. Spellright." When Mr. Spellright's ghost read that, he began moaning. Legend says that if any student can use ten of the following words correctly in a story, Mr. Spellright will stop moaning. See if you can send Mr. Spellright back to his eternal rest.

except	it's	lose	write	whether
already	knew	peace	their	who's
capitol	know	plane	they're	whose
hear	no	principle	to	your
its	lead	quite	two	you're
knot	led	quiet	too	waste

CUMULATIVE REVIEW
Capitalization, Punctuation, and Spelling

A. Using capitalization, punctuation, and spelling correctly Copy the following sentences, correcting the errors in capitalization, punctuation, and spelling.

1. Los angeles Montreal St. louis and mexico city have all hosted the Summer olympics
2. We could not here the speech accept for the end of it
3. Bjorn borg, a fameous swedish tennis pro, has one quiet a few titles at wimbledon
4. "havent you renewed you're subscription two national geographic" asked diane
5. Was philadelphia once the capitol of the united states
6. "Did jrr tolkien right the book The hobbitt? asked Joe
7. These knew tapes were realy inexpenseive
8. Ive all ready seen the movie star wars eight times
9. What an unbeleivably beautiful picture that is
10. "I fryed the fish said Tim. Lee choped the vegetables"

B. Using proofreading skills Proofread the following paragraph. Copy it, correcting the errors in capitalization, punctuation, and spelling.

Do you ever, have difficulty makeing decisions or solveing arguments. I did then i discovered that the toss of a coin can usualy solve this problem. its quick and simple. Most People do knot argue, with the results of a toss. For centurys, coins have been used for trade. Tossing was an early use two. did you no, that orville and Wilbur wright actualy tossed a coin, at Kitty hawk North carolina. They wanted to decide who would pilot the first Airplain. Orville one that toss. So practice tossing catching and fliping the coin. Head's or tails may help you solve an arguement or make a decision.

Writer's Guide

Topics for Writing
Discovery Techniques
Common Usage Problems

 McDougal, Littell & Company

Ideas for Writing

Sometimes writers need a little help getting started. Once you have an idea, you can then build upon it. The following lists of ideas can help you think of interesting topics to write about. Read over these lists. Then review the **Discovery Techniques** that appear in this **Writer's Guide.** They will help you think of other interesting ideas as well.

Ideas for Writing

Narrative

unknown danger
a new beginning
total confusion
a sudden discovery
on the parallel bars
no way out
the one that got away

a bicycle trip
a real winner
the cat ate it
on the way home from school
the disguise
a perfect day

Descriptive

a passing stranger
something left in the rain
a cookout
a storm at night
an amusement park
a deserted street
a park after a snowstorm

a fire
your private collection
someone riding a skateboard
radio-controlled car in motion
the view from a window
a new-born baby

Process

how a lie detector works
how bottles are recycled
how to become a gymnast
how animals hunt
how to make a pizza
how to perform a card trick

how to build a ship in a bottle
how an airplane flies
how baseballs are made
how to build a treehouse

Definition

Define one: the Aztecs, dwarf stars, haiku poetry, migrant workers, prejudice, rock-and-roll, "gold fever," computer chips, embarrassment

Opinion

Should students be allowed to wear anything they want?
Should the government provide free lunches in schools?
Should schools be open throughout the summer?
What should be done about young people who live on the streets?

Ideas for Writing in Subject Areas

The Arts

fixing the Statue of Liberty
today's comedians
building a home workshop
origins of country music

ancient Greek mythology
miniature furniture
why TV "soaps" are popular
how tap dancing began

Social Studies

going to school in Japan
hunger in America
how a police lab works
how to recognize fake money

America's immigrants today
what fossils tell about life in
    the past
problems in South Africa

Science

how a microwave oven works
How safe is tap water?
How does a battery work?
What formed the Grand
    Canyon?

Why are sunspots dark?
What causes a desert oasis?
Why do birds molt?
why animals hibernate

Discovery Techniques for Writing

When you are stumped for writing ideas and find yourself staring at a blank sheet of paper, what can you do? The following techniques can help you find or develop ideas for any writing assignment.

Brainstorming   Begin with one general idea. Then write down everything that comes to mind about that particular idea. For example, the general idea *fish* could lead to topics such as "Common Myths About Sharks," "How To Set Up a Home Aquarium," "Fishing for Trout," or "How To Cook Catfish."

Clustering   Clustering is another way to brainstorm for ideas. Start by writing a word or phrase in the center of a piece of paper. Circle this word or phrase. Think of other ideas connected to your first idea. Write these new ideas on your paper, circle them, and connect them with lines to your first idea. Keep branching off with new ideas. Circle them and draw connecting lines, as shown below.

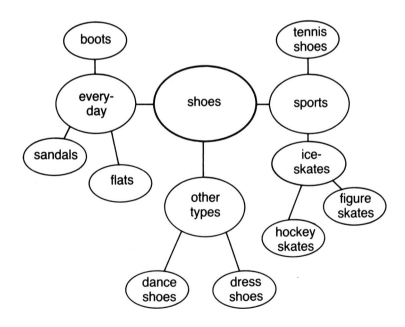

Freewriting Freewriting is a way to loosen up ideas. Start with any idea or subject. Then write without stopping for a given period of time, perhaps ten minutes. Write whatever comes to mind. Don't worry about grammar or spelling, or even about writing complete sentences. Simply keep writing for the entire period of time. Switch to new ideas as they occur to you, and let your mind and writing hand move freely. The following is an example of freewriting.

> Toys are fun for people of all ages—kids like dolls, blocks, etc.—adults like card games and gadgets of all kinds. Teenagers like skateboards, video games some board games. Some kids like models that you can put together. Not for me. Boring! Lots of games are fads . . . like one year everybody has to have one game and the next year nobody remembers its name. But some games seem to last . . . like Monopoly. That game has been around forever it seems. I wonder why. Why do kids still play Monopoly when there are so many more exciting games around these days . . . I wonder how Monopoly began. Did somebody invent it? Maybe there's a story here. . . .

Gleaning Gleaning means "collecting" or "gathering in." You do this every day of your life, but you may not have realized that gleaning can help you find writing ideas.

When you glean, you collect interesting or "writable" ideas. You may, for example, see a window washer hanging out of the fiftieth floor of a skyscraper. You wonder how on earth anyone gets into that line of work. You may see a dog threading its way through eight lanes of traffic. Now ask yourself how animals get street smarts. Either of these experiences can be used as a writing topic.

Another way to glean is to browse through books, newspapers, and magazines at home or in the library. Write down any ideas that interest you and that could make good writing topics.

Picturing Much of what is stored in your brain is in the form of pictures. To use the picturing technique, first close your eyes. Clear your mind of other thoughts. Concentrate on your subject.

What pictures come to mind? Are there people present? Who are they and what are they doing? What are they feeling? What sights, sounds, or smells are present? Allow yourself at least three minutes to picture your subject. Then describe it as fully as possible on paper. An example of picturing follows.

> I slowly walk to the free-throw line, my legs tired from four quarters of running. The referee calls out, "One shot." He hands me the ball. The grain of the leather feels coarse to the touch. The crowd is screaming "Air ball!" I tell myself to concentrate, focus, take a deep breath. I bounce the ball several times and am surprised at how light it feels compared to my heavy arms. Another deep breath and I eye the rim— try to relax. I feel sweat rolling down my forehead. Then I feel nothing. The ball is out of my hands, in the air, arching downward. Swish!

Listing Making a list can help you organize what you already know and find out what you don't. For example, you might want to list the steps in a process, such as washing a car. Making a list can also provide a framework for later writing, as in the following example.

Inventions That Changed America	Facts to Check
telephone	dates
cotton gin	inventors
electric light	effects
barbed wire	

Charting Making a chart can also help you organize your topic. In addition, a chart can help you see how one thing relates to another. A simple chart has columns of items listed under various headings. For example, the following chart lists several facts about squirrels: Common Name, Scientific Name, Gestation Period, Number of Young, and Life Span (in captivity). Beneath each heading, the details are given.

Common Name	Scientific Name	Gestation Period	Number of Young	Life Span (in captivity)
Flying Squirrel	Glaucomys	40 days	2–6	7–13 years
Fox Squirrel	Sciurus	45 days	2–4	9 years
Gray Squirrel	Sciurus	44 days	2–5	8–15 years
Red Squirrel	Tamiasciurus	40 days	4	8–9 years

Journalists' Questions   Ask yourself the kinds of questions reporters and other journalists ask. Prepare questions beginning with *who, what, when, where, why,* and *how.* Then answer these questions.

Creative Questions   To be creative, you need to let your imagination run freely. Just because you have always thought of a paper clip as something that holds papers together doesn't mean that it can't be used for other purposes. Start asking "What if?" questions such as the following, and be alert to any good writing ideas that your answers suggest.

1. What if I combined two subjects that are usually separate?
2. What if I used this object in a new or unusual way?
3. What if this person, place, object, event, or idea had never existed or happened?
4. What if I changed just one part of this thing or situation?
5. What if I changed what this object is made of? What if I changed its shape in some way?
6. What if the relationships between certain people, places, objects, or events were different?
7. What if I changed the location of something?
8. What if people changed their roles or actions in some way?

Common Usage Problems

Certain usage problems cause frequent problems in writing. Following are some of the most common errors. Study this list and try to avoid these errors in your writing. Also use the list whenever you revise your writing.

Abbreviations

In general, do not use abbreviations in any writing except personal letters and notes. The only exceptions to this rule are titles (Mr., Mrs., Ms., Dr., Rev.), dates (B.C., A.D.), and times (A.M., P.M.).

Double Negatives

Negatives are words such as *no, not, never, nothing,* and *none.* Two negatives in a sentence produce a **double negative.** Avoid this error. The problem usually occurs when using contractions such as *hasn't* or *couldn't.* Remember that the *n't* in these contractions means *not.* If you pair a contraction with another negative word such as *never,* you end up with a double negative such as *hasn't never.*

> Incorrect: The speed of a tornado has*n't never* been measured.
> Correct: The speed of a tornado *has never* been measured.
> Incorrect: When the storm began, I could*n't* see *nothing.*
> Correct: When the storm began, I could*n't* see *anything.*

Hardly or *barely* used with a negative word is also incorrect.

> Incorrect: Lauren had*n't hardly* fallen asleep when the phone rang.
> Correct: Lauren *had hardly* fallen asleep when the phone rang.

Modifiers

Adjective–Adverb Confusion   Both adjectives and adverbs are modifiers. Adjectives modify nouns or pronouns. Adverbs

modify verbs, adjectives, or other adverbs. Adverbs often end in
-*ly*. One problem you may have when using adverbs is deciding
when to turn an adjective into an adverb by adding -*ly*.

In general, add the -*ly* to modifiers that follow action verbs.

Incorrect: On July 20, 1969, Neil Armstrong climbed *careful*
down a ladder and onto the moon.

Correct: On July 20, 1969, Neil Armstrong climbed *carefully* down a ladder and onto the moon.

Bad and Badly   *Bad* is an adjective. Use it after a linking verb.
In the following cases *bad* modifies the subject.

Orlando felt *bad*. (*Bad* modifies *Orlando*.)
The milk tastes *bad*. (*Bad* modifies *milk*.)

Badly is an adverb. It is used with action verbs.

Alan skated *badly* yesterday. (*Badly* modifies *skated*.)
The magician performed *badly*. (*Badly* modifies *performed*.)

Good and Well   *Good* is used only as an adjective to modify
nouns and pronouns. It is used after linking verbs.

The movie was *good*. (*Good* modifies *movie*.)
The strawberry yogurt tastes *good*. (*Good* modifies *yogurt*.)

Well can be used as an adjective or an adverb. It is an adjective
when it means "in good health." When *well* is used as an adverb to
modify an action word, it means that the action was performed
properly or expertly.

My grandmother looks *well* today. (*Well* is an adjective
meaning "in good health.")
My grandmother played the piano *well* at the party. (*Well* is
an adverb modifying the action verb *played*.)

Comparisons   Use the **comparative** form to compare two
things. Use the **superlative** form to compare more than two

things. Superlatives can also be used to compare one thing to all others of its kind.

Basic form: The Earth is a *large* planet. (no comparison)
Comparative form: The Earth is *larger* in diameter than Mars. (The comparison is between two planets.)
Superlative form: Jupiter is the *largest* planet in our solar system. (The comparison is between Jupiter and all other planets in our solar system.)

Do not use *-er* and *more* or *-est* and *most* together.

Incorrect: Venus shines *more brighter* than Neptune.
Correct: Venus shines *brighter* than Neptune.

Incorrect: The moon is by far the *most brightest* object in the sky.
Correct: The moon is by far the *brightest* object in the sky.

Misplaced Modifiers   Sometimes a modifier is placed so that it appears to modify the wrong word. Then it is called a **misplaced modifier.** Usually this error happens with prepositional phrases and other types of phrases. To correct this kind of error, move the modifier as close as possible to the word that it modifies.

Misplaced phrase: Carla spotted a robin on the way to school hopping on the ground. (Was the robin going to school?)
Correct: On the way to school, Carla spotted a robin hopping on the ground.

Sometimes a modifier seems to refer to a word that is missing from the sentence. This is called a **dangling modifier.**

Dangling modifier: When stacking the video games on the shelf, they tumbled to the floor. (Who was doing the stacking?)
Correct: When *I* stacked the video games on the shelf, they tumbled to the floor.

Parallelism

When *and* is used to join the same type of sentence parts, such as noun and noun, verb and verb, or phrase and phrase, the sentence parts are said to be parallel. If *and* is used to join sentence parts of different kinds, there is a lack of parallelism.

Not parallel: In history class we learned about boom *towns,* ghost *towns,* and *how gold mines were found.* (two nouns and a clause)

Parallel: In history class we learned about boom *towns,* ghost *towns,* and gold *mines.* (three nouns)

Not parallel: The people who traveled to the West in search of gold were *excited, enthusiastic,* and *came to the area hopeful.* (two adjectives and a phrase)

Parallel: The people who traveled to the West in search of gold were *excited, enthusiastic,* and *hopeful.* (three adjectives)

Point of View

Person refers to the point of view a writer uses. A writer may use first-person (I, we), second-person (you), or third-person (he, she, they) point of view. Point of view should not change from sentence to sentence. This confuses the reader.

Incorrect: When a *photographer* takes pictures with a 35mm camera, *you* must set the film speed on the ISO dial.

Correct: When a *photographer* takes pictures with a 35mm camera, *he* or *she* must set the film speed on the ISO dial.

Pronouns

Agreement Pronouns must agree with, or match in number, the nouns they stand for. This means that when you use a singular pronoun, the noun that the pronoun stands for must also be singular. When you use a plural pronoun, the noun that the pronoun stands for must be plural.

Incorrect: A *student* sometimes has trouble balancing *their* school and work responsibilities. (The pronoun *their* is plural; *a student* is singular.)

Correct: *Students* sometimes have trouble balancing *their* school and work responsibilities. (Both pronoun and noun are plural.)

Indefinite pronouns sometimes cause problems in agreement. The following indefinite pronouns are always singular: *anyone, anybody, anything, each, either, everybody, everyone, everything, neither, nobody, no one, one, somebody,* and *someone.*

Incorrect: *Everybody* should bring *their* own lunch to the picnic.

Correct: *Everybody* should bring *his* or *her* own lunch to the picnic.

Subject or Object   Pronouns change forms, depending on their use in sentences. The subject form is used when a pronoun takes the place of a subject or follows a form of the verb *be.*

They rode their skateboards through the park. (subject form)

It was *she* who taught me how to play the guitar. (follows a form of the verb *be*)

When there are two or more subjects, be sure to use the subject form for all pronouns. Sometimes it helps to read each subject alone with the verb.

(*He,* Him) and (*I,* me) went bowling on Thursday. (*He* went bowling. *I* went bowling.)

Sara and (*she,* her) led our volleyball team to victory. (*Sara* led our volleyball team. *She* led our volleyball team.)

The object form is used when pronouns take the place of nouns used as objects.

Christine invited *me* to the party next weekend. (direct object)
Enrico sent *her* a bouquet of flowers. (indirect object)
Will you unlock the door for *me*? (object of preposition)

When there is more than one object, don't forget to use the object form for any pronouns. To decide which pronoun form to use in a compound object, try each object separately.

My mother drove Latania and (I, *me*) downtown. (My mother drove *Latania*. My mother drove *me*.)
The money was divided between (he, *him*) and (she, *her*). (Both pronouns are objects of the preposition *between*.)

Clear Referent   Make sure that your reader knows what noun your pronoun refers to. If there are two possibilities, your reader may be confused.

Unclear: After Donna connected the video recorder to the television, she turned *it* on. (Did Donna turn on the video recorder or the television?)
Clear: After Donna connected the video recorder to the television, she turned on the television.

Lack of Antecedent   The pronoun *it* causes a great deal of confusion. Do not use *it* unless there is an antecedent. Otherwise, your reader will not know what *it* means.

Unclear: She walked across the bridge and dropped *it* into the water. (What was dropped into the water?)
Clear: She walked across the bridge and dropped the *ring* into the water.

Repetition

A statement is repetitious if it contains the same words or ideas twice. Remove any repetitious words to improve your writing.

Repetitious: James Baldwin wrote an *autobiography of his life.*
Better: James Baldwin wrote an autobiography.

Repetitious: The oldest of nine children, Baldwin had *daily* responsibilities for his brothers and sisters *every day.*
Better: The oldest of nine children, Baldwin had daily responsibilities for his brothers and sisters.

Sentence Errors

Fragments   A **sentence fragment** is a group of words that is not a complete sentence. A sentence fragment is missing a subject, a verb, or both. To correct a sentence fragment, add the missing part or parts.

Fragment: Are the oldest of all living things in the world. (missing subject)
Sentence: Sequoia *trees* are the oldest of all living things in the world.

Fragment: These majestic trees more than three hundred feet tall. (missing verb)
Sentence: These majestic trees *grow* more than three hundred feet tall.

Fragment: In honor of Sequoya, a famous Indian chief. (missing subject and verb)
Sentence: *Sequoias were named* in honor of Sequoya, a famous Indian chief.

Run-on Sentences   A **run-on sentence** is two or more sentences written incorrectly as one. The most common run-on sentence joins two sentences with a comma. A run-on sentence can be easily corrected by using the proper capitalization and punctuation. The sentence below can be corrected with either a period or a semicolon.

Run-on sentence: Automobile accidents are the leading cause of death for people under age twenty-four, safety belts double the chances of surviving a collision.

Correct: Automobile accidents are the leading cause of death for people under age twenty-four. Safety belts double the chances of surviving a collision.

Correct: Automobile accidents are the leading cause of death for people under age twenty-four; safety belts double the chances of surviving a collision.

Another way to correct a run-on sentence is to join the two sentences with a comma and a coordinating conjunction. The coordinating conjunctions are *and, but,* and *or.*

Run-on sentence: A car traveling at thirty-five miles per hour can stop in about 100 *feet, a* train traveling at the same speed requires more than a mile to stop.

Correct: A car traveling at thirty-five miles per hour can stop in about 100 *feet, but* a train traveling at the same speed requires more than a mile to stop.

Stringy Sentences Stringy sentences occur when three or more sentences are "strung" or joined together by the word *and.* To correct stringy sentences, write each sentence separately or use other sentence-combining techniques.

Stringy sentence: The World Future Society predicts that Earth's largest cities will have more than 100 million residents by the end of the next century, *and* that some day there may be cities with more than a billion residents, *and* that society's most dangerous criminals may be shipped to faraway planets or underwater prisons.

Correct: The World Future Society predicts that Earth's largest cities will have more than 100 million residents by the end of the next century. Some day there may be cities with more than a billion residents. Society's most dangerous criminals may be shipped to faraway planets or underwater prisons. (One long stringy sentence becomes three shorter sentences.)

Subject–Verb Agreement

A verb must agree with its subject in number. Singular subjects take singular verbs. Plural subjects take plural verbs.

He (*doesn't,* don't) have his own car.
They (doesn't, *don't*) have the tickets either.

When making subjects and verbs agree, beware of phrases that appear between the subject and the verb. Always keep the subject in mind and make sure it agrees with the verb.

The *bottles* of cleaning fluid (is, *are*) full.
My *coach,* in addition to my parents, (agree, *agrees*) with me.

Shifting Tense

Tense means "time." Most verbs change their forms to show present, past, and future time. Each verb has three simple tenses and three perfect tenses.

Sometimes a writer confuses the reader by changing the verb tense in the middle of a sentence. Avoid this type of error.

Incorrect: I *heard* the siren, and then I *see* the flashing lights of the ambulance.
Correct: I *heard* the siren, and then I *saw* the flashing lights of the ambulance.

Use of *You*

Do not use the pronoun *you* in your writing unless you mean the reader.

Incorrect: *You* should gradually increase *your* distance when *you* train for a marathon. (The writer does not mean *you* personally.)
Correct: A *runner* should gradually increase *his* or *her* distance when training for a marathon.

in possessives, 314–315,
551–552
Articles, 412, 534
Assignments, understanding,
214–215
Audience, of a speaker, 256
Author card in card catalog,
207–208
Auxiliaries. *See* Helping verbs.

B

bad/badly, 486
bad/good, 419–420
Base words, 12–13
be, forms of, 323, 326–327, 333,
350. *See also is, was, are,
were.*
between/among, 447–448
Bibliographies, 194–195
Body of business letter, 242
Body of composition, 132–133,
138, 144–145
Body of friendly letter, 234–236
Books, finding and using in library.
See Library, using the.
Borrowed words, 2
Brainstorming, 64–65, 70–71
Bread and butter notes, 239–241
Brittanica Junior Encyclopedia,
211
Business letters, 242–244
block form, 242–244
modified block form, 242–244
buy/by, 577

C

Call numbers of library books, 205
can/may, 377
capital/capitol, 578
Capitalization, 521–540

abbreviations, 524
businesses, 527–528
clubs, 527–528
days, 525–526
direct quotations, 529–530
first words
of outlines, 531
of poetry lines, 531
of quotations, 529–530
of sentences, 529
holidays, 525–526
I, 522
initials, 523–524
languages, 527
in letters, 234, 532
months, 525–526
names, 523–524
nationalities, 527
organizations, 527–528
places and things, 526
proper adjectives, 522–523
proper nouns, 522–523
religions, 527
rules for, 521–534
titles of persons and their abbreviations, 524
written works, 534
Card catalogs, 207–209
author card, 207
subject card, 208
title card, 208
Characters, 148–149
Charts. *See* Graphic aids.
Chronological order, 72–73,
92–93, 151
in narrative compositions, 92–93
in paragraphs, 72–73
Closing of letters, 234–236, 244
commas with, 549
Collier's Encyclopedia, 211
Commas, 548–551
with adjectives, 407

with city, state, country, 548
in compound predicates,
288–289
in compound sentences,
492–493, 495, 550
with dates, 548
with direct address, 549
with direct quotations, 549
with introductory words, 549
in letters, 549
rules for use, 548–550
in a series, 549
after *yes, no,* 549
Common nouns, 522
Comparisons
of adjectives, 417–421, 424
of adverbs, 431–433, 437
Completion or fill-in-the-blank
tests, 230–231
Complete predicate of sentence,
279
Complete sentences, 271–272
Complete subject of sentence, 279
Compositions, 131–145
body in, 132–133, 138, 144–145,
166–167
characters in, 148
choosing topics for, 134–135
conclusion in, 132–133, 138,
144–145
definition of, 132–133
descriptive, 163–171
details in, 164–165
development of, 144–145
explanatory, 173–181
final copy of, 142–143
first drafts of, 138–139
first-person point of view in,
152–153
introduction in, 132–133, 138,
144–145
logical order in, 176–177, 254

narrative, 147–161
omniscient point of view in,
152–153
organizing ideas, 136–137
parts of, 132, 166–167
planning, 148–149
plot in, 150–151
point of view in, 152–153
revision of, 140–141, 145,
170–171, 180–181
sensory details in, 164–165
setting in, 148–149
step-by-step order, 176–177
third-person point of view in,
152–153
time sequence in, 150–151
title for, 142, 144
transitions in, 158–159, 178–179
See also Writing and Pre-writing.
Compound direct object, 453–454
Compound object of preposition,
453–454
Compound object of verb,
453–454
Compound predicate, 288–290
Compound predicate adjective,
453–454
Compound predicate noun,
453–454
diagraming, 508–509
Compound sentences, 487–499
commas with, 492–493, 495, 550
definition of, 489–490
diagraming, 514–515
punctuation of, 492–493, 495,
550
Compound subjects, 286–288
diagramming, 506–507
Compound verb, 453–454
diagraming, 506–507
Compound words, 2
Computers, 18

Conclusions, in composition,
132-133, 138, 144-145, 155,
168-169, 190
Conclusions, in paragraphs, 76-77
Conflict, in stories, 148, 149
Conjunctions, 452-455
  in compound sentence parts,
  452-454
  in compound sentences,
  489-493
  definition of, 452-453
  exercises, 453-454, 457,
  459-461
Context
  defined, 4
  learning word meanings from
  by definition, 6-7
  in dictionary entries, 30-31
  by examples, 8-9
  by restatement, 6-7
Contractions, 379-380
  apostrophe in, 379-380,
  552-554
  definition, 379
  list of, 379
  negatives, 380-382
  n't not included in verb,
  329-330
Cumulative review,
  capitalization, punctuation, spelling, 586
  parts of speech, 470-471
  sentence, 497-499
  usage, 486

D

Dates
  capitalization of, 525
  commas with, 548
Declarative sentences, 273-274
  defined, 273
  exercises for, 275-276, 291

periods with, 275-276
Definition, as context clue to
  meaning of word, 6-7
Definitions, 12-13, 14-15, 16-17,
  24-29, 30-31
Definitions in dictionary, 28-31
Demonstrations, 252-253, 254-255
Descriptions, 101-109, 163-171
Descriptive compositions, 163-171
Descriptive paragraph
  gathering sensory details,
  102-103
  revising, 108-109
  using spatial order, 104-105
  using transitional words,
  106-107
Details, 42, 56-57, 83, 90-91,
  102-103
  organizing, 72-73
  in paragraphs, 56-57
  sensory, 164-165
  in speeches, 254-255
Dewey Decimal System, 204-206
Diagraming, 500-520
  adjectives, 510-511
  adverbs, 513-514
  compound sentences, 514-515
  compound subjects and verbs,
  506-507
  direct objects, 507-508
  imperative sentences, 504
  possessive nouns, 512-513
  predicate adjectives, 509-510
  predicate nouns, 508-509
  questions, 503
  sentences, 500-519
  sentences with *there*, 505
  subjects in unusual order, 502
  verbs and their subjects, 501
Diagrams, *See* Graphic aids.
Dialogue, 156-157
Dictionary, 21-31

point of view in, 94–95
process of writing, 61–79
sensory details in, 102–103
spatial order in, 72–73, 104–105
specific verbs in, 98–99
step-by-step order in, 114–115
third-person point of view in,
  94–95
time sequence in, 72–73
topic for, narrowing, 66–67
topic sentence in, 54–55, 68–69
transitions in, 96–97, 106,
  116–117, 126–127
unity in, 52–53
Parts of speech, 27, 28, 29,
  462–471
definition of, 462
as shown in dictionary entries,
  27–29
using words as different,
  464–466
See also Adjectives, Adverbs,
  Conjunctions, Interjections,
  Nouns, Prepositions, Pronouns, Verbs.
Past participles of verbs, 348
Past tense of verbs, 337–338
peace/piece, 579
Period, 542–545
in abbreviations, 524, 542–544
and declarative sentences,
  275–276
and imperative sentences,
  275–276
after initials, 523–524, 542
in outlines, 544
with quotation marks, 556
in sentences, 542
Personal observation to attain information, 70–71
Personal point of view. *See* First-
  person point of view.

piece/peace, 579
plain/plane, 580
Plot in stories, 148, 149, 150–151
Plural forms
of nouns, 311–312
  shown in dictionary entries,
  312
of pronouns, 389
of verbs, 472–482
Poetry lines,
capitalization of first words in,
  531
Point of view, 94–95, 152–153
first-person, 94–95, 152–153
omniscient, 152–153
third-person, 94–95, 152–153
Possessive nouns, 313–315
diagraming, 512–513
Possessive pronouns, 398–399
Predicate
complete, 279
compound, 288–289
definition of, 277–278
exercises, 278, 280, 282, 289,
  292, 293, 295, 296, 297
simple, 279–281
Predicate adjectives, 334–336,
  413–414
compound, 453–454
definition of, 413
diagraming, 509–510
Predicate nouns, 334–336
compound, 453–454
definition of, 333
diagraming, 508–509
Predicate pronouns, 333–336
Predicate words
definition of, 333
or direct objects, 335–336
exercises, 335–336
Prefixes, 14–15
and spelling, 572, 573

S

s'/s, 313–314
Salutation in letters, 234–236,
 242–244
Schedules
 for study, 220–221
Senses, as base for detail in writing, 102–108
Sensory details, 102
Sentence fragments, 270, 272,
 299–300
Sentence patterns,
 N LV Adj., 341
 N LV N, 340
 NV, 316
 NVN, 339
Sentences, 39–47, 269–297
 capitalization in, 529
 combining, 46–47
 complete, 271–272
 complete predicate in, 279
 complete subject in, 279
 compound, 487–499
 compound predicate in, 288–290
 compound subject in, 286–288
 correct use of, 299–307
 declarative, 273–274
 definition of, 40–41, 270, 488
 diagraming, 500–519
 empty, 42–43
 ending, in paragraphs, 76–77
 end punctuation in, 542,
 546–548
 exclamatory, 273–274
 exercises, 272, 291, 296, 298,
 497–499
 fragments of, 270, 272, 299–301
 imperative, 273–274
 interrogative, 273–274
 kinds of, 273
 padded, 44–45
 in paragraphs, 50–51, 52–53

parts of, 276–289
patterns of, 316, 339–341, 345
punctuation of, 275–276, 542
run-on, 299, 302–303
simple, 488–489
simple predicate (the verb) in,
 277, 279–281
simple subject in, 277, 281–283
topic, 68–69, 167
writing, 39–48
set/sit, 378
Setting in stories, 148, 149
Short answer tests, 230–231
Signature in letters, 234–236,
 244
Simple predicate (the verb), 277,
 279–281
Simple sentences, 488–489
 definition of, 488
Singular forms
 of nouns, 311–312
 of pronouns, 476–477
 of verbs, 472–482
sit/set, 378
Skimming, 248–249
Slang, 36–37
Social notes. See Letters.
Source cards, 186–187
Special order in a composition,
 164–165
Specific verbs, 98–99
Speech, 251–265
 choosing topics, 256
 and eye contact, 258–259
 formal, 252–253, 256–257
 choosing a topic, 256
 deciding your purpose, 256
 gathering information, 256
 knowing the audience, 256
 organizing information, 256
 and gestures, 258–259
 guidelines for content, 264–265

Acknowledgments

Johnny Hart and News Group Chicago, Inc.: For BC cartoon; copyright © 1971 Publishers Newspaper Syndicate; copyright © 1977 by Fawcett Publications, Inc. The New Yorker Magazine, Inc.: For "Catalogue" by Rosalie Moore; copyright © 1940, 1968, The New Yorker Magazine, Inc.

Photographs

Jim Whitmer, ii, xvi, 32, 48, 80, 100, 110, 146, 162, 196, 202, 250, 266; Jacqueline Durand, 20; James L. Ballard, 38, 60, 172, 182, 212, 232; Brent Jones, 88, 120; Hillstrom Stock/Tom McCarthy, 130.

Cover

Sinjerli Variation I, 1977. Frank Stella. Petersburg Press, London and New York. © Vert Foncé, 1977.